# INTRODUCTION TO

# ACCOUNTANCY

# FOR

# BANKING STUDENTS

Also by the same authors

*Accountancy for Banking Students* (1983)

# INTRODUCTION TO ACCOUNTANCY FOR BANKING STUDENTS

by

**J. R. Edwards,** M.Sc(Econ.); FCA; ATII

and

**H. J. Mellett,** M.Sc(Econ.); FCA

## The Chartered Institute of Bankers

10 Lombard Street, London EC3V 9AS

First Published 1985
Reprinted 1988

Chartered Institute of Bankers (CIB) Publications are published by Bankers Books Limited under an exclusive licence and royalty agreement. Bankers Books Limited is a company owned by The Chartered Institute of Bankers.

Enquiries should be sent to the publishers at the undermentioned address:

BANKERS BOOKS LIMITED
The Chartered Institute of Bankers
10 Lombard Street
London
EC3V 9AS

© The Institute of Bankers 1985 and J. R. Edwards and H. J. Mellett.

ISBN 0 85297 138 9

 British Library Cataloguing in Publication Data

Edwards, J. R.
    Introduction to accountancy for banking students.
    1. Accounting    2. Banks and banking—Accounting
    I. Title    II. Mellett, H. J.
    657'.024332              AF5635

Typeset in 10pt Times by Commercial Typesetting.
Text Printed on 80gm² Commercial Print, Cover on 240gm² Euro Cote 'G'.
Printed and bound by Commercial Colour Press, Forest Gate, London E.7., England.

To
Ross, Katherine, Ewen, Helen, Catherine and Elizabeth

# Preface

This book is designed to meet the Stage 1 accountancy requirements of banking students; these are an ability to prepare basic accounting statements and to appreciate, at an elementary level, the significance of the information they contain. A full knowledge of the scope and potential of accounting is an essential requirement for the lending banker, and it is therefore necessary for the student to view this subject as a means of obtaining financial and analytical skills which will be of long-term benefit, rather than merely as an obstacle to progress which must be overcome. For this reason, *Introduction to Accountancy for Banking Students* has been written to provide readers with a sound *understanding* of accountancy, rather than simply to equip them with a series of unrelated techniques which will help them pass the next exam, provided the 'right' questions come up. At the same time, the text is essentially practical and makes reference to accounting theory only where relevant to provide an understanding of accounting practice.

We have become aware of the need for a Stage 1 accountancy text, specifically written for bankers, as the result of our experience as moderators of the bankers' conversion course. The papers we receive for moderation, although in many cases of a high standard, do not always provide an appropriate Stage 2 foundation for a variety of reasons: these include over-emphasis on the preparation of *routine* accounting statements; the failure to test whether students are able to show a written appreciation of the information they prepare; and the inclusion of *advanced* topics (such as DCF, SSAP's and the Companies Act) which must inevitably mean an inadequate coverage of Stage 1 material. We believe that this new text book, in conjunction with the teaching scheme, will help to clarify the level of expertise expected from students and the appropriate structure for the introductory course. We do not expect complete agreement from teachers regarding the level of emphasis attached to every topic, but we think we have achieved a reasonable balance which will, in due course, be reviewed on the basis of further experience.

Since we are concerned to emphasise understanding, and aware of the fact that we are addressing student bankers, not trainee accountants, we do not launch readers immediately into the intricacies of double entry. Instead Chapter 1 introduces the student to what is, for the banker, the principal accounting statement — the balance sheet. Information is provided about the various sources of finance and assets which appear in the balance sheet, and the relationship between the two sides of the statement is carefully explained by showing how they are affected by individual transactions entered into by a firm. Chapter 2 builds on Chapter 1 by showing how profit arises as the result of an increase in net assets and how profit can be measured by capital changes, provided account is taken of capital injected and withdrawn during the year. Chapter 3 introduces the student to profit as the difference between revenue and expenditure and explains how to prepare a trading and profit and loss account, and balance sheet, from cash records.

Chapters 4—6 explain the operation of the formal system for recording and reporting business transactions based on double entry procedures. Chapter 4 deals with the initial record of the transactions to be to be controlled and reported in the cash book, day books and the journal. Chapter 5 shows how this information is posted to the ledger and also deals with the use of the trial balance to summarise the balances outstanding in the ledger at the end of the accounting period. Chapter 6 deals with the preparation of the final accounts from the trial balance, taking account of necessary post-trial balance adjustments.

Chapter 7 goes into greater depth on a number of valuation and conceptual issues central to the text. For example, it discusses different methods of depreciation and shows how their use affects the level of reported profit. The significance for financial reports of the basic accounting concepts and conventions, e.g. prudence, is also explained. A number of specialised accounting techniques not previously discussed, such as the preparation of the manufacturing account and the method for recording a transfer of business, are considered in Chapter 8. Chapters 9 and 10 deal with a number of respects in which the accounts of partnerships and limited companies differ from those of the sole trader: for example, in the case of a partnership, an appropriation account is needed to show the division of the profit between the partners; in the case of a limited company, the legal requirement to record share issues at their nominal value produces a number of accounting complications. Chapter

11 deals with the preparation and interpretation of specialised reports to be used by management as the basis for resource allocation decisions, e.g. forecast accounts, while Chapter 12 introduces students to funds flow analysis as the basis for performance assessment.

The text of each chapter is fully illustrated with worked examples, and at the end of each chapter there are a number of questions designed to test the extent to which the subject matter has been understood. The final chapter of the book, Chapter 13, consists of 30 additional revision questions, and the order of these broadly follows the chapter sequence. Full solutions to *every* question are provided in the Appendix at the back of the book. It is recommended that the book is read, and the questions worked, in chapter order. Every attempt must be made to master both the theoretical and the practical aspects of the subject, as it is important for bankers to appreciate what lies behind any figures presented to them by their customers.

## Acknowledgements

We are grateful to The Institute of Bankers for permission to reproduce questions from past *Structure of Accounts* examination papers. We also wish to place on record our appreciation to Don Fiddes, FIB who encouraged us to write this book and, by regular telephone calls, ensured that we met our deadline. We are grateful to Stuart Crebo of National Westminster Bank for reading the original manuscript and making some helpful suggestions for improvement. Our thanks are also due to Sandie Edwards for coping magnificently with the task of typing a series of dispiritingly illegible manuscripts and to David Whelpton and Alexander Moffatt for completing the job at the Institute and thus ensuring prompt publication.

*J. R. Edwards.*
*H. J. Mellett.*
University College, Cardiff.

# Contents

## CHAPTER 3   The Preparation of Accounts from Cash Records

## CHAPTER 4   The Initial Record of Transactions

## CHAPTER 5  The Double Entry System

## CHAPTER 6  Periodic Accounting Reports

CHAPTER 7    **Asset Valuation, Profit Measurement and the Underlying Accounting Concepts**

## CHAPTER 8  Some Specialised Accounting Statements

## CHAPTER 9  Partnerships

# CHAPTER 10 Company Accounts

# CHAPTER 11 Decision-Making

CHAPTER 12   **Performance Assessment**

CHAPTER 13   **Revision Questions**

APPENDIX   **Solutions to Questions**

# CHAPTER 1

# The Balance Sheet Relationship between Assets and Sources of Finance

## 1.1 INTRODUCTION

You may have only recently joined the bank, but you have probably already discovered that the ability to analyse financial information and make quick calculations are valuable skills in your chosen profession. You will also find these abilities helpful in your accountancy studies, because numbers are at the foundation of the entire accounting process. An introductory text-book must include a definition of the topic under consideration and, for this purpose, we may define accountancy as follows:

*Accountancy is a system for recording and reporting business transactions, in financial terms, to interested parties who use this information as the basis for performance assessment and decision making.*

The two main elements of the accounting process are inter-related since accounting records are kept as the basis for preparing accounting reports. For instance, when the bank makes a loan to a customer, a record is made of this transaction, and the terms of the agreement provide for the loan to be repaid after a specified time period. Periodically, the bank manager will examine a list of loans outstanding and, if it transpires that the loan remains outstanding after the repayment date has fallen due, steps can be taken to insist on immediate repayment. We can therefore see both why the transaction is recorded and why the report is made. The loan is recorded so that it is not forgotten, i.e. it helps to protect money belonging to the bank, while the report brings to the bank manager's attention the fact that the loan is overdue. He can then take the necessary steps to ensure repayment takes place.

The loan report is an example of a *detailed* accounting statement since it contains full information relating to each advance. At the other extreme, accounting statements are prepared in a highly *summarised* form. A good example is the annual report published by banks for their shareholders. This report includes a number of accounting statements, amongst which the best known - the balance sheet and the profit and loss account - are the main subjects of this book. The profit and loss account is usually confined to a single sheet which summarises the financial effect of all the business transactions which produced either a profit or a loss for the bank during the year. The profit and loss account of the National Westminster Bank for 1984 showed a profit before tax of £671,000,000; the cumulative effect of many millions of individual transactions. The balance sheet, on the other hand, reports the assets belonging to the bank, at the end of the financial year, and the various ways in which those assets were financed at that date. The balance sheet of Barclays Bank, at 31 December 1984, reported total assets of £73,623,000,000 divided into just six major categories. The theory is that the shareholder needs financial information to judge the overall performance of his investment, as the basis for deciding whether to retain or sell his shares; the inclusion of vast amounts of detail would not help him in this endeavour and might even be positively damaging by obscuring the major financial developments.

We can therefore see that accountancy is a device for communicating relevant information as the basis for assessing performance and reaching decisions about how money should be invested. The accounting report is the means for communicating this information while the accounting record forms the basis for the report. The nature of the information and degree of detail contained in the report depend on the kind of decision which the recipient wishes to take.

## 1.2   THE ENTITY CONCEPT

Within the private sector of the economy there are three basic forms of business organisation:

*Sole trader.*   This is a business which has a single owner who also takes all the major managerial decisions. Examples are a shopkeeper or a plumber in business on his own account.
*Partnership.*   This exists where two or more people share the ownership and managerial functions. Professional people, such as accountants, solicitors and doctors, commonly

organise their business activities in the form of partnerships.
*Limited company.** A limited company may be private (Ltd.)
or public (plc). The main significance of the distinction is that
only the latter can make an issue of shares to the general public.
In the case of public companies, there is the further distinction
between quoted companies, whose shares are traded on the
stock exchange, and unquoted companies. In general, public
companies are larger than private companies and quoted
companies larger than unquoted.

There are two important differences between sole traders and
partnerships, sometimes referred to as 'firms', on the one hand and
limited companies on the other.

*1. The Relationship between ownership and management.*   In the
case of firms, the owner or owners also run the business, whereas in
the case of the limited company there may well be a significant
separation between the ownership and managerial functions. This is
particularly likely in the case of the public limited company where
the bulk of the finance is raised from the general public and the
business is run by professional managers who have only a relatively
small financial investment in the concern.

*2. The owner's liability for business debts.*   Sole traders and
partners normally have unlimited liability for the debts of their
firm, whereas the shareholders of limited companies are not
required to contribute beyond the amount of their original
investment. This distinction is significant when a business runs into
financial difficulties. In the case of firms, the creditors claim first
against the business assets but, if these are insufficient to satisfy the
amounts due, creditors can then claim against the owner's personal
wealth. In an extreme situation, the owner of a bankrupt firm could
be forced to sell his home and all other personal belongings to meet
demands from the firm's creditors. This contrasts starkly with the
respective positions of investors and creditors in a limited company,
where any deficiency of business assets compared with liabilities at
the date of liquidation is borne by the creditors.

---

* There are also a small number of unlimited companies in existence. For example, this
method of incorporation is sometimes used by professional firms who are not allowed to have
limited liability but want the tax advantages of being a company.

Company Law therefore regards a limited company as a separate legal entity. The creditor contracts with the company and can claim only against its assets. No such legal distinction is recognised where the business is carried on by a sole trader or by partners. *The position in accountancy is quite different*. It is always assumed, for accounting purposes, that the business entity has an existence separate and distinct from owners, managers, or any other individuals with whom it comes into contact during the course of its trading activities. The assumption of a separate existence, for accounting purposes, usually referred to as the *Entity Concept,* requires a careful distinction to be drawn between business affairs and personal transactions. One of the reasons for requiring this distinction to be made is that it facilitates performance assessment. A sole trader forms a business in the hope that it will earn him a satisfactory profit and, to discover whether this objective has been achieved, profit must be calculated on the basis of only business transactions.

### Illustration 1.1
On 1 January 19X1 Mr Little won a premium bond prize of £10,000 and used the cash in the following way:
  (i)    Purchased a mink coat for his wife, £1,900.
  (ii)   Holiday in Italy, £2,000.
  (iii)  Purchased a new cricket bat, £100.
  (iv)   Little decided to form a business called Little Enterprises and, as a first step, opened a business bank acount and paid in £6,000.

For accounting purposes Little Enterprises is immediately regarded as a separate entity from Little, It is therefore necessary to distinguish private transactions from business transactions. An examination of the above information shows (i) (ii) and (iii) to be private transactions and (iv) to be a business transaction.

Students should now work Question 1.1 at the end of the chapter. In all cases students should work the question *and then compare their answer with the solution provided at the end of the book.*

## 1.3 REPORTING CAPITAL IN THE BALANCE SHEET
Because the business is regarded as a separate accounting entity, business transactions must be recorded *twice:*

*First* to show the effect of the transaction on the assets belonging to the business and

*Secondly* to show the effect of the transaction on the relationship between the business, on the one hand, and providers of finance on the other.

Applying this rule to transaction (iv) in Illustration 1.1 we find that its effect is as follows:

| | |
|---|---|
| Effect on business assets: | Assets increase from zero to £6,000 as the result of the injection of cash. |
| Effect on relationship with providers of finance: | The business now owes Mr. Little £6,000. |

These facts are conventionally presented in the balance sheet in the following form:

## Illustration 1.2

*Balance Sheet of Little Enterprises at 1 January 19X1*

| SOURCES OF FINANCE | £ | ASSETS | £ |
|---|---|---|---|
| Capital: Mr. Little......... | 6,000 | Cash at bank................ | 6,000 |

The left side of the balance sheet shows that Mr Little has made a capital investment of £6,000 in the business. Put another way, the business owes Mr Little £6,000. The right side of the balance sheet shows that the assets belonging to the business, at present, consist of cash amounting to £6,000. Readers should note that there is numerical equality between the two sides of the balance sheet. This must always be the case since assets belonging to the business do not come out of 'thin air' and have been financed in some way or another. The corresponding finance is shown on the left side of the balance sheet and the fundamental equation SOURCES OF FINANCE = ASSETS therefore continues throughout the life of the business. We may therefore define the balance sheet as follows:

*The balance sheet is a financial statement which shows on the one hand the sources from which the business has raised finance and on the other the ways in which those resources are employed.*

It should also be noted that the balance sheet sets out the business's financial position *at a particular moment in time*: on 1 January 19X1 in the above example. It is for this reason that the balance sheet is sometimes described as an instantaneous financial photograph of the business. This description highlights both the major strength and major weakness of the balance sheet. It sums up, in a single statement, a large number of important financial facts, but only at one point in time; a day earlier or a day later the financial facts might be quite different.

## 1.4  RAISING FURTHER FINANCE

Before a business commences operations, arrangements should be made to raise finance sufficient to support the planned level of activity. Too many businesses begin their lives with insufficient cash resources and most of them fail before they get off the ground. At best, the early years of the firm's life will suffer from a continuous shortage of cash and much of management's time will be taken up coping with cash flow problems rather than being directed towards the development of profitable trading activities. A major portion of the initial financial requirement is, of course, provided by the owner, and this is described as his *capital investment* in the concern. It is, however, likely that an additional source of finance will have to be raised if the business is to be placed on a sound financial footing. Mr. Little has made a personal investment of £6,000 in Little Enterprises (see Illustration 1.2), and we will assume that he has estimated that a total initial investment of £10,000 is required to finance the planned level of business operations. He is £4,000 short and is likely to explore a number of avenues in the endeavour to obtain this sum. One possibility is to borrow from family or friends, another is to seek government aid, and a third might involve acquiring some of the business assets on hire purchase. We will assume that Little convinces his bank manager that there are sound prospects for Little Enterprises and on 2 January the bank lends him £4,000 secured by the deeds of his house. The effect of the transaction is as follows:

Effect on business assets:    Cash increases by £4,000.

Effect on relationship        Indebtedness to bank
with providers of finance:    increases from zero to
                              £4,000

The revised balance sheet becomes:

### Illustration 1.3

*Balance Sheet of Little Enterprises at 2 January 19X1*

| SOURCES OF FINANCE | £ | ASSETS | £ |
|---|---|---|---|
| Capital................... | 6,000 | Cash at bank (£6,000 + £4,000) | 10,000 |
| Loan from bank............ | 4,000 | | |
| | 10,000 | | 10,000 |

The equality between sources of finance and assets is retained with the increase in business assets financed by the bank loan. There are now, however, two different types of finance. The amount advanced by Little, his capital, is a permanent investment which will not usually be withdrawn until the business is wound up, whereas the amount advanced by the bank is a liability which must be repaid in due course. The relationship SOURCES OF FINANCE = ASSETS therefore needs to be extended, as follows, by dividing the sources of finance into the two component parts:

$$CAPITAL + LIABILITIES = ASSETS$$
which may be abbreviated to
$$C + L = A$$

Students should test their understanding of this relationship by working Question 1.2 at the end of this chapter.

## 1.5  THE INVESTMENT DECISION

It is the job of management to employ profitably the resources which have been placed at its disposal. To carry out this function many decisions have to be made, and these result in a continuous flow of cash and other assets into and out of the business. Accounting statements, amongst which the balance sheet is one of the most important, are prepared at regular intervals to enable management to monitor the results of their decisions and to gauge the extent to which they are achieving the objective of profit maximisation. Accounting statements are also prepared for the owners to enable them to assess the effectiveness with which the resources placed at management's disposal have been employed.

In firms, and often also private limited companies, management and ownership are in the hands of the same individuals, but the entity concept enables their separate roles to be clearly identified; the owners provide the finance and expect an adequate return on their investment, while management enjoys paid employment but is responsible for earning an adequate return on the resources entrusted to it. On the basis of results shown in the accounting statements, management makes decisions about the future conduct of the business while ownership decides whether to maintain or increase its investment in the business, withdraw from the undertaking, or, where management and ownership are different people, the owners may change the management team if they feel that the results could be improved.

In the case of Little Enterprises, Mr Little, when performing his managerial role, must decide how to employ the cash available to the business, i.e. he must make an *investment decision*. Little decides to go into business as a wholesaler specialising in the acquisition of stationery from manufacturers and its resale to retail shops. After careful enquiries, he purchases for cash premises for £7,000 and stock-in-trade for £2,500 on 10 January 19X1. The effect of these transactions is as follows:

| | |
|---|---|
| Effect on business assets: | Premises increase by £7,000, Stock-in-trade increases by £2,500. Cash at bank reduces by £9,500. |
| Effect on relationship with outsiders: | Zero |

**Illustration 1.4**

Balance Sheet of Little Enterprises at 10 January 19X1.

| SOURCES OF FINANCE | £ | ASSETS | £ |
|---|---|---|---|
| Capital .................... | 6,000 | Premises .................... | 7,000 |
| Loan from bank ............. | 4,000 | Stocks ..................... | 2,500 |
| | | Cash at bank (£10,000-£9,500) | 500 |
| | 10,000 | | 10,000 |

No additional sources of finance have been raised and the left hand side of the balance sheet remains unchanged. The effect of the investment decision is merely to cause a redistribution of available resources, and the above balance sheet shows the revised financial position at 10 January. Little Enterprises is now in a position where it is almost ready to commence trading. However, Little must first make sure that the firm is in possession of a stock of stationery sufficient to enable sales to be made and still leave available a full range of products to display to potential customers for this purpose. He estimates that further stocks costing £2,000 are required. The above balance sheet shows that the company has insufficient cash available and an additional source of finance must be obtained. In practice, very few businesses operate entirely on the cash basis; instead a proportion, often a high proportion, of purchases and sales are made on credit, i.e. a period of time elapses between the dates that goods are supplied and paid for. Normally businesses take the maximum period of credit allowed because, during this time, stock is financed by suppliers rather than by the firm itself. The period of credit allowed by suppliers varies a great deal but 30 days is most common.

Little Enterprises acquires stationery costing £2,000 on 11 January 19X1. The supplier allows 30 days credit. The effect of the transaction is as follows:

Effect on business assets:     Stock-in-trade increases by £2,000.

Effect on relationship with outsiders:     Trade creditors increase by £2,000.

## Illustration 1.5

*Balance Sheet of Little Enterprises at 11 January 19X1.*

| SOURCES OF FINANCE | £ | ASSETS | £ |
|---|---|---|---|
| Capital | 6,000 | Premises | 7,000 |
| Loan from bank | 4,000 | Stocks (£2,500 + £2,000) | 4,500 |
| Trade creditors | 2,000 | Cash at bank | 500 |
| | 12,000 | | 12,000 |

The above balance sheet shows that the firm now owns assets totalling £12,000 made up of premises, stock-in-trade (usually abbreviated to 'stocks') and cash at bank. The finance has been obtained from three sources: ownership, the bank and suppliers who are described as trade creditors for balance sheet purposes. The investment made by the owners is normally permanent, while the loan is likely to be the subject of a formal agreement which deals with such matters as the repayment date and the rate of interest payable. Trade creditors expect to be repaid in accordance with the normal practice of the particular trade, in this case 30 days. An important feature of trade credit is that it is a renewable source of finance in the sense that, provided the firm pays money currently owed, it will be able to acquire further supplies on credit, thereby maintaining a constant level of indebtedness.

Students should now work Question 1.3 at the end of the chapter.

## 1.6 BUSINESS DEVELOPMENT

Little Enterprises is now ready to start trading. Mr Little established the business in the expectation that it would earn profits, and stocks must therefore be sold for sums sufficiently in excess of their cost to convince Little that his captial is efficiently employed and would not yield a larger return if invested elsewhere.

On 12 January Little Enterprises sells stationery costing £2,000 to a local chain of newsagents for £3,500, payment to be made by the end of the month. Ignoring interest charges and other operating costs, a *profit* of £1,500 (sales price £3,500 minus cost £2,000) is earned which accrues to Mr Little and is added to his capital to show that the value of his investment in the business has increased. The effect of the transaction is as follows:

| | |
|---|---|
| Effect on business assets: | Stock-in-trade decreases by £2,000. |
| | Trade debtors increase by £3,500. |
| Effect on relationship with outsiders: | Capital increases by £1,500 |

**Illustration 1.6**

*Balance Sheet of Little Enterprises at 12 January 19X1.*

| SOURCES OF FINANCE | £ | ASSETS | £ |
|---|---|---|---|
| Capital.................... | 6,000 | Premises.................... | 7,000 |
| Add:   Profit | 1,500 | Stocks (£4,500-£2,000) | 2,500 |
| | 7,500 | Trade debtors.............. | 3,500 |
| Loan from bank............. | 4,000 | Cash at bank................ | 500 |
| Trade creditors.............. | 2,000 | | |
| | 13,500 | | 13,500 |

The total assets of Little Enterprises, alternatively described as the 'gross assets', have increased from £12,000, in Illustration 1.5, to £13,500 in Illustration 1.6. This is because one asset (stock) costing £2,000 has been replaced by a new asset (trade debtors) worth £3,500. A similar increase occurs in the sources of finance as the result of adding the profit earned to Mr Little's initial capital investment. It should be noticed that profit is recognised despite the fact that the cash due for the goods has not yet been received. This brings us to a second assumption made by accountants when preparing accounting statements, namely the *Realisation Concept.* This concept assumes that profit is earned or realised *when the sale takes place,* and the justification for this treatment is that Little

Enterprises now possesses a more valuable asset, since the £3,500 is a legally enforceable debt. The trading cycle is completed by Little Enterprises collecting £3,500 on 31 January 19X1 and paying £2,000 to its supplier on 8 February 19X1, 30 days after the goods were supplied. The effect of these transactions are as follows:

| | |
|---|---|
| Effect on business assets: | Trade debtors decrease by £3,500. |
| | Cash increases by £3,500. |
| | Cash decreases by £2,000. |
| Effect on relationship with outsiders: | Trade creditors decrease by £2,000. |

**Illustration 1.7**

*Balance Sheet of Little Enterprises at 8 February 19X1*

| SOURCES OF FINANCE | £ | ASSETS | £ |
|---|---|---|---|
| Capital.................... | 6,000 | Premises................... | 7,000 |
| Add: Profit................ | 1,500 | Stocks.................... | 2,500 |
| | 7,500 | Cash at bank (£500 + £1,500).. | 2,000 |
| Loan from bank............. | 4,000 | | |
| | 11,500 | | 11,500 |

Students should now work Question 1.4 at the end of this chapter.

## 1.7  THE TRADING CYCLE

The single trading cycle for Little Enterprises, examined above, is now complete, and can be expressed in the form of a diagram as on the following page.

The cycle consists of the following four stages:

Stage 1:  The purchase of goods on credit which gives rise to balance sheet entries for trade creditors and stock.

Stage 2:  The sale of stock results in a profit being realised or a loss incurred. At this stage some of the stock is replaced by trade debtors in the balance sheet.

Stage 3:  The collection of trade debts. This produces a change in the composition of the firm's assets, from debts to cash.

Stage 4:  The payment of the amounts due to suppliers.

## Figure 1.1
## The Trading Cycle

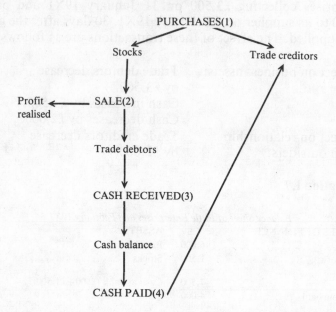

A comparison of the position before (Illustration 1.4) and after (Illustration 1.7) the trading cycle is undertaken shows just two differences: Cash rises by £1,500 and the owner's capital investment increases by a similar amount to reflect profit earned.

The trading cycle examined above is obviously a simplified version of what happens in practice. A company does not complete one cycle before commencing another, but is involved in a continuous series of overlapping business transactions. The purchases cycle consists of ordering goods, receiving them into stock as an asset, and paying for them by means of a cash outflow, while the sales cycle consists of making a sale, parting with the stocks sold as an asset outflow, and collecting the money due from the customer to produce a cash inflow. Therefore, even before one creditor is paid another is created and debtors are turned over in a similar manner. It is the responsibility of management to ensure that all of these flows are adequately controlled and recorded. Thus no payment should be made without ensuring that the related goods or services have in fact been received, and no goods should be allowed to leave the firm except in exchange for cash or by the creation of a debt. In the latter case there must be adequate follow up to ensure that the cash is subsequently collected.

A simplified version of the trading cycle occurs when purchases and/or sales are made for cash. There are just two stages: Stage 1, the purchase of goods, involves the exchange of cash for stocks; Stage 2, the sale of goods, involves the exchange of stock for cash of a greater or lesser value, with the amount of the difference recorded as a profit or a loss.

## 1.8 REPORTING CHANGES IN OWNER'S CAPITAL

Each enterprise is regarded as a separate entity for accounting purposes, and the statement of capital in the balance sheet records the indebtedness of the business to its owners. This indebtedness is initially created by ownership introducing finance into the business but the amount changes over time as the result of trading activity. A profit increases the indebtedness, whereas a loss reduces the value of the owner's capital investment. Because it shows the relationship between the business and its owner, the capital section of the balance sheet also reports all other transactions between these two entities. For instance, it reports any additional capital investments made by the owner during the life of the business, and also the regular withdrawals of cash and goods made for personal use. The manner in which these matters are reported is shown in Illustration 1.8. Because we are only interested in changes in capital, the remainder of the balance sheet is omitted.

### Illustration 1.8

C.Newman started in business on 1 January 19X1 and paid £2,000 into his business bank account. On 30 June he transferred to the business his car valued at £1,400. Each week he withdrew £60 from the business in cash. The accounts prepared for 19X1 showed that his business had earned a profit of £4,100 during the year.

*Extracts from Balance Sheet at 31 December 19X1*

|  |  | £ |
|---|---|---|
| Opening capital, 1 January 19X1 | | 2,000 |
| Add: Additional capital investment | | 1,400 |
| Profit for 19X1 | | 4,100 |
| | | 7,500 |
| Less: Drawings (£60 x 52) | | 3,120 |
| Closing capital, 31 December 19X1 | | 4,380* |

*The closing capital for 19X1 is the opening capital for 19X2.

The owner does not normally wait until profit is calculated before making withdrawals. Often he is dependent on the business for his livelihood and profits are withdrawn, for personal use, as they are earned during the year. Where profits exceed drawings, as is the case in Illustration 1.8, the surplus of £980 (profit £4,100 minus drawings £3,120) is retained in the business and increases the owner's capital by an equivalent amount. These extra resources may be used to finance an expansion in the level of business operations. Illustration 1.8 also demonstrates the fact that capital may be introduced in the form of assets other than cash. The motor vehicle, transferred to the business by Newman, appears as an asset in the balance sheet, and is matched by a corresponding increase in the value of his capital investment. Similarly, drawings may be made in a non-cash form (e.g. the family of a farmer is likely to consume some of the farm produce) though this has not happened in the above illustration. Readers should now work Question 1.5 at the end of the chapter.

## 1.9 CAPITAL + LIABILITIES = ASSETS

In the case of Little Enterprises we saw that the equality between sources of finance and assets was maintained throughout the trading cycle and, because all assets must be financed in some manner, we can be confident that this equality will continue throughout the firm's life. In this context there are four basic categories of business transaction:

1. Where an increase in a source of finance is matched by an increase in an asset. For example, extra capital invested by the owner which increases the cash balance by an equal amount.
2. Where an increase in a source of finance is matched by a decrease in another source of finance. For example, an increased overdraft to enable trade creditors to be paid the amount due to them.
3. Where a reduction in a source of finance is matched by a reduction in an asset. For example, trade creditors paid out of the balance of cash at bank.
4. Where an increase in an asset is matched by a reduction in another asset. For example, a new motor vehicle purchased for cash.

A complication occurs in the case of a transaction involving the sale of goods, since this gives rise to a profit or a loss which must also be recorded. For example, assume an item of stock which cost £80 is sold on credit for £100. In the balance sheet stock is replaced by debtors, i.e. a category 4 transaction takes place. In addition a category 1 transaction occurs, because the higher value of debtors, £20, gives rise to a profit which must be added to the owner's capital.

Readers should now work Questions 1.6 and 1.7 at the end of this chapter.

## 1.10 CLASSIFICATION OF ASSETS AND SOURCES OF FINANCE

**1.10.1 Assets** Business assets may be defined as resources owned by an entity which have the potential for providing it with future economic benefits in the sense that they help to generate future cash inflows or reduce future cash outflows. The fact that a business asset exists, however, does not necessarily mean that it will be reported in the balance sheet. For this to be done, the asset must satisfy the further requirement that the benefit it provides can be measured or quantified, in money terms, with a reasonable degree of precision. This rule is called the *Money Measurement Concept* . For example, stock-in-trade is reported as a business asset because it is owned by the firm, it has an identifiable monetary value (its cost) and it is expected to benefit the firm when it is sold. Expenditure incurred on training staff, on the other hand, presents a more difficult problem. While it is possible to identify the amount of the expenditure, it is not possible to forecast with a high degree of certainty whether the firm will benefit from the expenditure. Employees may be poorly motivated and fail to improve their competence as the result of attending training courses. In addition, they may leave the firm and take their new expertise elsewhere. Because of this uncertainty concerning the likely extent of any future benefit, such expenditure is not reported as a business asset but is instead written off against profit as it is incurred.

Assets reported in the balance sheet are divided into two categories:

1. Current Assets. These are defined as assets which are held for resale, conversion into cash or are cash itself. There are three main types of current assets: stock-in-trade, trade debtors and cash. A *temporary* investment of funds in the shares of a quoted company or in government securities should also be classified as a current asset. A characteristic of current assets is that the balances are constantly changing as the result of business operations.

2. Fixed Assets. These are assets which a firm purchases and retains to help carry on the business. It is not intended to sell fixed assets in the ordinary course of business and it is expected that the bulk of their value will be used up as the result of contributing to trading activities. Examples of fixed assets are premises, plant, machinery, furniture and motor vehicles. A characteristic of fixed assets is that they usually remain in the business for long periods of time and will only be sold or scrapped when they are of no further use. A fixed asset which a firm uses but does not own, e.g. rented premises, must *not* be reported in the balance sheet, but any expenses incurred to obtain the use of the asset must be treated as a business expense.

It is important for students to realise that it is possible to classify an asset as current or fixed only by examining the reason why it was purchased, i.e. was it purchased for resale or retention? Assets purchased by one company for resale may be purchased by another for retention. For example, a garage purchases motor vehicles for resale while a manufacturing concern acquires them as fixed assets to be used for example by sales representatives.

Assets are reported in the balance sheet in the order of increasing liquidity, i.e. the list starts with the items least likely to be turned into cash and ends with the items expected to be converted into cash in the near future. A typical balance sheet presentation of assets is given in Figure 1.2

## Figure 1.2

*Balance Sheet of the Nut and Bolt Engineering Company at 31 December 19X1*

| | £ | £ | | £ | £ |
|---|---|---|---|---|---|
| Capital | | 179,000 | *Fixed Assets* | | |
| | | | Land and buildings | | 75,000 |
| *Non-Current Liabilities* | | | Plant and machinery | | 49,000 |
| Loans repayable 19X8 | | 50,000 | Motor vehicles | | 21,500 |
| | | | | | 145,500 |
| *Current Liabilities* | | | | | |
| Trade creditors | 170,000 | | *Current Assets* | | |
| Expense creditors | 1,900 | | Stock-in-trade | 145,700 | |
| Bank overdraft | 36,700 | | Trade debtors | 143,700 | |
| | | | Investments | 2,600 | |
| | | 208,600 | Cash in hand | 100 | |
| | | | | | 292,100 |
| | | 437,600 | | | 437,600 |

**1.10.2  Sources of Finance**  We have seen that sources of finance are divided into the capital invested by the owners and liabilities due to non-ownership groups. These liabilities may be further classified into current liabilities, defined as amounts repayable within twelve months of the balance sheet date, and non-current liabilities. Typical examples of current liabilities are amounts owing to trade creditors for goods supplied, creditors for other business expenses and bank overdrafts which are normally repayable on call. Any loans repayable within the following year are also listed under current liabilities. The only loan outstanding in the case of Nut and Bolt Engineering is not repayable for another seven years (in 19X8), and is therefore classified as a non-current liability and positioned between the capital section and current liabilities in the balance sheet.

We can see from Figure 1.2 that sources of finance are listed in order of permanence, with the most permanent sources at the top and amounts repayable, or potentially repayable, in the near future at the bottom of the balance sheet. Most sources of finance are easily classified into one or other of the three categories, but certain items cause a little more difficulty. For example, the terms of a bank loan may provide for an advance of £100,000 repayable by five equal annual instalments of £20,000. In these circumstances the liability must be divided into two parts, with the next instalment repayable, of £20,000, shown as a current liability and the balance reported as a non-current liability. Therefore, at the end of the first year, £20,000 is reported as a current liability and £80,000 as a non-current liability.

Accountancy is a device for communicating relevant financial information to interested parties. It is therefore important that the information reported should not only be technically accurate but also be presented in an orderly fashion so that it can be readily understood by owners, managers and others who wish to assess progress. The balance sheet of the Nut and Bolt Engineering Company is drafted in a manner which helps to achieve this objective. It is divided into five sections and, for each of these, an appropriate description is given and a sub-total provided. Users of accounting statements are therefore able to see, at a glance, the amount of finance provided by the owners, the volume of long-term loans and the quantity of short-term finance. The statement also shows how the total finance has been allocated between fixed and current assets. If a firm is to be financially stable, it is normally important for long-term investments in fixed assets to be substantially financed by the owners and for current assets to be sufficient to meet current liabilities falling due over the next twelve months. A well prepared balance sheet enables these and other forms of financial analysis, examined in chapters 11 and 12, to be efficiently carried out.

Readers should now work Questions 1.8 - 1.10 at the end of this chapter.

## 1.11  QUESTIONS
### Question 1.1
Indicate which of the following transactions relate to Clive's business as a newsagent and which are his personal transactions:
   (i)    £50 win on premium bonds owned by Clive.
   (ii)   £100 paid for the following advertisement on a hoarding at the local football ground: 'Clive's for all the up to date news'.
   (iii)  Payment to the newspaper wholesaler, £1,260.
   (iv)   Sale of unsold newspapers to a local fish and chip shop.
   (v)    Purchase of a new car for family use, although it will be used each morning to collect papers from suppliers.

### Question 1.2
John decides to start up in business on 1 April 19X2, and pays £4,000 from his private bank account into a newly opened business bank account. On 2 April 19X2 John's father loans the firm £600 to help with the new venture, and this amount is paid immediately into the business bank account. On 4 April the firm borrows £150 from John's friend Peter. This amount is kept in the form of 'ready cash' to meet small business expenses.

*Required:*
Balance sheets for John's business after the transactions on:
   (a)    1 April
   (b)    2 April
   (c)    4 April

### Question 1.3
Roger starts up in business on 1 September with a capital of £1,200 which he pays into his business bank account on that day. The bank agrees to provide him with a business overdraft facility of £500 for

the first three months. The following business transactions take place:

| | |
|---|---|
| 2 September: | A machine is bought, on three months credit from Plant Suppliers Ltd., for £750. |
| | £1,000 is borrowed from the Endridge Local Authority which is keen to encourage this type of enterprise. |
| 3 September: | £1,820 is paid for a second hand machine. |
| | Stock is purchased, for cash, £420. |
| 4 September: | Stock is purchased, on credit, for £215. |

*Required:*
Balance sheets for Roger's business following the transactions on:
- (a)   1 September
- (b)   2 September
- (c)   3 September
- (d)   4 September

## Question 1.4

The following balance sheet was prepared for Jeff's business at 1 October 19X5. The firm has an overdraft facility of £700.

*Balance Sheet*

| | £ | | £ |
|---|---|---|---|
| Capital | 5,300 | Machinery | 2,200 |
| | | Stocks | 2,870 |
| Trade creditors | 690 | Debtors | 800 |
| | | Cash at bank | 120 |
| | 5,990 | | 5,990 |

Jeff enters into the following transactions:

| | |
|---|---|
| 2 October: | Sells goods which cost £120 for £200, cash. |
| | Sells goods which cost £240 for £315, on credit. |
| 3 October: | Collects £150 from customers. |
| | Purchases stock for £190, on credit. |
| 4 October: | Pays trade creditors £75. |
| | Purchases a machine for £600, cash. |

*Required:*
Balance sheets for Jeff's business following the transactions on:
  (a)   2 October
  (b)   3 October
  (c)   4 October

## Question 1.5

(a)   Prepare the balance sheet of Daley from the following list of assets and liabilities at 31 December 19X1:

|  | £ |
|---|---|
| Cash | 1,750 |
| Stock | 5,250 |
| Owed by customers | 3,340 |
| Owed to suppliers | 2,890 |
| Business premises | 9,000 |
| Loan from Weakly | 3,000 |

(b)   Prepare the balance sheet of Daley's business at the end of each of the first seven days of January taking account of the following transactions:

19X2:   January. 1.   Purchased, on credit, a typewriter for office use, £500
             2.   Received £190 from a customer.
             3.   Paid a supplier £670.
             4.   Purchased stock, on credit, £260.
             5.   Sold goods which had cost £350 for £530 cash.
             6.   Repaid Weakly £1,000 of the balance due to him (ignore interest).
             7.   Withdrew stock costing £100 for private use.

## Question 1.6

Examine separately the effect of each of the following transactions on the relationship $C + L = A$.
1.   The owner of a business received a legacy of £2,000 and paid it into his business bank account.
2.   Machinery costing £3,000 is purchased for cash.
3.   Stock-in-trade is purchased on credit for £800.
4.   A business computer is purchased for £5,000 and is financed by a loan from a friend.

5. Trade debts amounting to £750 are collected from customers.
6. Stock-in-trade costing £1,000 is sold for £1,400.
7. A supplier is paid £220 due to him.
8. Stock-in-trade is purchased for cash £350.
9. A filing cabinet is purchased for £60 by increasing an existing bank overdraft.
10. The owner of a business drew a cheque for £100 on his business bank account to meet private expenses.

You should present your answer in the following form:

| TRANSACTION | CAPITAL + | LIABILITIES | = ASSETS. |
|---|---|---|---|
| | £ | £ | £ |
| 1 | +2,000 | 0 | = +2,000 |
| 2 | 0 | 0 | = +3,000 |
| | | | −3,000 |

Note: In transaction 2, the machinery acquired increases assets by £3,000 but the payment reduces assets by the same amount. The net effect is zero.

## Question 1.7

Prepare balance sheets to determine the amount missing from each of the following lists of balances at 31 December 19X1:

| | A | B | C | D | E | F |
|---|---|---|---|---|---|---|
| | £ | £ | £ | £ | £ | £ |
| Capital at 1 January 19X1 | 2,500 | 2,000 | 3,000 | 4,000 | 3,800 | ? |
| Profit for 19X1 | 1,000 | 3,200 | ? | 5,700 | 2,300 | 7,000 |
| Drawings during 19X1 | 800 | 3,000 | 1,000 | 4,900 | ? | 4,500 |
| Current liabilities | 750 | ? | 600 | 1,300 | 1,700 | 2,100 |
| Fixed assets | 1,800 | 1,750 | 2,800 | ? | 3,700 | 8,500 |
| Current assets | ? | 850 | 1,200 | 1,900 | 1,600 | 3,500 |

## Question 1.8

Review your understanding of the following concepts and terms discussed in this chapter by writing a short explanation of each of them.

| | | | |
|---|---|---|---|
| (i) | Accountancy | (vii) | C+L=A. |
| (ii) | Entity concept | (viii) | Owner's capital |
| (iii) | Balance sheet | (ix) | Money measurement concept |
| (iv) | Realisation concept | (x) | Fixed assets |
| (v) | Trade credit | (xi) | Current assets |
| (vi) | Trading cycle, credit transactions | (xii) | Current liabilities |
| | | (xiii) | Gross assets. |

## Question 1.9

For a fish and chip shop, indicate which of the following items are current liabilities, which are current assets and which are fixed assets.

(i) Microwave oven.
(ii) 2,000 kilos of 'King Edward' potatoes.
(iii) Cash register.
(iv) Amount owing to the Fat Fishy Company Ltd.
(v) Capital investment of Mr V.Greasy, owner.
(vi) Mrs Greasy's pearl knecklace and gold wristwatch.
(vii) 250 Mackerel.
(viii) Loan from V.Greasy's father, repayable in two years time.
(ix) Last instalment due, in one month's time, on the microwave oven acquired on hire purchase.
(x) Shop rented from a property company.

For items not classified as current liabilities or current assets or fixed assets, describe how they would be reported in the balance sheet, if at all.

## Question 1.10

The following list of balances relates to the business of C.Forest at 31 December 19X3:

| | |
|---|---:|
| Plant and machinery | 26,500 |
| Stock in trade | 14,200 |
| Loan repayable June 19X4 | 2,500 |
| Capital of C.Forest at 1 January 19X3 | 52,380 |
| Trade creditors | 10,600 |
| Trade debtors | 14,100 |
| Cash-in-hand | 270 |
| Bank overdraft | 3,940 |
| Profit for 19X3 | 12,600 |
| Owner's drawings during 19X3 | 10,950 |
| Loan repayable 19X9 | 9,000 |
| Leasehold premises | 25,000 |

*Required:*
The balance sheet of C.Forest's business at 31 December 19X3 presented in good style.

# CHAPTER 2

# Profit Calculated as the Increase in Capital

## 2.1 PROFITABLE ACTIVITY

The maximisation of profit has been traditionally regarded as the principal factor motivating the individual to invest in a business venture. In recent years, however, businessmen have often appeared reluctant to justify business activity in quite so direct a manner. This is in many ways a healthy development which demonstrates an increasing awareness of the fact that business organisations, particularly the very large ones, have responsibilities other than to produce an adequate return for their investors. A list of the responsibilities acknowledged by businessmen today can be obtained by examining the corporate objectives declared by company chairmen in their annual reports to shareholders. These often include a wide range of items, amongst which earning a profit appears to be accorded no particular priority. Identified corporate goals include such matters as an increase in the market share, the improvement of product quality, a contented work force, pollution-free production processes, the maximisation of exports, and survival. It is difficult to say whether these aims are each of equal importance, but probably they are not. One view is that profit maximisation is the main objective, and all the other stated objectives have as their central purpose to contribute, either directly or indirectly, to the long-run achievement of that principal aim. This view may attach rather too much significance to profit, but widespread agreement that profit is an essential product of business activity in Great Britain can safely be assumed.

There are basically two competing claims on the profits generated by business activity.

*1. Withdrawals.* The owner requires a satisfactory return on his investment, in the form of drawings or dividends, and an inadequate return will result in the owner closing down the business and investing his money elsewhere.

*2. Reinvestment.* The second claim on profit arises from the fact that retained profits have historically been the major source of finance for business expansion. In earlier times, it was quite common for businesses to develop from small beginnings and become very large industrial undertakings, entirely on the basis of retained earnings. Today it is usual for companies to speed up their rate of expansion by calling on a wide range of additional sources of finance, including bank loans and overdrafts, but there remain many companies in which profits retained and reinvested over the entire life of the concern far exceed the capital initially subscribed by the shareholders. For example, the balance sheet of Williams & Glyn's Bank plc at 30 September 1984 shows share capital as £33.8 million whereas retained profits amount to £213.7 million, i.e. over six times more. The retention of profits increases the value of the owner's investment in the business, of course, and should produce higher profits and withdrawals in the future.

When trading conditions are difficult there may be insufficient profits to finance expansion or even to pay a return on the owner's investment and, in these circumstances, management must look elsewhere for the finance required to carry on business. This is not a situation which can persist indefinitely; just as consistent profitability generates the resources necessary for a healthy business, equally a succession of losses gradually deprives a company of the finance needed to support a continuation of business activity. Failure to restore an adequate level of profitability eventually results in the cessation of business activities. It is part of the accounting function to help management guard against such an outcome by enabling it to monitor progress and ensure that resources are efficiently employed.

## 2.2   PROFIT AND CHANGES IN GROSS ASSETS

The equivalence between assets and sources of finance was demonstrated in chapter 1, where we also discovered that when profit is earned a similar increase occurs in the assets under the control of management. This fact was illustrated by means of a series of balance sheets setting out the financial development of a firm called Little Enterprises. Readers should now revise their understanding of the relationship between profit and the level of business assets by working the following example:

## Example 2.1

*Balance Sheet of Larch at 31 December 19X1*

| SOURCES OF FINANCE | £ | ASSETS | £ | £ |
|---|---|---|---|---|
| Capital .................... | 2,000 | *Fixed Assets* | | |
| *Current Liabilities*.......... | | Plant and machinery......... | | 1,600 |
| Trade creditors.............. | 700 | *Current Assets* | | |
| | | Stocks..................... | 600 | |
| | | Trade debtors.............. | 300 | |
| | | Cash ..................... | 200 | 1,100 |
| | 2,700 | | | 2,700 |

On 1 January 19X2 Larch sold stock (cost price £140) on credit for £220.

*Required:*
The balance sheet of Larch following the transaction on 1 January.

## Solution

*Balance Sheet of Larch at 1 January 19X2*

| SOURCES OF FINANCE | £ | ASSETS | £ | £ |
|---|---|---|---|---|
| Capital .................... | 2,000 | *Fixed Assets* | | |
| Add:Net profit (220 - 140).... | 80 | Plant and machinery......... | | 1,600 |
| | 2,080 | *Current Assets* | | |
| *Current Liabilities* | | Stocks (600 - 140)........... | 460 | |
| Trade creditors.............. | 700 | Trade debtors (300 + 220)..... | 520 | |
| | | Cash ..................... | 200 | 1,180 |
| | 2,780 | | | 2,780 |

A comparison of the two balance sheets shows that the financial effects of the single trading transaction undertaken by Larch are as follows:

(i)  Gross assets have increased from £2,700 to £2,780 as the result of stock costing £140 being replaced by a debt due from a customer of £220.

(ii) Total sources of finance have increased by the same amount as the result of adding the profit realised, of £80, to Larch's opening capital.

## 2.3  BALANCE SHEET PRESENTATION: VERTICAL FORMAT

The balance sheets so far examined are presented in, what is conventionally described as, the horizontal format with sources of finance on the left and assets on the right.* Since the early 1960's industry has gradually discarded the horizontal format in favour of the vertical format, though many financial institutions continue to favour the former method of presentation. Lloyds Bank plc is one exception; it changed to the vertical format for its 1983 published accounts. The vertical presentation, to which we now turn attention, is illustrated below using the same information as appears in the balance sheets contained in Example 2.1.

**Example 2.2**

Vertical presentation of the balance sheets of Larch.

*Balance Sheet of Larch*

| | 1 Jan. 19X2 | | 31 Dec. 19X1 | |
|---|---|---|---|---|
| NET ASSETS | £ | £ | £ | £ |
| *Fixed Assets* | | | | |
| Plant and machinery............ | | 1,600 | | 1,600 |
| *Current Assets* | | | | |
| Stocks........................ | 460 | | 600 | |
| Trade debtors.................. | ·520 | | 300 | |
| Cash ......................... | 200 | | 200 | |
| | 1,180 | | 1,100 | |
| *Less: Current Liabilities* | | | | |
| Trade creditors................ | 700 | | 700 | |
| Working capital............... | | 480 | | 400 |
| | | 2,080 | | 2,000 |
| *Financed by:* | | | | |
| CAPITAL | | | | |
| Opening capital............... | | 2,000 | | ** |
| Add: Net profit.............. | | 80 | | ** |
| Closing capital................ | | 2,080 | | 2,000 |

**: figures not provided

The main advantage of the vertical presentation is that it is easier to compare the position of a business at a series of accounting dates. The above illustration gives the position at just two dates, but a columnar presentation dealing with five or even ten accounting dates would pose no particular difficulty, and it is then a relatively

* The Companies Act 1981 introduced a requirement for the published accounts of *Limited* companies, when presented in the horizontal format, to show assets on the *left* and liabilities on the *right*. In due course, it is likely that this presentation will be adopted, voluntarily, by those unincorporated enterprises which continue to use the horizontal format.

easy matter to glance across the series of figures to discover relevant changes and overall trends. For example, the analysis might show that large amounts of money are being spent each year on fixed assets, suggesting a policy of rapid expansion, whereas a continuous decline in the balance of cash, perhaps converting into a substantial overdraft, might be taken as an indication of the fact that the company is suffering from increasing cash difficulties.

A second advantage of the vertical presentation is that it contains an extra item of useful information which does not appear in the horizontal balance sheet, namely working capital, which is the balancing figure obtained by deducting current liabilities from current assets. A financially stable business is one which is able to meet its debts as they fall due for payment, and an adequate balance of working capital is an essential requirement if this desirable state of affairs is to exist. It is not possible to specify a figure for working capital which all firms should try to maintain. Much will depend on individual circumstances, such as the size of the firm, the speed with which creditors are paid, stocks are sold and cash is collected from customers. Neverthless managers, shareholders, creditors and other users of accounting statements normally hold firm views concerning what can be regarded as an acceptable balance for a particular business. Working capital is examined further in section 3 of chapter 12.

The vertical balance sheet contains the same basic financial information as does the horizontal balance sheeet, since the facts are in no way altered by adopting a different method of presenting them. Similarly, the overall financial relationship between sources of finance and assets, expressed in the formula Capital + Liabilities = Assets remains unchanged. The revised presentation does, however, focus attention on a different aspect of the relationship between the three magnitudes, since it emphasises the fact that capital is equal to assets (fixed plus current) minus liabilities, i.e:

$$Capital = Assets - Liabilities$$

In practice, the term 'assets minus liabilities' is normally shortened to 'net assets'. We can therefore see that capital equals net assets; indeed these are two different ways of describing the same financial total. The only difference is the way in which the figure is calculated. The figure for capital is computed by taking the owner's opening investment, adding profit earned and deducting withdrawals for private use to give his/her closing investment at a particular date. Net assets, on the other hand, are computed by adding together the values of the various assets owned on the date under consideration, and then deducting the amount of finance obtained in the form of liabilities. Since assets are, by definition, financed either from capital or from liabilities, the balance which remains must necessarily be equal, in value, to the owner's investment.

Students should now work Question 2.1 at the end of this chapter.

## 2.4 PROFIT AND THE INCREASE IN NET ASSETS

Example 2.1 demonstrates the fact that profit produces an equivalent increase in the gross assets of a firm; the profit of £80 resulted in gross assets increasing from £2,700 to £2,780. If you now examine the vertical balance sheets given in Example 2.2 you can see that profit also produces an equivalent increase in net assets which are up from £2,000 to £2,080. This is to be expected. The firm has earned a profit and this must be added to Larch's capital. We know that capital is equal to net assets, though calculated differently, so an increase in capital of £80 necesarily involves an increase in net assets of the same amount. In Example 2.2 liabilities are admittedly held constant at £700 but, even if these change, the equality of capital and net assets is in no way disturbed. This fact is illustrated in example 2.3.

### Example 2.3

The following additional transactions were undertaken by Larch's business:

2 January.   Suppliers paid £160.
3 January.   Stock purchased on credit for £270.

*Required:*
Separate balance sheets for Larch's business after the transactions on:
  (a)   2 January
  (b)   3 January

## Solution

*Balance Sheet of Larch*

| | 3 Jan 19X2 | | 2 Jan 19X2 | | 1 Jan 19X2 | |
|---|---|---|---|---|---|---|
| NET ASSETS | £ | £ | £ | £ | £ | £ |
| *Fixed Assets* | | | | | | |
| Plant and machinery..... | | 1,600 | | 1,600 | | 1,600 |
| *Current Assets* | | | | | | |
| Stocks ............... | 730 | | 460 | | 460 | |
| Trade debtors.......... | 520 | | 520 | | 520 | |
| Cash | 40 | | 40 | | 200 | |
| | 1,290 | | 1,020 | | 1,180 | |
| *Less:Current Liabilities* | | | | | | |
| Trade creditors......... | 810 | | 540 | | 700 | |
| Working capital........ | | 480 | | 480 | | 480 |
| | | 2,080 | | 2,080 | | 2,080 |
| CAPITAL | | | | | | |
| Opening capital......... | | 2,000 | | 2,000 | | 2,000 |
| Add: net profit......... | | 80 | | 80 | | 80 |
| Closing capital......... | | 2,080 | | 2,080 | | 2,080 |

Each change in the company's liabilities is matched by an equivalent change in the company's assets i.e. the first transaction causes both trade creditors and cash to fall by £160, whereas the second transaction causes both trade creditors and stocks to increase by £270. After each transaction, net assets remain unchanged at £2,080 as does Larch's capital.

The aim of a business is to earn a profit, but sometimes losses are suffered instead. This may be due to management inefficiency or, alternatively, events beyond their control for which they should not be blamed e.g. a dock strike which makes it impossible to obtain delivery of imported raw materials which are essential for production. Where a firm suffers a loss, net assets and, therefore, the owner's capital are reduced by the amount of the loss. These circumstances are illustrated in Example 2.4.

## Example 2.4

The following balance sheet is prepared in respect of Elm at 31 December 19X1.

*Balance Sheet of Elm at 31 December 19X1*

| SOURCES OF FINANCE | £ | ASSETS | £ | £ |
|---|---|---|---|---|
| Capital ................... | 7,600 | *Fixed Assets* | | |
| | | Plant and machinery...... | | 4,000 |
| *Current Liabilities* | | *Current Assets* | | |
| Trade creditors.............. | 1,200 | Stock.................... | 1,900 | |
| | | Trade debtors............ | 2,200 | |
| | | Cash ................... | 700 | 4,800 |
| | 8,800 | | | 8,800 |

On 1 January 19X2 Elm sold, on credit for £480, goods which cost £600 some weeks ago.

*Required:*

(a)   Calculations of:
(i)    Elm's net assets at 31 December 19X1.
(ii)   The profit or loss arising on the 1 January sale.
(iii)  Elms capital investment on 1 January after the above transaction.
(iv)   Elm's net assets on 1 January after the above transaction.
(b)   Elm's balance sheet at 1 January 19X2, presented in vertical format, to show the calculation of net assets at that date.

## Solution.

(a)

(i)

| | £ |
|---|---|
| Assets........................................... | 8,800 |
| Less: Liabilities..................................... | 1,200 |
| Net assets........................................ | 7,600 |

(ii)

| | |
|---|---|
| Cost of stock..................................... | 600 |
| Less: Sales proceeds................................ | 480 |
| Loss............................................ | 120 |

(iii)

| | |
|---|---|
| Capital at 31 December............................. | 7,600 |
| Less: Loss........................................ | 120 |
| Capital at 1 January................................ | 7,480 |

(iv)   ASSETS

| | |
|---|---:|
| Plant and machinery............................... | 4,000 |
| Stock (£1,900−£600)................................ | 1,300 |
| Trade debtors (£2,200 + £480)........................ | 2,680 |
| Cash............................................ | 700 |
| | 8,680 |

LIABILITIES

| | |
|---|---:|
| Trade creditors.................................... | 1,200 |
| NET ASSETS.................................... | 7,480 |

(b)

*Balance Sheet of Elm at 1 January 19X2*

| | £ | £ |
|---|---:|---:|
| NET ASSETS | | |
| *Fixed Assets* | | |
| Plant and machinery........................ | | 4,000 |
| *Current Assets* | | |
| Stocks.................................... | 1,300 | |
| Trade debtors............................. | 2,680 | |
| Cash..................................... | 700 | |
| | 4,680 | |
| *Less: Current Liabilities* | | |
| Trade creditors........................... | 1,200 | |
| Working capital............................ | | 3,480 |
| | | 7,480 |
| CAPITAL | | |
| Opening capital............................ | | 7,600 |
| Less:   Net loss (£600 - £480)................ | | 120 |
| Closing capital............................ | | 7,480 |

We can therefore conclude from the above examples that
    Profit = Increase in net assets (or capital)
    Loss   = Decrease in net assets (or capital)
An awareness of the relationship between a profit or a loss and changes in net assets is fundamental to a sound understanding of the financial effects of business activity. The relevant connections between the various financial magnitudes can be expressed diagramatically as shown in Figure 2.1.

**Figure 2.1**

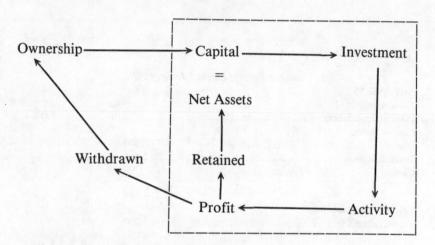

⟵——— denotes flows of resources
------- denotes the boundary of the business entity

The ownership group invests capital which is used to acquire business assets. These assets form the basis for business activity subsequently undertaken in order to generate profit Some of the profit is likely to be paid out to the owners as a return on their investment. The remainder is retained and this results in an increased volume of net assets to be used for trading purposes during the following accounting period. The re-investment takes place in the expectation that the greater volume of net assets will enable a higher profit to be earned in the future.

## 2.5 PROFIT MEASURED BY CAPITAL CHANGES
It sometimes happens that the accountant is faced with the task of

measuring profit despite the fact that no record exists of business transactions undertaken during the accounting period under review, e.g. because the records have been lost or destroyed by fire.* In these circumstances it is *not* possible to calculate profit by comparing the cost of stock sold with its selling price, as in the previous examples worked. Instead the calculation must be based on the fact, established in section 4 of this chapter, that profit produces an equivalent increase in net assets or owner's capital. Profit can therefore be found by comparing capital at the beginning of an accounting period with capital at the end of that period, i.e.

Profit = Closing capital − Opening capital

(If opening capital exceeds closing capital, the result of the calculation is a negative figure and this means that a loss has been suffered.)

When making this calculation, in practice, the accountant must first establish the proprietor's capital investment at the beginning and end of the period. This process usually involves a significant element of estimation and judgement, particularly in relation to assets owned at the earlier of the two accounting dates. The existence of fixed assets can usually be established by physical verification but the valuation of these items may prove more difficult. Evidence of the price paid may well be available in view of the large sums often involved; otherwise it is necessary to use information which can be obtained from suppliers of the relevant items or, alternatively, to arrange for a professional valuation. Reliable figures for stocks are difficult to obtain unless steps were taken to arrange for them to be physically counted and valued at each of the balance sheet dates. If this task has not been undertaken, then an estimate of the likely values is required from the proprietor of the business. Figures for trade debtors and trade creditors can be constructed if the sales and purchase invoices are retained and, where the company deals in products subject to value added tax, the likelihood of this information being readily available is much increased. The amount of money due to or from the bank can be etablished by an examination of the relevant bank statements.

The measurement of profit by capital changes is illustrated in Example 2.5.

* The procedure described in this section is also used by the Inland Revenue where existing records are unreliable but profit needs to be estimated because the taxpayer is believed to have understated his income in his tax return.

## Example 2.5

The following information is provided relating to the affairs of James who trades in fashionable garments from rented property.

| Assets and Liabilities | 31 Dec. 19X1 | 31 Dec. 19X2 |
|---|---|---|
| | £ | £ |
| Motor vehicles................................... | 1,800 | 1,350 |
| Fixtures and fittings............................... | 450 | 820 |
| Stocks........................................... | 1,060 | 1,610 |
| Trade creditors................................... | 730 | 810 |
| Trade debtors.................................... | 240 | 300 |
| Bank overdraft................................... | 920 | 760 |
| Cash in hand..................................... | 40 | 50 |

*Required:*
(a)  Calculations of James's capital investment in the business at the end of 19X1 and 19X2.
(b)  A calculation of the profit earned by James during 19X2.
(c)  The balance sheet of James's business at 31 December 19X2, presented in horizontal format.

## Solution

(a)  Capital is calculated at each date by deducting liabilities from assets:

Statement of Assets, Liabilities and Capital at 31 December

| | | 19X1 | | 19X2 |
|---|---|---|---|---|
| ASSETS | £ | £ | £ | £ |
| Motor vehicles................. | | 1,800 | | 1,350 |
| Fixtures and fittings............ | | 450 | | 820 |
| Stocks....................... | | 1,060 | | 1,610 |
| Trade debtors................. | | 240 | | 300 |
| Cash in hand.................. | | 40 | | 50 |
| | | 3,590 | | 4,130 |
| LESS: LIABILITIES | | | | |
| Trade creditors................ | 730 | | 810 | |
| Bank overdraft................ | 920 | 1,650 | 760 | 1,570 |
| CAPITAL | | 1,940 | | 2,560 |

(b)  Profit is calculated by deducting opening capital from closing capital:

| | £ |
|---|---|
| Closing capital................. | 2,560 |
| Less: Opening capital........... | 1,940 |
| Profit ........................ | 620 |

(c)                          *Balance Sheet at 31 December 19X2*

|  | £ | £ |  | £ | £ |
|---|---|---|---|---|---|
| Opening capital.... |  | 1,940 | *Fixed Assets* |  |  |
| Add: Net Profit.... |  | 620 | Motor vehicles........ |  | 1,350 |
|  |  |  | Fixtures and fittings.... |  | 820 |
| Closing capital..... |  | 2,560 |  |  |  |
|  |  |  |  |  | 2,170 |
| *Current Liabilities* |  |  | *Current Assets* |  |  |
| Trade creditors..... | 810 |  | Stocks.............. | 1,610 |  |
| Bank overdraft..... | 760 | 1,570 | Trade debtors......... | 300 |  |
|  |  |  | Cash in hand.......... | 50 | 1,960 |
|  |  | 4,130 |  |  | 4,130 |

Students should now work Question 2.2 at the end of the chapter.

## 2.6 CAPITAL INJECTIONS AND WITHDRAWALS

There are two categories of business transaction which cause capital to increase or decrease during an accounting period:
- (a) transactions which produce a profit or a loss
- (b) transactions involving the injection or withdrawal of capital by the owners.

Section 5 of this chapter demonstrates the measurement of profit by capital changes assuming that there are no capital injections or withdrawals. This assumption is now dropped. Where capital injections or withdrawals occur, their financial effects must be isolated if profit is to be measured accurately. This is because, although an investment or withdrawal of funds causes capital and, therefore, net assets to increase or decrease, these changes have not come about as the result of trading activity and therefore give rise to neither a profit nor a loss. The following adjustments must therefore be made:

1. *Drawings.* These reduce closing capital but, because they are not a business expense, they must be *added back* to the increase in capital arrived at by deducting opening capital from closing capital.
2. *Capital injections.* These increase closing capital but they are not business profits and so their effect must be eliminated by *deducting* the amount of the additional investment from the increase in capital arrived at by deducting opening capital from closing capital.

The calculation of profit therefore becomes:

$$\text{Profit} = \text{Closing capital} - \text{opening capital} + \text{drawings} - \text{capital introduced}$$

**Example 2.6**

Assume the same assets and liabilities as are given in Example 2.5. In addition you discover that James withdrew cash totaling £1,000 to meet living expenses during 19X2, while on 1 August he paid into his business bank account the first prize of £200 won in his golf club's raffle.

*Required:*

(a)   A calculation of the corrected profit earned by James during 19X2.
(b)   The capital section of James's balance sheet at 31 December 19X2.

**Solution**

(a)   Profit is calculated on the basis of the increase in capital as follows:

|  | £ |
|---|---|
| Closing capital................ | 2,560 |
| Less: Opening capital.......... | 1,940 |
| Increase in capital............ | 620 |
| Add: Drawings................. | 1,000 |
| Less: Capital introduced........ | (200) |
| Profit ....................... | 1,420 |

*Note:*   The assets and liabilities remain the same as in Example 2.5, and so the increase in capital is unchanged at £620 (£2,560 − £1,940). However, account must be taken of the two 'non-trading' transactions which have affected the value of closing capital and caused a net reduction of £800 (cash withdrawals of £1,000 partly compensated by a capital injection of £200). This amount must be added back to the observed increase in capital to produce a 'true' profit figure of £1,420.

(b)

*Balance Sheet Extract 31 December 19X2*

| Capital section | £ |
|---|---|
| Opening capital............... | 1,940 |
| Add: Capital injection........... | 200 |
| Net profit................ | 1,420 |
| | 3,560 |
| Less: Drawings................. | 1,000 |
| | 2,560 |

*Note:* The balance sheet now contains a full and accurate statement of transactions affecting the owner's capital during the year. It shows that James made an additional capital investment of £200, that he made personal withdrawals of £1,000 and that a profit figure of £1,420 (not £620) should be used as the basis for assessing the firm's performance and as a starting point for computing tax payable.

An injection of additional capital by the owner is an unusual event which is normally quite easy to identify. Sources of extra capital might include a legacy or gambling winnings or the sale of a non-business asset belonging to the proprietor. Drawings are usually more difficult to calculate as they occur more often, may well vary from week to week, and may comprise both cash and stock-in-trade, the latter being particularly likely in the case of a retail business. In the absence of a firm record of withdrawals, a careful estimate is required from the proprietor. The various matters discussed in this chapter are incorporated in the following example.

## Example 2.7

The following information is provided relating to the affairs of John who owns a tobacconist, confectionery and newspaper kiosk.

| Assets and Liabilities | 1 Jan. 19X3 | 31 Dec. 19X3 |
|---|---|---|
| | £ | £ |
| Kiosk..................................... | 2,000 | 2,000 |
| Stocks of tobaccco and confectionery.......... | 450 | 600 |
| Trade creditors............................. | 250 | 320 |
| Bank balance............................. | 160 | 940 |
| Cash in hand............................... | 20 | 30 |

During 19X3 John received a legacy of £800 which was paid into his business bank account. Cash drawings are estimated at £200 per week and, in addition, John took from the business goods worth £150 for his own use during the year.

## Required:
(a)   A calculation of the profit earned by John during 19X3.
(b)   The balance sheet of John's business at 31 December 19X3, presented in vertical format.

## Solution
(a)   (i)   Calculation of capital by deducting liabilities from assets.

Statement of Assets, Liabilities and Capital at:

|  | 1 Jan. 19X3 | 31 Dec. 19X3 |
|---|---|---|
| *Assets* | £ | £ |
| Kiosk....................................... | 2,000 | 2,000 |
| Stocks...................................... | 450 | 600 |
| Bank balance.............................. | 160 | 940 |
| Cash in hand.............................. | 20 | 30 |
|  | 2,630 | 3,570 |
| *Liabilities* | | |
| Trade creditors............................ | 250 | 320 |
| CAPITAL................................ | 2,380 | 3,250 |

(ii)   Calculation of profit on the basis of the increase in capital.

|  | £ |
|---|---|
| Closing capital.......................................... | 3,250 |
| Less: Opening capital.................................... | 2,380 |
| Increase in capital....................................... | 870 |
| Add: Drawings.......................................... | 10,550* |
| Less: Capital introduced................................. | (800) |
| Profit ................................................. | 10,620 |

*Drawings: Cash, £200 x 52 = 10,400
            Goods              150
                            ————
                            10,550

*Note:* John's capital has increased by only £870 during 19X3 (from £2,380 to £3,250). However, during 19X3 John withdrew goods and cash totalling £10,550 which must be added to the increase in capital to calculate profits generated from trading activity. Similarly the legacy, which is a non-trading receipt, must be deducted. The combined effect of these two adjustments is to produce a revised profit figure of £10,620.

(b)

*Balance Sheet at 31 December 19X3.*

| ASSETS | £ | £ |
|---|---|---|
| *Fixed Assets* | | |
| Kiosk......................................... | | 2,000 |
| *Current Assets* | | |
| Stocks........................................ | 600 | |
| Bank balance................................. | 940 | |
| Cash in hand................................. | 30 | |
| | 1,570 | |
| *Less: Current Liabilities* | | |
| Trade creditors................................ | 320 | |
| Working capital............................... | | 1,250 |
| | | 3,250 |
| | | |
| CAPITAL | | |
| Opening capital............................... | | 2,380 |
| Add:Capital introduced......................... | | 800 |
| Profit....................................... | | 10,620 |
| | | 13,800 |
| Less:Drawings-cash ........................... | 10,400 | |
| -goods........................... | 150 | 10,550 |
| | | 3,250 |

Students should now work Questions 2.3 and 2.4 at the end of this chapter.

## 2.7   QUESTIONS
### Question 2.1
The following balance sheet relates to the affairs of Columbus who works for the Government and also buys and sells second hand cars. The balance sheet of his second hand car business is as follows:

*Balance Sheet at 31 December 19X1*

| | £ | | £ | £ |
|---|---|---|---|---|
| Capital............ | 6,500 | Fixed assets..... | | 2,000 |
| *Current Liabilities:* | | *Current Assets* | | |
| Trade creditors...... | 200 | Stock of cars | 2,700 | |
| | | Debtors........ | 1,000 | |
| | | Bank .......... | 1,000 | 4,700 |
| | 6,700 | | | 6,700 |

Transactions undertaken in January 19X2:
  1. Columbus collects the £1,000 owing in respect of the second hand car sold in December 19X1.

2. Columbus wins £500 on the football pools and pays the proceeds into his business bank account.
3. Columbus sells for £1,200 a car which was in stock on 31 December 19X1 at a value of £1,300.
4. Columbus withdraws £50 for private use.
5. Columbus purchases a friend's car for £150, and promises to pay him in February.
6. Columbus purchases a new machine for £700 and pays in cash.

*Required:*
(a) Give the totals for gross assets, net assets and working capital based on the figures in the above balance sheet.
(b) Taking each of the transactions listed above separately, give their effect (increase or decrease) on:
(i) Profit.
(ii) Net Assets.
(iii) Gross assets.
(iv) Working capital.

## Question 2.2
The balance sheet of Paul at 30 June 19X3 is as follows:

*Balance Sheet as at 30 June 19X3*

|  | £ | £ |  | £ | £ |
|---|---|---|---|---|---|
| Capital........... |  | 10,330 | Fixed assets........ |  | 7,500 |
|  |  |  | *Current Assets* |  |  |
| *Current Liabilities* |  |  | Stock............. | 3,280 |  |
| Trade creditors... | 1,220 |  | Debtors........... | 1,750 | 5,030 |
| Bank overdraft | 980 | 2,200 |  |  |  |
|  |  | 12,530 |  |  | 12,530 |

During the year to 30 June 19X4, Paul received a loan of £3,000 from a friend. The loan is interest free and repayable at the end of 19X6. On 1 December 19X3 Paul purchased fixed assets costing £2,350. At 30 June 19X4, trade creditors amounted to £1,890, stock was valued at £4,270 and debtors amounted to £1,450. In addition Paul had £570 in his bank account and cash in hand of £30.

*Required:*
(a)  A calculation of Paul's capital investment in the business at 30 June 19X4.
(b)  A calculation of the profit earned by Paul's business during the year to 30 June 1984.
(c)  The balance sheet of Paul's business at 30 June 19X4, presented in vertical format.

## Question 2.3
The balance sheet of Burnley's business as at 31 December 19X7 was as follows:

*Balance Sheet as at 31 December 19X7*

|  | £ | £ |  | £ | £ |
|---|---|---|---|---|---|
| Capital........... |  | 23,496 | Fixed assets........ |  | 17,700 |
| *Current Liabilities* |  |  | *Current Assets* |  |  |
| Creditors |  |  | Stock............. | 5,062 |  |
| Goods.......... | 4,032 |  | Debtors........... | 3,728 |  |
| Expenses........ | 204 | 4,236 | Bank............. | 1,242 | 10,032 |
|  |  | 27,732 |  |  | 27,732 |

The following information about Burnley's financial position at 31 December 19X8 was extracted from his books

|  | £ |
|---|---|
| Stock | 6,536 |
| Debtors | 4,864 |
| Bank overdraft | 2,492 |
| Creditors: |  |
| Goods | 4,236 |
| Expenses | 168 |
| Fixed assets | 15,930 |

Burnley drew £10,800 from his business during 19X8 for private purposes.

*Required:*
(a)  A calculation of Burnley's capital at 31 December l9X8.
(b)  A calculation of the firm's profit for 19X8.
(c)  The firm's balance sheet at 31 December 19X8 presented in vertical format.

## Question 2.4

The following information is obtained in connection with the business of G. Haze, a trader.

|  | 31 December | |
| --- | --- | --- |
|  | 19X3 | 19X4 |
|  | £ | £ |
| Fixed assets at book value.................... | 9,000 | see below |
| Stocks.................................... | 2,650 | 3,710 |
| Trade debtors............................. | 5,200 | 5,600 |
| Trade creditors............................ | 1,710 | 1,210 |
| Bank balance (overdraft)................... | (360) | 50 |

During 19X4 motor vehicles were purchased at a cost of £3,144, part of which was met by G. Haze trading in his private motor car at an agreed valuation of £600. Cash drawings made by G. Haze amounted to £150 per week and, in addition, stocks valued at £300 were taken during the year for personal use.

*Required:*
(a)   A calculation of the profit earned by G. Haze's business during 19X4.
(b)   The balance sheet of the firm at 31 December 19X4 presented in the horizontal format.

# CHAPTER 3

# The Preparation of Accounts from Cash Records

## 3.1 ACCOUNTING SYSTEMS AND INFORMATION REQUIREMENTS

The complexity of the accounting system for recording and reporting business transactions is principally a function of the size of the firm.* The large number of transactions undertaken each day and the separation of the management group from the ownership group, which is likely to occur in the case of a substantial business concern, will require sophisticated accounting systems for the dual purposes of *control* and *assessment*. These conditions do not apply in the small firm and, accordingly, the accounting system will be far more rudimentary. Effective protection of valuable resources is achieved, in this latter situation, as a result of the owner's close personal contact with all aspects of the firm's business activities. Certain of the firm's most vulnerable assets, e.g. the cash balance and the bank account, are likely to remain under the direct control of the owner. Other resources, e.g. stocks, which may be in the custody of trusted personnel will, nevertheless, remain under the close scrutiny of the proprietor.

Neither is it necessary, in the small firm, to employ formal reporting procedures as a basis for performance assessment. The number of trade creditors and customers will be relatively small, and any difficulties associated with the supply of, or demand for, the firm's products will quickly come to the attention of a diligent proprietor. Similarly, in the absence of a significant level of capital expenditure, changes in the bank balance are likely to provide a fairly reliable indication of progress; the function of accounting reports, in these circumstances, is often confined to the identification of the annual increase in wealth as a basis for agreeing tax liabilities with the Inland Revenue and, where there are a

* The position is different in the case of limited companies because, irrespective of their size, they are legally required to keep accounting records.

number of proprietors, as a means of allocating profit between the partners. Although an increase in the scale of a firm's activities implies a need for a more formal system of accounting, it does not necessarily follow that transactions will be recorded daily in accordance with the system of double entry described in chapter 5. It is essential that accounting systems be judged in terms of their usefulness, and a decision to invest the time and money required to operate a complex system must be justified in terms of the benefits it produces.

There is a certain minimum amount of financial information which must be made available, however, to enable the accountant to prepare a full set of final accounts consisting of both a trading and profit and loss account, which gives a detailed list of business revenues and expenditures arising during the year (see section 3 of this chapter), and a balance sheet. The information required consists of:

1. Assets at the beginning and at the end of the year.
2. Liabilities at the beginning and at the end of the year.
3. Cash receipts and payments during the year.

The steps which must be taken to obtain details of assets and liabilities were discussed in section 5 of chapter 2. This information is used to compile the closing balance sheet, and also the opening balance sheet unless this statement has previously been prepared. Details of cash transactions are required as the starting point for preparing the trading and profit and loss. The business bank statements fulfil an essential role in this context, since they contain a wealth of reliable information concerning cash transactions during the year. There is, of course, usually a large number of bank statements and the analysis of these documents is a lengthy process, particularly because the statements provide few details. For example, the only information usually given in respect of cheque payments is the amount and the cheque number, while in the case of receipts only a brief description, indicating the source of the lodgement, is provided. It is therefore important for cheque books and paying in books to be retained so that a full and accurate description of the various items appearing on the bank statements is available. Details must also be obtained of any cash transactions which have *not* gone through the bank. This information may be recorded in a 'petty' cash book (see section 2.5 of chapter 4); alternatively it may be possible to build up the relevant figures from files of cash receipts and payments. In examination questions the analysis work has generally been done already, and figures for receipts and payments are given in a summary form similar to the following:

**Figure 3.1**

*Cash Transactions During 19X1*

| Receipts | £ | Payments | £ |
|---|---|---|---|
| Opening balance | | Payments to | |
| of cash.................. | 510 | supplier................. | 17,380 |
| Sales of goods............ | 23,750 | Wages.................. | 2,560 |
| | | Rent and rates........... | 840 |
| | | Lighting and | |
| | | heating................. | 620 |
| | | General expenses......... | 375 |
| | | | 21,775 |
| | | Closing balance of | |
| | | cash.................... | 2,485 |
| | 24,260 | | 24,260 |

The receipts side of the summary shows cash receipts from customers of £23,750 which, when added to the sum available at the start, of £510, means that cash resources amounting to £24,260 became available to the business during 19X1. From this total, cash payments of £21,775 must be deducted, leaving a cash balance at the year end of £2,485.

Provided the rudimentary financial facts referred to in this section can be assembled, it will be possible to prepare a full set of final accounts. The process, described as the preparation of accounts from cash records, is examined in this chapter.

## 3.2 THE MATCHING CONCEPT: PROFIT = REVENUE – EXPENDITURE

Chapter 2 demonstrated how profit can be measured in the absence of detailed information concerning trading transactions undertaken during a particular accounting period, i.e. it is computed by calculating the owner's capital the beginning and the end of the accounting period and measuring the change which has occurred. Where there exists an adequate accounting record of transactions undertaken, during the year, profit is instead computed in accordance with the *matching concept*, i.e. the accountant measures profit by comparing or 'matching' the total cost of the many trading transactions undertaken during an accounting period with the total revenues arising therefrom.

## Example 3.1

Mex Cars Ltd. is a motor vehicle distributor which makes up its accounts on the calendar year basis. Ten cars are purchased during 19X1 for £4,500 each and sold for £6,000 each.

*Required:*
Calculate profit by matching revenues with expenditures.

## Solution

|  | £ |
|---|---|
| Revenue:   Proceeds from sale of cars (£6,000 x 10) . . . . . . . . . . | 60,000 |
| Less:   Expenditure:   Cost of cars sold (£4,500 x 10) . . . . . . . . . | 45,000 |
| Profit . . . . . . . . . . . . . . . . . . . . . . . . . . . . . . . . . . . . . . . . . . . . . . . . . . . . . | 15,000 |

## 3.3   GROSS PROFIT AND NET PROFIT

The balance of profit, which is arrived at by matching sales proceeds with the actual cost of goods sold, is called *gross profit*. In practice many other costs will also be incurred: salaries will be paid to employees, commissions may be paid to salesmen, rent and rates may well be paid on the showroom and office accommodation, and there will be many other incidental expenses such as telephone costs, stationery, etc. Since these outlays are incurred to help generate sales revenue, they must also be deducted to leave a final balance called *net profit*. Revenues and expenditures are matched against one another in the *trading account and the profit and loss account,* (usually abbreviated to trading and profit and loss account) and a common method of presenting this accounting statement is illustrated in Figure 3.2.

**Figure 3.2**
The trading and profit and loss account of Mex Cars Ltd. for 19X1 is
as follows:

*Trading and Profit and Loss Account for 19X1*

| EXPENDITURE | £ | REVENUE | £ |
|---|---|---|---|
| Cost of cars sold.......... | 45,000 | Sales................ | 60,000 |
| Gross profit............. | 15,000 | | |
| | 60,000 | | 60,000 |
| Salaries................. | 6,200 | Gross profit.......... | 15,000 |
| Commissions............ | 600 | | |
| Rent and rates........... | 1,400 | | |
| Lighting and heating...... | 250 | | |
| Telephone............... | 150 | | |
| Postage and stationery.... | 220 | | |
| Advertising.............. | 370 | | |
| General expenses......... | 500 | | |
| | 9,690 | | |
| Net profit............... | 5,310 | | |
| | 15,000 | | 15,000 |

The gross profit is calculated in the trading account and the
remaining expenses are deducted in the profit and loss account. It
might occur to students that the calculation of profit on the basis of
changes in capital is a rather more straightforward process than by
comparing revenue with expenditure. The accumulation of figures
for sales revenue and the various items of expenditure is a far more
laborious and time consuming task than the identification of figures
for capital on the basis of assets minus liabilities. Part of the
justification for the extra work is that trading transactions entered
into during an accounting period are recorded, not only to enable
profit to be measured, but also to facilitate effective control over
inflows and outflows of cash and goods, e.g. to ensure that cash is
collected from customers and that employees are paid the amounts
due to them. Therefore, even though an accurate measurement of
profit may be achieved by comparing capital at two different dates,
day-to-day records of trading transactions are still required to fulfil
the essential control function.

In practice, detailed accounting records also enable management
to make a more useful calculation of profit because, although the
end result may be the same, the advantage of preparing a trading

and profit and loss account is that a comprehensive statement of *how* the net profit balance has been achieved is readily available. This document which includes, in addition to the net profit figure, both a calculation of gross profit and a detailed list of expenses, is a valuable means for assessing performance, e.g. by comparing this year's results with those achieved last year, and for reaching decisions concerning the future allocation of resources. The significance of the distinction between gross profit and net profit, as the basis for performance assessment, is examined in section 4 of chapter 11.

### 3.4  THE PROBLEM OF PERIODIC PROFIT CALCULATION

The frequency with which the trading and profit and loss account and balance sheet are prepared varies depending on the circumstances of the particular business. As a minimum, however, accounts must be prepared once a year: limited companies are legally required to prepare annual accounts for publication, while sole traders and partnerships are under an effective legal obligation to prepare annual accounts for tax purposes. To provide the information needed to take day-to-day decisions designed to achieve the most effective use of available resources, management requires more frequent calculations of profit, and the preparation of quarterly or even monthly management accounts is a common feature within commerce and industry today.

The calculation of *periodic* profit causes difficulties because business activity is continuous. For example, a business may run for ten years but, for accounting purposes, it must be split into at least ten accounting periods, each lasting one year. The problem is how to deal with the transactions which cannot be completely identified with a particular accounting period. Many transactions cause no difficulties. For example, assuming accounts are prepared on the calendar year basis, an item of stock purchased and paid for in January 19X1 and sold for cash in February 19X1 is taken into account in computing the profit for 19X1. Problems arise with transactions which *overlap* the end of one accounting period and the beginning of another. For example, consider the following cases assuming a 31 December accounting date:

1.  Stocks are delivered to a customer in December 19X1 but are not paid for until January 19X2.

2. Stocks are purchased and paid for in November 19X1 but not sold until March 19X2.
3. Rates are paid on 1 October 19X1 for the six months to 31 March 19X2.
4. Machinery is purchased and paid for in 19X1 which will last for eight years.

The problem of deciding whether these transactions give rise to revenues and expenditures in 19X1 or 19X2 or another accounting period is solved by the accountant making certain assumptions and applying a range of accounting conventions to the factual information generated by the accounting system. These procedures are examined in sections 5-7 of this chapter.

## 3.5   THE IDENTIFICATION OF REVENUE: THE REALISATION CONCEPT

Revenue is obtained mainly from the sale of goods purchased or manufactured in the case of an industrial concern and, for accounting purposes, it is assumed to arise *at the point of sale*. For a cash sale this occurs when the goods are exchanged for cash; for a credit sale, it occurs when the goods and sales invoice are delivered to the customer. The assumption that revenue, and therefore profit, arises when the sale takes place is called the *Realisation Concept*, and it is a good illustration of how accounting procedures are based on generally agreed conventions rather than indisputable facts.

For example, consider the case of a manufacturer of motor vehicles where demand exceeds supply. A great deal of work goes into building the car and by the time manufacture is complete there is little more to do. Demand exceeds supply and so delivery to a motor vehicle distributor is likely to take place fairly soon in order to satisfy consumer requirements. No profit is recognised, however, during the course of the prodution process and the motor vehicle remains in the books at cost until the sale takes place. This procedure demonstrates the rather cautious approach towards profit measurement which the accountant generally adopts. It might be argued that, during the course of the productive process, profit is being gradually earned which should be recognised in the accounts, but the accountant prefers to wait until the expected profit is validated by a sale. He takes this view partly because it would be difficult to decide how much profit to recognise at any interim stage and partly because he considers it imprudent to anticipate sales which may not occur. At the other extreme, it might be argued that, in the case of a credit sale, it would be even safer to wait until the cash is actually collected before recognising a profit. But although the accountant rightly has the reputation of being cautious, he is not that cautious. The sale has taken place and the business has a legally enforceable debt against the customer. The collection of cash will in most cases be a mere formality and no further delay in the recognition of revenue is thought to be justified (the complication of bad debts is examined in section 7 of chapter 6).

### 3.5.1 Calculating Sales from Records of Cash Receipts

Where accounting records are incomplete, the sales figure will not usually be available and it must be built up from cash records and figures for the opening and closing balances of trade debtors.

**Example 3.2**

During 19X1, John received £17,500 from customers in respect of credit sales. At 1 January 19X1, his trade debtors amounted to £3,600 and at 31 December 19X1 they were £4,720.

| Calculation of sales: | £ |
|---|---|
| Cash received in respect of credit sales | 17,500 |
| Less: Opening trade debtors | 3,600 |
| | 13,900 |
| Add: Closing trade debtors | 4,720 |
| Sales | 18,620 |

Of the £17,500 received during the year, £3,600 was collected from customers to whom goods were sold in 19X0 and which would have been reported as revenue in the trading account for that year. The difference, £13,900, represents the cash received in respect of sales during 19X1. To this must be added closing debtors for goods sold during 19X1, but not yet paid for, to produce the sales figure of £18,620.

The rule to remember is therefore:

SALES = CASH RECEIVED FROM CUSTOMERS −
           OPENING DEBTORS + CLOSING DEBTORS.

## 3.6 MATCHING EXPENDITURE WITH REVENUE: THE BENEFIT PRINCIPLE

The first step in the calculation of profit for the year is to compute revenue; the second step involves identifying the expenditures which must be matched against revenue. The basic test is: 'Which accounting period benefits from the expenditure?' If the answer is the current accounting period then the expenditure is charged against revenue for the current year. If the answer is a future accounting period, then the expenditure must be carried forward as an asset in the balance sheet and charged against the revenue of the future accounting period which benefits. If the answer is both the current period and one or more future periods, an apportionment must be made. This process, which bases the charge on *benefits received* during the year rather than payments made during the year is called the *Accruals Concept*. The application of this concept to specific business facts is now examined in sections 6.1 to 6.3.

**3.6.1 Accounting for Stock** The calculation of the figure for cost of goods sold, to be compared with sales revenue for the purpose of computing gross profit, involves two steps:

1. Calculate purchases. The procedure is analogous to that followed when computing sales, and may be expressed in the following formula:

PURCHASES = CASH PAID TO SUPPLIERS – OPENING CREDITORS + CLOSING CREDITORS.

2. Calculate cost of goods sold. It is unlikely that all the goods purchased during the year will have been sold by the end of the year. Some items will remain in stock and should be deducted from purchases and carried forward, in the balance sheet, to the following accounting period which will benefit from their sale. In a similar manner, stocks brought forward from the previous year and sold during the current accounting period must be added to purchases and matched with the current year's sales proceeds. The calculation which must be memorised in this case is:

COST OF GOODS SOLD = PURCHASES + OPENING STOCK – CLOSING STOCK.

## Example 3.3

James made payments by cheque to suppliers of goods on credit amounting to £27,300 during 19X2. In addition, he made cash purchases of £1,600. Trade creditors at 1 January 19X2 and 31 December 19X2 amounted respectively to £4,750 and £6,100. Opening stocks were £10,250 while closing stocks amounted to £9,640.

### Required:

Calculate (a) purchases and (b) cost of goods sold for 19X2.

### Solution

| | £ |
|---|---|
| (a) Calculation of purchases: | |
| Cash paid to suppliers: Credit purchases................... | 27,300 |
| Cash purchases....:............... | 1,600 |
| | 28,900 |
| Less: Opening creditors................................ | 4,750 |
| | 24,150 |
| Add: Closing creditors................................. | 6,100 |
| Purchases......................................... | 30,250 |

| | £ |
|---|---|
| (b) Calculation of cost of goods sold: | |
| Opening Stock........................................ | 10,250 |
| Add: Purchases....................................... | 30,250 |
| | 40,500 |
| Less: Closing stock.................................... | 9,640 |
| Cost of goods sold.................................... | 30,860 |

The calculations discussed and illustrated in sections 5.1 and 6.1 of this chapter are central to the measurement of profit by matching revenue with expenditure. Readers should test their understanding of these calculations by working Example 3.4 before examining the solution.

## Example 3.4

The following information is provided relating to Peter's business for 19X3:

£

Cash collected from customers in respect of:

| | |
|---|---|
| credit sales | 41,750 |
| cash sales | 12,350 |
| Payments to suppliers | 36,590 |

| Balances at | 1 January | 31 December |
|---|---|---|
| | £ | £ |
| Trade debtors | 12,650 | 11,780 |
| Trade creditors | 6,540 | 8,270 |
| Stock | 9,150 | 9,730 |

## Required:

(a) Calculations for 19X3 of    (i)    Receipts from customers.
       (ii)    Sales.
       (iii)    Purchases.
       (iv)    Cost of goods sold.

(b) The trading account of Peter's business for 19X3.

## Solution.

£

(a)    (i)    Cash collected in respect of:

| | | £ |
|---|---|---|
| credit sales | | 41,750 |
| cash sales | | 12,350 |
| Receipts from customers | | 54,100 |

(ii)

| | | £ |
|---|---|---|
| Receipts from customers | | 54,100 |
| Less: Opening debtors | | (12,650) |
| Add: Closing debtors | | 11,780 |
| Sales | | 53,230 |

(iii)

| | | £ |
|---|---|---|
| Payments to suppliers | | 36,590 |
| Less: Opening creditors | | (6,540) |
| Add: Closing creditors | | 8,270 |
| Purchases | | 38,320 |

(iv)

| | | £ |
|---|---|---|
| Opening Stock | | 9,150 |
| Add: Purchases | | 38,320 |
| Less: Closing stock | | (9,730) |
| Cost of goods sold | | 37,740 |

(b)

*Trading Account for 19X3*

| | £ | | £ |
|---|---|---|---|
| Purchases.............. | 38,320 | Sales.......... | 53,230 |
| Add: Opening stock....... | 9,150 | | |
| Less: Closing stock....... | (9,730) | | |
| | | | |
| Cost of goods sold........ | 37,740 | | |
| Gross profit............ | 15,490 | | |
| | | | |
| | 53,230 | | 53,230 |

Students should note that it is conventional practice to show the calculation of cost of goods sold on the face of the trading account, but not the calculations of purchases and sales.

**3.6.2 Accounting for Services: Accruals and Prepayments** When preparing accounts from incomplete records, it is also necessary to adjust cash payments for services rendered to the company, so that the amount charged in the profit and loss acount reflects the cost of benefits actually consumed during the year.

For certain services, payments are made before the associated benefits are received, i.e. the payment is made *in advance.* In the case of rent and rates, advance payments are made for the right to occupy the property for a fixed future period of time. Where the period of occupation covers the end of one accounting year and the beginning of another, an arithmetic apportionment of the amount paid must be made between the two consecutive accounting periods. For example, if a rental of £600 is paid on 1 April 19X1 for the forthcoming twelve months, and the accounts are made up on the calendar year basis, nine months (or three-quarters) of the total benefit is received during 19X1 and three months (or one-quarter) of the benefit is received during 19X2. Therefore, $3/4 \times £600 = £450$ is charged against revenue arising during 19X1 and $1/4 \times £600 = £150$ is carried forward in the balance sheet as a 'prepaid expense' and charged against revenue arising during 19X2.

The majority of expenses are, however, paid *in arrears,* mainly because the amount charged depends on the extent to which the service is utilised. Examples are electricity charges, telephone charges and the wage bill. In these cases, it is necessary to raise an 'accrual', at the end of the acounting period, representing the value of the benefit received but not yet paid for. The amount of the accrual may be estimated on the basis of past experience. Alternatively, where the bill is received by the time the accounts are prepared, an apportionment may be made in the manner described in the previous paragraph. This will not necessarily produce strictly accurate results because the service will not have been utilised at an even rate throughout the period under consideration. However, the error is unlikely to be significant, and the extra work and cost involved in obtaining a more precise apportionment would not be justified. The amount of the accrual is carried forward in the balance sheet as a current liability under the heading 'accrued expense'.

## Example 3.5
The following information is provided relating to Mark's business for 19X4:

|  |  | £ |
|---|---|---|
| Payments during the year for: rates | | 500 |
| telephone | | 375 |

| Balances at | 1 January | 31 December |
|---|---|---|
|  | £ | £ |
| Rates paid in advance | 100 | 125 |
| Telephone charges outstanding | 50 | 62 |

*Required:* Calculations of the amount to be charged against revenue for 19X4 in respect of (i) rates (ii) telephone.

## Solution.

|  |  |  | £ |
|---|---|---|---|
| (i) Rates | Payments during 19X4 | | 500 |
| | Add:Amount prepaid at 1 January 19X4 | | 100* |
| | | | 600 |
| | Less:Amount prepaid at 31 December 19X4 | | 125 |
| | Charge for the year | | 475 |

* This amount was paid in 19X3, but it relates to the occupation of the premises during 19X4 and must be charged against revenue arising during 19X4.

|  |  | £ |
|---|---|---|
| (ii) Telephone Payments during 19X4..................................... | | 375 |
| Less: Amount accrued at 1 January 19X4.............. | | 50** |
| | | 325 |
| Add: Amount accrued at 31 December 19X4........... | | 62 |
| | | 387 |

** This amount was paid in 19X4, but it relates to services received during 19X3 and it will have been charged against revenue arising during 19X3.

### 3.6.3 Accounting for depreciation of fixed assets

Fixed assets are usually paid for at the date of acquisition, or soon afterwards, but they are expected to *benefit* the firm for many years. For example, a motor vehicle used by a sales representative might last five years, a machine ten years, and a building fifty years or more. It would therefore be unreasonable to burden revenue arising during the year that the asset is acquired with its entire cost. At the same time, most fixed assets have a limited useful life, and it would be equally wrong to keep these items indefinitely in the books at cost.

The term accountants use to describe the fall in the value of a fixed asset between the date it is acquired and the date it is sold or scrapped is 'Depreciation'. It may be defined as the fall in the value of a fixed asset due to the passage of time, usage or obsolesence. This reduction in value is acknowledged, in the accounts, by making an annual depreciation charge designed to spread the loss over the periods which benefit from using the asset. There are many different methods of charging depreciation, and we will concentrate on the one which is most common and easy to apply for the purpose of illustration, namely the straight line method (sometimes called the equal instalment method). This method assumes that each accounting period benefits to the same extent from using the asset and the total decline in its value is therefore spread equally over the period of ownership. The formula used to calculate the depreciation charge for one year is as follows:

$$\text{STRAIGHT LINE DEPRECIATION} = \frac{\text{ORIGINAL COST} - \text{ESTIMATED VALUE AT END OF USEFUL LIFE}}{\text{ESTIMATED LIFE}}$$

## Example 3.6

Paul purchased a machine for £130,000 on 1 January 19X1. It is estimated that the machine will have a useful life of 6 years and then be sold for £10,000. Calculate the annual depreciation charge.

### Solution

Straight line depreciation charge $= \dfrac{£130,000 - £10,000}{6} = £20,000$ per annum.

Each year, for 6 years, a depreciation charge of £20,000 will be made against revenue and the machine will appear in the year end balance sheets as follows:

| 31 December | 19X1 | 19X2 | 19X3 | 19X4 | 19X5 | 19X6 |
|---|---|---|---|---|---|---|
| | £000 | £000 | £000 | £000 | £000 | £000 |
| Machine at cost......... | 130 | 130 | 130 | 130 | 130 | 130 |
| Less: Accumulated depreciation ...... | 20 | 40 | 60 | 80 | 100 | 120 |
| | 110 | 90 | 70 | 50 | 30 | 10 |

The effect of charging depreciation is that the balance sheet value of the machine is gradually reduced to its disposal value. If everything works out as planned, on 31 December 19X6 the machine will be removed from the balance sheet and replaced by cash of an equal value. Events may not progress quite so smoothly, and it may turn out that the estimates on which the calculation was based prove to be wrong, i.e. the machine might not last for six years or sell for £10,000 at the end of its useful life. These complications are considered in section 5 of chapter 6 and section 3.1 of chapter 7.

## 3.7 THE PREPARATION OF ACCOUNTS FROM CASH RECORDS: A WORKED EXAMPLE

### Example 3.7

William is a trader who has carried on business for a number of years. In the past a friend has prepared accounts which were sufficient to enable William to agree his tax liabilities. William's friend has now left the country and is therefore unable to help. William maintains separate files of invoices received from suppliers and issued to customers.

The following summary has been prepared from William's paying in books, cheque books and bank statements for 19X2.

*Bank Summary*

| | £ | | £ |
|---|---|---|---|
| Cash sales............... | 39,640 | Opening balance......... | 3,520 |
| Proceeds from credit | | Payments to suppliers.....| 31,910 |
| sales................... | 18,500 | Rates................... | 2,800 |
| | | Personal drawings........ | 6,500 |
| | | Wages for part-time staff.. | 5,930 |
| | | General expenses......... | 3,180 |
| | | Vehicle................. | 4,000 |
| | | Closing balance.......... | 300 |
| | 58,140 | | 58,140 |

The following additional information has been obtained from the files of invoices and other books and records of William:

1.  William has paid all sales proceeds into his bank except for £200 which was used to pay additional part-time staff over the busy Christmas period.
2.  Assets and liabilities at 31 December, based on an analysis of the invoice files, and from discussions with William, were as follows:

| | 19X1 £ | 19X2 £ |
|---|---|---|
| Premises at cost........................... | 6,600 | 6,600 |
| Furniture at book value..................... | 3,000 | Note 3 |
| Stocks..................................... | 4,250 | 5,760 |
| Trade creditors............................. | 4,630 | 4,920 |
| Trade debtors.............................. | 2,140 | 2,320 |
| Rates paid in advance...................... | 180 | 200 |
| General expenses accrued................... | 320 | 290 |

3.  William charges depreciation at 10% on the book value of furniture owned at the end of the year.
4.  The vehicle was purchased on 1 July 19X2 and is to be written off over 5 years assuming a resale value of £1,000 at the end of that period. Ignore depreciation of premises.

The preparation of accounts from cash records involves the following four steps:

Step 1:  Establish the financial position at the beginning of the year by preparing an opening balance sheet. This shows the proprietor's opening capital which is needed when preparing the balance sheet at the year end.

Step 2: Calculate revenues and expenditures for inclusion in the trading and profit and loss account.
Step 3: Prepare the trading and profit and loss account.
Step 4: Prepare the closing balance sheet.

These procedures are now applied to the financial facts and information provided by William:

## *Step 1*

*Balance Sheet at 1 January 19X2*

| | £ | £ |
|---|---:|---:|
| **Fixed Assets** | | |
| Premises............................... | | 6,600 |
| Furniture ............................... | | 3,000 |
| | | 9,600 |
| **Current Assets** | | |
| Stocks................................ | 4,250 | |
| Trade debtors.......................... | 2,140 | |
| Prepaid expenses....................... | 180 | |
| | 6,570 | |
| **Less: Current Liabilities** | | |
| Trade creditors......................... | 4,630 | |
| Accrued expenses....................... | 320 | |
| Bank overdraft......................... | 3,520 | |
| | 8,470 | |
| Working capital........................... | | (1,900) |
| Capital................................... | | 7,700 |

## *Step 2*

*Workings*

| 1. Sales: | £ | 2. General expenses: | £ |
|---|---:|---|---:|
| Paid into bank: | | Paid during year........ | 3,180 |
|    cash sales....... | 39,640 | Less:Opening accrual... | (320) |
|    credit sales...... | 18,500 | Add:Closing accrual.... | 290 |
| Proceeds not paid in.... | 200 | | 3,150 |
| Total cash received..... | 58,340 | 3. Wages: | |
| Less:Opening debtors.. | (2,140) | Paid by cheque........ | 5,930 |
| Add:Closing debtors... | 2,320 | Paid in cash........... | 200 |
| | 58,520 | | 6,130 |

4. Purchases:

| | |
|---|---:|
| Payments to suppliers.. | 31,910 |
| Less:Opening creditors. | (4,630) |
| Add:Closing creditors.. | 4,920 |
| | 32,200 |

5. Rates:

| | |
|---|---:|
| Paid during year....... | 2,800 |
| Add:Opening advance payment | 180 |
| Less:Closing advance payment ......... | (200) |
| | 2,780 |

6. Depreciation of furniture:

$£3,000 \times 10\% = £300$

7. Depreciation of vehicle:

$(£4,000 - £1,000) \div 5 \times \frac{1}{2}* = £300$

\* The vehicle has only been owned for 6 months.

## Step 3        Trading and Profit and Loss Account for 19X2

| | £ | | £ |
|---|---:|---|---:|
| Purchases.............. | 32,200 | Sales ................... | 58,520 |
| Add:   Opening stock..... | 4,250 | | |
| Less:   Closing stock...... | (5,760) | | |
| Cost of goods sold....... | 30,690 | | |
| Gross profit............ | 27,830 | | |
| | 58,520 | | 58,520 |
| Rates................... | 2,780 | Gross profit............. | 27,830 |
| General expenses......... | 3,150 | | |
| Wages.................. | 6,130 | | |
| Depreciation:   furniture.. | 300 | | |
|                      vehicle.... | 300 | | |
| | 12,660 | | |
| Net profit.............. | 15,170 | | |
| | 27,830 | | 27,830 |

*Step 4*                                   *Balance Sheet at 31 December 19X2*

| | £ | £ | | | £ |
|---|---|---|---|---|---|
| Opening capital....... | | 7,700 | *Fixed Assets* | | |
| Add:Net profit........ | | 15,170 | Premises at cost....... | | 6,600 |
| Less: Drawings........ | | (6,500) | Furniture ............ | 3,000 | |
| | | | Less: Depreciation..... | 300 | 2,700 |
| | | 16,370 | | | |
| *Current Liabilities* | | | Vehicle at cost | 4,000 | |
| Trade creditors........ | 4,920 | | Less: Depreciation..... | 300 | 3,700 |
| General expenses | | | | | |
| accrued.............. | 290 | 5,210 | | | 13,000 |
| | | | *Current Assets* | | |
| | | | Stocks.............. | 5,760 | |
| | | | Trade debtors......... | 2,320 | |
| | | | Prepaid rates......... | 200 | |
| | | | Bank ............... | 300 | 8,580 |
| | | 21,580 | | | 21,580 |

### 3.7.1 Trading and profit and loss account presented in vertical format

Section 3 of chapter 2 drew attention to the fact that today the balance sheet is often presented in the vertical format rather than the horizontal format, and the same is the case with the trading and profit and loss account. The reasons are similar: the layout is thought to be more easily comprehended by the non-accountant; it is possible to present a number of years results on a single sheet; and comparison of results between years is made much easier. The trading and profit and loss account of William is now reproduced in vertical format for the purpose of illustration.

## Figure 3.3

*Trading and Profit and Loss Account of William for 19X2*

| | £ | £ |
|---|---:|---:|
| Sales..................................... | | 58,520 |
| Less: Purchases .......................... | 32,200 | |
| Add: Opening stock.................... | 4,250 | |
| Less:Closing stock.................... | (5,760) | |
| Cost of goods sold.......................... | | 30,690 |
| Gross profit.............................. | | 27,830 |
| Less: Rates............................... | 2,780 | |
| General expenses...................... | 3,150 | |
| Wages............................... | 6,130 | |
| Depreciation:furniture................. | 300 | |
| vehicle.................. | 300 | 12,660 |
| Net profit................................ | | 15,170 |

In exam. questions, instructions to use either the horizontal format or vertical format must be complied with but, where no instruction is given, either presentation may be followed.

Readers should now work Questions 3.1, 3.2, and 3.3 at the end of this chapter.

## 3.8 CLUBS AND SOCIETIES

Clubs and societies are a common feature of most local communities. Such organisations are often formed as the result of a group of individuals, possessing a common interest, voluntarily joining together with the objective of providing a social facility otherwise not available. For instance, most towns have their own tennis club, parent/teacher association and childrens' playgroup. Such clubs and societies are usually described as *non-profit making organisations* whose objectives are to further recreational or religious activities. This description is a little misleading. Most clubs and societies will aim to generate an excess of revenue over expenditure but, unlike commercial concerns, this is not their principal objective. Furthermore, any profit which does arise is not distributed to members but instead viewed as a source of finance for extending their activities. These facts should be clearly spelled out in the rules governing the activities of the club or society. Provided this is done, the organisation is exempted from taxation which would otherwise be levied on profits arising.

The scale of the activities undertaken by many, though by no means all, clubs and societies is relatively small. The officers of these organisations, namely the chairman, secretary, treasurer etc. are unpaid volunteers. For these reasons a comprehensive accounting system is unlikely to exist. Indeed, in the majority of clubs and societies, the accounting system is unlikely to consist of more than a record of receipts and payments during the year. At the year end, a decision must be taken concerning the form that the final accounts should take. Perhaps because of the absence of necessary expertise, and also perhaps because there is little demand for accounting information from the members, the treasurer may simply prepare a 'Receipts and Payments Account' for the year. This is an analysed list of total cash coming into and going out of the club during the year; no attempt is made to take account of debts and liabilities outstanding at the balance sheet date and no balance sheet is prepared. This form of account may be satisfactory for the very small club or society, but is totally inadequate for the larger organisation where there exist valuable assets or substantial outstanding liabilities (perhaps because a bank loan has been raised to build a new squash court) of which the members should be made aware. For the larger organisations, the accounts must be prepared in accordance with the *accruals concept*, and the procedure then followed is almost exactly the same as that described for industrial and commercial concerns earlier in this chapter.

**3.8.1 Accounting terms used by clubs and societies** The only distinction, of any significance, between properly prepared final accounts of clubs and societies, on the one hand, and those of industrial and commercial concerns on the other, is that different terms are used to describe certain essentially similar financial magnitudes. The main differences are as follows:

| Industrial and Commercial Concerns | Club/ Society | Comment |
|---|---|---|
| Profit and Loss Account | Income and Expenditure Account | These differences reflect the fact that clubs and societies are not profit orientated. When computing income and expenditure, however, the accruals concept is applied in exactly the same way as when calculating figures for inclusion in the profit and loss account |
| Net profit/ Net loss | Surplus/ Deficit | |

| Industrial and Commercial Concerns | Club/ Society | Comment |
|---|---|---|
| Capital | Accumulated Fund | The term capital denotes a proprietorial interest which does not exist in clubs and societies, e.g. if a member resigns he has no right to reclaim his joining fee |

Readers should now work Question 3.4 at the end of this chapter.

**3.8.2   Treatment of subscriptions** A main source of revenue for clubs and societies is the subscriptions received from members, but it is often considered inappropriate to apply the full force of the accruals concept to this item. At the end of any accounting period, it is likely that there will be subscriptions which remain unpaid for that year and subscriptions received in advance for the following year. Strict application of the accruals concept would require the subscriptions outstanding to be credited to income and treated as a debt due to the club. This treatment will not usually be followed in practice. Although there may be no doubt that an individual has made use of the club's facilities during the year, the fact that his subscription remains unpaid at the end of the year is probably a fairly clear indication that it will never be collected. The former member has probably now left the club and the amount outstanding would be insufficient to justify the costs of any legal action needed to achieve recovery. Subscriptions received in advance, on the other hand, should be shown as a liability in the balance sheet and treated as income of the following accounting period.

**Example 3.8**
At the end of 19X2 subscriptions outstanding amounted to £300 and subscriptions received in advance for 19X3 amounted to £90. During 19X3 subscriptions received amounted to £5,400. This included the £300 outstanding at the end of 19X2 and £120 in advance for 19X4. Subscriptions outstanding at the end of 19X3 amounted to £500.

*Required:*

Calculate the amount to be credited to the income and expenditure account for 19X3 assuming that subscriptions are accounted for on (i) the cash basis, and (ii) the accruals basis, and (iii) the prudent basis described above.

## Solution.

| | | |
|---|---|---:|
| (i) Cash basis............................................ | | £5,400 |
| (ii) Accruals basis: | | £ |
| Cash received in 19X3.................................. | | 5,400 |
| Add: | Received in 19X2 for 19X3......................... | 90 |
| | Outstanding at end of 19X3........................ | 500 |
| | | 5,990 |
| Less: | Outstanding at end of 19X2........................ | (300) |
| | Received in 19X3 for 19X4......................... | (120) |
| | | 5,570 |
| (iii) Prudent basis (subscriptions outstanding ignored): | | £ |
| Cash received in 19X3.................................. | | 5,400 |
| Add: Received in 19X2 for 19X3........................ | | 90 |
| | | 5,490 |
| Less: Received in 19X3 for 19X4........................ | | (120) |
| | | 5,370 |

Many clubs charge new members an entry fee. These receipts may be credited either to income or direct to the accumulated fund. Either treatment is acceptable, but the method chosen should be applied consistently from year to year with the amount involved clearly disclosed. Life membership fees may also be accounted for in a variety of ways. There are three main alternatives:

i. Credit to the accumulated fund.
ii. Credit in full to the income and expenditure account in the year received.
iii. Credit initially to a life membership account, and transfer the fee to the income and expenditure account, in instalments, over an agreed number of years.

The third alternative is theoretically superior, since it attempts to relate income to the periods when the member uses the club's facilities, but it is also the most time-consuming accounting treatment.

### 3.8.3 Identifying the results of separate activities

It is always important, when deciding what form the annual acounts will take, to consider carefully the information which is likely to be of interest to the recipients of these reports. For this reason the accounts should be designed to reflect the particular nature of the organisation's activities. It is quite usual for clubs and societies to have a number of spheres of interest. For instance, a recreation club may provide facilities for lawn tennis, squash, table tennis, bowls, rugby and cricket. It will usually be considered useful to identify the contribution of each section, whether positive or negative, to the overall finances of the club. This information is not, however, necessarily required as a basis for deciding to extend or discontinue particular facilities. It must be remembered that it is the aim of clubs to provide recreational facilities not to make a profit.

However, the extent to which the profitable sections can subsidise the unprofitable is not unlimited and, if a succession of poor results reflects a decline in the demand for a particular sport, the facility may have to be withdrawn in the interests of the club members as a whole. More likely, significant deficits in certain areas will be interpreted as evidence of the need to revise subscriptions upwards. For these reasons a separate income and expenditure account should be prepared for each section, and the balances transferred to a general income and expenditure account where they will be combined with any unallocated items of income and expenditure arising from the club's activities.

Many clubs provide bar facilities at which drinks and perhaps tobacco and refreshments are sold and, where this occurs, the relevant items of income and expenditure are collected together in the bar trading account. The balance of this account, whether a profit or a loss, is also transferred to the general income and expenditure account.

In the case of industrial and commercial organisations, separate identification of the results of different product lines in order to show whether they are operating at a profit or a loss is a principal basis for management decisions on whether to expand or close down an area of activity The information made available for the purpose of this type of management decision is examined in section 2 of chapter 11.

Readers should now attempt Question 3.5 at the end of this chapter.

## 3.9 QUESTIONS

The preparation of accounts from incomplete records involves fundamental accounting procedures which must be mastered before students can expect to make progress in their accounting studies. It is for this reason that questions testing the students' understanding of these procedures are extremely common in examinations. Such questions often follow a pattern similar to William (Example 3.7 in this chapter), and solutions should consist of the same four steps recommended for answering that question. Questions 3.1, 3.4 and 3.5 below are of this type. Some variation is of course possible, and the remaining two questions in this section include certain innovations. The opening balance sheet is provided in question 3.2 so that only steps 2, 3 and 4 need to be processed. Question 3.3 is a revision question which deals with matters covered in chapter 2 as well as the present chapter.

### Question 3.1

Stoll, a trader, pays all his business takings into his bank account. All business payments are made by cheque. The following is a summary of his bank account for the year 19X5.

*Bank Summary*

| | £ | | £ |
|---|---|---|---|
| Balance 1 January 19X5... | 480 | Trade creditors........... | 24,800 |
| Received from debtors.... | 31,560 | General expenses......... | 2,524 |
| | | Rent ................... | 300 |
| | | Drawings .............. | 3,600 |
| | | Balance 31 December 19X5.................. | 816 |
| | 32,040 | | 32,040 |

The following information is obtained from the available records:

| | 31 Dec.19X4 | 31 Dec.19X5 |
|---|---|---|
| | £ | £ |
| Debtors for goods sold..................... | 1,900 | 2,344 |
| Trade creditors............................ | 1,630 | 1,930 |
| Stock..................................... | 2,040 | 1,848 |
| Furniture and fittings: | | |
| at cost less depreciation.................... | 400 | 360 |

*Required:*

    (a)   Calculate the balance of Stoll's capital at 31 December 19X4.

    (b)   Prepare the trading and profit and loss account for the year 19X5 and the balance sheet at 31 December 19X5. Present these accounting statements in vertical format.

## Question 3.2

Bennett commenced business as a retail trader at the beginning of 19X0. He maintains no formal system of ledger accounts for recording business transactions. An accountant was called in during 19X2 to prepare accounts for 19X1, in order to enable tax liabilities to be agreed. The following balance sheet was prepared as at 1 January 19X1:

*Balance Sheet, 1 January 19X1*

| | £ | | £ |
|---|---|---|---|
| Capital . . . . . . . . . . . . . . . . . | 8,720 | Motor vehicles at cost . . . . . | 10,000 |
| Loan at 15% . . . . . . . . . . . . . | 2,000 | Less: Accumulated | |
| Creditors . . . . . . . . . . . . . . | 850 | depreciation . . . . . . . . | 2,000 |
| Accrued expenses . . . . . . . . | 260 | | 8,000 |
| Bank overdraft . . . . . . . . . . | 2,030 | Stock . . . . . . . . . . . . . . . . . . . | 3,750 |
| | | Debtors . . . . . . . . . . . . . . . . | 1,060 |
| | | Prepaid expenses . . . . . . . . . | 400 |
| | | Bank deposit account . . . . . | 650 |
| | 13,860 | | 13,860 |

The following information is provided regarding 19X1:

1.  An analysis of the business bank accounts provided the following information:

| Receipts | £ | Payments | £ |
|---|---|---|---|
| Cash sales . . . . . . . . . . . . . . | 32,100 | Paid to suppliers . . . . . . . . . | 20,850 |
| Proceeds from credit sales . . | 7,560 | General expenses . . . . . . . . . | 7,560 |
| Legacy from relative . . . . . . | 2,650 | Drawings . . . . . . . . . . . . . . . | 12,500 |
| Bank interest received . . . . . | 50 | Motor vehicle . . . . . . . . . . . . | 4,000 |
| | 42,360 | | 44,910 |

2.  During the year a new motor vehicle was purchased for £4,000; Bennett depreciates vehicles at the rate of 20% on cost.

3.  Debtors outstanding at the end of 19X1 amounted to £1,840, none of which was considered to be bad or doubtful.

4.  Amounts due to suppliers at the end of 19X1 totalled £1,140 and stock was valued at £4,600.

5.  Accruals and prepayments of general expenses, at the end of 19X1, amounted to £310 and £520 respectively.

*Required:*
The trading and profit and loss account of Bennett's business for 19X1 and the balance sheet at 31 December 19X1.

## Question 3.3

The following is the balance sheet of Stondon, a trader, at 31 December 19X2:

*Balance Sheet*

| | £ | | £ |
|---|---|---|---|
| Capital................ | 7,940 | Furniture and fittings..... | 800 |
| | | Stock................... | 5,384 |
| Trade creditors........... | 3,294 | Trade debtors............ | 4,162 |
| | | Balance at bank.......... | 888 |
| | 11,234 | | 11,234 |

In January 19X3 Stondon sold certain private investments for £4,200; he purchased a motor van for business use for £3,000 and paid the balance of the proceeds into his business bank account.

At 31 December 19X3, trade debtors amounted to £4,124, stock in trade was valued at £6,891 and trade creditors amounted to £3,586. Stondon's business bank account was overdrawn by £782. His drawings during 19X3 were £12,840.

The total of running expenses charged to the profit and loss account for the year 19X3 amounted to £14,420; this total included £500 for depreciation of the motor van.

Stondon's gross profit is at the rate of 25% of selling price for all goods sold during 19X3.

*Required:*
   (a) Prepare Stondon's balance sheet at 31 December 19X3.
   (b) Calculate Stondon's net profit for 19X3 on the basis of changes in capital.
   (c) Reconstruct the trading and profit and loss account of Stondon's business for the year 19X3.

**Note:** Ignore depreciation of furniture and fittings.

## Question 3.4

The following details are extracted from the books of the Fellowship Club:

| Balances at: | 31 Dec.19X7 | 31 Dec.19X8 |
|---|---|---|
| | £ | £ |
| Bar Stock.......................... | 8,200 | 11,936 |
| Creditors for bar supplies.............. | 4,080 | 4,568 |
| Creditors for expenses................ | 160 | 248 |

Summary of Bank Account for 19X8

| | £ | | £ |
|---|---|---|---|
| Balance 1 January 19X8... | 13,280 | Bar purchases........... | 80,760 |
| Subscriptions received..... | 12,400 | Salaries................ | 16,840 |
| Bar sales............... | 107,600 | Rent of club premises...... | 2,800 |
| Interest on investments.... | 4,160 | Rates.................. | 2,000 |
| | | General expenses........ | 5,360 |
| | | Cost of new investments... | 26,000 |
| | | Balance 31 December 19X8.................. | 3,680 |
| | 137,440 | | 137,440 |

On 1 January 19X8 the club held temporary investments which it had purchased for £49,200, and the furniture in use was valued at £30,400. The club is building up its investments to enable it to purchase its own clubhouse in due course. Depreciation should be charged on the furniture at the rate of 10 per cent per annum on the opening value.

*Required:*
(a) A bar trading account for 19X8.
(b) A general income and expenditure account for 19X8.
(c) A balance sheet as at 31 December 19X8.

## Question 3.5

The Ridlingham Recreation Club consists of a tennis section and a rugby section. The following information has been obtained relating to the position of the club on 1 January 19X1:

|  | £ |
|---|---:|
| Club house at cost | 38,000 |
| Creditors for bar purchases | 3,720 |
| Creditors for general expenses | 500 |
| Tennis courts at cost (£40,000), less depreciation to date | 24,000 |
| Furniture and equipment at book value | 5,000 |
| Bar stocks | 4,400 |
| Bank balance | 1,500 |

The club's bank statements for 19X1 have been analysed and the following summary prepared:

*Bank Account, 19X1*

| | £ | | £ |
|---|---:|---|---:|
| Balance 1 January | 1,500 | New tennis court | 16,000 |
| Ten year membership | 12,000 | Repairs to tennis courts | 2,520 |
| Other subscriptions: tennis | 6,400 | Prizes for tennis tournaments | 140 |
| rugby | 1,300 | Rugby kit | 900 |
| Tennis tournament entry fees | 240 | Rental of rugby pitch | 400 |
| Bar sales | 69,660 | Rates on clubhouse | 1,100 |
| Collections at rugby matches | 180 | Payments for bar supplies | 48,400 |
| Tennis court fees | 5,700 | Wages of bar steward | 7,800 |
| | | General expenses | 17,300 |
| | | Balance 31 December | 2,420 |
| | 96,980 | | 96,980 |

You discover that all cash received is paid into the club bank account and all payments are made by cheque.

During the year a new tennis court was built which was first used on 1 July 19X1. In order to help pay for the new court, ten year memberships were offered for sale, at the beginning of the first year, at £400 each.

At 31 December 19X1 creditors for bar purchases and general expenses amount to £4,300 and £640 respectively. Bar stocks are valued at £5,280. It is the club's policy to write off the cost of the

tennis courts over a ten year period. Furniture is depreciated at 10%
on the balance at the year end. For the purpose of the accounts the
rugby kit is considered to possess a nil value.

*Required:*
(a) The bar trading account and a general income and
    expenditure account for 19X1. The general income and
    expenditure account should show the net surplus or deficit
    arising separately from the tennis section and the rugby
    section.
(b) The balance sheet at 31 December 19X1.

CHAPTER 4

# The Initial Record
# of Transactions

## 4.1 INTRODUCTION
Accounting reports are based on summarised information, and are
accurate only if the initial record of the individual transactions is
correct. The operation of a company results in numerous individual
transactions taking place; in the case of large companies there is
likely to be a massive volume of these. Inflows and outflows of
goods, services and cash occur, and it is the responsibility of
management to ensure that there is an efficient system of accounting. This system must be designed both to record and control individual transactions and to enable the production of summarised
results in the form of accounting reports. For example, a retail shop
which makes a large number of relatively small sales must have controls to ensure that all items which leave the shop are paid for and
that all cash received is recorded; summaries showing the total value
of sales, possibly analysed by product, are then produced for
management so that the shop's progress can be monitored. This
chapter covers the detailed recording of the separate items in such a
way as to provide an adequate foundation for the remainder of the
accounting process.

## 4.2 CASH FLOWS
Control of cash receipts and payments is obviously of particular importance to the company as resources which are in the form of cash
are vulnerable to misappropriation; the cash book, in which all
receipts and payments are recorded, is the central element of this
control. The objective is to ensure that all cash due to the company
is received and retained until its subsequent, properly authorised,
disbursement takes place. A simple way to establish this control is
to ensure that:
    (i)   all cash receipts are recorded as they are received;

(ii) all cash receipts are paid with little delay into the company's bank account; and

(iii) only senior personnel are permitted to authorise the bank to make payments from the account.

One result of using a bank account is to create an additional source of information on cash flows since all the entries in the cash book have a corresponding entry on the statement of account which is provided periodically by the bank. (The importance of this is discussed in section 2.2 of this chapter, the Bank Reconciliation).

The initial record of cash receipts is usually in the form of a memorandum list which should be prepared at the point and time of receipt. The necessary documentation is completed as each sale is made when the goods are exchanged directly for cash, as is the case with a retail shop, or at some other point where goods are sold on credit and the cash is received some time after the sale. For example, if it is usual for cheques to be received in the post, a reliable employee should be made responsible for opening all letters, removing and listing the cheques enclosed, and passing them to the cashier for prompt payment into the bank. The inclusion of a number of different people in this line of control reduces the possibility of undetected theft since the list produced by the person responsible for opening the post is independent of, and can be checked with, the sum accounted for by the cashier. On the payments side it must be ensured that only a limited number of senior people are authorised to sign documents, such as cheques and standing order mandates, which are accepted by the bank as instructions to pay sums of money out of the account. The official signing the document, for example the cheque, should require evidence to warrant its completion, such as a valid invoice received from a supplier. In this example, the invoice should be referenced to the cash payment and retained so that the transaction's validity can, if required, be subsequently verified. This involves a system of cross-referencing, with the payment recorded in the cash book cross-referenced to a supplier's account in which the liability has been recorded on the previous receipt of a valid invoice.

**4.2.1 The Cash Account** The cash account is used to record the inflows and outflows of cash and is kept in an accounting record called the cash book. The account consists of two lists of figures, one of which gives details of cash receipts and the other cash payments; in accordance with the rules of *double entry book keep-*

*ing* (explained in detail in chapter 5) the receipts are known as 'debits' and are placed on the left hand page of the cash book, while the payments are recorded on the right hand page and are termed 'credits'. (The terms debit and credit are often abbreviated to 'dr' and 'cr' respectively). A period of time, such as a week or a month, is covered by the lists, and, as well as the cash flows which take place during the period, the opening cash position is included so that the closing balance of cash can be determined. If the company starts the period with cash in hand, the amount is entered at the top of the cash received (debit) column, while an overdraft is entered at the top of the payments (credit) column.

To find the closing balance of cash the account is 'balanced'. This is done by finding the difference between the total values of debits and credits. The closing balance of one period, known as the 'Balance Carried Down', is the opening balance for the following period, when it is termed the 'Balance Brought Down'; this balance appears in the company's balance sheet.

**Example 4.1**
Wire Ltd. balances its cash book each week, and at the end of week 8 of 19X7 held cash of £782. During week 9 the following receipts and payments took place.

|  |  | £ |
|---|---|---:|
| Receipts: | Sales | 5,769 |
|  | Loan from Newbank Ltd | 2,000 |
| Payments: | Purchase of goods for resale | 3,150 |
|  | Wages | 790 |
|  | Rent | 126 |
|  | Advertising | 75 |
|  | Delivery Van | 3,500 |

*Required:*
Prepare the cash account for week 9 of Wire Ltd. as it would appear in the company's cash book and show the balance carried forward to week 10.

## Solution

*Cash Account*

| | Cash in = Receipts Debit | | | Cash Out = Payments Credit | |
|---|---|---|---|---|---|
| | | £ | | | £ |
| Week 9 | Balance brought | | Week 9 | Purchases ......... | 3,150 |
| | down ........... | 782 | | Wages ............. | 790 |
| | Sales .............. | 5,769 | | Rent .............. | 126 |
| | Loan .............. | 2,000 | | Advertising ........ | 75 |
| | | | | Van .............. | 3,500 |
| | | | | | 7,641 |
| | | | | Balance carried | |
| | | | | down ........... | 910 |
| | | 8,551 | | | 8,551 |
| Week 10 | Balance brought | | | | |
| | down ........... | 910 | | | |

*Notes:*
1. Although the £910 is a debit balance, ie, debit items exceed credit items by this amount, it is conventionally added to the list of credits so that the two columns add up to £8,551. The surplus is then brought down as the opening balance for week 10. As, in this case, the balance brought down is on the debit side of the account, it is a debit balance; credit balances are those brought down on the credit side of the account.
2. The terms 'balance carried down' and 'balance brought down' are often abbreviated to 'balance b/d' and 'balance c/d' respectively.

You should now work Question 4.1 at the end of this chapter to test your understanding of the preparation of the cash account.

**4.2.2 The Bank Reconciliation** A company's cash account should contain exactly the same receipts and payments as pass through its bank account. A valuable check on the accuracy of the cash account is provided by the routine preparation of the Bank Reconciliation Statement which agrees the cash account's balance with that shown on the bank statement. To provide additional control, the reconciliation should ideally be prepared or checked by an official of the company who is otherwise independent of the control and recording of the flows of cash.

The Bank Reconciliation Statement is prepared by comparing items in the cash account with those in the bank statement. Entries which appear in both during the period under examination are checked off, but usually these records, although covering the same period of time, do not correspond exactly. This is the result of some or all of the following:

(a) Payments in the cash account not on the bank statement. These mainly result from the fact that there is a delay between the issue of the cheque, at which time it is entered in the cash account, and its clearance by the bank, when it appears on the bank statement.

(b) Receipts in the cash account not on the bank statement. A company may enter the cash received each day in the cash account, but pay it into the bank the following day, or even allow it to accumulate for short period of time. This causes a lapse of time between the cash account record and the bank statement entry. For security reasons, the delay should be kept to a minimum.

(c) Payments on the statement not in the cash account. Some payments, such as those for bank charges, are generated by the bank; the company may know that they have been paid only when a statement is received, and they would not have been previously entered in the cash book. Other items which fall into this category are payments made by standing order and direct debits.

(d) Receipts on the statement not in the cash account. It is common nowadays for sums to be paid directly into the recipient's bank account, and sometimes they are identifiable only when the statement is received.

Items (a) and (b) above are merely timing differences and, although appearing in the bank reconciliation, require no further entry in the cash account. Items (c) and (d), however, are additional items which, if valid, should be entered in the cash account when the statement is received.

The procedure for preparing a bank reconciliation statement is to take the entries in the cash account for a certain period of time and mark off in both records those which also appear on the bank statement for the same period. Any items which are left unmarked must be examined and classified into types (a), (b), (c) and (d). Items of types (c) and (d) are entered in the cash account from which the balance is then extracted. This balance will still differ from that shown on the bank statement if there are any items of types (a) and (b), and so a memorandum statement is drawn up which adjusts the balance on the statement for these items, after which it should agree with that shown on the cash account.

## Example 4.2

The following information relates to Check Ltd. for the month of March:

### Cash Account

| Receipts (debit) | | £ | Payments (credit) | | £ |
|---|---|---|---|---|---|
| March | | | March | | |
| 1 | Balance brought down.... | 1,000 | 4 | Cheques issued: No.11.... | 150 |
| 9 | Receipts paid into bank.... | 350 | 9 | No.12.... | 225 |
| 16 | Receipts paid into bank.... | 200 | 15 | No.13.... | 75 |
| 23 | Receipts paid into bank.... | 475 | 22 | No.14.... | 445 |
| 30 | Receipts paid into bank.... | 150 | 30 | No.15.... | 160 |
| | | | 31 | No.16.... | 330 |
| | | | 31 | Balance carried down..... | 790 |
| | | 2,175 | | | 2,175 |

### Bank Statement

| | | Debit £ | Credit £ | Balance £ |
|---|---|---|---|---|
| March | | | | |
| 1 | Balance brought forward........... | | | 1,000 Cr. |
| 6 | Cheque no. 11.................... | 150 | | 850 |
| 11 | Lodgement...................... | | 350 | 1,200 |
| | Cheque no. 12.................... | 225 | | 975 |
| 17 | Cheque no. 13.................... | 75 | | 900 |
| 18 | Lodgement...................... | | 200 | 1,100 |
| 24 | Cheque no. 14.................... | 445 | | 655 |
| 25 | Lodgement...................... | | 475 | 1,130 |
| | Standing Order.................. | 60 | | 1,070 |
| 26 | Direct Credit.................... | | 50 | 1,120 |
| 31 | Bank Charges.................... | 100 | | 1,020 |
| | Balance carried forward........... | | | 1,020 |

*Note* As the bank statement is prepared from the point of view of the bank, payments made by the company are shown as debits and deposits with the bank as credits, ie, the terms are the opposite way round compared with the cash account in the company's books.

## Required:

(i) Make the necessary adjustments to the cash account for the month of March.

(ii) Prepare the bank reconciliation statement at the end of March.

## Solution

When the entries in the cash account are checked with those on the statement, the following differences are found:

(a) Payments in the cash account not on the bank statement:

Cheque no. 15............ £160

Cheque no. 16........... £330

(b) Receipts in the cash account not on the bank statement:

Lodgement............... £150

(c) Payments on the bank statement not in the cash account:

Standing order........... £ 60

Bank Charges........... £100

(d) Receipts on the bank statement not in the cash account:

Direct Credit............ £ 50

Items (c) and (d) are used to complete the cash account, and items (a) and (b) appear in the bank reconciliation statement.

(i) *Completion of the Cash Account for March*

| Receipts (debit) | | | Payments (credit) | | |
|---|---|---|---|---|---|
| March | | £ | March | | £ |
| 31 | Balance brought down...... | 790 | 31 | Standing order............. | 60 |
| 31 | Direct credit............... | 50 | 31 | Bank charges.............. | 100 |
| | | | 31 | Balance carried down....... | 680 |
| | | 840 | | | 840 |

(ii) *Bank Reconciliation Statement at 31 March*

| | | £ | £ |
|---|---|---|---|
| | Balance per bank statement..................... | | 1,020 |
| less: | Outstanding cheques No. 15..................... | 160 | |
| | No. 16..................... | 330 | 490 |
| | | | 530 |
| plus: | Outstanding lodgement....................... | | 150 |
| | Balance as per cash account.................... | | 680 |

*Notes:*

1. Subsequent bank statements should be checked to ensure that all outstanding items are cleared without undue delay.

2. It is possible for banks to make mistakes. Any unexplained entry on the bank statement should be queried as it may have been entered in the company's account in error. Until a satisfactory explanation is obtained, such items should be shown as part of the reconciliation statement and not entered in the cash book.

Readers should now attempt Question 4.2 at the end of this chapter to test their understanding of the preparation of bank reconciliation statements.

**4.2.3  The Double Column Cash Book**  It was stated above that all cash receipts should be paid into the firm's bank account, without delay, and that all disbursements should be made from the bank account. Although this is a very good rule to observe in practice, there are occasions when it is not applied, especially in the case of small businesses. In these circumstances it is particularly important to ensure that all cash flows are recorded so that none are overlooked. For example, a trader may make sales of £100 for cash and out of the proceeds pay wages of £30 and motor expenses of £5 before banking the residual £65. It is incorrect merely to record in the books of the firm the lodgement of £65 in respect of sales, since this ignores the receipt of the additional £35 which was paid out on wages and motor expenses. The effect of the omission would be to understate sales, wages and motor expenses.

Where sums are paid out of cash takings before they are banked, it is therefore necessary to maintain two cash accounts, one to deal with the flows of cash which take place through the bank account, called the 'cash at bank account', and one to deal with other cash flows, called the 'cash in hand account'. Transfers between the two accounts are made in the usual way, so that, for example, when cash is banked a payment is entered in the cash in hand account and a receipt recorded in the cash at bank account. Although it is possible to maintain two completely separate accounts, it is usual in these circumstances to modify the traditional cash book format and use what is known as a Double Column Cash Book.

**Example 4.3**
Glue Ltd. undertook the following transactions between 1 and 10 June.

| Date | Details | Value |
|------|---------|-------|
| June | | £ |
| 1 | Cash balance in hand............................................. | 50 |
| 1 | Balance at bank................................................. | 200 |
| 3 | Received from cash sales........................................ | 1,275 |
| 4 | Cash paid into bank............................................. | 1,000 |
| 7 | Pay wages in cash............................................... | 100 |
| 8 | Make cash purchases............................................. | 200 |
| 9 | Draw cash from bank............................................. | 300 |
| 10 | Pay for purchases by cheque..................................... | 150 |
| 10 | Pay rent in cash................................................ | 175 |

*Required:*

Prepare the double column cash book to record the above transactions, carrying down the balance on 10 June.

## Solution

*Double Column Cash Book*

| Date | Detail | Cash in | Cash at | Date | Detail | Cash in | Cash at |
|------|--------|---------|---------|------|--------|---------|---------|
| June | | hand | bank | June | | hand | bank |
| | | £ | £ | | | £ | £ |
| 1 | Balances b/d........ | 50 | 200 | 4 | Cash to bank......... | 1,000 | |
| 3 | Sales............... | 1,275 | | 7 | Wages .............. | 100 | |
| 4 | Cash paid in....... | | 1,000 | 8 | Purchases ........... | 200 | |
| 9 | Cash from bank..... | 300 | | 9 | Cash withdrawn....... | | 300 |
| | | | | 10 | Purchases ........... | | 150 |
| | | | | 10 | Rent................. | 175 | |
| | | | | 10 | Balances c/d......... | 150 | 750 |
| | | 1,625 | 1,200 | | | 1,625 | 1,200 |
| 10 | Balances b/d........ | 150 | 750 | | | | |

Note that the accounts shown above comply with the usual convention that debits are recorded on the left and credits on the right, but it differs from the usual format as there are two columns on each side, one to record the flows of cash into the business and the manner of its disposition while the other contains details of the cash flows which take place through the bank account. The opening balances are respectively the cash in hand and at the bank on 1 June, and the first transaction increases cash held by £1,275 which is debited in the cash column to represent a cash receipt. £1,000 of this cash is paid into the bank on June 4: cash in hand is credited with this amount to show that the payment was made out of cash, while the bank is debited to show the corresponding receipt. Conversely, when cash is drawn from the bank to be used for cash payments, cash at bank is credited and the cash in hand column debited.

Readers should now work Question 4.3 at the end of this chapter.

**4.2.4  The Analysed Cash Book**  To enable accounting reports to be prepared it is necessary to ascertain why particular cash flows have taken place. For example, cash from sales and the receipt of a loan are both recorded as cash inflows, but the former is an element in the calculation of profit while the latter is entered in the balance sheet as a liability. A simple way to break down cash flows into their constituent parts is to maintain an analysed cash book. This has columns not only for cash inflows and outflows, but also further columns for different types of flows. When a type of receipt or payment occurs on a regular basis, such as payments for goods or wages, a separate column is devoted to this category of transaction; infrequent transactions are entered in a sundry column. An advantage of the use of an analysed cash book is that the nature of each item must be ascertained at the time it is recorded; errors are more likely to occur if there is delay in this process, due for example to a lapse of memory.

## Example 4.4

The following cash transactions were undertaken by Thorn & Co:

| Day | Receipts | | | Payments | |
|-----|----------|---|---|----------|---|
| | | £ | | | £ |
| 1 | Sales | 250 | | Purchases of stock | 125 |
| 2 | Sales | 300 | | Wages | 76 |
| 3 | Sales | 270 | | Purchases of stock | 150 |
| 4 | Sales | 315 | | Wages | 79 |
| 4 | Loan | 150 | | Rent | 50 |
| 4 | | | | Purchase of fixed asset | 200 |

## Required:

Prepare the company's analysed cash book to record the above transaction.

## Solution

### Cash Account

| | Receipts (debit) | | | | Payments (credit) | | | | |
|---|---|---|---|---|---|---|---|---|---|
| Day Detail | | Total | Sales | Sundry | Day Detail | Total | Purchases of stock | Wages | Rent | Sundry |
| | | £ | £ | £ | | £ | £ | £ | £ | £ |
| 1 | Sales | 250 | 250 | | 1 Purchases | | | | | |
| 2 | Sales | 300 | 300 | | of stock.. | 125 | 125 | | | |
| 3 | Sales | 270 | 270 | | 2 Wages.... | 76 | | 76 | | |
| 4 | Sales | 315 | 315 | | 3 Purchases | | | | | |
| | Loan | 150 | | 150 | of stock.. | 150 | 150 | | | |
| | | | | | 4 Wages.... | 79 | | 79 | | |
| | | | | | Rent...... | 50 | | | 50 | |
| | | | | | Purchase of | | | | | |
| | | | | | fixed asset | 200 | | | | 200 |
| | | 1,285 | 1,135 | 150 | | 680 | 275 | 155 | 50 | 200 |

The fact that the aggregate of the totals of the analysis columns is equal to the total of 'Total' column provides a useful check of arithmetical accuracy.

Readers should now work Question 4.4 at the end of this chapter.

**4.2.5 The Petty Cash Account** All businesses have to meet small incidental expenses in the course of operating and, as it is often inconvenient to pay these by cheque, it is usual to maintain a petty cash float. The normal procedure is to adopt the 'Imprest' system which uses a fixed sum as a float from which money is paid in return for a properly authorised petty cash voucher. The size of the float should be sufficient to cover the normal level of disbursements during the length of time between replenishments. At regular intervals the petty cashier exchanges the petty cash vouchers for a cheque equal to their total value which is then used to restore the fund to its designated amount. An advantage of using this system is that at any time the cash in hand plus that represented by vouchers should total the amount of the initial float. This facilitates spot checks by an appropriate official.

Although petty cash expenditure, by definition, covers only relatively small amounts it is still necessary to ensure that it is properly controlled and accounted for. The use of the Imprest system gives control, and to ensure that a proper record exists it is usual to maintain a petty cash book, in which are entered the details of the receipts and payments of petty cash. The petty cash book also acts as the petty cash account. Example 4.5 shows entries in a petty cash account recording the transactions of an imprest petty cash fund of £50.

## Example 4.5

*Petty Cash Account*

| Receipts (debit) | | | | | *Payments (credit)* | | | | |
| Date | | | Date | Voucher No. | Total | Postage | Travel | Cleaning |
| June | | £ | June | | £ | £ | £ | £ |
| 1 | Balance b/d.. | 12 | 4 | 11 | 10 | | 10 | |
| 3 | Bank........ | 38 | 11 | 12 | 7 | | | 7 |
| | | | 18 | 13 | 5 | 5 | | |
| | | | 24 | 14 | 8 | | 8 | |
| | | | 29 | 15 | 4 | 4 | | |
| | | | | | 34 | 9 | 18 | 7 |
| | | | 30 | Balance c/d.. | 16 | | | |
| | | 50 | | | 50 | | | |
| July | | | | | | | | |
| 1 | Balance b/d.. | 16 | | | | | | |
| 2 | Bank........ | 34 | | | | | | |

The opening balance of £12 shows that expenditure of £38 has been made in the previous period and should be represented by vouchers to support the amount of cash drawn from the bank. The debit entry in the petty cash account of £38 shows the receipt of cash and will correspond with a credit in the cash at bank account from which the payment is made. The fund stands at £50 immediately after reimbursement; withdrawals of cash are entered as payments on the credit side of the book in the cash column and this has the effect of reducing the petty cash balance. Analysis columns are used to provide a summary of the amount spent for each purpose. Vouchers 11 to 15 account for £34, and this sum is drawn from the bank to replenish the fund at the beginning of July.

Question 4.5 at the end of this chapter should now be worked.

## 4.3  FLOWS OF GOODS AND SERVICES

Accounts are designed to reflect the economic activity which takes place during a period of time, and this is not accurately shown by simply reporting cash movements. This is because it is usual for sales and purchases to be made on credit and, in these circumstances, the movement of goods is not immediately accompanied by equivalent transfers of cash. Companies must therefore keep records of inflows and outflows of goods and services as well as for flows of cash. For example, the fact that goods have been purchased on credit must be reported, even if they have not yet been paid for.

One reason for making a record of flows of goods and services is because control is needed to ensure that cash is subsequently collected from credit customers and that suppliers are paid on time. This section deals with the initial record of economic events; the control of debtors and creditors is dealt with in section 5 of chapter 5.

**4.3.1 Day Books** In its simplest form a day book is a list of sales or purchases which have taken place on credit with the name of the customer or supplier entered next to each item. The total of each list gives the value of purchases or sales which have taken place during a period of time.

To make certain that all sales are recorded, steps should be taken to ensure that a sales invoice is made out each time goods are supplied. A number of copies of the sales invoice are normally required, one of which goes to the customer and another to the accounts section as the basis for entering the transaction in the sales day book. A final control, such as pre-numbering, should be used to ensure that copies of all invoices are entered in the day book; any missing numbers should be investigated.

The purchases day book is written up on the basis of invoices received from suppliers. To ensure that payment is made only for goods received, a record should be kept of goods delivered to the company against which the invoice can be checked; the record of goods received is cancelled after checking the invoice to prevent the possibility of paying twice for one delivery. The invoice should also be matched with its originating order to make sure that goods delivered are actually required by the company. An invoice not supported by both evidence of receipt of the goods and a purchase order should be investigated and not passed for entry in the books until there is sufficient proof that it relates to a valid transaction. Invoices for services, such as cleaning, should be supported by an order or contract and passed for payment only by an authorised official.

To produce final accounts and provide management with relevant information the inflows and outflows of goods and services must be broken down, and this is achieved by adding analysis columns to the day books as was done in the case of the cash book. The analysis headings are determined on the basis of which aspects of the organisation are to be monitored. Excessive detail impairs comprehension and so too many headings should not be used; on the other hand, significant matters may be masked if the headings are too broad. Management needs to identify areas of strength and weakness, and this is achieved if, for example, sales and purchases are analysed by type of product, and the department or branch in which they originate.

**Example 4.6**

House Ltd. owns a shop which consists of two distinct departments, one selling bricks and the other mortar. All purchases are made on credit and management requires reports which show the individual results of each department.

*Required:*

Prepare from the following details the purchases day book in a manner which provides the information needed by management.

Purchases: March 1st. from Builder Ltd. — bricks £100; mortar £75 (supplied on one invoice)
March 2nd. from Cement Ltd. — mortar £50
March 3rd. from Jerry Ltd. — bricks £65

**Solution**

*Purchases Day Book*

| Date | Supplier | Total | Bricks | Mortar |
|------|----------|-------|--------|--------|
| March | | £ | £ | £ |
| 1 | Builder Ltd........ | 175 | 100 | 75 |
| 2 | Cement Ltd....... | 50 | | 50 |
| 3 | Jerry Ltd........ | 65 | 65 | |
| | | 290 | 165 | 125 |

The use of day books is not restricted to purchases and sales; they can be used for any routine transactions, such as the return of goods from customers or to suppliers. In all cases appropriate controls must be established to ensure that only valid entries are made in the records.

Readers should now work Question 4.6 at the end of this chapter to test their understanding of the preparation of day books.

**4.3.2 Computerisation** It is possible for a business of any size, from the small to the multinational company, to acquire a computer facility on which to maintain its accounting records. These installations are versatile and can provide a variety of memorandum analyses; this represents a great advance on manual analysis.

Information to be entered in the computer is coded to indicate such features as the type of product sold, the area of the sale or the branch or sales-person making the sale. The computer can then produce memorandum analyses of the total sales figure under whichever headings are required. An important point to note with all systems is that the required analysis headings should be chosen in advance so that, as each transaction is recorded at the prime entry stage, it is analysed or coded as a matter of routine. If this is not done, each analysis would involve returning to the prime documents to re-analyse or code them, a process which is likely to be laborious. It is also possible that the basic data has not been recorded, for example, a sale could only be analysed on the basis of the sales-person who made it if a note is placed on the invoice at the time of sale to indicate the person responsible; often such information could not be reconstructed after the lapse of a period of time.

## 4.4 QUESTIONS
### Question 4.1
Mr. Wall decided to set up in business as a sole trader on 1 January 19X1. He opened a business bank account into which he pays all the takings and from which he pays all business costs. His transactions for January 19X1 were:

(a) Pay £5,000 into bank as capital on the 1st.
(b) Buy for cash a second-hand delivery van for £4,000 on the 2nd.
(c) Pay one month's rent on premises £100 on the 3rd.
(d) Sell goods for £2,250 cash during the month.
(e) Collect £450 from debtors and pay £2,500 to creditors during the month.
(f) Withdraw £110 on the 15th.
(g) Pay insurance for one year, from 1 January 19X1 of £120 on the 30th.

*Required*
Write up the business cash account for January 19X1.

### Question 4.2
The accounts of Storm Ltd. for the year to 30 June 19X1 showed a year end debit balance at the bank of £1,296, and the bank state-

ment showed an overdraft of £87. Investigation revealed the following facts:

- (a) Cheques received from customers, amounting to £1,350, in respect of credit sales were entered in the cash book on 30 June, but did not appear on the bank statement until 1 July.
- (b) Cheques drawn by Storm Ltd. on 28 June in favour of trade creditors to the value of £682 were not cleared through the bank until after 30 June.
- (c) No entry was made in the cash account to record rent for the year of £500 which was paid by the bank in accordance with a standing order on 22 June.
- (d) On 28 June a customer paid £160 direct to the company's bank account.
- (e) A cheque from a customer for £200 was recorded in the cash book and was paid into the bank on 25 June. The bank returned the cheque on 30 June marked "Refer to drawer"; no entry was made in respect of this return in the cash book.
- (f) Bank charges of £175 were charged on the bank statement on 30 June, but were not entered in the cash book.

*Required*
- (i) Write up the cash account to record the matters detailed above.
- (ii) Prepare a reconciliation between the revised cash account balance and the balance shown by the bank statement.

## Question 4.3
Ray Gunne set up in business on 1 January 19X3. The firm's transactions for the first week of January 19X3 were:

- (a) Pay capital of £10,000 into the bank
- (b) Buy premises for £8,000 and equipment for £2,750; both paid by cheque
- (c) Borrow £5,000 from Gunne's brother; he provided this sum in cash of which £4,000 was used to buy a delivery van and £750 was paid into the bank
- (d) Buy trading stock: £3,000 by cheque and £1,000 for cash
- (e) Make cash sales of £5,500
- (f) Pay wages of £100 in cash
- (g) Take cash drawings of £150
- (h) Pay rates by cheque of £250
- (i) Pay £4,250 of cash into the bank.

*Required*

Prepare the double column cash book of Gunne's business for the first week of January 19X3 and carry down the balances at the end of the week.

## Question 4.4

At the start of a trading week the cash account of Laser Ltd showed that the company was £6,510 overdrawn. During the week the company undertook the following cash transactions:

| Day | Receipts | £ | Payments | £ |
|---|---|---|---|---|
| 1 | Sales | 1,790 | Purchases | 2,250 |
| 2 | Sales | 2,190 | Wages | 380 |
| 3 | Sales | 1,250 | | |
| 3 | Sale of fixed asset | 1,000 | | |
| 4 | Sales | 3,720 | Interest on loan | 400 |
| 5 | Sales | 1,540 | Purchases | 3,140 |
| 6 | Sales | 2,710 | Wages | 450 |

*Required*

Prepare the analysed cash book of Laser Ltd to record the above information and carry down the balance at the end of the week.

## Question 4.5

Zapper Ltd maintains its petty cash using the imprest system with a float of £100. On 1 December the petty cash account showed a balance of £14 and the petty cashier was authorised to draw £86 from the bank to replenish the float. The following amounts were then paid out:

| Date Dec. | Voucher No. | Detail | £ |
|---|---|---|---|
| 2 | 37 | Stationery | 5 |
| 2 | 38 | Postage | 7 |
| 3 | 39 | Travelling | 22 |
| 4 | 40 | Stationery | 19 |
| 5 | 41 | Travelling | 13 |
| 5 | 42 | Postage | 5 |
| 6 | 43 | Travelling | 12 |

*Required*

(a)  Prepare the petty cash account to record and analyse the above transactions.

(b)   Calculate the amount to be drawn from the bank to replenish the float after the above amounts have been paid.

## Question 4.6

Office Ltd owns a shop which sells typewriters and stationery and also repairs office equipment. The following credit sales took place:

Day 1   Sold a typewriter for £300 and stationery for £75 to Gum Ltd.
        Repaired Glue Ltd's typewriter for £100.
Day 2   Sold stationery to Stick Ltd for £70.
Day 3   Sold a typewriter to Fast Ltd. for £450.
        Repaired Stick Ltd's typewriter for £50.

*Required*
Prepare an analysed sales day book for Office Ltd. to record the above transactions. The results of each separate activity are to be ascertained.

# CHAPTER 5

# The Double Entry System

## 5.1 INTRODUCTION

The previous chapter explained the manner in which the primary record of flows of goods, services and cash is compiled. Checks and controls must be established to ensure accuracy as this information, held in memorandum form, is the basis on which the rest of the accounting system relies. If the initial records are incorrect, accounting statements based on them will contain errors and wrong decisions may be made. This chapter examines how the information on inflows and outflows of goods, services and cash is analysed and converted into accounting statements by means of the system of double entry book-keeping.

## 5.2 THE INTERLOCKING EFFECT OF TRANSACTIONS

In chapter 1 the impact on the balance sheet of a number of transactions was examined. Sources of finance remained equal in value to assets after each transaction, and the relationship, C(capital) + L(liabilities) = A(assets), remains true in all circumstances. The interlocking effect of transactions is fundamental to the system of double entry book-keeping, and is now given further consideration.

To maintain the relationship $C + L = A$, each transaction must have two equal, but opposite effects. The alternatives are shown in Figure 5.1.

**Figure 5.1**

| *Effect 1 (Debit)* | *Effect 2 (Credit)* |
|:---:|:---:|
| Increase Asset | Decrease Asset |
| OR | OR |
| Decrease Liability | Increase Liability |
| OR | OR |
| Decrease Capital | Increase Capital |

A single transaction can affect any of the items listed as *Effect 1* and be paired with any item from the *Effect 2* list. The interlocking effect means that the total value of either of the two impacts must be the same as that of the other.

Figure 5.1 covers changes in assets, liabilities, and capital; it can be extended to include revenues and expenses. Items of revenue and expense are recorded separately; the impact of an expense is to decrease capital, and so it is recorded as an *Effect 1*, while revenue increases capital and so is an *Effect 2*. The effects of revenues and expenses are compared to calculate the firm's net profit or loss. A net profit is then added to capital and any net loss is deducted from it. Figure 5.2 extends Figure 5.1 to include revenues and expenses.

## Figure 5.2

| Effect 1 (Debit) | Effect 2 (Credit) |
|:---:|:---:|
| Increase Asset | Decrease Asset |
| OR | OR |
| Decrease Liability | Increase Liability |
| OR | OR |
| Decrease Capital | Increase Capital |
| OR | OR |
| Increase Expense | Decrease Expense |
| OR | OR |
| Decrease Revenue | Increase Revenue |

A practical application of the interlocking effect is given in Illustration 5.1.

### Illustration 5.1

The following transactions were undertaken by Bernard Egin, a sole trader, when starting his business:

| Transaction Number | Description | Value £ |
|---|---|---|
| 1 | Introduce cash as capital | 1,000 |
| 2 | Raise a loan for cash | 500 |
| 3 | Buy plant for cash | 1,000 |
| 4 | Buy stock for cash | 250 |
| 5 | Buy stock on credit | 350 |
| 6a | Sell stock on credit | 550 |
| 6b | Cost of stock sold | 350 |
| 7 | Collect cash from debtor | 550 |
| 8 | Pay cash to creditors | 350 |
| 9 | Pay general expenses in cash | 80 |

The twofold effect of each of these transactions is as follows:

| Transaction Number | Value £ | Effect 1 (Debit) | Effect 2 (Credit) |
|---|---|---|---|
| 1 | 1,000 | + Asset (cash) | + Capital |
| 2 | 500 | + Asset (cash) | + Liability (loan) |
| 3 | 1,000 | + Asset (plant) | – Asset (cash) |
| 4 | 250 | + Asset (stock) | – Asset (cash) |
| 5 | 350 | + Asset (stock) | + Liability (creditor) |
| 6a | 550 | + Asset (debtor) | + Revenue (sales) |
| 6b | 350 | + Expense (cost of goods sold) | – Asset (stock) |
| 7 | 550 | + Asset (cash) | – Asset (debtor) |
| 8 | 350 | – Liability (creditor) | – Asset (cash) |
| 9 | 80 | + Expense (General expenses) | – Asset (cash) |

Trading transactions 6a and 6b have the combined effect of producing a gross profit of £200 from which general expenses of £80 (item 9) are deducted to leave a net profit of £120. The net profit is added to capital when the balance sheet is prepared.

Both Effect 1 and Effect 2 have the same value and so their combined impact on the relationship C + L = A is to leave it in balance. For example, transaction 1 adds £1,000 to each side, while transaction 3 both adds and subtracts £1,000 from the same side; the asset cash is exchanged for the asset plant. Readers should now revise their understanding of the relationship C + L = A by preparing the balance sheet of B.Egin as it appears after each individual transaction has been completed.

The dual effect of each transaction has given rise to the system of *double entry book-keeping*, under which each transaction is recorded twice: its *Effect 1* is recorded as a debit and its *Effect 2* is a credit. The equality between debits and credits holds true even if more than two elements are affected by a single deal. For example, a customer buys and takes away goods for £250; the price is settled by an immediate cash payment of £100, and an agreement to pay the remaining £150 in one month's time. The facts to be recorded at the time of sale together with their impact are:

|  | Value £ | Effect 1 | Effect 2 |
|---|---|---|---|
| Sales............. | 250 | | 250 + Revenue (sales) |
| Cash received...... | – 100 | 100 + Asset (cash) | |
| Creation of debtor.. | 150 | 150 + Asset (debtor) | |
| | | 250 | 250 |

There is a credit of £250 and total debits of £250; equality has been sustained.

## 5.3  LEDGER ACCOUNTS

The practical operation of a set of double entry books to record transactions involves the use of a separate record for each type of revenue, expenditure, asset and liability. Each record is named according to the item to which it relates, and is known as an 'account', for example, each company maintains a cash account, as described in section 2.1 of chapter 4, in which inflows and outflows of cash are recorded. The guiding principle which must be followed, when designing a system of accounts, is that it must provide the information needed to prepare the accounting statements, which comprise at least a trading and profit and loss account and a balance sheet. The complete set of accounts kept by a firm is called its 'ledger', and this term is also used to refer to particular groups of the accounts, such as the 'debtors' ledger' and the 'nominal ledger'.

**5.3.1  'T' Accounts**  The ledger accounts in which business transactions are recorded are known as 'T' accounts, a name derived from each account's appearance, as is apparent from the following examples. The T account represents an open ledger and has two sides; the left is used to record debits and the right credits. An example, containing no accounting entries, is shown in Figure 5.3

**Figure 5.3**

*A "T" Account*

| Debit | Credit |
|---|---|
| £ | £ |

We can now return to the transactions of Bernard Egin given in Illustration 5.1. The first was the introduction into his firm of capital in the form of cash of £1,000. The two accounts needed to record this transaction are "cash" and "capital"; cash, an asset, is increased by an inflow of £1,000 and so is *debited* with this sum, while capital, the liability to ownership, is increased by £1,000 and the account is *credited*. The accounts appear as follows when the transaction has been entered:

| | Cash | | | | Capital | |
|---|---|---|---|---|---|---|
| Debit | | Credit | | Debit | | Credit |
| | £ | | £ | | £ | | £ |
| Capital | 1,000 | | | | | Cash | 1,000 |

Note that a system of cross-reference is used whereby, in each account, the location of the corresponding entry is named. Thus, for this transaction, the credit entry corresponding to the debit entry in the cash account can easily be traced to the capital account. This referencing is necessary as the separate accounts would not necessarily be adjacent to each other in the ledger.

**Example 5.1**

The transactions undertaken by Bernard Egin, given in Illustration 5.1, are reproduced for ease of reference:

| Transaction Number | Description | Value £ |
|---|---|---|
| 1 | Introduce cash as capital . . . . . . . . . . . . . . . . . . . . . . | 1,000 |
| 2 | Raise a loan for cash . . . . . . . . . . . . . . . . . . . . . . . . . | 500 |
| 3 | Buy plant for cash . . . . . . . . . . . . . . . . . . . . . . . . . . . | 1,000 |
| 4 | Buy stock for cash . . . . . . . . . . . . . . . . . . . . . . . . . . . | 250 |
| 5 | Buy stock on credit . . . . . . . . . . . . . . . . . . . . . . . . . . | 350 |
| 6a | Sell stock on credit . . . . . . . . . . . . . . . . . . . . . . . . . . | 550 |
| 6b | Cost of stock sold . . . . . . . . . . . . . . . . . . . . . . . . . . . | 350 |
| 7 | Collect cash from debtors . . . . . . . . . . . . . . . . . . . . . . | 550 |
| 8 | Pay cash to creditors . . . . . . . . . . . . . . . . . . . . . . . . . | 350 |
| 9 | Pay general expenses in cash . . . . . . . . . . . . . . . . . . . . | 80 |

## Required:

Record the transaction of B. Egin in a set of T accounts. Insert the transaction number before each item.

(The impact of each item is given in Illustration 5.1).

## Solution

| Cash | | | | | |
|---|---|---|---|---|---|
| **Debit** | | | **Credit** | | |
| | | £ | | | £ |
| 1 Capital | | 1,000 | 3 Plant | | 1,000 |
| 2 Loan | | 500 | 4 Stock | | 250 |
| 7 Debtor | | 550 | 8 Creditor | | 350 |
| | | | 9 General | | |
| | | | expenses | | 80 |

| Capital | | | | |
|---|---|---|---|---|
| **Debit** | | **Credit** | | |
| | £ | | | £ |
| | | 1 Cash | | 1,000 |

| Loan | | | | |
|---|---|---|---|---|
| **Debit** | | **Credit** | | |
| | £ | | | £ |
| | | 2 Cash | | 500 |

| Plant | | | | |
|---|---|---|---|---|
| **Debit** | | **Credit** | | |
| | £ | | | £ |
| 3 Cash | 1,000 | | | |

| Stock | | | | |
|---|---|---|---|---|
| **Debit** | | **Credit** | | |
| | £ | | | £ |
| 4 Cash | 250 | 6b Cost of | | |
| 5 Creditors | 350 | goods sold | | 350 |

| Creditors | | | | |
|---|---|---|---|---|
| **Debit** | | **Credit** | | |
| | £ | | | £ |
| 8 Cash | 350 | 5 Stock | | 350 |

| Debtors | | | | |
|---|---|---|---|---|
| **Debit** | | **Credit** | | |
| | £ | | | £ |
| 6a Sales | 550 | 7 Cash | | 550 |

| Sales | | | | |
|---|---|---|---|---|
| **Debit** | | **Credit** | | |
| | £ | | | £ |
| | | 6a Debtor | | 550 |

| Cost of Goods Sold* | | | | |
|---|---|---|---|---|
| **Debit** | | **Credit** | | |
| | £ | | | £ |
| 6b Stock | 350 | | | |

| General Expenses | | | | |
|---|---|---|---|---|
| **Debit** | | **Credit** | | |
| | £ | | | £ |
| 9 Cash | 80 | | | |

\* In this example the asset 'stock' is converted to the expense 'cost of goods sold' at the time of sale; in practice, the cost of goods sold is usually found by preparing a trading account in which purchases are adjusted for opening and closing stocks. See section 3 of chapter 6 for the explanation of how to achieve this using double entry techniques.

At the end of the accounting period, the accountant prepares the profit and loss account and balance sheet and, at this stage, it is necessary first to balance each of the accounts in the manner described in section 2.1 of chapter 4. The balances on the accounts which relate to items of revenue and expense are then transferred to the trading and profit and loss account where the net result of trading is calculated; the balances remaining, together with the net result of trading, are then used to compile the balance sheet.

## Example 5.2
*Required:*
(a) List the balances from the ledger accounts in Example 5.1 in two columns, one for debit balances and one for credit balances.
(b) Prepare B. Egin's Trading and Profit and Loss Account and Balance Sheet from the balances listed in answer to part (a).

## Solution
(a)

|  | Debit £ | Credit £ |
|---|---|---|
| Cash........................................... | 370 | |
| Capital......................................... | | 1,000 |
| Loan .......................................... | | 500 |
| Plant .......................................... | 1,000 | |
| Stock .......................................... | 250 | |
| Sales........................................... | | 550 |
| Cost of Goods Sold............................... | 350 | |
| General Expenses................................. | 80 | |
| | 2,050 | 2,050 |

*Notes*
1. There are no debtors or creditors as, in this instance, their inflows and outflows are exactly equal in value and so cancel each other out.
2. The debit balances are equal in value to the credit balances; this provides a check of accuracy, the importance of which is discussed in section 6 of this chapter.

(b)

*Trading and Profit and Loss Account*

|  | £ |
|---|---|
| Sales | 550 |
| Less: Cost of Goods Sold | 350 |
| Gross Profit | 200 |
| Less: General Expenses | 80 |
| Net Profit | 120 |

*Balance Sheet of B. Egin*

| CAPITAL | £ | £ | FIXED ASSETS | £ | £ |
|---|---|---|---|---|---|
| At start of period | | 0 | Plant | | 1,000 |
| Introduced | | 1,000 | | | |
| Profit for period | | 120 | CURRENT ASSETS | | |
| | | | Stock | 250 | |
| At end of period | | 1,120 | Cash | 370 | |
| | | | | | |
| LOAN | | 500 | | | |
| | | | | | 620 |
| | | 1,620 | | | 1,620 |

It should be noted that no balances are carried forward in the sales, costs of goods sold and general expenses accounts. The transactions which were entered in them relate to a period of time; at the end of the period the accounts are cleared to the trading and profit and loss account and appear as follows:

*Sales*

| | £ | | £ |
|---|---|---|---|
| Transfer to Trading Account | 550 | Balance b/d | 550 |

*Cost of Goods Sold*

| | £ | | £ |
|---|---|---|---|
| Balance b/d | 350 | Transfer to Trading Account | 350 |

*General Expenses*

| | £ | | £ |
|---|---|---|---|
| Balance b/d................. | 80 | Transfer to Profit and | |
| | | Loss Account................ | 80 |

The balances on all accounts cleared to the trading and profit and loss account revert to zero and these accounts are used to accumulate information for the next period. The assets and liabilities shown in the balance sheet are carried forward to the next accounting period where they are adjusted for any changes which then occur.

**5.3.2 Alternative Formats for Ledger Accounts** The advent of machine and, more recently, computer based systems of accounting has resulted in a move away from the use of T accounts, although all of the rules of double entry are still complied with. There are a number of possible alternatives, for example, there may be separate columns for debits and credits or the transactions in any account may be listed with credits identified by an asterisk. One rule which must be observed is that, irrespective of the method used to distinguish debits from credits, it must be consistently applied. The following example lists three ways for recording the same information in a mechanised or computerised cash account:

| | (1) | | (2) | (3) | | |
|---|---|---|---|---|---|---|
| | *Debit* | *Credit* | | *Debit* | *Credit* | *Balance* |
| | £ | £ | £ | £ | £ | £ |
| Opening balance..... | 500 | | 500 DR | | | 500 DR |
| Cash from Sales...... | 1,250 | | 1,250 DR | 1,250 | | |
| Cash for Purchases... | | 1,000 | 1,000 CR | | 1,000 | |
| Closing balance...... | 750 | | 750 DR | | | 750 DR |

### 5.3.3   The Ledger in Practice   Accounts can be classified into the following types:

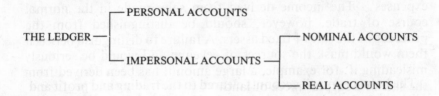

*Personal Accounts* are those which record the relationship between the entity and outsiders such as debtors, creditors and investors. There should be a separate account for each individual who owes money to or is owed money by the company so that it can be established how much to demand or pay respectively in each instance.

*Impersonal Accounts* are either Nominal Accounts or Real Accounts:

> *Nominal Accounts* contain all of the items which are transferred to the trading and profit and loss account and so include such items as sales, purchases, wages and expenses.
> *Real Accounts* are used for the non-personal assets of the company, such as cash, stock and fixed assets.

Personal accounts should be first classified according to general type such as trade debtors, trade creditors, debenture holders and capital. Normally total, or control, accounts are maintained in the main ledger for each of these classes, and subsidiary, or memorandum ledgers kept for individual details (see section 5 of this chapter). Some of the real accounts can be treated in the same way, so that while the main ledger contains such general accounts as plant and machinery or stock, they are backed up by a register of plant and machinery or stock records to show the detail that comprises their total values.

The decision on which nominal accounts to use should be based on a compromise between providing information which is of little use because it is too general or alternatively giving too much detail. The exact selection is based on the type of activity which the business undertakes and the items which management wishes to monitor and control, but in general the rule applies that accounts should be opened in respect of all items which are likely to be material (see section 5.10 of chapter 7). For example, it would not be deemed important in normal circumstances to identify individually the costs of petrol and motor insurance since they are both consequent upon running a vehicle and are reported under the heading "motor expenses". The income derived from sales made in the normal course of trade, however, should be distinguished from the proceeds of the sale of fixed assets. A failure to distinguish between them would mask the sources of revenue and would be seriously misleading if, for example, a large amount has been derived from the sale of a surplus piece of land.

## 5.4 BOOKS OF PRIME ENTRY

It is unwieldy to attempt to enter each individual flow of cash, goods or services in the accounts ledger. To overcome this problem each transaction is entered, in the first instance, in a "Book of Prime Entry". The initial record of transactions is made in either a day book, the cash book or the journal; each of these is now considered in turn.

**5.4.1 Day Books** The sales and purchases day books were described in section 3 of chapter 4. It is also advisable to use a day book for any type of transaction which occurs frequently, such as the return of goods sold from customers who decide not to keep them (returns inwards) and the return of goods purchased to suppliers (returns outwards). Day books are used to summarise the flows of goods and services in to and out of the company in order to generate entries for the appropriate ledger accounts. The sales day book must produce: (a) the value of debtors created from sales to be debited to the debtors account; and (b) the value of credit sales to be credited in the sales account, possibly analysed according to type of sale. The purchases day book creates: (a) the total to be credited to the creditors account; and (b) the values to be debited to the various expense and asset accounts. For example, the following are the totals from a purchase day book:

| Total £ | Goods for Resale £ | Stationery £ | Motor Van (Fixed Asset) £ |
|---|---|---|---|
| 2,000 | 1,500 | 50 | 450 |

The totals of the analysis columns add up to the total value, and are entered in the following ledger accounts:

|  | Debit | Credit |
|---|---|---|
| Goods for resale (increase asset)............................ | 1,500 | |
| Stationery  (expense)....................................... | 50 | |
| Motor Van (increase asset)................................ | 450 | |
| Creditors (increase liability)............................... | | 2,000 |
|  | 2,000 | 2,000 |

There should be clear cross referencing between the books of prime entry and the accounts so that the trail can be retraced if necessary. A note should be made in the day book of the account, and its location, to which the figures are posted; the entry in the accounts should refer to the source of the figure, preferably also stating the page in the book of prime entry on which it can be found.

### 5.4.2   The Cash Book and Discounts

The cash book, unlike the day books, is itself a ledger account; it is therefore necessary only to complete the corresponding double entry for the transactions it contains. At the end of the accounting period the cash book is balanced and the result entered in the balance sheet. Again, only the analysis totals need to be posted and not each separate transaction. For example, the following are the totals from an analysed cash book:

Cash Book

| Receipts | | | Payments | | | |
|---|---|---|---|---|---|---|
| Total | Debtors | Cash Sale | Total | Wages | Creditors | Rent |
| £ | £ | £ | £ | £ | £ | £ |
| 5,000 | 3,500 | 1,500 | 4,000 | 1,000 | 2,500 | 500 |

The total of cash received, £5,000, is already debited to the ledger as the result of including it in the total column of the cash book, and so the double entry is completed by making the following credit entries:

|  | £ |
|---|---|
| Sales (revenue) | 1,500 (credit) |
| Debtors (reduce asset) | 3,500 (credit) |

The entries to complete the record of the effect of cash payments are:

|  | £ |
| --- | --- |
| Wages (Expense) | 1,000 (debit) |
| Creditors (Reduce liability) | 2,500 (debit) |
| Rent (Expense) | 500 (debit) |

The petty cash book (see section 2.5 of Chapter 4) is also part of the double entry accounts, and is operated in the same way as the main cash book. The totals of its analysis columns are posted to the ledger accounts, and its balance is entered in the balance sheet.

*Discounts.* The full value of each sale made on credit is entered in the debtors account, and in some cases this may be cleared by the receipt of cash together with the grant of a discount for prompt payment, that is, the cash received is less than the value of the debt. To remove the full amount of indebtedness shown in the debtor's account it is necessary to credit the account with the value of the discount; the corresponding debit is to the 'Discounts Allowed Account' in which all such discounts are accumulated. The balance on this account is transferred to the profit and loss account when the periodic accounting reports are prepared. If, alternatively, the company takes a discount offered by a supplier, the creditor account is debited and the 'Discounts Received Account' credited; the balance on the latter account is income and is credited to the profit and loss account. Where, as is the case with discounts given for purchasing large quantities, the discount is received as a reduction in price, that is, a trade discount, no entry in the discount column is needed as the amount invoiced is reduced by the discount. The procedure for recording discounts for prompt payment is illustrated in Example 5.3.

**Example 5.3**
Seller sells goods on credit to Buyer for £500. A discount of 4% may be taken if the debt is settled within ten days. On the assumption that the discount is taken, prepare:
(a) The debtor and discount accounts in Seller's books; and
(b) The creditor and discount accounts in Buyer's books.

(a)   *The books of Seller*

| Debtor Account | | | | Discounts Allowed Account | | | |
|---|---|---|---|---|---|---|---|
| | £ | | £ | | £ | | £ |
| Sales .......... | 500 | Cash ....... | 480 | Debtor ......... | 20 | | |
| | | Discounts | | | | | |
| | | Allowed ..... | 20 | | | | |
| | 500 | | 500 | | | | |

(b)   *The books of Buyer*

| Creditor Account | | | | Discounts Received Account | | | |
|---|---|---|---|---|---|---|---|
| | £ | | £ | | £ | | £ |
| Cash .......... | 480 | Purchases ... | 500 | | | Creditor ..... | 20 |
| Discounts | | | | | | | |
| Received ....... | 20 | | | | | | |
| | 500 | | 500 | | | | |

It is quite likely that a large number of discounts will be received and allowed during an accounting period. To save time, each transaction is not recorded separately; instead, discounts allowed and received are accumulated in the cash book and transferred to the ledger at the end of the period. Example 5.4 shows how this method is operated; it should be noted that the cash book record of discounts is purely memorandum.

## Example 5.4
Disco owes £400 to Dancer and £760 to Tapper. He is owed £540 by Jumper and £880 by Runner. Prepare the cash book for Disco on the assumption that all of the above debts are settled subject to a 5% prompt payment discount.

## Solution

Cash Book — Disco

| | Discount Allowed | Cash | | Discount Received | Cash |
|---|---|---|---|---|---|
| | £ | £ | | £ | £ |
| Jumper — Debtor | 27 | 513 | Dancer — Creditor | 20 | 380 |
| Runner — Debtor | 44 | 836 | Tapper — Creditor | 38 | 722 |
| | 71 | 1,349 | | 58 | 1,102 |

The cash received of £1,349 is credited to the debtors account and the £1,102 cash paid debited to the creditors account; this completes the double entry in both cases. Since the columns in which the discounts are recorded are only memorandum, it is necessary to make both debit and credit entries in respect of their contents. The total of discounts allowed, £71, is debited to the discounts allowed account and credited to the debtors account while the £58 of discounts received is debited to the creditors account and credited to discounts received. In all cases the value of the discount plus the amount of the cash flow is equal to the total amount of indebtedness.

It is useful to keep the discounts received and discounts allowed in separate accounts, rather than net them, so that the cost of granting discounts and the benefit of taking them can be easily identified and their impact assessed. If discounts allowed rise in value, the question should be asked whether the terms are too generous, and the benefit of taking discounts must be weighed against the alternative advantages of retaining the cash in the business for a longer period of time.

**5.4.3 The Journal** There are a few transactions which are not entered in the cash or day books, and these are instead initially entered in the 'Journal'. The use of a journal ensures that every entry in the ledger first passes through a book of prime entry which fully explains the nature of the transaction. Each entry in the journal should be authorised to ensure that no unsanctioned changes are made in the ledger. Journal entries are likely to be relatively small in number, and include such items as:

(a) *Transfers* These occur when it is necessary to transfer value from one account to another, for example, to correct a mistake made in the original posting which placed the entry in the wrong account.

(b) *Adjustments* The original entry may be made in the correct account in the light of prevailing knowledge, but circumstances may change and require a further entry. For example a debtor is created when a credit sale is made but if, at a later date, it becomes apparent that the money will not be collected, the debt must be written off by transfer to the Bad Debts Account, since it no longer represents an asset. (Bad debts are considered further in section 7 of chapter 6).

(c) *Closing entries* Adjusting entries must be made at the accounting date to enable the periodic accounts to be drawn up. (These are dealt with in chapter 6).

The debit and credit entry for each transaction is entered in the journal together with a brief narrative to explain its purpose. Example 5.5 shows some specimen entries.

**Example 5.5**

A. Jones, a trader, wishes to record the following in his firm's ledger:
   (a) The correction of a wrong posting which entered the purchase of a fixed asset costing £1,000 in the purchase of goods for resale account.
   (b) The accrual of rent due for three months of £50.
   (c) The introduction by A Jones of capital in the form of a fixed asset worth £2,500.

*Required*

Prepare the journal entries to enter the above facts in the firm's ledger accounts.

**Solution**

The journal entries are:

### A. Jones — Journal

|  |  | Debit (DR*) £ | Credit (CR*) £ |
|---|---|---|---|
| (a) | Fixed Assets.............................. | 1,000 | |
| | Purchases................................. | | 1,000 |
| | Narrative: Transfer to fixed assets of incorrect posting | | |
| (b) | Rent...................................... | 50 | |
| | Landlord.................................. | | 50 |
| | Narrative: Rent due for three months | | |
| (c) | Fixed Assets.............................. | 2,500 | |
| | A. Jones — Capital........................ | | 2,500 |
| | Narrative: Introduction of capital in the form of a fixed asset | | |

* "DR" and "CR" are usual abbreviations for the words "debit" and "credit" respectively.

Although for practical purposes, the use of the journal is restricted to those cases where there is no other appropriate book of prime entry, it is theoretically possible to record all entries in journal form, and an exercise on these lines provides a useful way for examiners to test students understanding of double entry accounting without calling for the preparation of a full set of T accounts. For example, the transactions of B. Egin given in Illustration 5.1 can be recorded in journal form:

*B. Egin — Journal*

| Transaction No. | | Debit £ | Credit £ |
|---|---|---|---|
| 1. | Cash................................... | 1,000 | |
| | Capital................................ | | 1,000 |
| | Receipt of capital in the form of cash | | |
| 2. | Cash................................... | 500 | |
| | Loan.................................. | | 500 |
| | Loan raised | | |
| 3. | Plant.................................. | 1,000 | |
| | Cash.................................. | | 1,000 |
| | Purchase of plant for cash | | |
| 4. | Stock.................................. | 250 | |
| | Cash.................................. | | 250 |
| | Purchase of stock for cash | | |
| 5. | Stock.................................. | 350 | |
| | Creditor............................... | | 350 |
| | Purchase of stock on credit | | |
| 6a & 6b | Debtor................................ | 550 | |
| | Sales.................................. | | 550 |
| | Cost of goods sold..................... | 350 | |
| | Stock................................. | | 350 |
| | Sale of goods on credit | | |
| 7. | Cash.................................. | 550 | |
| | Debtors............................... | | 550 |
| | Collection of cash from debtors | | |
| 8. | Creditors.............................. | 350 | |
| | Cash.................................. | | 350 |
| | Payment of cash to creditors | | |
| 9. | General Expenses...................... | 80 | |
| | Cash.................................. | | 80 |
| | Payment of general expenses in cash | | |

These entries can be checked to the T accounts in Example 5.1

## 5.5 CONTROL ACCOUNTS FOR DEBTORS AND CREDITORS

Businesses require two types of information about debtors and creditors:

1.    Their total values must be made available both to provide a record of the total amount due to and by the company and to provide the figures for inclusion in the balance sheet.

2.   The amount owed to each individual creditor and by each debtor is needed for day to day control; the correct amount must be paid or claimed in each case.

The required information is produced by maintaining two records; in the main double entry ledger 'control' or 'total' accounts are kept which provide the overall values of debtors and creditors, while memorandum debtors and creditors ledgers contain a separate account for each individual debtor and creditor. (The debtors ledger is also referred to as the sales ledger and the creditors ledger is also known as the purchase ledger). The debtors and creditors ledgers are referred to as "memorandum" as they are subsidiary to, and do not form part of, the main double entry system.


### 5.5.1  Records of Debtors and Creditors

The memorandum accounts for debtors and creditors are written up from the day books and cash book using the entries for each separate transaction. The control acounts in the double entry ledger are compiled using totals from the books of prime entry. Example 5.6 shows the operation of this system for sales; the same method is applicable to purchases.


### Example 5.6

Use the following information to prepare (a) a single column Sales Day Book, (b) the Cash Book (receipts side only), (c) the Debtors Control Account, and (d) the Individual Memorandum Debtor Accounts.

| Customer | Balance 1 March | Sales during March | Goods Returned | Cash Received | Discounts |
|---|---|---|---|---|---|
| | £ | £ | £ | £ | £ |
| Page.......... | 100 | 150 | — | 98 | 2 |
| Book......... | 125 | 130 | 10 | 79 | 1 |
| Volume....... | 150 | 160 | — | 150 | — |
| | 375 | | | | |

## Solution

(a)

*Sales Day Book*

|  | £ |
|---|---|
| Page | 150 |
| Book | 130 |
| Volume | 160 |
|  | 440 |

The total figure for credit sales is credited to the Credit Sales Account and debited to the Sales Ledger Control Account. The individual transactions are debited to the individual memorandum debtor accounts.

(b)

*Cash Book (Debit Side)*

|  | Cash | Discount |
|---|---|---|
|  | £ | £ |
| Page | 98 | 2 |
| Book | 79 | 1 |
| Volume | 150 | — |
|  | 327 | 3 |

The total figure for cash received is credited to the Sales Ledger Control Account; the individual amounts are credited to the memorandum debtor accounts. The total discount figure is credited to the Sales Ledger Control Account and debited to the Discounts Allowed Account; the individual amounts are credited to the individual memorandum debtor accounts.

(c)

*Sales Ledger (Debtors) Control Account*

|  | £ |  | £ |
|---|---|---|---|
| Balance b/d | 375 | Cash Book | 327 |
| Sales Day Book | 440 | Discounts Allowed | 3 |
|  |  | Returns Inwards | 10 |
|  |  | Balance c/d | 475 |
|  | 815 |  | 815 |

(d)                                   *Page Account*

| | £ | | £ |
|---|---|---|---|
| Balance b/d | 100 | Cash | 98 |
| Sales Day Book | 150 | Discounts Allowed | 2 |
| | | Balance c/d | 150 |
| | 250 | | 250 |

*Book Account*

| | £ | | £ |
|---|---|---|---|
| Balance b/d | 125 | Cash | 79 |
| Sales Day Book | 130 | Discounts Allowed | 1 |
| | | Returns Inwards | 10 |
| | | Balance c/d | 165 |
| | 255 | | 255 |

*Volume Account*

| | £ | | £ |
|---|---|---|---|
| Balance b/d | 150 | Cash | 150 |
| Sales Day Book | 160 | Balance c/d | 160 |
| | 310 | | 310 |

**5.5.2 Reconciling the Control Account** The use of control accounts for customers and suppliers reduces the number of entries in the main ledger and enables a cross-check to be performed. The total of the balances on the individual memorandum accounts should agree with the single balance of the control account. Agreement on these lines based on the figures in Example 5.6 is:

| | | £ |
|---|---|---|
| Balances from individual accounts: | Page | 150 |
| | Book | 165 |
| | Volume | 160 |
| Balance as per control account | | 475 |

The maintenance of the memorandum debtors and creditors ledgers can be delegated to a responsible person who has no access to the main ledger, which is likely to contain many confidential entries. Where this system is operated, the personnel in charge of the debtors and creditors ledgers should periodically supply a list of balances to the official responsible for the control accounts who can then check that the totals agree. Any difference must be investigated, but there is the possibility that the totals may agree despite the fact that an error has been made, for example, an invoice may have been posted to the wrong debtor account; however such an error should be identified when the incorrect amount is demanded from a customer who has been wrongly charged for the goods in question.

## Example 5.7

A list of the balances on the memorandum individual personal accounts in a company's sales ledger at 31 December 19X6 had a total of £305,640. This did not agree with the balance on the Sales Ledger Control Account at that date of £325,000. The following errors were discovered:

(a) A sales invoice of £12,900, included in the Sales Day Book, had not been posted to the personal account in the sales ledger.

(b) Discounts allowed to customers of £1,260 had been credited to the individual accounts in the sales ledger, but no other entries had been made in the books.

(c) The Returns Inwards Day Book had been wrongly totalled; it was over-cast by £3,000.

(d) A sales invoice of £9,400 had been entirely omitted from the books.

(e) A debit balance of £7,400 on the personal account of a customer had been included in the list of balances as £4,700.

(f) The balance on a customer's account in the sales ledger of £5,500 had been omitted from the list of balances.

*Required:*

(i) Write up the control account to correct it for those errors by which it is affected.

(ii) Revise the total value of the list of balances in respect of those errors by which it is affected.

## Solution

(i)

### Sales Ledger Control Account

| 19X6 | £ | 19X6 | £ |
|---|---|---|---|
| 31 Dec Balance b/d.......... | 325,000 | 31 Dec Discounts | |
| Returns Inwards (c)..... | 3,000 | Allowed (b).......... | 1,260 |
| Sales (d).............. | 9,400 | Balance c/d.......... | 336,140 |
| | 337,400 | | 337,400 |

(ii)

|  | £ |
|---|---|
| Value of list of balances........................................ | 305,640 |
| Invoice not in memorandum account (a)............................ | 12,900 |
| Invoice omitted (d)............................................ | 9,400 |
| Balance wrongly extracted (7,400−4,700) (e)..................... | 2,700 |
| Balance omitted (f)............................................ | 5,500 |
| Correct value of Debtors....................................... | 336,140 |

Note that the same closing balance now appears in the control account and the list of balances; the results obtained from the two separate sources of information have therefore been reconciled.

Monthly statements should be sent to customers reminding them of the amount due and requesting payment. The customer can then compare this document with the information contained in his own ledger. The balances on the statement and in the customer's books are unlikely to be the same, for example, the customer may not have received certain goods appearing on the statement, and so a reconciliation must be prepared. In the same way, the company should receive details of their account from suppliers, and these should be checked with the creditor's account in the company's books. The bank statement is a good example of the exchange of information on individual accounts (the bank reconciliation is dealt with in section 2.2 of chapter 4.)

The control account is likely to include the following entries in addition to those for sales, cash and discounts:

(a)   Credit balances on the debtors ledger and debit balances on the creditors ledger. For example, if a customer overpays, the account in the debtors ledger will be a credit. These balances should be carried down separately in the control account and added to creditors in the balance sheet.

(b)   Bad debts. Some debtors are unable to pay, and the amounts they owe are known are known as bad debts. These balances must be removed from debtors, by a journal entry, as they no longer represent an asset.

(c)   Settlement by contra. A firm may both buy from and sell to another company; this gives rise to a debtor account and a creditor account in the same name. The balances on the two accounts may be set off, and the net balance settled for cash.

(d)   Interest on overdue debts. When a debtor is very slow to pay, a firm may, by agreement, charge interest on the debt; this is added to the amount owed.

(e)   Returns. Goods may be returned either to or by the company; the related debt must be cancelled.

## Example 5.8

The following particulars relate to the year 19X1 and were extracted from the books of Singer Ltd. The company maintains memorandum debtors and creditors ledgers in which the individual accounts of customers and suppliers are maintained. You are required to prepare the debtors control account and the creditors control account as they would appear in the company's ledger at 31 December 19X1 on the basis of the following information which relates to 19X1:

|  | £ |
|---|---|
| Debit balance on Debtors Control Account 1 January 19X1 | 66,300 |
| Credit balance on Creditors Control Account 1 January 19X1 | 50,600 |
| Sundry credit balances on Debtors Ledger 1 Jan. 19X1 | 724 |
| Goods purchased on credit | 257,919 |
| Goods sold on credit | 323,614 |
| Cash received from debtors | 299,149 |
| Cash paid to creditors | 210,522 |
| Discounts received | 2,663 |
| Discounts allowed | 2,930 |
| Cash purchases | 3,627 |
| Cash sales | 5,922 |
| Bad debts written off | 3,651 |
| Interest charged on overdue debtor accounts | 277 |
| Returns outwards | 2,926 |
| Returns inwards | 2,805 |
| Accounts settled by contra between Debtor and Creditor Ledgers | 1,106 |
| Sundry credit balances on Debtors Ledger 31 December | 815 |
| Sundry debit balances on Creditors Ledger 31 December | 698 |

## Solution

### Debtors (Sales Ledger) Control Account

| 19X1 | | £ | 19X1 | | £ |
|---|---|---|---|---|---|
| 1 January | Balance b/d....... | 66,300 | 1 January | Balance b/d....... | 724 |
| | Sales............. | 323,614 | | Cash............. | 299,149 |
| | Interest.......... | 277 | | Discounts allowed.. | 2,930 |
| 31 December | Balance c/d...... | 815 | | Bad debts......... | 3,651 |
| | | | | Returns inwards... | 2,805 |
| | | | | Contra-Creditors .. | 1,106 |
| | | | 31 December | Balance c/d...... | 80,641 |
| | | 391,006 | | | 391,006 |
| 19X2 | | | 19X2 | | |
| 1 January | Balance b/d....... | 80,641 | 1 January | Balance b/d....... | 815 |

### Creditors (Purchase Ledger) Control Account

| 19X1 | | £ | 19X1 | | £ |
|---|---|---|---|---|---|
| | Cash............. | 210,522 | 1 January | Balance b/d | 50,600 |
| | Discounts received. | 2,663 | | Purchases......... | 257,919 |
| | Returns outwards.. | 2,926 | 31 December | Balance c/d...... | 698 |
| | Contra Debtors.... | 1,106 | | | |
| 31 December | Balance c/d...... | 92,000 | | | |
| | | 309,217 | | | 309,217 |
| 19X2 | | | 19X2 | | |
| 1 January | Balance b/d....... | 698 | 1 January | Balance b/d....... | 92,000 |

Note that the cash sales and cash purchases do not appear in the control accounts. They do not affect the recorded value of debtors or creditors.

## 5.6   THE TRIAL BALANCE

A set of books maintained in accordance with the double entry method provides a comprehensive and appropriately analysed record of all the transactions undertaken by an entity. This record not only enables the day to day control of such items as debtors and creditors, but also provides the basis from which the final accounting statements, namely the trading and profit and loss account and balance sheet, are prepared.

The process by which an economic event becomes included in the final accounting statements is:

| Economic Event eg. sale | → | Book of Prime Entry eg. sales day book | → | Double Entry Ledger | → | Trial Balance | → | Final Accounts |
|---|---|---|---|---|---|---|---|---|

It can be seen that the stage prior to the production of the statements from the ledger (covered in chapter 6) is the preparation of a Trial Balance. This is a list of all the balances remaining at the end of the accounting period on the many accounts contained in the main ledger; the balances are entered in separate columns according to whether they are debit balances or credit balances. The two columns should possess the same total value şince each entry in the books consists of a debit and a credit of equal value and, as described in section 2 of this chapter, leaves the relationship C + L = A in balance. Although it was not described as such, Example 5.2 part (a) shows the trial balance of B.Egin.

Readers should now work Questions 5.1 to 5.6 at the end of this chapter.

The fact that the trial balance shows equal totals for both debit and credit balances does not necessarily mean that it is correct, since there are some errors which are not revealed as an imbalance. These are:

(a) *Error of Principle.* An entry may be made in the wrong account, for example, wages may be debited to purchases.

(b) *Duplication.* Both the debits and credits for a transaction could be entered in the accounts twice.

(c) *Ommissions.* A transaction may be omitted altogether.

(d) *Compensatory Errors.* There may be two or more errors, the effects of which cancel each other out.

(e) *Error in the Original Entry.* An incorrect figure may be used as the basis of the double entry record.

**5.6.1 The Suspense Account** The trial balance, when it is first extracted, does not always balance, and it is then obvious that some error has been made. The first step to discover the mistake is to review all the balances to ensure that they have been extracted correctly from the books. The next step is to check that subsidiary memorandum ledgers, for such items as debtors and creditors, have been reconciled with their control accounts; any discrepancy would indicate a likely area in which the error is to be found. Finally, if the difference is material enough to make its discovery essential, a more thorough checking of the records of prime entry to the ledger must be carried out. So as not to delay the preparation of the accounts, a difference on the trial balance may be placed in a Suspense Account which is cleared after investigations have been completed. This procedure is shown in Example 5.9

### Example 5.9
The trial balance of Wrong at 31 December, as first compiled, contained total debits of £197,500 and total credits of £210,000. The difference of £12,500 was placed to the debit of a suspense account to balance the trial balance. Subsequent investigation revealed the following errors:

(a)   The balance from the cash book of £3,750 had not been entered in the trial balance.
(b)   The debtors balance had been wrongly recorded as £71,560 instead of £75,160.
(c)   A fixed asset purchased for £10,000 had been credited to the fixed asset account instead of being debited.
(d)   The previous year's profit of £14,850 had not been added to the profit and loss account balance brought forward.

*Required:*
Prepare the suspense account to record the corection of the errors.

### Solution

*Suspense Account*

| | £ | | £ |
|---|---|---|---|
| Difference on Trial Balance .................... | 12,500 | Cash (a)..................... | 3,750 |
| | | Debtors (b)................. | 3,600 |
| Profit and Loss Account (d)................. | 14,850 | Fixed Assets (c).............. | 20,000 |
| | 27,350 | | 27,350 |

*Note:*

The Suspense Account now has no value left on it, and the double entry is completed within the Trial Balance with the following effects:

(a)     Cash of £3,750 appears as an asset.

(b)     Debtors are increased by £3,600, to their correct value of £75,160.

(c)     The incorrect credit entry in the fixed asset account of £10,000 is cancelled and the correct debit entry of £10,000 is substituted. Note that the total effect of this error was to understate fixed assets by £20,000.

(d)     The profit and loss account balance is increased by £14,850, being the previous year's profit omitted.

## 5.7 ADVANTAGES OF DOUBLE ENTRY

The double entry system is very flexible. In this chapter, reference has been made to books of account and pages within these books. The records could, in practice, be kept on separate cards or be produced as computer print outs. Whichever method of operation is employed, however, the benefits derived from the use of double entry are:

(a)     It enables all types of transactions undertaken by the business, which can be expressed in monetary terms, to be recorded; provided an economic event has a measurable financial impact on the entity it can be fitted into the double entry framework.

(b)     It enables large numbers of transactions to be recorded in an orderly manner; similar transactions are grouped together.

(c)     Economic events are recorded both from the personal point of view, that is their impact on the relationship between the entity and outsiders, and also from the impersonal aspect, that is, their effect on the company itself in terms of assets owned, revenue and expenses.

(d)     The debits entered to record a particular transaction must be of equal value to the credits. This equality enables a Trial Balance to be prepared which gives an initial check on the arithmetical accuracy of the records, although there are errors which are not revealed.

(e)     The Trial Balance, an end product of the double entry system, is the basis for the preparation of the trading and profit and loss account and balance sheet. The former of these gives an indication of the return made by the entity on the resources invested in it, while the latter presents a picture of the extent to which management has carried out its custodial duties in the form of a statement of the financial position.

Readers should now work Questions 5.7 to 5.10 at the end of this chapter.

## 5.8 QUESTIONS

Questions 5.1 to 5.6 which follow trace the transactions of a business from the opening balances of the accounting period through to the closing trial balance. The remaining questions test other aspects covered in this chapter.

## Question 5.1

The following are the balances on the accounts of Radio on 1 January.

*Credit Balances*

|  | £ | £ |
|---|---|---|
| Capital................................................ | | 8,500 |
| Trade Creditors: Tele............................... | 2,300 | |
| Trany............................... | 1,000 | |
| Valve.............................. | 1,300 | |
| | | 4,600 |
| | | 13,100 |

*Debit Balances*

|  | £ | £ |
|---|---|---|
| Plant and Machinery at Written Down Value............. | | 4,500 |
| Stock................................................. | | 2,700 |
| Debtors: Vision...................................... | 2,500 | |
| Sister...................................... | 1,500 | |
| Batty....................................... | 1,200 | |
| | | 5,200 |
| Cash.................................................. | | 700 |
| | | 13,100 |

*Required:*
Prepare the Journal Entries to record the opening balances in Radio's books on 1 January.

# Question 5.2

## During January Radio undertook the following transactions:

*Credit Transactions with Customers during January*

| Customer | Sales | Returns Inwards | Cash Received | Prompt Payment Discount |
|---|---|---|---|---|
|  | £ | £ | £ | £ |
| Vision | 7,000 | 300 | 6,350 | 50 |
| Sister | 4,000 | — | 3,500 | 40 |
| Batty | 2,700 | 200 | 2,600 | 25 |
| Flat | 200 | — | — | — |
| Broke | 300 | — | — | — |

*Credit Transactions with Suppliers during January*

| Supplier | Detail | Purchases | Returns Outwards | Cash Paid | Prompt Payment Discount |
|---|---|---|---|---|---|
|  |  | £ | £ | £ | £ |
| Tele | Goods for resale | 3,000 | — | 2,950 | 55 |
| Trany | Goods for resale | 2,000 | 100 | 1,950 | 35 |
| Valve | Goods for resale | 2,400 | 150 | 2,200 | 20 |
| Garage | Motor expenses | 100 | — | — | — |
| Paper | Office supplies | 50 | — | — | — |

*Other Cash Transactions during January*

| Payee | Detail | £ |
|---|---|---|
| Plantmax | Purchase of plant | 1,000 |
| Cash | Wages | 1,500 |
| Acom | Rent for 6 months to 30 June | 600 |
| Supplies | Office expenses | 250 |
| Garage | Motor expenses | 300 |

£100 was received from Scrap for some machinery which was disposed of.

## Required:

Enter this information in the books of prime entry, i.e. the day books and cash book.

## Question 5.3

Use the information in questions 5.1 and 5.2 to prepare the ledger accounts, other than cash, in Radio's main ledger.

## Question 5.4

Use the information in questions 5.1 and 5.2 to prepare the memorandum debtors and creditors ledger.

## Question 5.5

Use the information in questions 5.3 and 5.4 to prepare reconcilations of the purchases and sales control accounts with their memorandum ledgers.

## Question 5.6

Prepare Radio's Trial Balance at 31 January from the accounts produced in question 5.2 and 5.3.

## Question 5.7

(a) Define and distinguish, with examples, the following three classifications of ledger accounts:
i.     Real Accounts
ii.    Personal Accounts
iii.   Nominal Accounts

(b) Give the appropriate classification for each of the following account balances:
i.     Fixed asset at cost £10,000
ii.    Wages paid £700
iii.   Discounts received £1,400
iv.    Balance due from Double Ltd £1,500

## Question 5.8

Explain how the accountant makes use of the trial balance.

## Question 5.9

The following particulars have been extracted from the books of a trading concern for the year ended 30 September, 19X5:

|  |  | £ |
|---|---|---|
| 1. | Sales ledger debit balances 1 October 19X4................... | 102,300 |
| 2. | Sales ledger credit balances 1 October 19X4 ................... | 340 |
| 3. | Credit sales............................................. | 630,800 |
| 4. | Cash sales.............................................. | 140,100 |
| 5. | Cash received from debtors .............................. | 498,660 |
| 6. | Returns outwards ....................................... | 8,300 |
| 7. | Returns inwards ........................................ | 2,700 |
| 8. | Discounts received....................................... | 15,200 |
| 9. | Discounts allowed ....................................... | 11,790 |
| 10. | Accounts settled by contra to purchase ledger ................ | 5,200 |
| 11. | Bad debts written off .................................... | 3,950 |
| 12. | Sales ledger credit balances 30 September, 19X5 .............. | 510 |

*Required:*

Prepare the Sales Ledger Control Account for the year to 30 September, 19X5

## Question 5.10

Ian Error has produced a trial balance for his business for the year to 30 June 19X2 which does not balance and the difference has been placed in a suspense account. An examination of the company's books reveals the following errors:

(a) An invoice from Zed amounting to £1,000, for goods purchased, has been omitted from the purchase day book and posted direct to the purchases account in the nominal ledger and to Zed's account in the memorandum purchase ledger. It has not been included in the creditors control account in the trial balance.

(b) The sales day book has been undercast by £2,400.

(c) Discounts allowed for the month of June amounting to £4,890 have not been debited to the ledger.

(d) Goods received from Wye on 30 June 19X2 which cost £24,100 have been included in the stock but the invoice has not yet been received and entered in the books.

(e) A cheque for £1,920 received from Exe, a debtor, has been debited to cash and credited to the sales account in the nominal ledger.

*Required:*

(i)   Prepare the journal entries to correct these errors.

(ii)  Prepare a statement which shows the effect of the corrections on the company's profit for the year; and

(iii) Calculate the difference between the sides of the trial balance which was placed to suspense account.

CHAPTER 6

# Periodic Accounting Reports

## 6.1 PERIODIC ACCOUNTS

The preparation of accounting statements should be a routine procedure as they are regularly needed by management, ownership, and other interested parties, such as bankers, to monitor the progress and position of the company. The principal accounting statements used for these purposes are the trading and profit and loss account and the balance sheet. The frequency with which these statements are produced varies according to individual circumstances, but it is normal to prepare them at least once a year to comply with legal and taxation requirements. Their usefulness depends firstly on the ability of the recipients to base decisions on them and secondly on the time lags between the occurrence of events, their financial effects being reported, and decisions taken. If decisions are delayed due to lack of financial information, then opportunities may be missed, possibly with disasterous consequences. For this reason management, and sometimes other interested parties, are provided with statements more frequently than once a year, usually monthly, but possibly even more often. For example, when losses are being made it is important to realise this fact at an early stage; this is helped by the frequent and prompt production of a profit and loss account. The first evidence that losses are being incurred may otherwise be the collapse of the company, an eventuality which might have been avoided if the losses had been identified earlier and remedial action taken.

The procedures described in chapters 4 and 5 provide the foundations of the accounting process as they are used to record the flows of cash, goods and services and provide a summary of these flows in the form of the Trial Balance. This chapter deals with the adjustments necessary to the information contained in the Trial Balance to enable the production of the Trading and Profit and Loss Account and Balance Sheet where a system of double entry is in operation.

## 6.2   ADJUSTMENTS TO THE TRIAL BALANCE

Adjustments to the trial balance are necessary because the transactions in the ledger accounts do not reflect precisely the economic events which have occurred during the period covered by the accounting statements. Adjustments are therefore needed to take account of:

*1. Timing differences* These occur when an item recorded in the books during an accounting period has significance for the business not only in that accounting period, but also in previous or subsequent ones. In these circumstances an adjustment must be made to distribute the item accordingly. For example, the purchase of a fixed asset is initially recorded at cost in the year of purchase, but it is necessary to apportion this cost over the years which derive benefit from the expenditure. (For a fuller explanation see section 3 of chapter 7). Timing differences also operate in the opposite direction. For example, there may be an interval between the receipt of goods and the arrival of the related invoice. (See section 3 of this chapter).

*2. Incomplete information* The entries in the books may not reflect all of the economic changes which must be reported, since some events are not supported by a documented flow of value on which a day book entry is based. For example, a debtor may be unable to pay the sum due to the company (see section 7 of this chapter), or a machine may be scrapped unsold (see section 5 of this chapter). The routine documentation procedures do not apply in these cases, and care must be taken to ensure that allowance has been made for them when the accounts are prepared. The accountant must satisfy himself that he has included all items that relate to the period under review and also excluded items that are not relevant.

The adjustments made to the trial balance must comply with the rules of double entry; each must comprise a debit and a credit of equal value. The implementation of the adjustments which routinely arise when periodic accounts are prepared are examined in this chapter; the principles of valuation on which the adjustments are based are dealt with in chapter 7.

## 6.3   STOCKS (INVENTORIES)

Profit is measured by comparing the value of sales for a period of time with their related costs, and so it is necessary to determine the value of goods consumed in the manner described in section 6.1 of chapter 3. Companies may hold many different types of stock, such as raw materials, work in progress and finished goods, and the general equation to find the cost of items consumed is:

Cost of goods consumed = Opening Stock + Inflow of goods
− Closing Stock

Care must be taken to ensure that all inflows of goods are included. Any items received prior to the accounting date and included in stock, but which have not been entered as purchases as they have not yet been invoiced, must be identified. An adjustment in the form of an accrual is then made which increases the value of purchases (debit) and is shown as a liability in the balance sheet (credit).

In a system of double entry accounting, it is usual to enter the opening stock in one account and to accumulate in another account, called purchases, the cost of all acquisitions made during the accounting period. The effect of this procedure is that the trial balance contains separate balances for opening stock and purchases; these provide two elements of the formula given above. The missing element is the figure for closing stock, and this is usually determined by means of a physical stock-take to find the quantities of each type of stock which are then valued.

To find the Cost of Goods Sold in the Trading Account it is necessary to transfer to the debit of this account the values of opening stock and purchases contained in the trial balance. The accounting entry to record closing stock in the final accounts must then be made:

| Debit | Credit | With |
| --- | --- | --- |
| Stock Account | Trading Account | Value of Closing Stock |

The closing balance on the Stock Account appears as an asset in the Balance Sheet and is subsequently included as opening stock in the trading account for the following accounting period.

Example 6.1 involves the preparation of final accounts from the trial balance where an adjustment has to be made for closing stock.

## Example 6.1

The trial balance of Button, a sole trader, at 31 December 19X4 was:

|  | £ | £ |
|---|---:|---:|
| Capital | | 10,000 |
| Drawings | 10,000 | |
| Sales | | 75,500 |
| Purchases | 45,250 | |
| Stock 1 January 19X4 | 6,750 | |
| Debtors | 4,300 | |
| Creditors | | 3,200 |
| Cash | 1,125 | |
| Delivery Costs | 875 | |
| Wages | 11,225 | |
| Sundry Expenses | 3,000 | |
| Freehold Premises | 6,175 | |
| | 88,700 | 88,700 |

The stock at 31 December 19X4 was £7,150

*Required*

Prepare the Trading and Profit and Loss Account of Button for the year to 31 December 19X4 and a Balance Sheet at that date. The accounts should be presented in vertical format.

## Solution

Trading and Profit and Loss Account
Year to 31 December 19X4

|  | £ | £ |
|---|---:|---:|
| Sales | | 75,500 |
| Stock 1 January | 6,750 | |
| Purchases | 45,250 | |
| Stock 31 December | (7,150) | |
| Cost of Goods Sold | | 44,850 |
| Gross Profit | | 30,650 |
| Wages | 11,225 | |
| Delivery Costs | 875 | |
| Sundry Expenses | 3,000 | |
| | | 15,100 |
| Net Profit | | 15,550 |

*Balance Sheet at 31 December 19X4*

|  | £ | £ |
|---|---|---|
| Fixed Assets |  |  |
| Freehold premises......................... |  | 6,175 |
| Current Assets |  |  |
| Stock.................................... | 7,150 |  |
| Debtors................................. | 4,300 |  |
| Cash.................................... | 1,125 |  |
|  | 12,575 |  |
| Current Liabilities |  |  |
| Creditors.............................. | 3,200 |  |
|  |  | 9,375 |
|  |  | 15,550 |
| Capital |  |  |
| At 1 January............................. |  | 10,000 |
| Profit for 19X4.......................... |  | 15,550 |
|  |  | 25,550 |
| Drawings............................... |  | 10,000 |
|  |  | 15,550 |

Readers should now attempt Question 6.1 at the end of this chapter.

## 6.4 DEPRECIATION

Fixed assets and their related accumulated depreciation are recorded in the double entry ledger by using an account for each type of fixed asset at cost and another for each type of fixed asset's accumulated depreciation. The number of accounts to be opened depends on the nature of the business, but usually separate accounts for land and buildings, plant and machinery, motor vehicles, and furniture and fittings suffice. Further accounts can be used if appropriate, for example, computer equipment or assets out on hire may have a value significant enough to warrant separate identification. The totals of these accounts should be backed up by detailed analysis in a fixed asset register so that the individual assets can be identified.

When the trial balance is extracted it contains for each type of fixed asset, as a debit, the cost and, as a credit, the accumulated balance of depreciation brought forward at the start of the accounting period. The value of the depreciation charge for the period for each class of asset has then to be calculated, and the amounts are debited to the profit and loss account and credited to the accounts containing the opening balances of accumulated depreciation. (The calculation of the depreciation charge is dealt with in section 3 of chapter 7). The debit balance on each of the fixed asset (at cost) accounts is entered in the balance sheet, and from it the credit balance on the related accumulated depreciation account is deducted to give the written down value, that is, the portion of cost not yet written off and therefore carried forward to the next accounting period. It is helpful to the users of the accounts if both the total cost and the total related depreciation are shown in the balance sheet, rather than just the net figure; this procedure indicates how much of the value has been used up and therefore how long it is likely to be before replacement becomes necessary. In the case of a limited company, such disclosure is a legal requirement (see section 5.1 of chapter 10).

**Example 6.2**
The following information relates to the machinery owned by Clip Ltd:

|  | £ |
|---|---|
| At cost, 1.1.19X1 | 65,000 |
| Accumulated depreciation at 1.1.19X1 | 25,000 |
| Acquired during 19X1 | 10,000 |
| Depreciation charge for 19X1 | 8,000 |

*Required:*
a) Prepare the ledger accounts for 19X1 to record the above information.
b) Show the balance sheet extract for Machinery at 31.12.19X1.

## Solution
a)

### Machinery at Cost Account

| | £ | | £ |
|---|---|---|---|
| 1.1.19X1 Balance b/d..... | 65,000 | 31.12.19X1 Balance c/d... | 75,000 |
| 19X1 Purchases.......... | 10,000 | | |
| | 75,000 | | 75,000 |

### Accumulated Depreciation Account — Machinery

| | £ | | £ |
|---|---|---|---|
| 31.12.19X1 Balance c/d... | 33,000 | 1.1.19X1 Balance b/d..... | 25,000 |
| | | 31.12.19X1 Profit and | |
| | | Loss Account.. | 8,000 |
| | 33,000 | | 33,000 |

b)

### Balance Sheet Extract 31.12.19X1

| | £ | £ |
|---|---|---|
| Machinery at Cost............................... | 75,000 | |
| Less: Accumulated Depreciation................... | 33,000 | |
| | | 42,000 |

Readers should now attempt Questions 6.2 and 6.3 at the end of this chapter. The former question tests the entries for fixed assets and depreciation in the books of account, and the latter puts them in the context of preparing final accounts from the trial balance.

## 6.5  DISPOSAL OF FIXED ASSETS

When a fixed asset is disposed of, its cost and related depreciation must be eliminated from the books and any profit or loss on disposal calculated. Any proceeds from disposal must not be included in the company's sales figure as they do not relate to routine trading activity. Instead, the proceeds are credited to a Disposal of Fixed Assets Account, the balance on which appears as a credit entry in the trial balance. The calculation of the profit or loss arising on disposal may then be made in the Disposal of Fixed Assets Account using the following entries:

| Account Debited | Account Credited | With |
|---|---|---|
| Disposal of Fixed Assets | Fixed Assets at Cost | Historical Cost of the Asset Sold or Scrapped |
| Accumulated Depreciation | Disposal of Fixed Assets | Accumulated Depreciation on the Asset |

## Example 6.3

In 19X3 Case Ltd. sold for £6,500 cash a piece of machinery which had cost the company £25,000. At the time of sale, the accumulated depreciation on the asset was £20,000.

*Required:*
Prepare the disposal of fixed assets account to record the sale of the machinery.

## Solution

*Disposal of Fixed Assets Account*

| | £ | | £ |
|---|---|---|---|
| Machinery at cost......... | 25,000 | Cash.................... | 6,500 |
| Profit on sale*........... | 1,500 | Accumulated depreciation. | 20,000 |
| | 26,500 | | 26,500 |

*Balancing figure credited to the profit and loss account

Sometimes a Disposal of Fixed Assets Account is not maintained during the year and instead any proceeds are credited to the Fixed Assets at Cost Account. This happens especially where a 'trading in' allowance is received, for example, when changing motor vehicles, as a reduction in the amount paid for the new asset. In these circumstances, the proceeds or trading in allowance must be transferred to the disposal account by the following entry:

| Account Debited | Account Credited | With |
|---|---|---|
| Fixed Assets at Cost | Disposal of Fixed Assets | Proceeds of Disposal or Trading in Allowance |

Instead of making the appropriate entries in a Disposal of Fixed Assets Account, the profit or loss on the disposal of an individual asset may alternatively be calculated by using the following formula:

$$\text{Proceeds on Disposal} - \left( \text{Historical Cost} - \text{Accumulated Depreciation} \right) = \text{Profit/Loss on Disposal}$$

Questions can be framed so that any one element from this equation is unknown and has to be found as the balancing figure after the others have been determined and entered.

**Example 6.4**

Shed Ltd. bought a fixed asset for £10,000 in 19X1 which was sold for £6,250 in 19X5 to give a profit on disposal of £1,250.

*Required:*

(a) Calculate the accumulated depreciation which had been charged on the asset up to the time it was sold.

(b) Explain why, when the amount of profit on disposal is known, it is necessary to calculate the depreciation figure.

**Solution**

(a) £6,250 (proceeds) − (£10,000 (cost) − accumulated depreciation)
= £1,250 (profit)
∴ £6,250 − £10,000 + accumulated depreciation = £1,250
∴ accumulated depreciation = £10,000 − £6,250 + £1,250 = £5,000

(b) It is necessary to know the value of accumulated depreciation as, when an asset is disposed of, all the related entries in the books must be removed. This is done by using double entry procedures to complete a disposal of fixed assets account:

*Disposal of Fixed Assets Account*

| | £ | | £ |
|---|---|---|---|
| Fixed assets at cost........... | 10,000 | Proceeds................... | 6,250 |
| Profit on disposal........... | 1,250 | Accumulated depreciation.... | 5,000 |
| | 11,250 | | 11,250 |

When a fully depreciated asset is scrapped, and no proceeds are received, its cost and accumulated depreciation may be eliminated from the books without using a disposal of asset account. This is achieved by the entries:

| Account Debited | Account Credited | With |
|---|---|---|
| Accumulated Depreciation | Fixed Assets at Cost | Historical Cost of Asset Scrapped |

Readers should now work Question 6.4 at the end of this chapter which tests all the aspects of asset disposal described in this section.

## 6.6   PREPAYMENTS AND ACCRUALS

A business makes a number of payments which give a right to enjoy certain benefits over a period of time. Some of these payments, such as rates on the occupation of property, are paid in advance of the receipt of the benefit and give rise to a prepayment, while others, such as for the consumption of gas or electricity, are made in arrears and create accruals. The accruals concept, as explained in section 6 of chapter 3, is applied, and so, unless the period of time covered by these payments coincides exactly with the accounting period, an adjustment is needed to take account of the asset created where payments are made in advance, and the liability which arises when benefits are paid for in arrears. The value of accruals and prepayments for items which relate to a period of time is found by apportioning the cost on a time basis.

*Prepayments*   The entries in the accounts to record a prepayment are:

| Account Debited | Account Credited | With |
|---|---|---|
| Prepayment | Expense | Value of prepayment |

The credit of the prepayment in the expense account reduces the expense, and the prepayment is shown in the balance sheet as a current asset. In practice, the prepayment may be carried down in the expense account to which it relates. This is illustrated in Example 6.5.

## Example 6.5

Gelco Ltd. makes up its accounts to 31 December, and made the following cash payments in respect of rates:

| Year | Month | Payment |
|---|---|---|
| | | £ |
| 19X0 | October................. | 900 |
| 19X1 | April................... | 1,000 |
| 19X1 | October................. | 1,000 |

The payments for rates relate to the six month period starting with the month in which they are paid.

*Required:*
Prepare the rates account for 19X1

## Solution

Rates Account

| | £ | | £ |
|---|---|---|---|
| 1.1.19X1 Balance b/d..... | 450 | 31.12.19X1 Balance c/d... | 500 |
| April Cash.............. | 1,000 | Profit and Loss | |
| October Cash............ | 1,000 | Account...... | 1,950 |
| | 2,450 | | 2,450 |
| 1.1.19X2 Balance b/d..... | 500 | | |

The balance brought down at the start of the year is half of the payment of £900 made in October 19X0 and covers January, February and March 19X1. The balance of £500 carried down at the end of 19X1 is an asset since it pays in advance for the first three months of 19X2 and will appear as a current asset in the balance sheet at 31 December 19X1. The transfer to the profit and loss account is found as a balancing figure once all the other entries have been made. The balance brought down on 1 January 19X2 will be charged against profit as an expense in 19X2, even though payment was made in 19X1.

*Accruals*   The entries in the accounts to record an accrual are:

| Account Debited | Account Credited | With |
|---|---|---|
| Expense | Accruals | Value of Accrual |

The accrual increases the expense figure charged in the profit and loss account (debit) and is included as a current liability in the balance sheet (credit). In practice the accrual may be carried down in the expense account to which it relates. This is illustrated in Example 6.6.

## Example 6.6

Gelco Ltd. makes up its accounts to 31 December, and made the following payments in respect of electricity:

| Year | Month | Payment £ |
|------|-------|-----------|
| 19X0 | October................. | 400 |
| 19X1 | January................. | 600 |
| 19X1 | April................... | 630 |
| 19X1 | July.................... | 400 |
| 19X1 | October................. | 500 |
| 19X2 | January................. | 750 |

The payments are for electricity consumed during the three months immediately prior to the months in which they are made.

### Required:

Record the above transactions in the company's electricity account for 19X1 and 19X2.

### Solution

*Electricity Account*

| | £ | | £ |
|---|---|---|---|
| 19X1 | | 1.1.19X1 Balance b/d........ | 600 |
| January Cash.............. | 600 | 31.12.19X1 Profit and Loss | |
| April Cash............... | 630 | Account......... | 2,280 |
| July Cash................. | 400 | | |
| October Cash.............. | 500 | | |
| 31.12.19X1 Balance c/d...... | 750 | | |
| | 2,880 | | 2,880 |
| 19X2 | | 1.1.19X2 Balance b/d........ | 750 |
| January Cash.............. | 750 | | |

The credit balance of £600 brought down would have appeared in the balance sheet at 31 December 19X0 as a liability and relates to the electricity consumed in the last three months of 19X0. It can be seen that it is cancelled by the actual cash payment made in January 19X1 and at that point the balance on the account is zero. The same reasoning relates to the £750 carried down at the end of 19X1.

Readers should now attempt Question 6.5 at the end of this chapter.

## 6.7   BAD DEBTS

When a company makes sales on credit there is a possibility that some of the customers will not be able to pay their debts, with the result that bad debts are suffered. Although known bad debts may be written off during the year, it is usual to review carefully the list of debtors outstanding when the annual accounts are prepared and write off any additional bad debts likely to arise. The fact that a debt is likely to prove bad becomes apparent when a great deal of time has elapsed since the goods were supplied and no cash has been received despite repeated efforts to collect the amount outstanding. This emphasises the importance of monitoring debtors on a routine basis so that, when the terms for payment are exceeded, further supplies can be stopped; such action encourages the customer to pay the amount owed and also minimises the loss if the debt should prove to be bad. When it becomes apparent that the full amount of the debt will not be received from the debtor, it is necessary to remove the value of the irrecoverable debt from the total debtors account and record the loss. The double entry to achieve this is:

| Account Debited | Account Credited | With |
|---|---|---|
| Bad Debts | Debtors Control | Value of Bad Debt |

The amount is also credited to the individual personal account of the debtor in the memorandum debtors ledger. The balance on the bad debts account appears as a debit balance in the Trial Balance, and is written off to the profit and loss account when the annual accounts are prepared since it represents the loss of an asset, and, therefore, is an expense.

In addition, a company may know, from experience, that a stable proportion of the debts outstanding at the balance sheet date will prove to be bad, although it is not possible to tell in advance which specific debts will remain unpaid. Prudence suggests that, in these circumstances, an allowance should be made for the likely bad debts contained in the value of debtors outstanding at the year end by the introduction of a provision for *doubtful* debts. When the amount to be allowed for has been determined, the provision is created by a debit to the Doubtful Debts Account with the corresponding credit to a Provision for Doubtful Debts Account; this credit balance is offset against the value of debtors in the balance sheet to show the net amount which is expected to be collected. The fact that this provision is general, or non-specific, means that no consequential adjustments are made in the debtor's individual memorandum personal accounts.

Once a provision has been created, it appears as a credit balance in the Trial Balance prepared at the end of the subsequent accounting period, and it is necessary only to adjust its value from year to year, rather than charge annually the full required value. This is because the provision created at the end of one year is carried forward to the next, and any debts which in fact prove bad are debited to the bad debts account and then written off to the profit and loss account. The double entry to record adjustments to the doubtful debts account is:

| Account Debited | Account Credited | With |
|---|---|---|
| Doubtful Debts | Doubtful Debt Provision | Increase in Provision |
| Doubtful Debt Provision | Profit and Loss | Decrease in Provision |

## Example 6.7

The following balances appeared in the books of Fifth Ltd. at the end of 19X1:

|  | Debit £ | Credit £ |
|---|---|---|
| Bad debts written off during 19X1................... | 950 |  |
| Provision for doubtful debts brought forward................................ |  | 900 |
| Debtors Control Account......................... | 125,000 |  |

It is decided, after a review of the debtors' balances at the end of the year, to write off a further £1,000 of bad debts and create a provision of 1% of the value of the remainder for Doubtful Debts.

*Required:*
Write up the T accounts to deal with these matters and show the appropriate extracts from the profit and loss account and balance sheet.

## Solution

### Bad Debts Account

|  | £ |  | £ |
|---|---|---|---|
| 19X1 Debtors.............. | 950 | 31.12.19X1 Profit and Loss... | 1,950 |
| 31.12.19X1 Debtors......... | 1,000 |  |  |
|  | 1,950 |  | 1,950 |

*Debtors Control Account*

| | £ | | £ |
|---|---|---|---|
| 31.12.19X1 Balance.......... | 125,000 | 31.12.19X1 Bad Debts........ | 1,000 |
| | | 31.12.19X1 Balance c/d...... | 124,000 |
| | 125,000 | | 125,000 |

*Provision for Doubtful Debts Account*

| | £ | | £ |
|---|---|---|---|
| 31.12.19X1 Balance c/d...... | 1,240* | 31.12.19X1 Balance b/d...... | 900 |
| | | 31.12.19X1 Doubtful debts... | 340 |
| | 1,240 | | 1,240 |

\* 1% of £124,000 = £1,240

*Doubtful Debts Account*

| | | £ | | | £ |
|---|---|---|---|---|---|
| 31.12.19X1 | Provision for doubtful debts | 340 | 31.12.19X1 | Profit and Loss | 340 |

*Profit and Loss Account (extract)*

| | £ | £ |
|---|---|---|
| Bad debts..................................... | 1,950 | |
| Doubtful debts................................ | 340 | |
| | | 2,290 |

*Balance Sheet (extract)*

| | £ | £ |
|---|---|---|
| Debtors...................................... | 124,000 | |
| less:Provision for doubtful debts.................. | 1,240 | |
| | | 122,760 |

*Notes*
1. The bad debts of £950 have already been written off the value of debtors and so no further adjustment to the debtors control account is required in respect of this loss.
2. All bad debts arising during 19X1 have been written off against profit. It is therefore necessary only to increase the provision to the revised value, that is, by £340 to £1,240. In some cases the review of debtor balances results in a reduction of the provision and hence a credit to the profit and loss account.

Readers should now work Question 6.6 at the end of the chapter which tests the book entries related to bad debts, and Question 6.7 which revises the preparation of final accounts from the trial balance with some additional adjustments.

## 6.8   THE ADJUSTED TRIAL BALANCE

The adjustments made to the trial balance when the trading and profit and loss account are prepared must be carried out in a systematic manner which complies with double entry procedures. Example 6.8 shows how this can be done.

### Example 6.8

The following trial balance was extracted from the books of T.Jones on 31 December 19X5:

|  | £ | £ |
|---|---|---|
| Sales | | 100,000 |
| Purchases | 50,000 | |
| Stock — 1 January | 10,000 | |
| Rent | 5,000 | |
| Wages | 12,000 | |
| Electricity | 1,500 | |
| Debtors | 9,000 | |
| Trade creditors | | 8,000 |
| Cash | 1,000 | |
| Fixed assets at cost | 34,000 | |
| Accumulated depreciation — 1 January | | 13,000 |
| Other expenses | 6,000 | |
| Capital — 1 January | | 17,000 |
| Drawings | 9,500 | |
|  | 138,000 | 138,000 |

The following additional information is provided:
1. Goods which cost £1,000 were received during 19X5 and were included in closing stock. No invoice was included in purchases for them in 19X5.
2. Rent of £500 is prepaid.
3. Electricity of £350 is accrued.
4. The depreciation charge for the year is £6,000
5. Jones took stock for his own use which cost £450. No entry was made in the books in respect of this.
6. The closing stock is £12,000.
7. Bad debts of £150 are to be written off.
8. A provision for doubtful debts of £100 is to be created.

*Required:*
(a) Prepare the adjusted trial balance of T. Jones as at 31 December 19X5.
(b) Prepare the Trading and Profit and Loss Account of T. Jones for the year to 31 December 19X5 and the Balance Sheet as at that date.

## Solution:

### (a) Adjusted Trial Balance

| | Original Trial Balance at 31.12.X5 | | Adjustments | | Final Trial Balance | | | |
| | | | | | Trading and Profit and Loss Account | | Balance Sheet | |
| | £ DR | £ CR | £ DR | £ CR | £ DR | £ CR | £ DR | £ CR |
|---|---|---|---|---|---|---|---|---|
| Sales | | 100,000 | | | | 100,000 | | |
| Purchases | 50,000 | | 1,000(1) | 450(5) | 50,550 | | | |
| Stock | 10,000 | | 12,000(6) | 12,000(6) | 10,000 | 12,000 | 12,000 | |
| Rent | 5,000 | | | 500(2) | 4,500 | | | |
| Wages | 12,000 | | | | 12,000 | | | |
| Electricity | 1,500 | | 350(3) | | 1,850 | | | |
| Debtors | 9,000 | | | 150(7) | | | 8,850 | |
| Creditors | | 8,000 | | 1,000(1) | | | | 9,000 |
| Cash | 1,000 | | | | | | 1,000 | |
| Fixed assets at cost | 34,000 | | | | | | 34,000 | |
| Accumulated depreciation 1 January | | 13,000 | | 6,000(4) | | | | 19,000 |
| Other Expenses | 6,000 | | | | 6,000 | | | |
| Capital 1 January | | 17,000 | | | | | | 17,000 |
| Drawings | 9,500 | | 450(5) | | | | 9,950 | |
| Accruals | | | | 350(3) | | | | 350 |
| Prepayments | | | 500(2) | | | | 500 | |
| Depreciation charge | | | 6,000(4) | | 6,000 | | | |
| Bad and doubtful debts | | | { 100(8) 150(7) } | | 250 | | | |
| Provision for Doubtful debts | | | | 100(8) | | | | 100 |
| | _138,000_ | _138,000_ | _20,550_ | _20,550_ | 91,150 | 112,000 | 66,300 | 45,450 |
| | | | | | | − 91,150 | | 20,850 |
| | | | | | 20,850 | | 66,300 | 66,300 |

*Notes*

i.    The 'adjustments' columns show the debit and credit entries needed to give effect to the additional information. The number in brackets by such figures refers to the note in the question on which it is based.

ii.   The opening balance of each line is taken, adjusted, and then entered in the Final Trial Balance.

iii.  The fact that the two adjustment columns have the same total shows that the double entry rules have been complied with.

iv.   The Final Trial Balance is separated into the Trading and Profit and Loss Account and the Balance Sheet. This is to aid the preparation of the final accounts. The proof of the trial balance in this format is that each section has an equal, but opposite, difference. This is the profit figure.

v.    The accrual of £1,000 for the goods received but not invoiced at the year end represents a trade creditor and so is added to the existing balance of £8,000.

(b)

### Trading and Profit and Loss Account
### Year to 31 December 19X5

|  | £ | £ |
|---|---|---|
| Sales | | 100,000 |
| Opening stock | 10,000 | |
| Purchases | 50,550 | |
| Closing stock | (12,000) | |
| Cost of goods sold | | 48,550 |
| Gross profit | | 51,450 |
| Rent | 4,500 | |
| Wages | 12,000 | |
| Electricity | 1,850 | |
| Other Expenses | 6,000 | |
| Depreciation | 6,000 | |
| Bad and doubtful debts | 250 | |
| | | 30,600 |
| Net Profit | | 20,850 |

*Balance Sheet at 31 December 19X5*

| | £ | £ | £ |
|---|---|---|---|
| **FIXED ASSETS** | | | |
| Fixed assets at cost......................... | | | 34,000 |
| Less: Accumulated depreciation.............. | | | 19,000 |
| | | | 15,000 |
| **CURRENT ASSETS** | | | |
| Stock..................................... | | 12,000 | |
| Debtors................................... | 8,850 | | |
| Less: Provision for doubtful debts........... | 100 | | |
| | | 8,750 | |
| Prepayment............................... | | 500 | |
| Cash..................................... | | 1,000 | |
| | | 22,250 | |
| **CURRENT LIABILITIES** | | | |
| Creditors................................. | 9,000 | | |
| Accruals.................................. | 350 | | |
| | | 9,350 | |
| WORKING CAPITAL..................... | | | 12,900 |
| | | | 27,900 |
| **CAPITAL** | | | |
| Balance at 1 January....................... | | | 17,000 |
| Profit for Year............................ | | | 20,850 |
| | | | 37,850 |
| Less: Drawings........................... | | | 9,950 |
| | | | 27,900 |

An adjusted trial balance, as used in Example 6.8 above, should be prepared for inclusion in a set of permanent working papers when final accounts are prepared in practice. In examinations it is often too time consuming to prepare, but, with practice, this process can be avoided. The important requirement is that students should adopt a systematic approach so as to ensure that all necessary adjustments are properly made. One useful technique is to note the double entry effects of all the adjustments to the trial balance on the question paper. The adjusted balances are then used to prepare the final accounts. This approach is now illustrated in Example 6.9 which uses the data given in Example 6.8 for T.Jones. The notes on the trial balance which would in practice be made by hand are shown in italics, and the final accounts include notes on how the figures have been calculated.

## Example 6.9

The following trial balance was extracted from the books of T.Jones on 31 December 19X5 and shows the adjustments needed to prepare the final accounts:

|  | £ |  | £ |
|---|---|---|---|
| Sales............................ |  |  | 100,000 |
| Purchases...................... | 50,000 | *+1,000 − 450* |  |
| Stock—1 January.............. | 10,000 |  |  |
| Rent......................... | 5,000 | *−500* |  |
| Wages......................... | 12,000 |  |  |
| Electricity..................... | 1,500 | *+350* |  |
| Debtors....................... | 9,000 | *−150* |  |
| Trade creditors................ |  |  | 8,000 + *1,000* |
| Cash......................... | 1,000 |  |  |
| Fixed assets at cost.............. | 34,000 |  |  |
| Accumulated depreciation—1 January...................... |  |  | 13,000 + *6,000* |
| Other expenses................ | 6,000 |  |  |
| Capital—1 January............. |  |  | 17,000 |
| Drawings..................... | 9,500 | *+450* |  |
|  | 138,000 |  | 138,000 |
| *Stock — 31 December* .......... | *12,000* |  | *12,000* |
| *Prepayments* .................. | *500* |  |  |
| *Accruals*..................... |  |  | *350* |
| *Depreciation  charge*............ | *6,000* |  |  |
| *Bad  debts*.................... | *150* |  |  |
| *Doubtful debts*................. | *100* |  |  |
| *Provision for doubtful debts* ..... |  |  | *100* |

The additional information on which the adjustments, in italics, are based is given in Example 6.8.

Care must be taken to include workings with the answer submitted to ensure that the examiner understands how the figures were derived. In this example, the workings are given in brackets on the face of the accounts.

*Trading and Profit and Loss Account Year to 31 December 19X5*

|  | £ | £ |
|---|---|---|
| Sales........................................... |  | 100,000 |
| Opening stock................................. | 10,000 |  |
| Purchases  (50,000 + 1,000 − 450).................. | 50,550 |  |
| Closing stock.................................. | (12,000) |  |
| Cost of goods sold............................. |  | 48,550 |
| Gross profit................................... |  | 51,450 |
| Rent (5,000 − 500)............................. | 4,500 |  |
| Wages........................................ | 12,000 |  |
| Electricity  (1,500 + 350)....................... | 1,850 |  |
| Other expenses................................ | 6,000 |  |
| Depreciation.................................. | 6,000 |  |
| Bad and doubtful debts (100 + 150)................ | 250 | 30,600 |
| Net Profit..................................... |  | 20,850 |

*Balance Sheet at 31 December 19X5*

|  | £ | £ | £ |
|---|---|---|---|
| **FIXED ASSETS** |  |  |  |
| Fixed assets at cost.......................... |  |  | 34,000 |
| Less:   Accumulated |  |  |  |
| Depreciation  (13,000 + 6,000).......... |  |  | 19,000 |
|  |  |  | 15,000 |
| **CURRENT ASSETS** |  |  |  |
| Stock..................................... |  | 12,000 |  |
| Debtors (9,000-150)....................... | 8,850 |  |  |
| Less:   Provision for doubtful debts........... | 100 | 8,750 |  |
| Prepayment.............................. |  | 500 |  |
| Cash..................................... |  | 1,000 |  |
|  |  | 22,250 |  |
| **CURRENT LIABILITIES** |  |  |  |
| Creditors  (8,000 + 1,000)................... | 9,000 |  |  |
| Accruals................................. | 350 | 9,350 |  |
| WORKING CAPITAL...................... |  |  | 12,900 |
|  |  |  | 27,900 |
| **CAPITAL** |  |  |  |
| Balance at 1 January...................... |  |  | 17,000 |
| Profit for Year........................... |  |  | 20,850 |
|  |  |  | 37,850 |
| Less:   Drawings (9,500 + 450)............... |  |  | 9,950 |
|  |  |  | 27,900 |

Readers should now work Question 6.7 at the end of this chapter.

Errors may come to light during the examination of the books which takes place when the periodic accounts are prepared. The correction of these errors must be made in accordance with the double entry techniques described in this chapter. This aspect of preparing final accounts is tested in Question 6.8 at the end of this chapter which readers should now work also.

## 6.9 QUESTIONS
### Question 6.1
The trial balance of Finis, a sole trader, at 31 December 19X4, was:

|  | £ Debit | £ Credit |
|---|---|---|
| Sales | | 130,000 |
| Returns inwards | 250 | |
| Stock 1 January 19X4 | 15,000 | |
| Returns outwards | | 150 |
| Purchases | 80,000 | |
| Capital at 1 January 19X4 | | 27,600 |
| Cash at bank | 3,100 | |
| Debtors | 15,400 | |
| Creditors | | 5,000 |
| Premises | 8,000 | |
| Wages | 17,300 | |
| Discounts received | | 300 |
| Rent and rates | 3,000 | |
| Delivery costs | 2,750 | |
| Cash withdrawn by Finis | 12,000 | |
| Heat and light | 3,500 | |
| Sundry expenses | 2,750 | |
| | 163,050 | 163,050 |

*Note:* The value of stock at 31 December, 19X4 was £17,750.

*Required:*
(a) State the location in the final accounts of each item in the Trial Balance, ie, whether it is entered in the trading account, the profit and loss account or the balance sheet.
(b) Prepare the Trading and Profit and Loss Account of Finis for the year to 31 December 19X4 and a Balance Sheet at that date.

## Question 6.2

Tip Ltd. was established and started trading on 1 January 19X1 and draws up its accounts to 31 December each year. Its purchases and disposals of fixed assets over the subsequent three years were as follows:

| Asset | Date of Purchase | Cost £ | Date of Disposal | Proceeds on Disposal £ |
|---|---|---|---|---|
| A | 1 January 19X1...... | 5,000 | — | — |
| B | 1 January 19X1...... | 2,500 | 1 January 19X3 | 900 |
| C | 1 January 19X3 | 7,000 | — | |

*Required:*
Use this data to:
(a) Prepare the Fixed Assets at Cost, Accumulated Depreciation, and Disposal of Fixed Assets Accounts based on straight line depreciation of 20% per year for 19X1, 19X2 and 19X3.
(b) Show the Fixed Asset extracts from the balance sheets at the end of each year.

## Question 6.3

The following is the trial balance of Push, a sole trader, at 30 June 19X7:

|  | £ | £ |
|---|---|---|
| Capital | | 30,350 |
| Sales | | 108,920 |
| Purchases | 72,190 | |
| Drawings | 12,350 | |
| Debtors | 7,350 | |
| Creditors | | 6,220 |
| Cash | 1,710 | |
| Stock | 9,470 | |
| Plant and machinery at cost | 35,000 | |
| Accumulated depreciation at 1 July 19X6 | | 12,500 |
| Rent | 1,000 | |
| Wages | 14,330 | |
| Other costs | 4,590 | |
| | 157,990 | 157,990 |

*Notes:*
1. The value of stock at 30 June 19X7 was £9,960
2. The depreciation charge for the year to 30 June 19X7 was £3,000

*Required:*
Prepare the Trading and Profit and Loss Account of Push for the year to 30 June 19X7 and the Balance Sheet at that date.

## Question 6.4

At 31 December 19X3 the Trial Balance of Damp Ltd. contained the following balances in respect of Motor Vehicles:

|  | Debit £ | Credit £ |
|---|---|---|
| Motor Vehicles at cost | 127,000 | |
| accumulated depreciation at 1 January 19X3 | | 76,000 |
| Disposal of motor vehicles | | 1,600 |

You ascertain that during 19X3:
1. A delivery van which was fully depreciated and had cost £2,000 was scrapped. No proceeds were received,
2. A car which cost £5,000 on which accumulated depreciation

was £3,000 had been traded in for a new model with a full cost of £8,000. A trade in allowance of £1,500 was received, and only the net cost of the new car, £6,500, has been entered in the books.

3. A car which cost £4,000 and had a written down value of £1,250 was sold for £1,600 (credited to the disposals account)
4. A delivery van was sold for £2,500. This vehicle had cost £10,000 and a loss of £750 was made on its sale. The proceeds have been credited to the fixed asset account.
5. The depreciation charge for the year is £25,000.

*Required:*
(a) Prepare the Motor Vehicles at Cost Account, Motor Vehicles Accumulated Depreciation Account and Disposal of Motor Vehicles Account for 19X3 to show the effect of the above information and the transfer to the Profit and Loss Account.
(b) Show the extract for Motor Vehicles which would appear in the company's balance sheet at 31 December 19X3.

**Question 6.5**
Prepac Ltd. prepared its accounts to 31 December. The following facts relate to 19X8

|  | £ |  |
|---|---|---|
| Balance on Insurance Account 1 January | 450 | (Debit) |
| Balance on Electricity Account 1 January | 300 | (Credit) |
| Balance on Rates Account 1 January | 290 | (Debit) |
| Balance on Gas Account 1 January | 600 | (Credit) |
| February — pay for electricity consumed during quarter to 31 January | 900 | |
| March—pay for gas consumed during quarter to 28 February | 850 | |
| —pay rates for the half year to 30 September | 780 | |
| May—pay for electricity consumed during quarter to 30 April | 820 | |
| June—pay for gas consumed during quarter to 31 May | 840 | |
| —pay insurance for the year to 30 June 19X9 | 1,020 | |
| August—pay for electricity consumed during quarter to 31 July | 690 | |
| September—pay for gas consumed during quarter to 31 August | 610 | |
| —pay rates for 6 months to 31 March 19X9 | 780 | |
| November—pay for electricity consumed during quarter to 31 October | 550 | |
| December—pay for gas consumed during quarter to 30 November | 960 | |
| Electricity consumed in November and December 19X8 | 390 | |
| Gas consumed in December 19X8 | 680 | |

*Required:*
Prepare the Insurance Account, Electricity Account, Rates Account and Gas Account for 19X8 as they appear in the books of Prepac Ltd. and showing clearly in each case the transfer to Profit and Loss Account.

## Question 6.6
At 31 December 19X0 the following balances were shown in the books of E. Rider Ltd.

|  | £ |
|---|---|
| Sales Control Account............................ | 156,937 (Dr) |
| Provision for Doubtful Debts....................... | 2,600 (Cr) |
| Bad Debts........................................ | 750 (Dr) |

The list of debtors contained balances which were considered to be bad or doutbful as indicated in the "remarks" column of the schedule below:

*Schedule of Bad and Doubtful Debts, 31 December 19X0*

| Customer | Account Number | Account Balance | Remarks |
|---|---|---|---|
| B.Clyde | C6 | £560 | Irrecoverable |
| S.Wars | W2 | £680 | In liquidation. At least 50p in the £ is anticipated, but full recovery is a possibility |
| M.Poppins | P4 | £227 | Irrecoverable |
| M.Express | E9 | £390 | This debt is doubtful to the extent of 20% |
| M.Ash | A1 | £240 | A provision of £80 is to be made against this debt. |

The general provision for doubtful debts in respect of debts other than those dealt with individually above is to be raised to £3,750.

*Required:*
(a)  Prepare the Sales Ledger Control Accounts, Bad Debts Account, Doubtful Debts Account and Provision for Doubtful Debts Account as they appear after recording the above transactions.
(b)  Show the balance sheet extract for Debtors at 31 December 19X0.

## Questions 6.7

The following trial balance was extracted from the books of Dellboy, a retail trader, at 31 December, 19X6:

|  | £ | £ |
|---|---|---|
| Capital account............................... |  | 193,894 |
| Freehold land and buildings at cost................. | 114,000 |  |
| Motor vans at cost.............................. | 37,500 |  |
| Provision for depreciation on motor vans at |  |  |
|     1 January 19X6............................ |  | 15,450 |
| Purchases.................................... | 164,770 |  |
| Sales......................................... |  | 234,481 |
| Rent and rates................................ | 3,000 |  |
| General expenses.............................. | 7,263 |  |
| Wages........................................ | 26,649 |  |
| Bad debts.................................... | 693 |  |
| Provision for doubtful debts at 1 January 19X6........ |  | 876 |
| Drawings..................................... | 18,000 |  |
| Debtors and creditors........................... | 20,911 | 13.006 |
| Stock in trade at 1 January 19X6.................... | 32,193 |  |
| Bank balance.................................. | 32,728 |  |
|  | 457,707 | 457,707 |

You are given the following additional information:
(i)     wages outstanding at 31 December, 19X6 amounted to £271
(ii)    the provision for doubtful debts is to be increased by £104
(iii)   stock in trade at 31 December, 19X6 was £34,671
(iv)    rent and rates amounting to £300 were paid in advance at 31 December, 19X6
(v)     during 19X6 Dellboy took stock costing £1,250 for his own use. No entry has been made in the books in respect of this
(vi)    during 19X6 a motor van which had cost £2,500 and had a written down value of £1,000 was sold for £1,500. No entry had been made in the books to record this, other than to credit the cash received to the motor vehicles account
(vii)   the depreciation charge for the year is £7,000

*Required:*
A trading and profit and loss account for the year 19X6 and a balance sheet as at 31 December, 19X6.

## Question 6.8

During the preparation of the accounts from the books of S. Top, a sole trader for the year to 30 June, 19X7, the following items were found:

1. Included in the Repairs to Machinery Account was £2,750 which was paid on 29 June 19X7 and was for the purchase of a new lathe.
2. Manufacturing Wages Account included £350 paid to an employee for time spent repairing a machine.
3. A debt of £1,290 due from J. Jones was included in debtors, but in fact was irrecoverable.
4. The rates on S. Top's private house of £200 had been paid by the business and charged to the Rates Account.
5. Goods worth £1,500 had been received into stock on 30 June and included in the value of stock for accounts purposes. No entry had been made in the books to record this purchase.
6. An old machine which had cost £1,000 and was fully depreciated had been scrapped during the year. This fact had not been recorded in the books.
7. S. Top had taken stock to the value of £150 for his own use during the year. No entry appeared in the books in respect of this usage.
8. A payment of £125 for delivery of goods to customers had been entered in the Purchases Account.

*Required:*
(a) Prepare the Journal entries to record the adjustments.
(b) Prepare a statement to show the effect of these adjustments on the profit for the year to 30 June, 19X7.

CHAPTER 7

# Asset Valuation, Profit Measurement and the Underlying Accounting Concepts.

The figure for profit appearing in published accounts depends on the amounts at which assets, reported in the balance sheet, are valued. Any errors made when valuing assets have a corresponding effect on the level of reported profit and, therefore, reduce its usefulness as a basis for assessing performance. For example, if closing stock is overvalued by £1,000, the figure for cost of goods sold is understated and reported profit overstated by this amount. Great care should therefore be taken when calculating asset values for inclusion in the accounts. The procedures which are followed, in practice, are examined below.

## 7.1 STOCK VALUATION METHODS
For a trading organisation which purchases and sells goods, but does not process them, stock consists of goods purchased but not sold at the end of the accounting period whereas, in the case of a manufacturing concern, the term covers raw materials, work-in-progress and finished goods awaiting sale. For many businesses stock is a large proportion of gross assets. For example, the accounts of Rolls-Royce Ltd., for 1983, included stock amounting to £153,000,000 and this represented 47.5% of its total assets.

The calculation of the figure for stock involves two steps: firstly the physical quantities of stocks must be established; secondly these physical quantities must be valued.

The quantity of stock on hand is usually established by a physical count after close of business at the end of the accounting period.

Because of the importance of the 'stock count', stocktaking procedures should be worked out well in advance and the exercise undertaken in a systematic manner by reliable employees who are fully aware of their responsibilities. In these circumstances the likelihood of error, as the result of items being mis-described, counted twice, or completely omitted, is reduced to a minimum. It is also necessary for management to take steps to ensure that all goods sold and invoiced to customers on the last day of the accounting period have been despatched from the premises by the time the count takes place. Failure to ensure this happens may mean that profit will be substantially over-stated as the result of including certain items *both* in sales for the year and in the year-end stock figure. For similar reasons management operates controls designed to ensure that all goods on the premises, and included in stock, are recorded in the books as purchases made during the year.

The way in which the quantities of stock are valued is now examined.

### 7.1.1 The Basic Rule

The fundamental rule is that stock should be valued at 'the *lower* of cost and net realisable value'. Readers will be broadly familiar with what is meant by cost (examined further in section 1.2 of this chapter), but the term 'net realisable value'(NRV) is met here for the first time. Basically, NRV is the market selling price of stock less any further costs to be incurred by the firm.

### Example 7.1

The following information is provided relating to a vehicle held in stock by Thornhill Carsales Ltd.

|  | £ |
|---|---|
| Cost | 3,700 |
| Market selling price | 5,000 |

Salesmen are paid a commission of 2% on market selling price, and it is the company's policy to allow the customer a full tank of petrol at an estimated cost of £20.

*Required:*
Calculate the net realisable value of the vehicle.

## Solution

|  | £ | £ |
|---|---|---|
| Net realisable value: | | |
| Market selling price........................... | | 5,000 |
| Less:Further costs - Commission............... | 100 | |
|                - Petrol | 20 | 120 |
| | | 4,880 |

NRV normally exceeds cost in a profitable concern, and this is the case in the above example; NRV (£4,880) exceeds cost (£3,700) by £1,180. Sometimes NRV is below cost. For example, where an existing model of car is to be replaced, the firm will be anxious to clear its 'old' stock before it becomes unsaleable, and is likely to accept a low price.

## Example 7.2
The following information is provided for three vehicles held in stock by Reliable Cars Ltd.

| Vehicle | Cost | NRV |
|---|---|---|
| | £ | £ |
| A | 5,400 | 6,200 |
| B | 5,200 | 8,500 |
| C | 7,100 | 6,200 |

*Required:*
Calculate the value of Reliable Cars Ltd's stock for the purpose of its accounts.

## Solution.

| Vehicle | Cost | NRV | Value for the Accounts: Lower of Cost and NRV |
|---|---|---|---|
| | £ | £ | £ |
| A | 5,400 | 6,200 | 5,400(cost) |
| B | 5,200 | 8,500 | 5,200(cost) |
| C | 7,100 | 6,200 | 6,200(NRV) |
| | 17,700 | 20,900 | 16,800 |

The total cost of the three vehicles is £17,700 compared with a total NRV of £20,900, i.e. total NRV exceeds total cost. It is to ensure that the fall in value of vehicle C is not ignored that the test is applied to each vehicle separately. Where the comparison between the cost and net realisable value of stock on an individual items basis would be excessively time-consuming, e.g. because of the large number of items involved, groups of similar items of stock may be compared.

Most of a company's stock is usually valued at cost, with a small number of items reduced to net realisable value either because they are damaged or because they are no longer popular with customers.

**7.1.2 Calculating Cost** The calculation of the cost of stock is a straightforward matter in the case of a trading organisation, and normally consists of the price paid to the supplier plus delivery charges where these are not included in the purchase price. The calculation is more difficult for a manufacturing organisation because, in these businesses, cost consists of the price paid for raw materials *plus* the processing costs incurred to convert these materials into finished goods. This raises the question: 'Which processing costs should be included?' Clearly the wages paid to employees working with the materials should be included as part of the cost of the finished item, but what about the wages paid to supervisors and other essential manufacturing costs such as lighting and heating, rent and rates of the factory and depreciation of the machinery? In practice one of the following two procedures is followed.

1. Include only those costs which can be traced directly to the item manufactured. This is called the 'marginal cost basis', and the costs included are normally materials costs and the wages paid to those employees directly involved in processing the materials.

2. Include all manufacturing costs i.e. marginal costs plus a fair proportion of incidental manufacturing expenses, called 'manufacturing overheads'. This is called the 'total cost basis'.

   The total cost figure for stock therefore exceeds the marginal cost figure by the amount of the fixed manufacturing overhead costs.

**Example 7.3**
The following data are provided relating to the manufacture of 'Nexo' for the month of January 19X1.

| | £ |
|---|---|
| Raw materials used (£5 per unit)............................... | 6,000 |
| Wages paid to staff directly involved in manufacture................ | 8,400 |
| Salary paid to supervisor....................................... | 850 |
| Rent and rates................................................ | 420 |
| Light and heat................................................ | 670 |
| Depreciation of machinery..................................... | 460 |

During January 1,200 items were manufactured of which 1,000 were sold. There was no opening stock and no work in progress at the beginning or end of the month. Closing stock consists of 200 completed items.

*Required:*

Valuations of closing stock on the:
  (a)  Marginal cost basis
  (b)  Total cost basis

**Solution.**

(a) Marginal cost basis:

| | | £ |
|---|---|---|
| Direct manufacturing costs: | Raw materials................ | 6,000 |
| | Labour...................... | 8,400 |
| | | 14,400 |

Marginal cost per unit manufactured, £14,400 ÷ 1,200 = ...... | 12

Marginal cost of unsold stock, £12 x 200 = ................. | 2,400

(b)  Total cost basis:

| | £ | £ |
|---|---|---|
| Direct manufacturing costs.............................. | | 14,400 |
| Manufacturing overheads: Salary........................ | 850 | |
| Rent and rates.................. | 420 | |
| Light and heat.................. | 670 | |
| Depreciation................... | 460 | 2,400 |
| | | 16,800 |

Total cost per unit manufactured, £16,800 ÷ 1,200 = | 14

Total cost of stock, £14 x 200 = | 2,800

The total cost basis produces a cost per unit which is £2 more (£14 - £12). This results from the inclusion of a proportion of manufacturing overheads which amount, in total, to £2,400, or £2,400 ÷ 1,200 = £2 per unit manufactured.

A company must be able to cover all its costs if it is to survive and flourish in the long run and, for this reason, companies are required to use the total cost basis when valuing stock for inclusion in the accounts published for external use. For internal reporting purposes, however, either total costs or marginal costs can be used and management may well regard the latter as the more relevant basis for *short-run* business decisions. For example, a business operating below its full productive capacity may find it worthwhile to accept orders at prices below total costs, provided marginal costs are covered, since overhead costs will be incurred anyway.

### 7.1.3   First In first Out (FIFO) and Last In First Out (LIFO) We saw in section 2 of chapter 3 that profit is calculated by matching costs with revenues arising during an accounting period. The difficulty, in the case of stocks, is to decide which costs to match with sales revenue in view of the large number of items acquired, probably at different prices. It is theoretically possible to identify the actual items sold and, where a firm deals in a relatively small number of high value items which can be easily identified, e.g. cars, this procedure is followed in practice. Where there are a large number of transactions, however, the heavy additional cost involved in keeping such detailed records rules out this option. Instead the matching process is facilitated by making one of a number of arbitary *assumptions* concerning the flow of goods into and out of the business. Two of the most common assumptions are :

1.   First in first out (FIFO). This assumes that the first items purchased are the first items sold. The items in stock are therefore the most recent acquisitions.
2.   Last in first out (LIFO). This assumes that the last items purchased are the first sold. The items in stock are therefore likely to have been purchased months or even years ago.

### Example 7.4
The following information is provided for Frame Ltd. for 19X2.

|  | £ |
|---|---|
| Opening stock, 200 units at £5 each............... | 1,000 |
| Purchases during 19X2, 1,000 units at £6 each...... | 6,000 |
| Sales during 19X2, 900 units at £10 each........... | 9,000 |
| Closing stock, 300 units | |

*Required:*
Calculate the value of Frame's closing stock using:
  (a)  FIFO
  (b)  LIFO

**Solution.**

(a)  FIFO, 300 units at £6 . . . . . . . . . . . . . . . . . . . . . . . . . . . . . . . . . £1,800

Note:   The 900 items sold are assumed to be made up of the opening stock of 200 units, plus 700 units purchased during the year. Closing stock therefore consists of the remaining 300 units purchased during the year and these are therefore valued at £6 each.

(b)  LIFO: 200 units at £5 . . . . . . . . . . . . . . . . . . . . . . . . . . . . . . . £1,000
        100 units at £6 . . . . . . . . . . . . . . . . . . . . . . . . . . . . . . .    600
                                                                            ———
                                                                            1,600

Note:   The 900 items sold are assumed to have been made entirely from purchases during the year. Closing stock is therefore assumed to consist of the opening stock of 200 units, plus the 100 units purchased during the year which were not sold.

If sufficient details are available management may choose to match purchases with sales on *the transaction basis* rather than on the basis of total purchases and sales during the accounting period (*the periodic basis*), which was a year in Example 7.4. Where the transaction basis is adopted, a slightly different value for stock will result if, as sometimes happens, the quantity of stock on hand falls below the opening balance at some stage during the accounting period.

**Example 7.5**
The following purchases and sales are made by Trader Ltd during the first two weeks of January 19X1. There are no opening stocks.

|  |  | *Purchases* | | *Sales* | |
|---|---|---|---|---|---|
|  |  | *Units* | *Price per Unit* | *Units* | *Price per Unit* |
|  |  |  | £ |  | £ |
| January: | 1 | 100 | 7 | 10 | 9 |
|  | 2 |  |  | 20 | 9 |
|  | 5 |  |  | 50 | 9 |
|  | 7 | 75 | 8 |  |  |
|  | 10 |  |  | 20 | 9 |
|  | 12 |  |  | 50 | 10 |
|  |  | 175 |  | 150 |  |

The physical stock-take confirmed that there were 25 units in stock at the year end.

*Required:*
Calculate the values of stock on both the FIFO and LIFO bases assuming:
  (a)   Purchases are matched with sales monthly, i.e. the periodic basis.
  (b)   Purchases are matched with sales on the transaction basis.

**Solution.**
(a)   Periodic basis.
      FIFO values stock at 25 x £8 (most recent purchase price) = £200
      LIFO values stock at 25 x £7 (earliest purchase price) = £175
(b)   Transaction basis.

|                        |      |
|------------------------|------|
| FIFO: as above         |      |
| LIFO: 20 units at £7 . . . . . . . . . . . | £140 |
| 5 units at £8 . . . . . . . . . . . | 40 |
|                        | 180  |

*Note:* The transaction basis produces a different figure for closing stock under the LIFO basis. This is because the transaction basis recognises the fact that 80 (50 + 20 + 10) of the original 100 units were issued *before* the second delivery took place. Therefore, only 20 units remain from the first delivery (100 - 80), and these are valued at the earlier price; the remaining 5 units are left over from the second delivery (75 - 20 - 50), and these are valued at the later price.

Whether stock is valued on the periodic basis or on the transaction basis, FIFO and LIFO have the following different effects on the figure for cost of goods sold and the valuation of stock during a period of rising prices:
1.   Cost of goods sold. This is higher under LIFO due to the fact that most recent purchases are matched with sales.
2.   Stock.This is valued at a higher figure under FIFO due to the fact that the most recent purchases are assumed to remain in stock.

The effect on the gross profit of Trader Ltd. of using the two different methods (Example 7.5) is shown in the following summarised trading accounts (transaction basis used for illustration):

*Summary Trading Accounts: Transaction Basis*

|  | FIFO | | LIFO | |
|---|---|---|---|---|
|  | £ | £ | £ | £ |
| Sales(100 x £9) + (50 x £10) |  | 1,400 |  | 1,400 |
| Less: Purchases (100 x £7) |  |  |  |  |
| + (75 x £8) | 1,300 |  | 1,300 |  |
| Closing stock | (200) |  | (180) |  |
| Cost of goods sold |  | 1,100 |  | 1,120 |
| Gross profit |  | 300 |  | 280 |

The above example shows that, when prices are rising, reported profit is higher using the FIFO cost flow assumption. The opposite is the case when prices are falling. It is important that students should recognise that actual events are unaffected by the choice of valuation method, but the selection usually alters the level of reported profit.

**7.1.4 Perpetual Inventory** Many large companies maintain detailed stock records which contain information concerning quantities, and sometimes also values, of the various types of stock on hand. The advantages of such records are:

1. They provide an element of control by showing the quantity of goods which *should* be in stock at a particular point in time. Any discrepancies compared with *actual* holdings can then be investigated.
2. Steps can be taken, in good time, to replenish stocks when they fall to a pre-determined minimum level.
3. A further advantage of stock records, where they show prices as well as quantities, is that values for the items in stock are readily available for the pupose of management accounts, which are perhaps prepared monthly, and the annual accounts published for external use. At least once a year, however, and perhaps more often, it is necessary to have a physical stock take to check the accuracy of the stock records.

Where detailed stock records are maintained, information is readily available to enable purchases and sales to be matched on *the transaction basis* for the purpose of valuing stock as described in section 1.3 of this chapter.

## Example 7.6

Using the information given in Example 7.5, write up detailed stock records for Trader Ltd. assuming issues from stock are made on (a) the FIFO basis, and (b) the LIFO basis.

## Solution.

(a)   FIFO basis:

*Stock Card.*

| Date | Receipts | | | Issues | | | Balance | | |
|------|-------|-------|-------|-------|-------|-------|-------|-------|-------|
|      | Units | Price | £ | Units | Price | £ | Units | Price | £ |
| Jan.1 | 100 | 7 | 700 | 10 | 7 | 70 | 90 | 7 | 630 |
| Jan.2 |     |   |     | 20 | 7 | 140 | 70 | 7 | 490 |
| Jan.5 |     |   |     | 50 | 7 | 350 | 20 | 7 | 140 |
| Jan.7 | 75 | 8 | 600 |    |   |     | 20 | 7 | 140 |
|       |    |   |     |    |   |     | 75 | 8 | 600 |
| Jan.10 |   |   |     | 20 | 7 | 140 | 75 | 8 | 600 |
| Jan.12 |   |   |     | 50 | 8 | 400 | 25 | 8 | 200 |
|       | 175 |  | 1,300 | 150 |  | 1,100 |    |   |     |

(b)   LIFO basis:

*Stock Card.*

| Date | Receipts | | | Issues | | | Balance | | |
|------|-------|-------|-------|-------|-------|-------|-------|-------|-------|
|      | Units | Price | £ | Units | Price | £ | Units | Price | £ |
| Jan.1 | 100 | 7 | 700 | 10 | 7 | 70 | 90 | 7 | 630 |
| Jan.2 |     |   |     | 20 | 7 | 140 | 70 | 7 | 490 |
| Jan.5 |     |   |     | 50 | 7 | 350 | 20 | 7 | 140 |
| Jan.7 | 75 | 8 | 600 |    |   |     | 20 | 7 | 140 |
|       |    |   |     |    |   |     | 75 | 8 | 600 |
| Jan10 |    |   |     | 20 | 8 | 160 | 20 | 7 | 140 |
|       |    |   |     |    |   |     | 55 | 8 | 440 |
| Jan.12 |   |   |     | 50 | 8 | 400 | 20 | 7 | 140 |
|       |    |   |     |    |   |     | 5 | 8 | 40 |
|       | 175 |  | 1,300 | 150 |  | 1,120 |    |   |     |

**7.1.5   Weighted Average Cost (AVCO)**   A third alternative is for firms to value cost of goods sold and closing stock at its weighted average cost (AVCO). This is fairly popular with companies and produces results which fall between those achieved by using FIFO or LIFO. The procedure is illustrated in Example 7.7.

## Example 7.7

Using the information given in Example 7.5:

(a)   Calculate the AVCO value of Trader's stock using (i) the periodic basis and (ii) the transaction basis where the company operates a system of perpetual inventory.

(b)   Prepare a summary trading account for Trader Ltd. using AVCO on the transaction basis.

## Solution

*(a) (i) Periodic basis:*

|  | Units | Price | £ |
|---|---|---|---|
| Purchases: 1 January | 100 | £7 | 700 |
| 7 January | 75 | £8 | 600 |
|  | 175 | 7.43* | 1,300 |

*£1,300 ÷ 175 = £7.43 per unit.
Stocks are therefore valued at £7.43 x 25 = £186

*(a) (ii)   Transaction basis, using perpetual inventory*
Stock Card.

| Date | Receipts | | | Issues | | | Balance | | |
|---|---|---|---|---|---|---|---|---|---|
|  | Units | Price | £ | Units | Price | £ | Units | Price | £ |
| Jan.1 | 100 | 7 | 700 | 10 | 7 | 70 | 90 | 7 | 630 |
| Jan.2 |  |  |  | 20 | 7 | 140 | 70 | 7 | 490 |
| Jan.5 |  |  |  | 50 | 7 | 350 | 20 | 7 | 140 |
| Jan.7 | 75 | 8 | 600 |  |  |  | 95 | 7.79† | 740 |
| Jan.10 |  |  |  | 20 | 7.79 | 156 | 75 | 7.79 | 584 |
| Jan.12 |  |  |  | 50 | 7.79 | 389 | 25 | 7.79 | 195 |
|  | 175 |  | 1,300 | 150 |  | 1,105 |  |  |  |

† £740 ÷ 95 (units)

(b)

*Summary Trading Account — AVCO*
*(Transaction basis)*

|  | £ | £ |
|---|---|---|
| Sales |  | 1,400 |
| Less: Purchases | 1,300 |  |
| Closing stock | (195) |  |
| Cost of goods sold |  | 1,105 |
| Gross profit |  | 295 |

## 7.2 THE DISTINCTION BETWEEN CAPITAL EXPENDITURE AND REVENUE EXPENDITURE

All expenditure incurred by a business must be accounted for as *either capital expenditure or revenue expenditure.* The basic test which is applied to distinguish between the two types of expenditure is the effect that the outlay has on the company's *long run ability to earn profits.* If it is enhanced, the expenditure is capital whereas, if the expenditure merely maintains the business's ability to operate, it is revenue. The distinction is of crucial importance because it affects how the expenditure is reported in the profit and loss account and balance sheet. Capital expenditure is recorded in the balance sheet at cost, and is subsequently charged against revenue over the period of years which benefit from using the asset. Revenue expenditure is normally charged against revenue arising during the period when the cost is incurred. The purchase of fixed assets is capital expenditure whereas the cost of acquiring or manufacturing stock for resale and the cost of running the business are revenue expenditures. It is important to classify expenditure properly as either capital or revenue, otherwise the reported balances for profit and net assets are incorrectly stated, and wrong conclusions may be reached regarding the performance and position of the firm.

### Figure 7.1.

*Effect of wrongly allocating Expenditure to Capital or Revenue.*

|  | Effect on. | |
| --- | --- | --- |
|  | *Profit.* | *Net Assets.* |
| Capital expenditure wrongly allocated to revenue | understated | understated |
| Revenue expenditure wrongly allocated to capital | overstated | overstated |

Most items of expenditure are easily classified as capital or revenue, but there are some 'grey areas' where judgement is needed to help make a proper allocation in the light of all the available facts. The main grey areas are:

*1. Stock*   The cost incurred in acquiring or manufacturing stock is a revenue expense. The gap between the purchase and sale of stock is relatively short, and most stock acquired will be re-sold by the end of the accounting year. These items are correctly debited to the trading account for that year. There will, however, be a balance of stock, unsold at the year-end, and this is carried forward in the balance sheet, as a current asset, and written off against revenue in the following accounting period.

*2. Fixed Assets*    The cost of fixed assets acquired or built by the firm itself, to form the basis for business activity, is clearly capital expenditure. Difficulties arise in connection with expenditure incidental to the acquisition of the fixed asset and expenditure on fixed assets currently in use. The following rules should be followed to achieve a proper allocation.

1.  Expenditure incurred in getting a new fixed asset ready for business use is a capital expense. This includes, for example, any transport costs, import duties and solicitors' fees. In addition, costs incurred in modifying existing premises to accommodate a new fixed asset should also be capitalised.
2.  Expenditure on an existing fixed asset which enhances its value to the business, e.g. by increasing its capacity, effectiveness or useful life, should be capitalised.
3.  Expenditure on an existing fixed asset intended to make good wear and tear and keep it in satisfactory working order is a revenue expense. It is possible that an expenditure contains both elements of repair and of improvement in which case an apportionment between capital expenditure and revenue expenditure must be made.

**Example 7.8**
Indicate for each of the following items whether it is capital or revenue expenditure:
1.  Legal expenses incurred when acquiring a new building.
2.  Giving the factory a fresh coat of paint.
3.  Repacing 200 tiles on a roof damaged by a gale.
4.  Expenditure incurred demolishing part of a wall to make room for a recently purchased machine.
5.  Replacing wooden office windows by double-glazed metal windows.
6.  Installing a system of ventilation in the factory.

**Solution.**
1.  Capital. This is part of the cost of acquiring the new asset.
2.  Revenue. This makes good wear and tear.

3.    Revenue. This merely restores the roof to its pre-gale condition.
4.    Capital. This is part of the cost of bringing the fixed asset into use.
5.    Part capital/part revenue. The new windows should be more effective in eliminating draughts and making the office sound proof.
6.    Capital. Working conditions and employee performance should improve.

*3. Advertising*   It is necessary to distinguish between expenditure designed to launch a new product (capital) and expenditure designed to maintain the level of sales by keeping the product in 'the public eye' (revenue). The former type of expenditure is likely to involve a heavy initial outlay which, if successful, will benefit the firm for a number of years. Such expenditure may be 'capitalised' and written off over the accounting periods which benefit from the sale of the new product. In the balance sheet, the amount not yet written off is reported under the heading 'deferred revenue expenditure' to emphasise the fact that special circumstances justify carrying forward a type of expenditure which is normally charged immediately against revenue.

## 7.3  DEPRECIATION METHODS
Section 6.3 of chapter 3 draws attention to the fact that depreciation is charged in the accounts to reflect the fact that the business has benefitted from using fixed assets which, as a result, have declined in value. The pattern of benefit which arises differs from one type of fixed asset to another. For example, some fixed assets produce a greater benefit in the early years of ownership, when the asset is more efficient, whereas other fixed assets make a fairly steady contribution over their entire useful life. There are a number of different methods of charging depreciation and management should chose the one which most closely reflects the pattern of benefits received.

### 7.3.1 Straight Line (Equal Instalment) Method   Under this method the difference between original cost and ultimate disposal value is spread equally over the asset's estimated useful life. This method is described and illustrated in section 6.3 of chapter 3 and has been used in all previous examples and questions requiring a

charge to be calculated. The method assumes that each accounting period benefits to an equal extent from using the fixed asset, and the annual charge is calculated on the basis of the following formula:

$$\frac{\text{Original cost} - \text{Estimated disposal value}}{\text{Estimated life}}$$

An attraction of this method is that it is easy to apply once the initial estimates have been made and, for this reason, it is widely used in Great Britain.

**Example 7.9**
On 1 January 19X1 a manufacturing company acquired a new lathe for £23,000. It is estimated to have a useful life of 4 years during which time it will produce 100,000 units of output: 50,000 units in 19X1; 10,000 units in 19X2; 10,000 units in 19X3 and 30,000 units in 19X4. The lathe is expected to be sold for £3,000 at the end of 4 years.
The annual straight-line charge is calculated as follows:

$$\text{Depreciation charge} = \frac{£23,000 - £3,000}{4}$$

$$= £5,000$$

**7.3.2 Reducing (Declining) Balance Method** This is the second most popular method. A depreciation rate is decided upon and then applied to the *net* book value (original cost less accumulated depreciation) of the asset brought forward at the beginning of each accounting period. The charge is highest in year 1 and then falls, each year, because the fixed depreciation rate is applied to a declining balance. The appropriate depreciation rate is usually given in examinations. Where it is not provided it may be calculated, as a percentage, using the following formula:

$$r = \left(1 - n\sqrt{\frac{s}{c}}\right) \times 100$$

where r is the depreciation rate, n is the expected useful life, s is the expected scrap value and c the original cost.

Applying this formula to the facts provided in Example 7.9 gives the following results:

$$r = \left( 1 - 4\sqrt{\frac{3,000}{23,000}} \right) \times 100$$
$$= 39.9\%$$

Depreciation charges, 19X1-19X4

|  | £ |
|---|---|
| Original cost.............................................. | 23,000 |
| 19X1 depreciation charge, £23,000 x 39.9%...................... | 9,177 |
| Net book value at 31 December 19X1........................... | 13,823 |
| 19X2 depreciation charge, £13,823 x 39.9%...................... | 5,515 |
| Net book value at 31 December 19X2........................... | 8,308 |
| 19X3 depreciation charge, £8,308 x 39.9%...................... | 3,315 |
| Net book value at 31 December 19X3........................... | 4,993 |
| 19X4 depreciation charge, £4,993 x 39.9%...................... | 1,993 |
| Net book value at 31 December 19X4........................... | 3,000 |

It should be noticed that the charge for 19X1 (£9,177) is over four times higher than the charge for 19X4 (£1,993). Clearly the method is appropriate only when the bulk of the benefit arises early on. An argument sometimes put forward for this method (and the sum of the digits method, see section 3.3 of this chapter) is that repair and maintenance costs normally increase as a fixed asset gets older and the reducing balance basis therefore helps to ensure that the total annual charge (depreciation + maintenance) remains steady over the asset's useful life.

**7.3.3  Sum of the Digits Method**  This method also produces larger charges in the early years, but the differences which occur are less dramatic than with the reducing balance method. Each year of the asset's life is represented by a digit, beginning with 1, and the depreciation charge for each year is calculated by applying the following formula:

$$\frac{\text{Original cost - Disposal value}}{\text{Sum of the year's digits}} \times \frac{\text{Number of years' life remaining}}{\text{at beginning of year.}}$$

Applying the formula to the facts provided in Example 7.9 gives the following results:

Depreciation charge: 19X1 $= \dfrac{£20,000}{(1+2+3+4)} \times 4 = £8,000$

$\qquad\qquad$ 19X2 $= \dfrac{£20,000}{(1+2+3+4)} \times 3 = £6,000$

$\qquad\qquad$ 19X3 $= \dfrac{£20,000}{(1+2+3+4)} \times 2 = £4,000$

$\qquad\qquad$ 19X4 $= \dfrac{£20,000}{(1+2+3+4)} \times 1 = £2,000$

**7.3.4 The Units of Service Method** This method relates the charge to the extent that the asset is used during an accounting period. For this purpose usage may be measured on the basis either of the number of units produced or the number of hours in service. The formula used to calculate the depreciation cost per unit (or hour) is as follows:

$$\dfrac{\text{Original cost} - \text{Disposal value}}{\text{Estimated number of units (hours)}}$$

Applying the formula to the facts provided in Example 7.9 produces the following results:

$$\text{Depreciation per unit} = \dfrac{£23,000 - £3,000}{100,000} = £0.20$$

Depreciation charge: 19X1 $= £0.20 \times 50,000 = £10,000$
$\qquad\qquad\quad$ 19X2 $= £0.20 \times 10,000 = £2,000$
$\qquad\qquad\quad$ 19X3 $= £0.20 \times 10,000 = £2,000$
$\qquad\qquad\quad$ 19X4 $= £0.20 \times 30,000 = £6,000$

This depreciation method is considered to be the most rational because it produces a variable charge which depends on the level of activity. The lathe is capable of producing 100,000 units, of which 50,000 are produced in 19X1. Half of the total benefit provided by the asset arises in 19X1 and half of its net cost to the business (£20,000 x 1/2) should therefore be charged against revenue arising during that year. Only the units of service method produces this result. In the following year, 19X2, when 10,000 units are produced, 1/10th of the asset's net cost, i.e. £2,000, is charged against revenue. The disadvantage of this method is the difficulty of estimating the units of service that a fixed asset will provide, and it is not widely used.

**7.3.5 Comparing the Methods** The charges made under each of the four methods are as follows:

| | 19X1 | 19X2 | 19X3 | 19X4 | Total |
|---|---|---|---|---|---|
| | £ | £ | £ | £ | £ |
| Straight line | 5,000 | 5,000 | 5,000 | 5,000 | 20,000 |
| Reducing balance | 9,177 | 5,515 | 3,315 | 1,993 | 20,000 |
| Sum of the digits | 8,000 | 6,000 | 4,000 | 2,000 | 20,000 |
| Units of service | 10,000 | 2,000 | 2,000 | 6,000 | 20,000 |

It can be seen that the pattern of charges differs a great deal depending on the method used. For example, the highest charge arises in 19X1 from using the units of service method; in 19X2 from using the sum of the digits method; in 19X3 from using the straight line method; and in 19X4 again from using the units of service method. Within particular years the difference is also marked. For example, in 19X1 the units of service method produces a charge which is twice as high as under the straight line method. Looked at another way, reported profit for 19X1 is £5,000 more if the straight line basis is used. This shows that great care should be taken when choosing the depreciation method as this can have a substantial effect on the level of reported profit. The choice is rarely easy, however, as the depreciation policy must be decided upon when the asset is acquired and management does not know, at that stage, the precise benefit that will arise in each future accounting period. The decision is therefore to some extent arbitrary and, if an error is made, profit will be either under-or over-stated.

**7.3.6 Estimation Errors** In addition to the difficulty of selecting the most appropriate method, there is the problem of making accurate estimates of the useful life of the fixed asset, measured in terms of years or output, and its disposal value at the end of that period. Care should be exercised when making these estimates as errors produce an incorrect charge for depreciation and a consequent understatement or overstatement of profit.

**Example 7.10**

(a) A machine is purchased for £60,000 on 1 January 19X1. It is estimated that the machine will last for 5 years and then have a zero disposal value . Management believes that each accounting period will benefit equally from the use of the machine and the straight line method of depreciation is therefore considered appropriate.

*Required:*
Calculate the depreciation charge to be made each year, 19X1-19X5.

**Solution.**
$$\text{Depreciation charge} = \frac{£60,000}{5} = £12,000$$

(b) Assuming it turns out that all management's estimates are correct, except that it totally misjudges the second hand demand for the machine which eventually sells for £20,000.

*Required:*
Calculate the depreciation charge which would have been made each year if the disposal value had been accurately estimated.

**Solution.**
$$\text{Depreciation charge} = \frac{£60,000 - £20,000}{5} = £8,000$$

Because the disposal value was wrongly estimated, the annual charge is overstated and profit is understated by £4,000 during each of the five years of ownership. This is balanced by crediting £20,000 to the profit and loss account when the fixed asset, by this time completely written off, is sold for that figure.

## 7.4  GOODWILL

Business assets may be classified as either tangible or intangible. Tangible assets possess a physical existence; the most common examples are stocks and fixed assets, considered earlier in this chapter. Intangible assets possess no physical existence but they are valuable because they help the firm to earn a profit. The most common example of an intangible asset is goodwill which was defined as follows by Lord MacNaughton in CIR v Muller (1901):

> *It is the benefit and advantage of the good name, reputation and connection of a business. It is the attractive force which brings in custom. It is the one thing which distinguishes an old established business from a new business at its first start*

Goodwill is therefore built up gradually over the years and, when a businessman 'sells up', he expects the buyer to pay a price which covers not only the tangible assets but also goodwill. In these circumstances it is useful to value goodwill as a basis for negotiations. The following are two examples of the methods which may be used.

*Weighted average profits basis* Goodwill may be valued as a multiple of past profits. For this purpose a number of years' profits may be averaged and 'weights' attached to the profits arising each year.

### Example 7.11
The profits of a partnership for the last 3 years are as follows: 19X1, £20,000; 19X2, £26,000 and 19X3, £31,000.

*Required:*
Calculate goodwill on the basis of 1.5 times the weighted average profits of the last three years, using weights of 3 for the most recent year, 2 for the previous year and 1 for the earliest year.

### Solution.
Weighted average profits are calculated as follows:

| Year | Weight | Profits £ | Total £ |
|------|--------|-----------|---------|
| 19X1 | 1 | 20,000 | 20,000 |
| 19X2 | 2 | 26,000 | 52,000 |
| 19X3 | 3 | 31,000 | 93,000 |
| | 6 | | 165,000 |

$$\text{Weighted average} = \frac{£165,000}{6} = £27,500$$

Goodwill = £27,500 x 1.5 = £41,250.

*Super profit basis* This method seeks to identify the 'extra' profit earned by the firm because of the existance of good connections. It then values goodwill on the basis of this surplus.

### Example 7.12
Leake Ltd has earned profits averaging £20,000 per annum in recent years. It is estimated that £17,000 represents a reasonable return on the existing tangible assets.

| | £ |
|------|-----|
| Actual profit.................. | 20,000 |
| Normal profit.................. | 17,000 |
| Super profit.................. | 3,000 |

The amount a buyer is willing to pay for the 'super profit' depends on what is considered a reasonable rate of return in this line of business. If a return of 20% is considered reasonable, goodwill is worth:

$$\text{Goodwill} = £3,000 \times \frac{100}{20} = £15,000$$

i.e. At a 20% rate of interest, £15,000 must be invested to give an annual return of £3,000.

Each of the above approaches enables goodwill to be valued, but it does not necessarily follow that a buyer will be willing to pay either of these amounts or that the seller will accept them. The price actually paid for goodwill depends on negotiation between these two parties, and the main use of the above calculations is that they produce measures of value which can be referred to during discussions.

In examinations the total price paid for the business is often given, and the students are able to calculate goodwill by subtracting the value of tangible assets from this figure.

## Example 7.13

Ted Anthony who had been in business for many years decided to retire and sold his business assets, other than cash and debtors, to William Jones for £30,000. At the date of sale Anthony's tangible assets consisted of premises worth £20,000, machinery worth £3,500 and stocks valued at £2,500.

*Required:*
Calculate goodwill arising on the sale of the business.

## Solution.

|  | £ | £ |
|---|---|---|
| Purchase price................ |  | 30,000 |
| Less: Tangible assets: |  |  |
| Premises................ | 20,000 |  |
| Machinery.............. | 3,500 |  |
| Stock.................. | 2,500 | 26,000 |
| Goodwill..................... |  | 4,000 |

The total value of the tangible assets is £26,000, and we can therefore conclude that William Jones was willing to pay an extra £4,000 to cover the goodwill built up by Ted Anthony over the years.

In the above example, goodwill is the 'balancing' figure which results from comparing the agreed purchase price with the total value of the tangible assets acquired. The price paid for goodwill is initially recorded in the books of the acquiring company at cost, but goodwill does not last forever, e.g. the range of customers supplied gradually changes and those 'taken over' with the business eventually leave. Goodwill must therefore be written off either immediately against reserves, or gradually against profits over its estimated useful life of the asset. The latter approach is theoretically more sound as it complies with the accruals concept by attempting to match costs with revenues. Immediate write off is often the option selected, however, because it is favoured by the accounting profession, and because of the great difficulty of estimating the likely future life of this particular asset.

## 7.5 ACCOUNTING CONCEPTS
Accounting records and statements are based on a number of assumptions, called accounting concepts. The ten considered most important are examined below. The treatment is brief in those cases where the concept has already been discussed in an earlier chapter.

### 7.5.1 Entity Concept
This fixes the boundary for the financial affairs contained in an accounting statement and was examined in section 2 of chapter 1. The boundary is often the business, but it may be a smaller or even a larger unit. For instance, a business may be split into a number of departments, each of which is treated as a separate entity for the purpose of preparing accounting statements for management (see section 2 of chapter 11). At the other extreme, a number of companies may be regarded as a single entity for accounting purposes. This occurs where a company owns the shares of one or more other companies. The connected companies together form a 'group', and their separate accounts are 'consolidated' for the purpose of reporting to shareholders. This topic is examined in Stage 2 'Accountancy' and is discussed in *Accountancy for Banking Students,* chapter 5.

**7.5.2   Money Measurement Concept**   A business asset is reported in the balance sheet only if its value can be measured, in money terms, with a reasonable degree of precision. This concept was discussed in section 10.1 of chapter 1. A good example of the application of this concept concerns the accounting treatment of goodwill. We saw, in section 4 of this chapter, that goodwill consists of the reputation and business connections built up over a period of time. Most firms enjoy an element of goodwill, but its value continuously fluctuates, and is therefore difficult to quantify with any degree of precision. For this reason the existence of goodwill is usually acknowledged by an entry in the accounts *only* when its value is proved by a market transaction involving its purchase and sale.

**7.5.3   Matching Concept**   The accountant measures profit for a period of time, such as a year, by comparing or 'matching' revenue and expenditure identified with that period. The first step is to identify revenues and the second step is to deduct the expenditures incurred in producing the revenues. This concept was examined in section 2 of chapter 3. It should be noted that many of the concepts are closely inter-related. For example, the matching concept is put into effect by applying the realisation concept and the accruals concept. These are considered next.

**7.5.4   Realisation Concept**   Revenue is assumed to be earned when a sale takes place and a legally enforceable claim arises against the customer. The effect of this rule is that stock usually remains in the books at cost until the sale takes place, at which stage a profit arises or a loss is incurred. This concept was discussed in section 5 of chapter 3.

**7.5.5   The Accruals Concept**   Costs are matched against revenues when the benefit of the expenditure is received rather than when the cash payment is made. Where the benefit is received *before* the payment is made, the amount owed is treated as a *liability* in the balance sheet. Where the benefit is received *after* the payment is made, the amount paid is treated as an *asset* in the balance sheet, and charged against revenues arising during whichever future accounting period benefits from the payments. This concept was examined in section 6 of chapter 3.

**7.5.6 Historical Cost Concept**   Assets are initially recorded at the price paid to the supplier. In certain circumstances further costs may be added. For example, in the case of a manufacturing concern a proportion of the production costs should be added to the cost of raw materials to arrive at the cost of finished goods (see section 1.2 of this chapter). In the case of fixed assets their recorded cost includes not only the price paid to the supplier but also all incidental costs incurred to make the item ready for use (see section 2 of this chapter). A major advantage of this concept is that the accounting records are based on objective facts. A disadvantage of using historical cost is that, during a period of rising prices, the reported figures may significantly understate the asset's true value to the business. It is for this reason that some companies periodically revalue their fixed assets and/or publish supplementary accounts designed to take account of the effects of inflation (see further discussion in section 12 of chapter 10).

**7.5.7 Going Concern Concept**   This assumes that the business is a permanent venture and will not be wound up in the foreseeable future. Many fixed assets have low resale values e.g. machinery might cost many thousands of pounds but, because it is specially designed for a particular business, there may be no possibility of selling it other than as scrap metal. The going concern concept allows accountants to ignore this low resale value and instead spread the cost of an asset over the accounting periods which benefit from its use. The assumption that the business will continue indefinitely as a going concern is, however, in certain circumstances false and must be dropped. For example, if a company is about to be liquidated, forecasts of the amounts likely to be received by various providers of finance should be based on estimates of what the business assets are expected to realise in the market rather than their historical book value.

**7.5.8 Consistency Concept**   The same valuation methods should be used each year when preparing accounting statements. We have seen that there exist a number of methods for valuing fixed assets and stocks. There are arguments in favour and against most of them and, to some extent, an arbitrary choice must be made. The effect on reported profit is unlikely to be significant, however, provided similar procedures are adopted each year. For example, when prices are rising the FIFO method of matching stock purchased with stock sold produces a higher figure for stock than the LIFO method, but it does not necessarily produce a higher profit figure. Businesses have both opening and closing stock and use of the FIFO approach produces a higher figure for stock at both dates.

## Example 7.14

The following information is provided for one of the products traded in by Ridgeway Ltd.

|  | £ |
|---|---|
| Opening stock, 100 units valued as follows: | |
| LIFO basis, £5 per unit x 100............... | 500 |
| FIFO basis, £8 per unit x 100............... | 800 |
| Purchases during January 19X1, 300 units at £8.............. | 2,400 |
| Sales, 300 units at £11.................................. | 3,300 |

*Required:*
(a) Valuations of stock using (i) LIFO and (ii) FIFO.
(b) Trading account for January 19X1 using (i) LIFO and (ii) FIFO.

## Solution.

(a)  Valuation of closing stock:
  Opening stock is 100 units and, as the same number of items are purchased as are sold, closing stock is also 100 units, although these will almost certainly be different items from those owned at the beginning of the month.
(i)  LIFO (this approach assumes that the 300 items sold are the 300 items purchased during January), 100 × £5 = £500
(ii)  FIFO (this approach assumes that the 300 items sold includes the opening stock of 100 units), 100 × £8 = £800

(b)

### Trading Account, January 19X1

|  | (i)LIFO | | (ii)FIFO | |
|---|---|---|---|---|
|  | £ | £ | £ | £ |
| Sales |  | 3,300 |  | 3,300 |
| Less: Opening stock | 500 | | 800 | |
| Purchases | 2,400 | | 2,400 | |
| Closing stock | (500) | | (800) | |
| Cost of goods sold |  | 2,400 |  | 2,400 |
| Gross profit |  | 900 |  | 900 |

The higher opening and closing valuations, on the FIFO basis, cancel out, and gross profit is unaffected by the valuation method adopted. It should be noted, however, that the balance sheet figure for stocks and, therefore, gross assets and net assets are higher if FIFO is used. It should also be noted that reported profit *does vary* when there are *changes* in the level of stock because, in these circumstances, the opening and closing balances no longer cancel out. However, the difference is unlikely to be large unless the change in the level of stock is substantial, such as occurs when new business operations commence.

The level of reported profit can be significantly inflated or deflated if a company changes from one method to another.

**Example 7.15**
Assume the same facts as for example 7.14, except that LIFO is used at the beginning of the year and FIFO at the end.

*Required:*
The trading account for January 19X1.

**Solution.**

*Trading Account, January 19X1.*

|  |  | £ | £ |
|---|---|---:|---:|
| Sales |  |  | 3,300 |
| Less: | Opening stock (LIFO) | 500 |  |
|  | Purchases | 2,400 |  |
|  | Closing stock (FIFO) | (800) |  |
|  | Cost of goods sold |  | 2,100 |
| Gross profit |  |  | 1,200 |

Gross profit is £1,200 in Example 7.15 as compared with £900 in Example 7.14. Profit is therefore inflated by £300 as the result of switching from one valuation method to another and using the FIFO closing stock figure, £800, instead of the LIFO closing stock figure, £500. As the result of the change, reported profits are greater than actual profits and wrong conclusions may be reached concerning the performance of Ridgeway Ltd. It is therefore important for valuation procedures to be consistently applied so that reported results fairly reflect performance during the year, and valid comparisons can be made with results achieved in previous accounting periods.

While consistency is a fundamental accounting concept, it does not mean that methods, once adopted, should never be changed, but sound and convincing arguments must be put forward to justify departures from existing practice. The essential test is whether management can show that the new procedures result in a fairer presentation of the financial performance and position of the concern. If it is decided that a change should be made to a previously accepted method of valuation, the impact on comparability between two sets of figures must be noted and, wherever possible, also quantified, so that it can be taken into account when measuring performance. For example, when a firm switches from LIFO to the far more popular FIFO, relevant balances for the previous year, which are also reported, must be recomputed, using FIFO, so that a proper assessment of comparative performance can be made.

It must be emphasised that inconsistent accounting methods can have a marked effect on the information contained in accounting statements. The changes are not always explained as clearly as they should be, and the banker must scrutinise the accounts vigilantly to ensure that distorted financial information does not cause him to make a wrong investment decision.

**7.5.9 Prudence Concept** The prudence concept (sometimes called the concept of conservatism) requires the accountant to make full provision for all expected losses and not to anticipate revenues until they are realised. A good example of how this concept affects accounting practice is the basic rule that stock should be valued at the lower of cost and net realisable value (NRV). Where NRV is above cost, the profit likely to arise in the near future is ignored and stock remains in the accounts at the lower figure until the sale occurs, i.e. revenue is not anticipated. On the other hand, where NRV is below cost, stock must be immediately re-stated at the lower figure so that full provision is made for the likely future loss.

Approval of a prudent approach to profit measurement is based on the potential dangers of an over-optimistic calculation which may be used as the basis for an excessive withdrawal of funds, by ownership, which deprives the concern of much needed resources. Another possible pitfall is that an attractive presentation of the current position, not justified by the underlying facts, may cause management wrongly to expand the level of operations and, when this happens, heavy losses can result. New projects often involve a substantial commitment of resources, the bulk of which is tied up in fixed assets. The only way that the firm is likely to get its money back is by using these assets to produce and sell goods at a profit. Caution is therefore highly desirable when management is considering whether to make an investment, and any accounting statement used to help reach this decision should be prepared on a prudent basis. This may mean that, occasionally, good opportunities are missed, but this will not happen often, and the likely loss from an ill-conceived investment will be many times greater than the profit possibly forgone.

It is important, however, not to take the prudence concept too far. Where there are a number of likely outcomes, it is usually wise to choose the lower figure, but profit should not be deliberately under-stated. Accounting statements are used as the basis for decision-making, and they should contain realistic not excessively pessimistic financial information. Understatement can be just as misleading as overstatement and, although the potential loss from the misallocation of resources which may result is less, it can be avoided by preparers of accounting reports exercising a reasonable level of caution.

**7.5.10 Materiality** Accounting statements should contain only those financial facts which are material, or relevant, to the decision being taken by the recipient of the report. It is therefore important for the accountant to be familiar with the user's requirement so that he can decide which information should be included and excluded. For example, if an accounting statement is prepared to help management assess which departments are most successful, it is clearly important for the report to show the profits earned by each of them. This means identifying the revenues and expenditures which relate to each department, but unnecessary detail is omitted. For example, a manager is interested in knowing the individual amounts expended on materials, wages, power, depreciation etc, but not on Christmas gratuities, the ingredients for morning coffee and paper towels. Trivial items are therefore grouped together under the heading 'sundry expenses'. For similar reasons balance sheets contain values for the various main categories of assets and liabilities but do not give figures for each item of plant, stock etc.

Accounting statements prepared for shareholders of limited companies contain even less detail. This is partly because such information is of little interest to them. It is management's job to decide how to allocate resources between various investment opportunities, while the shareholder is primarily interested in assessing whether the overall performance is satisfactory. It is therefore considered desirable to keep to a minimum detailed facts which may be difficult to assimilate, and instead concentrate on the broad overall pattern of developments. It must be admitted that the sophisticated institutional investor would welcome far more detail than is provided in the published accounts, but there is a natural reluctance to publish sensitive material which could be of use to competitors. The banker is in a different position. Although he is an external user of accounting statements, confidential information can be made available to him, on an individual basis, and is normally insisted upon as one of the pre-conditions for a loan decision.

There is another aspect of materiality, and this concerns the amount of detail which the accountant goes into when measuring profit. A good example is the use of FIFO and LIFO instead of attempting to match individual purchases with sales. Another example is the failure of the accountant to distinguish between capital and revenue expenditure where the amount spent on a fixed asset is small. For example, minor items of office equipment such as staplers and punches last for a number of years, but it is not usually considered worthwhile to capitalise and depreciate them systematically over their expected useful life. Instead they are written off immediately against revenue. A detailed treatment is justified only if the extra cost involved produces a significant improvement in the quality of the information contained in accounting statements. When applying this test, it must be remembered that, because of the need for estimates to be made and judgement to be exercised, the reported profit figure is at best an approximation and is unlikely to be improved by making precise adjustments for trivial items.

## 7.6 QUESTIONS.

### Question 7.1

Give the basic rule for valuing stock. Apply this rule to the facts provided below and calculate the total value of stock to be included in the accounts.

| Product | Cost | Net Realisable Value |
|---------|------|----------------------|
|         | £    | £                    |
| A       | 2,400 | 2,760 |
| B       | 1,290 | 740 |
| C       | 3,680 | 750 |
| D       | 2,950 | 4,760 |
| E       | 6,280 | 9,730 |

## Question 7.2

What do you understand by the terms perpetual inventory and periodic stock take? In the case of a trader, how is the figure for cost of goods sold obtained under each of these systems?

## Question 7.3

Seconds Ltd. started trading on 1 January and during that month undertook the following transactions in respect of product Alpha:

| Date-Jan | Purchases Units | Cost per Unit | Sales Units | Price per Unit |
|----------|-----------------|---------------|-------------|----------------|
|          |                 | £             |             | £              |
| 8        | 100             | 20            | —           | —              |
| 13       | 60              | 25            | —           | —              |
| 14       | —               | —             | 125         | 40             |
| 17       | 75              | 30            | —           | —              |
| 22       | —               | —             | 30          | 42             |

*Required:*

Using the 'periodic basis' for matching purchases with sales, calculations of the figures for (a) closing stock, (b) cost of goods sold, and (c) gross profit on each of the following bases:
  (i)   FIFO
  (ii)  LIFO
  (iii) AVCO
Calculations to the nearest £.

## Question 7.4

Stoval Ltd started to trade on 1 January 19X1. Its purchases of trading stock, at cost, during the first three years of business were:

|        | £ |
|--------|---|
| 19X1........................ | 240,000 |
| 19X2........................ | 252,000 |
| 19X3........................ | 324,000 |

The values of stock at 31 December, under different valuation methods, were:

| 31 December | LIFO cost | FIFO cost | Lower of FIFO cost and Net Realisable value |
|---|---|---|---|
| 19X1 | £ 96,480 | £ 96,000 | £ 88,800 |
| 19X2 | £ 87,360 | £ 86,400 | £ 81,600 |
| 19X3 | £100,320 | £105,600 | £105,600 |

*Required:*
(a) Assuming that in any one year prices moved either up or down, but not both in the same year:
    (i)   Did prices go up or down in 19X1?
    (ii)  Did prices go up or down in 19X3?
(b) Which stock valuation method would show the highest profit for 19X1?
(c) Which stock valuation method applied to opening and closing stock would show the highest profit for 19X3?
(d) Which stock valuation method would show the lowest profit for all three years combined?

## Question 7.5
(a) How would you distinguish between capital and revenue expenditure and why is it important to make a correct allocation?
(b) State, with reasons, in which of the two caterories you would place the following items:
    (i)      Replacement of the blade on a cutting machine which was damaged as the result of using poor quality raw material inputs.
    (ii)     A feeding device costing £1,000 which is fixed to a machine so as to enable a 20% increase in throughput each hour.
    (iii)    The cost of transporting, to the factory, a new machine supplied by a Japanese company.
    (iv)    Second hand plant purchased at a cost of £1,500.
    (v)     Repairs to the plant mentioned in (iv) above before it is ready for use £300.

## Question 7.6
Simon is a surveyor who purchases old properties in poor condition. He incurs expenditure on improving these properties which he then resells. His balance sheet at 31 December 19X2 was as follows:

|  | £ |  | £ |
|---|---|---|---|
| Capital.......... | 79,000 | Properties on hand (including expenses on purchase): |  |
|  |  | 1..................... | 30,250 |
|  |  | 2..................... | 29,350 |
|  |  | Bank Balance................. | 19,400 |
|  | 79,000 |  | 79,000 |

## During 19X3 he bought three more properties:

|  | Cost | Legal expenses borne by Simon | Cost of improvement |
|---|---|---|---|
|  | £ | £ | £ |
| 3 | 36,250 | 1,000 | 260 |
| 4 | 24,000 | 750 | 1,000 |
| 5 | 25,000 | 800 | 520 |

## and sold the following three properties:

|  | Sale price | Legal expenses borne by Simon |
|---|---|---|
|  | £ | £ |
| 1 | 34,000 | 400 |
| 3 | 42,500 | 500 |
| 4 | 31,250 | 350 |

General expenses incurred and paid during 19X3 amounted to £2,500.

*Required:*
(a)  Simon's bank account for 19X3.
(b)  A profit and loss account for the year 19X3 covering Simon's property deals and a balance sheet at 31 December 19X3.

*Notes:*
1.  Cash due from the sale of property 4 was not received until 5 January 19X4.
2.  There were no other transactions during the year and all receipts and payments were by cheque.

## Question 7.7
A machine was purchased on 1 January 19X1 for £20,000. It is estimated to be operational for 76,000 hours over a five year working life, at the end of which it will possess a residual value of £1,000. The number of hours of operation is estimated to be 20,000

hours per annum for the first three years and 8,000 per annum thereafter.

*Required:*
(a) Calculate the depreciation charge for each year and the net book value of the fixed asset at the end of each year using:
   (i) The straight line method.
   (ii) The units of service method.
   (iii) The reducing balance method, applying a depreciation rate of 45%.
(b) Indicate which depreciation method would produce the highest reported profit for each of the years 19X1-X5, and for the entire 5 year period.

## Question 7.8
Buy Ltd paid Mr Sale £120,000, cash, to acquire his business, Sale & Co., as a going concern on 1 January 19X1. The assets taken over were considered to be worth the following amounts:

|  | £ |
| --- | --- |
| Fixed assets.................... | 71,500 |
| Stock........................ | 20,000 |
| Debtors...................... | 10,000 |

In addition, Buy Ltd assumed responsibility for paying Sale & Co's. outstanding creditors which amounted to £5,000. The policy of Buy Ltd is to write off goodwill over a 5 year period.

*Required:*
(a) Calculate the goodwill arising on the acquision of Sale & Co.
(b) Show how goodwill will appear in the balance sheet of Buy Ltd as at 31 December 19X1.

## Question 7.9
Where accounts are prepared in accordance with the *accruals concept,* cash receipts and payments may precede, coincide with, or follow the period in which revenues and expenses are recognized. Give two examples of each of the following:
(a) A cash receipt that precedes the period in which revenue is recognised.
(b) A cash receipt that coincides with the period in which revenue is recognised.

(c) A cash receipt that follows the period in which revenue is recognised.
(d) A cash payment that precedes the period in which expense is recognised.
(e) A cash payment that coincides with the period in which expense is recognised.
(f) A cash payment that follows the period in which expense is recognised.

**Question 7.10**
The summarised trading account of Change Ltd for 19X1 contained the following information:

*Trading Account for 19X1*

|  | £ | £ |
|---|---:|---:|
| Sales | | 100,000 |
| Less: Opening stock | 7,000 | |
| Purchases | 80,000 | |
| Closing stock | (11,000) | |
| Cost of goods sold | | 76,000 |
| Gross profit | | 24,000 |

Opening stock is valued at marginal cost, but the directors have now decided that total cost is more suitable, and this basis was used for the purpose of valuing closing stock. The value of opening stock, on the total cost basis, is found to be £10,000.

*Required:*
(a) Prepare a revised trading account for Change Ltd. complying with the consistency concept.
(b) Indicate the effect of the revision on the *net* profit figure reported by Change Ltd for 19X1.

# CHAPTER 8

# Some Specialised Accounting Statements

## 8.1 INTRODUCTION

The techniques of information collection and analysis described so far have related mainly to:
(a) Trading concerns which buy and sell goods without further processing;
(b) Transactions where the amount due is settled in one payment, either immediately or in the near future; and
(c) The 'going' concern.

There are many instances when the activities of a business or the information requirements of ownership, management or other interested parties, such as bankers, do not fit into this framework. For example:
(a) Many businesses are concerned with manufacturing. They buy raw materials and other supplies and spend further sums to process them into finished goods. The additional accounting requirements which these events give rise to are considered in section 2 of this chapter.
(b) Transactions are sometimes entered into on terms which involve the receipt of the total sum due in a number of instalments spread over a fairly long period of time; this occurs especially in the retail trade. The accounting consequences of such transactions are considered in section 3 of this chapter.
(c) Businesses are themselves sometimes the subjects of purchase and sale or are dissolved. This aspect of activity is dealt with in section 4 of this chapter.

The system of double entry book keeping, described in chapter 4, is extremely flexible and can be extended to meet not only the circumstances described above, but also many others which may arise. However, extensions of the system often introduce complications of data accumulation, recording and interpretation, and the cost of these additional impositions should be weighed against the benefits derived from the possession of additional information to decide whether the extra effort is justified. Finally, in section 5 of this chapter, consideration is given to the steps which must be taken to identify losses of stock and cash when the basic records are lost or are considered unreliable.

## 8.2   THE MANUFACTURING ACCOUNT

Where a company manufactures the product in which it trades, the cost of the goods produced is found by combining all the maufacturing costs in a Manufacturing Account. The total cost of completed items is then transferred to the Trading Account, where it takes the place of purchases and is adjusted for the opening and closing stocks of finished goods to calculate the cost of goods sold.

Only factory costs must be included in the Manufacturing Account, and the analysis of costs carried out in the day books must be designed to produce the necessary figures. Separate accounts are opened in the ledger to record the individual costs on the basis of the day book analysis. In due course the various revenues and expenses of the concern are summarised in the trial balance which is then examined to determine which relate to manufacturing; these are transferred to the manufacturing account. Typical manufacturing costs are raw materials and depreciation of plant, and these can be identified directly with the production process. However, in some cases it is not possible to relate a cost entirely to one function, for example, a single rent payment may be made for premises which contain a factory, warehouse, transport depot and offices. When this occurs, the total cost recorded in the trial balance may be apportioned, that is, the proportion which relates to the factory is shown in the manufacturing account and the remainder in the profit and loss account. Such apportionments should be made on a rational basis, for example, rent can be divided on the basis of the area occupied by each section. (The usefulness and limitations of apportionments are discussed in section 3.2 of chapter 11).

The costs entered in the manufacturing account should be divided between prime costs and production overhead costs. Prime costs are the materials and labour used directly in the production process; they vary with the level of production and would not be incurred at all if output fell to zero. Overhead costs are those which do not usually vary with the rate of production, for example, the rent must be paid whether the factory is producing very little or operating at full capacity. (The importance of the behaviour of costs in response to changes in output is discussed in section 4 of chapter 11) The sum of the prime costs and overhead costs is the total production cost, or factory cost, of the output.

To determine the cost of raw materials consumed, the value of purchases during a period must be adjusted by the opening and closing stocks by applying the formula:

$$\text{Opening stock of raw materials} + \text{Purchases} - \text{Closing stock of raw materials} = \text{Cost of materials consumed}$$

There may also be stocks of 'Work in Progress', that is, units of output which are partly completed at the accounting date; these are valued and used to adjust the total factory cost to give the cost of completed production. The adjustment is made by applying the formula:

$$\text{Opening work in progress} + \text{Total factory cost} - \text{Closing work in progress} = \text{Cost of completed items}$$

Work in progress is carried forward to the next period, when further costs are incurred to complete the items involved and make them ready for sale; work in progress appears in the balance sheet as part of the stock included in Current Assets.

## Example 8.1

The following balances were among those extracted from the books of Worker, a manufacturing business, on 31 December 19X4:

|  | Debit £ | Credit £ |
|---|---|---|
| Sales | | 270,000 |
| Production wages | 50,000 | |
| Purchase of raw materials | 100,000 | |
| Depreciation of manufacturing equipment in 19X4 | 10,000 | |
| Production overhead expenses | 7,500 | |
| Rent | 9,000 | |
| Depreciation of office equipment in 19X4 | 2,000 | |
| Salaries of salesmen | 16,000 | |
| Delivery costs | 12,000 | |
| Advertising costs | 6,000 | |
| General administration expenses | 22,000 | |
| Stocks at 1 January: Raw materials | 15,000 | |
| Work in progress | 1,500 | |
| Finished goods | 20,000 | |

*Notes:*
1. Stocks at 31 December were:                      £
   Raw materials....................      12,500
   Work in progress.................       2,500
   Finished goods...................      27,000
2. Two thirds of the rent charge relates to the factory.

## *Required:*
## Prepare the Manufacturing, Trading and Profit and Loss Accounts of Worker for 19X4.

**Solution.**   *Manufacturing, Trading and Profit and Loss Account of Worker for 19X4*

|  | £ | £ |
|---|---:|---:|
| Stock of raw materials 1 January.................... | 15,000 | |
| Purchases of raw materials......................... | 100,000 | |
| Less: Stock of raw materials 31 December............. | (12,500) | |
| | | |
| Raw materials consumed......................... | 102,500 | |
| Production wages.............................. | 50,000 | |
| | | |
| PRIME COST................................. | 152,500 | |
| Production overhead costs: | | |
| Depreciation................................ | 10,000 | |
| Expenses.................................... | 7,500 | |
| Rent........................................ | 6,000 | |
| | | |
| TOTAL FACTORY COST....................... | 176,000 | |
| Work in progress 1 January....................... | 1,500 | |
| Less: Work in progress 31 December................ | (2,500) | |
| | | |
| COST OF COMPLETED ITEMS TRANSFERRED | | |
| TO TRADING ACCOUNT....................... | 175,000 | |
| | | |
| Sales........................................... | | 270,000 |
| Stock of finished goods 1 January.................. | 20,000 | |
| Transferred from production...................... | 175,000 | |
| | | |
| | 195,000 | |
| Less: Stock of finished goods 31 December ............ | (27,000) | |
| Cost of goods sold............................... | | 168,000 |
| | | |
| GROSS PROFIT................................ | | 102,000 |
| Rent........................................... | 3,000 | |
| Depreciation of office equipment.................... | 2,000 | |
| Salesmens' salaries............................. | 16,000 | |
| Delivery costs.................................. | 12,000 | |
| Advertising.................................... | 6,000 | |
| General administration.......................... | 22,000 | |
| | | |
| | | 61,000 |
| | | |
| NET PROFIT................................. | | 41,000 |

The manufacturing account is used by management because it shows how much it has cost to produce the goods sold during a period. It enables management to compare individual elements of cost with the results of previous periods for control purposes. Also, the total cost of production can be compared with the cost of purchasing similar completed products to give an indication of the efficiency of the manufacturing section. If finished goods can be purchased elsewhere at a total cost lower than that of internal manufacture, then the cessation of manufacturing should be investigated and the possibility of simply buying the completed product for resale examined. Alternatively, such comparisons may give an incentive to achieve improved levels of productivity to match the costs of outside suppliers. On the other hand, a comparison with outside costs might reveal that additional profit is made by producing the goods internally. Management may wish to identify separately the manufacturing profit, or loss, by making the transfer from the manufacturing account to the trading account at the market value for which similar finished goods could be purchased. The manufacturing profit or loss is then transferred to the profit and loss account where it is combined with the gross profit on trading.

**8.2.1 Provision for Unrealised Profit on Manufacture** The technique of making transfers at other than historical cost can be extended. For example, a company may make sub-assemblies for incorporation into a finished product; these may be charged to production at 'outside' prices to allow the performance of the various departments to be assessed. This process may be illustrated by reference to a car manufacturer which produces its own gear boxes; the cost of these can be compared with that of those purchased complete from an outside supplier; the market price is used for transfers from the gear box department to the main car assembly section to show the profit or loss on internal production. The greater the number of separate departments which it is desired to monitor, then the more detailed the analysis of costs has to be. The result is useful information for management, but a problem arises when preparing final accounts for external use. For this purpose, the realisation concept (see section 5 of chapter 3) allows profit to be recognised only when a sale takes place, and this means that unsold stock must be valued at cost. Where transfers of stock have been made within the firm at a value in excess of cost, an adjustment must be made to remove any unrealised profit at the year end. This is done by creating a provision for unrealised profit which is set off against the stock value reported in the balance sheet. As was the case with the provision for doubtful debts (see section 7 of chapter 6), once a provision has been created it is only necessary to adjust its value each year with one of the following entries:

|  | Debit | Credit | With |
|---|---|---|---|
| EITHER: | Profit and Loss Account | Provision for Un- realised Profit | An increase in the provision |
| OR: | Provision for Un- realised Profit | Profit and Loss Account | A decrease in the provision |

**Example 8.2**

Doer Ltd was established on 1 January 19X8. The summarised Trading and Profit and Loss Accounts at historical cost for the first year of operations to 31 December 19X8 are:

|  | £ | £ |
|---|---:|---:|
| Cost of Manufacture: Prime..................... |  | 150,000 |
| Overheads................... |  | 75,000 |
| Factory cost of completed items................... |  | 225,000 |
| Sales......................................... |  | 375,000 |
| Transfer from Manufacturing Account.............. | 225,000 |  |
| *Less*: Closing stock of finished goods |  |  |
| at cost.................................. | (50,000) |  |
| Cost of goods sold.............................. |  | 175,000 |
| Gross profit.................................... |  | 200,000 |
| All other costs................................. |  | 150,000 |
| Net Profit...................................... |  | 50,000 |

The company's management wishes to know the profit on manufacturing. It discovers that it could have purchased a similar product at a price 10% greater than its own cost of manufacture. Prices were stable throughout the period, and there was no work in progress at the accounting date.

*Required:*
  (a)  Prepare the Manufacturing, Trading and Profit and Loss Accounts of Doer Ltd for the year to 31 December 19X8, making the transfer from the manufacturing account at cost plus 10%.
  (b)  Show the entry in the balance sheet at 31 December 19X8 for the stock of finished goods.

*Note:* A provision should be made, in the Profit and Loss Account, for the unrealised profit on unsold stock.

## Solution.

(a)

| | | £ | £ |
|---|---|---:|---:|
| Costs of Manufacture: | Prime.................. | | 150,000 |
| | Overhead.............. | | 75,000 |
| Factory cost of completed items................. | | | 225,000 |
| Profit on manufacturing....................... | | | 22,500 |
| Transfer to Trading Account................... | | | 247,500 |
| Sales....................................... | | | 375,000 |
| Transfer from Manufacturing Account........... | | 247,500 | |
| less: Stock at 31 December at | | | |
| transfer price (cost + 10%).............. | | (55,000) | |
| Transfer price of goods sold................... | | | 192,500 |
| Gross profit on trading....................... | | | 182,500 |
| Profit on manufacturing...................... | | | 22,500 |
| | | | 205,000 |
| less: All other costs......................... | | 150,000 | |
| Provision for unrealised profit........... | | 5,000 | |
| | | | 155,000 |
| Net Profit.................................. | | | 50,000 |

(b)

### Balance Sheet Extract

| | £ |
|---|---:|
| Stock of finished goods...... | 55,000 |
| less: Provision for unrealised | |
| profit.................... | 5,000 |
| | 50,000 |

*Notes*

1. The identification of the manufacturing profit results in the following double entry: a debit to the manufacturing account and a credit to the profit and loss account of £22,500.
2. The revised accounts show that the company makes £22,500 profit by manufacturing its own product, and £182,500 profit from trading.
3. The value of net profit, after providing for an unrealised profit on manufacture, remains unchanged.

Readers should now attempt Question 8.1 at the end of this chapter which combines the various aspects of the Manufacturing

Account dealt with in this section. Note that the presentation of the Profit and Loss Account is improved if similar items are grouped together under such headings as 'Finance Costs' and 'Selling Costs' and their sub-totals calculated.

## 8.3  INSTALMENT CREDIT AND HIRE PURCHASE

The application of the Realisation Concept (explained in section 5 of chapter 3) means that profit is recognised at the point of sale, and this rule applies even in the case of credit sales where the goods are exchanged for debts to be settled in the near future. There are some circumstances where the strict application of this rule is not, however, believed to portray fairly the underlying economic facts, such as, when a sale is made under a hire purchase or instalment credit agreement whereby the debt is settled by a number of payments spread over a long period of time. It is possible to determine the point of sale for such transactions in strictly legal terms: in the case of hire purchase it is at the time of the last instalment; in the case of instalment credit, the sale is deemed to take place at the outset when the entire debt is created. However, to recognise the whole profit at either the beginning or the end of the entire transaction is generally thought to be misleading; the economic fact is that completion of the sale takes place over a period of time, and this should be recognised when profit is measured.

A rational basis of apportionment is required to spread the profit on transactions settled by a series of cash payments, and a good measure of the degree of completeness is the proportion of the total sales price received during the period for which profit is to be calculated. The application of this approach is shown in example 8.3.

### Example 8.3

A company's accounting date is 31 December. On 1 June 19X1 it made a sale under an instalment credit agreement. The total value of the sale is £480 to be settled by a deposit of £96 and 24 monthly instalments of £16, the first to be made on 30 June 19X1. The cost of the goods sold is £360.

### Required:

Calculate the profit to be recognised on the sale in 19X1, 19X2 and 19X3 assuming that profit is recognised as cash is received.

## Solution
The total gross profit on the sale is £480 - 360 = £120

| | Cash Received | Proportion of Total Cash Received | Profit Taken | |
|---|---|---|---|---|
| | £ | | £ | £ |
| 19X1 | £ 96 + (6x£16) = 192 | 40% | 40% x 120 = | 48 |
| 19X2 | 12x£16 = 192 | 40% | 40% x 120 = | 48 |
| 19X3 | 6x£16 = 96 | 20% | 20% x 120 = | 24 |
| | 480 | | | 120 |

The phased recognition of profit on instalment credit transactions can be entered in the books of account in a number of ways. Two of the most common are: (a) to credit the total value of the sale to the trading account in the accounting period during which the sale takes place and create a provision for unrealised profit; and (b) to credit each period's trading account with the cash received during the period and assign a value to stock on the basis of cash not yet collected. In both cases it is best to operate a separate trading account in which to enter all instalment credit sales so that their results can be separately monitored.

### (a) The Provision for Unrealised Profit Method
With this method, the full value of the sale is entered in the trading account and recorded as a debtor. At the accounting date the value of unrealised profit is calculated and debited to the profit and loss account. The credit balance on the provision account is deducted from the value of Instalment Sales Debtors which should be disclosed separately in the balance sheet.

### Example 8.4
*Required:*
Prepare the Trading and Profit and Loss Account for 19X1 based on the information given in Example 8.3, using a provision for unrealised profit, and show the relevant extract from the balance sheet.

## Solution.

*Trading and Profit and Loss Account*

|  | £ |
|---|---|
| Sales | 480 |
| Cost of goods sold | 360 |
| Gross profit | 120 |
| Provision for unrealised profit (£48 + £24) | 72 |
| Profit | 48 |

*Balance Sheet Extract*

|  |  |
|---|---|
| Instalment sales debtors | 288* |
| Provision for unrealised profit | 72 |
|  | 216 |

*£480 (Total selling price) − £96 (Deposit) − (£16x6)(19X1 instalments)

*Notes*
1. In 19X2 £48, and in 19X3 the remaining £24, of the provision are credited to the profit and loss account.
2. There will usually be a number of transactions each year and the provision is adjusted at the year end in the same way as the provision for doubtful debts (see section 7 of chapter 6).

### (b) The Cash Receipts Method

The cash received as a deposit and the instalments receivable during the accounting period are entered in the Trading Account, and 'Stock out on Instalment Sales' is carried down as an asset in the balance sheet; no entry for debtors appears in the balance sheet other than for any instalments due but unpaid at the accounting date.

The value of the stock out on instalment sales is found by applying the proportion of sales price still outstanding to the cost of stock sold. The following formula may be used:

$$V = \frac{I}{S} \times C$$

Where:
V = Value of stock out on instalment sales
I = Instalments due in future accounting periods
S = Total selling price
C = Cost of stock sold

## Example 8.5
*Required:*
Prepare the Instalment Sales Trading Account for 19X1, 19X2 and 19X3 based on the information given in Example 8.3, using the 'cash receipts' method.

## Solution.

| To value stock at 31 December: | 19X1 | 19X2 |
|---|---|---|
| I (Instalments due in future accounting periods) = ..... | 288 | 96 |
| S (Total selling price) = ............................ | 480 | 480 |
| C (Cost of goods sold) = ............................ | 360 | 360 |
| $V = \dfrac{I}{S} \times C$ = ................................. | 216 | 72 |

*Instalment Sales Trading Accounts*

| | 19X1 | | 19X2 | | 19X3 | |
|---|---|---|---|---|---|---|
| | £ | £ | £ | £ | £ | £ |
| Deposit and instalments receivable .............. | | 192 | | 192 | | 96 |
| Stock out on instalment credit b/f .............. | | — | | 216 | | 72 |
| Cost of goods sold .......... | 360 | | — | | — | |
| Stock out on instalment credit c/f .............. | (216) | | (72) | | — | |
| | | 144 | | 144 | | 72 |
| Gross profit .............. | | 48 | | 48 | | 24 |

The examples in this section have dealt with only a single sale. Readers should now work Question 8.2 which extends the principle to multiple sales.

## 8.4   TRANSFER OF BUSINESS
It is possible for a business to grow by acquiring an existing undertaking. This is known as 'external' expansion and contrasts with 'internal' expansion which involves the purchase of new trading assets and the creation of additional activity to utilise them. An advantage of external expansion is that management does not have to develop new products or outlets. For example, the owner of a shop may wish to open a branch in another town: internal expansion involves acquiring premises and stock, training staff and attracting customers; external expansion involves the purchase of

an existing shop together with its stock, as a going concern, and possibly the retention of the bulk of its staff and customers.

The accounting entries which result from the transfer of a business can be divided into three areas:

(a)   The record of the assets and liabilities taken over in the books of the purchaser;
(b)   The record of any transactions carried out by the purchaser on behalf of the vendor of the business; and
(c)   The record of the sale of the business in the vendor's books.

**8.4.1 Purchaser's Books**   The agreement under which an existing business is acquired must contain a clear statement of which assets and liabilities are to be transferred under the deal. This is to avoid any future disputes about, for example, where the responsibility lies for such liabilities as an overdraft or trade creditors created before the takeover, or whether a specific piece of property is included in the price.

The transferred assets should be recorded in the purchaser's books at the agreed price, which is unlikely to be the same as the historical cost at which they are recorded in the vendor's books as they are acquired at current values. A difficulty may arise because a global figure is paid for the acquired business which is not allocated between specific assets taken over. In these circumstances, the price paid must be apportioned between the tangible assets and liabilities acquired, on the basis of their current values, with any excess recorded as goodwill. (See section 4 of chapter 7 for a full discussion of goodwill).

**Example 8.6**
The balance sheet of Firefly at 31 December 19X4 was:

| | £ | | £ | £ |
|---|---|---|---|---|
| Capital .......... | 20,000 | Premises ......... | | 14,000 |
| Creditors ........ | 15,000 | Stock ............ | 12,000 | |
| | | Debtors .......... | 7,000 | |
| | | Cash ............ | 2,000 | |
| | | | | 21,000 |
| | 35,000 | | | 35,000 |

Gloworm agreed to buy the business on 1 January 19X5 for £30,000 cash. The cash balance was not part of the deal and was to be retained by Firefly. The current value of the premises was £20,000; the other assets and liabilities are fairly stated at their balance sheet values.

*Required:*
   (a)   Calculate the value of Goodwill purchased from Gloworm.
   (b)   Show the journal entry made in Gloworm's books to record the acquisition.

## Solution

(a)

*Calculation of Goodwill*

| | £ | £ |
|---|---:|---:|
| Price paid............................................ | | 30,000 |
| Acquired:   Premises.............................. | 20,000 | |
| Stock................................. | 12,000 | |
| Debtors............................... | 7,000 | |
| | 39,000 | |
| Less: Liabilities assumed.......................... | 15,000 | |
| Net assets acquired at current value.................. | | 24,000 |
| Goodwill............................................ | | 6,000 |

(b)

*Journal*

| | Debit £ | Credit £ |
|---|---:|---:|
| Premises........................................ | 20,000 | |
| Stock............................................ | 12,000 | |
| Debtors.......................................... | 7,000 | |
| Creditors........................................ | | 15,000 |
| Goodwill......................................... | 6,000 | |
| Cash............................................. | | 30,000 |
| | 45,000 | 45,000 |

Readers should now work Question 8.3 at the end of this chapter.

**8.4.2 Transactions on Behalf of The Vendor** The purchasing company may carry out some transactions on behalf of the vendor, such as collecting debtors or paying creditors which are not taken over. This is a useful way of maintaining continuity with customers and suppliers. All such transactions are entered in a separate account, in the name of the vendor, and a net settlement made as agreed. Care must be exercised not to confuse these transactions with the trading activity which takes place after the acquisition.

### Example 8.7

Hotter purchased the business of Colder on 31 December 19X5. It was agreed that the following items should *not* be included in the acquisition:

|  |  | £ |
|---|---|---|
| Debtors | ......................... | 15,000 |
| Creditors | ...................... | 6,000 |
| Overdraft | ...................... | 1,700 |

Hotter agreed to collect the sums due from debtors, use this cash to settle the creditors and overdraft, and pay the remaining balance to Colder. By 31 January 19X6, £14,500 had been collected from debtors, the rest being considered bad debts, and Hotter had settled the agreed liabilities of Colder.

### Required:

Prepare the account of Colder in the books of Hotter and show the balance due to Colder on 31 January 19X6.

### Solution.

Colder's Account

| | £ | | £ |
|---|---|---|---|
| Cash paid to creditors..... | 6,000 | Cash collected | |
| Cash paid - overdraft...... | 1,700 | from debtors............ | 14,500 |
| Balance due to Colder..... | 6,800 | | |
| | 14,500 | | 14,500 |

Readers should now work question 8.4 at the end of this chapter.

**8.4.3 The Vendor's Books** When the business of a sole trader is sold, entries must be made in the firm's books to calculate the resulting profit or loss and to record the dissolution of the undertaking. A 'Realisation Account' is opened for this purpose, and the following entries are made:

   1.  Transfer the assets and, if applicable, the liabilities taken

over by the purchaser to the Realisation Account.

2. Debit the purchasing company's account and credit the realisation account with the agreed purchase price.

3. Credit the purchasing company's account and debit the relevant asset accounts with the purchase consideration when it is received. The consideration may be in the form of cash or partly or wholly in the form of shares in the purchasing company.

4. Any assets not taken over by the purchasing company are either sold for cash or taken over by the vendor, and any liabilities not taken over by the purchaser are settled. Profits or losses arising from any of these transactions are calculated in the relevant account and transferred to the realisation account.

5. The balance on the realisation account, representing the profit or loss on realisation, is transferred to the sole trader's capital account.

6. Debit the sole trader's capital account and credit the relevant asset accounts, usually cash and shares in the purchasing company, with the amounts available for distribution.

The effect of these entries is to close all the accounts in the books, and so the firm ceases to exist as an accounting entity.

**Example 8.8**

The following is the balance sheet of Punch, a trader, at 31 December 19X7:

| | £ | | £ | £ |
|---|---|---|---|---|
| Capital .............. | 28,000 | Fixed Assets....... | | 16,000 |
| Trade creditors........ | 12,000 | Stock............. | 13,000 | |
| | | Debtors........... | 8,000 | |
| | | Cash ............. | 3,000 | |
| | | | | 24,000 |
| | 40,000 | | | 40,000 |

It is agreed that all the assets and liabilities of Punch, other than cash, are to be taken over by Judy Ltd on 1 January 19X8.

*Required:*

Prepare the Realisation Account, Purchaser's Account, Cash Account and Capital Account in the books of Punch on the

alternative assumptions that the purchase consideration is:
(a)  £40,000 cash
(b)  £25,000 cash and £15,000 of shares in Judy Ltd.


## Solution

(a)

### Realisation Account

| | £ | | £ |
|---|---|---|---|
| Fixed Assets............. | 16,000 | Creditors .............. | 12,000 |
| Stock................... | 13,000 | Purchaser's Account...... | 40,000 |
| Debtors................ | 8,000 | | |
| Profit - transferred to | | | |
| Capital Account.......... | 15,000 | | |
| | 52,000 | | 52,000 |

### Purchaser's Account

| | £ | | £ |
|---|---|---|---|
| Realisation Account...... | 40,000 | Cash .................. | 40,000 |

### Cash Account

| | £ | | £ |
|---|---|---|---|
| Balance b/d............. | 3,000 | Punch - Capital.......... | 43,000 |
| Purchaser............... | 40,000 | | |
| | 43,000 | | 43,000 |

### Capital Account

| | £ | | £ |
|---|---|---|---|
| Cash .................. | 43,000 | Balance b/d............. | 28,000 |
| | | Realisation Account...... | 15,000 |
| | 43,000 | | 43,000 |

(b)

### Realisation Account

| | £ | | £ |
|---|---|---|---|
| Fixed Assets............. | 16,000 | Creditors .............. | 12,000 |
| Stock................... | 13,000 | Purchaser's Account...... | 40,000 |
| Debtors................ | 8,000 | | |
| Profit - transferred to | | | |
| Capital Account.......... | 15,000 | | |
| | 52,000 | | 52,000 |

*Purchaser's Account*

| | £ | | £ |
|---|---|---|---|
| Realisation Account...... | 40,000 | Cash.................. | 25,000 |
| | | Shares in Judy Ltd........ | 15,000 |
| | 40,000 | | 40,000 |

*Cash Account*

| | £ | | £ |
|---|---|---|---|
| Balance b/d............ | 3,000 | Punch - Capital.......... | 28,000 |
| Purchaser............... | 25,000 | | |
| | 28,000 | | 28,000 |

*Capital Account*

| | £ | | £ |
|---|---|---|---|
| Cash................... | 28,000 | Balance b/d............. | 28,000 |
| Shares................. | 15,000 | Realisation Account...... | 15,000 |
| | 43,000 | | 43,000 |

Readers should now work Question 8.5 at the end of this chapter.
A realisation account is also used when the business being dissolved is a partnership (see section 5.3 of chapter 9) or a limited company. In the case of a limited company, any surplus or deficit in the realisation account is added to or deducted from the accumulated balance on the profit and loss account. After all liabilities have been paid, each ordinary shareholder receives a share of the cash, and any other assets which remain, on the basis of the proportion of shares owned.

## 8.5 LOSSES OF STOCK AND CASH

The accounts of businesses only reflect those economic events which the initial data collecting process has been designed to record. Some activity remains unrecorded, such as losses of stock or cash. Stock may be lost through theft or accident, such as fire, and cash may be lost if, for example, the employee responsible for handling it steals some before recording the amount received. It is possible, where such losses are known or suspected, to calculate their value by using the techniques of incomplete records described in chapter 3. This ability relies on the fact that the accounting process uses known relationships between the elements which it reports, and if all the elements are known, except one, then the unknown value can be determined. For example, if all of the balances in a balance sheet are known with the exception of capital, the missing figure can be found as the amount needed to balance the balance sheet. (See section 5 of chapter 2 where this technique is used). This technique is now used to identify losses of stock and cash.

**8.5.1 Stock Losses** The value of stock lost is calculated by constructing the Trading Account from the date at which reliable data was last available to the time of the suspected loss. A theoretical value for closing stock is estimated as the balancing figure in the account and is compared with the actual value found by a physical stock check; the difference between these two figures is the amount of the loss. The figures in the Trading Account are determined as follows:

(a) *Sales*

Sales are known where a business maintains a system of double entry ledger accounts; alternatively, it may be necessary to convert cash received into the value of sales by adjusting for such matters as opening and closing debtors and discounts given to customers.

(b) *Purchases*

The value of purchases is known where a business maintains a systems of double entry ledger accounts; alternatively, it may be necessary to convert cash paid into purchases by adjusting it for opening and closing creditors and discounts received.

(c) *Opening Stock*

This is taken from the closing balance sheet of the previous period, the date of which must be the starting point from which sales and purchases are measured.

(d) *Gross Profit*

The difference between the selling price and the cost of goods sold is the 'gross profit' and can be assumed with some accuracy for a particular trade. The gross profit, expressed as a percentage, for the trade concerned is assumed to apply to the business under consideration. Care must be taken to ascertain whether the percentage relates to the value of Sales or to the Cost of Goods Sold. For example, if sales are £100 and the cost of goods sold £80, then the gross profit is £20; this is 20% of the value of sales, or 25% of the cost of goods sold.

The value of stock lost may now be calculated as follows:

1.  Calculate the expected gross profit by applying the assumed

mark up to the value of sales.
2. Calculate the cost of goods sold by deducting the expected gross profit (found in 1) from sales.
3. Calculate the theoretical closing stock by using the formula:
   Closing Stock = Opening Stock + Purchases
   $\qquad$ − Cost of Goods Sold (found in 2)
4. Calculate the value of stock lost by deducting the value of any stock which remains from the theoretical value of stock (found in 3).

### Example 8.9

During the night of 14 March 19X2 a fire occurred in the premises of Smoke and Company which destroyed a large quantity of stock and all the stock records. The following information was found from the remaining accounting records:

|  | £ |
| --- | --- |
| Stock at 31 December 19X1 as shown in the balance sheet............... | 15,865 |
| Sales 1 January to 14 March 19X2.................................. | 78,640 |
| Purchases 1 January to 14 March 19X2............................. | 57,103 |
| Value of stock not destroyed as counted on the morning of 15 March 19X2.............................................. | 2,856 |

The company makes a gross profit of 25% calculated on selling prices.

### Required:
Calculate the value of stock lost in the fire.

### Solution.
*Step*
1 Expected profit = 25% x 78,640 = 19,660
2 Cost of goods sold = 78,640 − 19,660 = 58,980
3 Theoretical closing stock = 15,865 + 57,103 − 58,980
   $\qquad\qquad\qquad$ = 13,988
4 Stock lost = 13,988 − 2,856 = £11,132

*Note*

Alternatively it is possible to reconstruct directly the theoretical closing stock from the trading account:

|  | £ | £ |
|---|---|---|
| Sales........................................ |  | 78,640 |
| Opening stock................................ | 15,865 |  |
| Purchases.................................... | 57,103 |  |
| Closing stock................................ | (13,988)*** |  |
| Cost of goods sold........................... |  | 58,980** |
| Gross Profit................................. |  | 19,660* |

    *   Calculated as 25% of sales
  **  Found as first balancing figure
***  Found as second balancing figure

   Readers should now work Question 8.6 at the end of this chapter which tests the calculation of the value of lost stock with adjustments for debtors and creditors.


**8.5.2 Cash Losses** Businesses must establish adequate control over their cash as it is a mobile asset which is difficult to trace and is easily exchanged. Receipts from cash sales are potentially vulnerable because control is not established until the sale has been recorded; prior to that point theft would not be highlighted by, for example, the failure of the amount of money taken from the till to agree with the till roll recording receipts. The value of suspected losses can be calculated as follows:

1. Calculate the Cost of Goods Sold as:
   Opening stock + Purchases − Closing stock
2. Calculate the theoretical value of sales by applying the expected mark up to the cost of goods sold (found in 1).
3. Deduct recorded sales from theoretical sales (found in 2) to calculate the shortfall in recorded sales, and hence cash.

**Example 8.10**

The manager of a shop suspects that takings are being stolen. He ascertains the following for the month of July 19X9:

|  | £ |
|---|---|
| Stock 1 July.......................... | 15,762 |
| Purchases during July.................. | 68,570 |
| Stock 31 July......................... | 17,056 |
| Recorded Sales........................ | 80,840 |

All goods are sold at a price to yield a gross profit of 20% on selling price.

*Required:*

Calculate the value of any cash discrepancy.

**Solution.**

Step

1. The cost of goods sold is: £15,762 + £68,570 − £17,056 = £67,276

2. 20% of the selling price is gross profit, and so the cost of goods sold is 80% of the selling price. The theoretical value of sales is therefore:
   £67,276 x 100/80 = £84,095 (ie, goods are sold at cost plus 25%)

3. The value of takings stolen is: £84,095 − £80,840 = £3,255

*Note:* The usefulness of this technique is reliant on the accuracy of the assumed gross margin.

## 8.6 QUESTIONS

### Question 8.1

Note: This question tests the principles dealt with in section 2 of this chapter.

The following is the Trial Balance of Midwich, a manufacturer, at 31 March 19X6:

| | £ | £ |
|---|---|---|
| Capital | | 50,000 |
| Sales | | 208,000 |
| Loan | | 30,000 |
| Raw materials: Purchases | 40,000 | |
| Stock at 1 April 19X5 | 12,000 | |
| Production wages | 30,000 | |
| Production equipment: at cost | 70,000 | |
| provision for depreciation at 1 April 19X5 | | 14,000 |
| Rent | 6,400 | |
| Light, heat and power | 12,000 | |
| Production overhead expenses | 17,500 | |
| Administration expenses | 7,500 | |
| Administration salaries | 15,000 | |
| Work in progress 1 April 19X5 | 2,000 | |
| Finished goods stock at 1 April 19X5 | 11,500 | |
| Provision for unrealised profit at 1 April 19X5 | | 1,500 |
| Hire of office equipment | 7,000 | |
| Postage and telephone | 5,350 | |
| Loan interest | 3,000 | |
| Bank charges | 1,250 | |
| Overdraft | | 10,000 |
| Hire of delivery vans | 2,000 | |
| Van driver's wages | 7,000 | |
| Petrol and other van expenses | 1,000 | |
| Debtors | 20,000 | |
| Creditors | | 5,000 |
| Drawings | 48,000 | |
| | 318,500 | 318,500 |

*Notes*
1. The production equipment has a life of 10 years and a zero scrap value.
2. Stocks at 31 March 19X6 were:

| | £ |
|---|---|
| Raw Materials | 14,000 (at cost) |
| Work in Progress | 7,000 (at cost) |
| Finished Goods | 13,800 (at transfer price) |

3.  75% of the Rent and Light, Heat and Power relates to the factory.
4.  Transfers are made from the Manufacturing Account at cost plus 15%.

*Required:*
The Manufacturing, Trading and Profit and Loss Account of Midwich for the year to 31 March 19X6 and the Balance Sheet at that date.

## Question 8.2

Lingwood commenced business as a hire purchase trader on 1 January 19X5, with a cash capital of £10,000. He decided to sell vacuum cleaners (VC) and electric polishers (EP) and his terms were that payment should be made in eight equal instalments, the first payable on the date of sale, and the remainder at quaterly intervals thereafter.

The following information is extracted from Lingwood's books at the end of 19X5:

|  | Numbers purchased £ | Numbers sold | Cost per unit £ | Cash selling price per unit £ | Total Selling price per unit £ |
|---|---|---|---|---|---|
| VCs | 300 | 250 | 96 | 144 | 168 |
| EPs | 250 | 200 | 144 | 216 | 252 |

### Bank Account for 19X5

| | | | |
|---|---|---|---|
| Opening balance......... | 10,000 | Purchases: | |
| Receipts in respect of sales: | | VCs-250 at £96......... | 24,000 |
| VCs-250 at £84........ | 21,000 | EPs-250 at £144........ | 36,000 |
| EPs-200 at £63........ | 12,600 | Expenses................ | 1,980 |
| | ―――― | Drawings .............. | 3,500 |
| | 43,600 | Bank interest........... | 1,086 |
| Overdraft at 31.12.X5..... | ⁻22,966 | | ―――― |
| | ―――― | | 66,566 |
| | ⁻66,566 | | |

All instalments due from customers were received on due date. On 31 December, 19X5, Lingwood still owed his suppliers for 50 VCs; creditors for expenses were £460.

*Note:* Credit for profit on sales is only to be taken in respect of instalments received.

*Required:*
The hire purchase trading and profit and loss account of Lingwood for 19X5 and his balance sheet at 31 December.

## Question 8.3

The following are the balance sheets of Sharpner and Pencil at 31 December 19X7.

|  | Sharpner | | Pencil | |
| --- | --- | --- | --- | --- |
|  | £ | £ | £ | £ |
| Fixed Assets |  |  |  |  |
| Land and buildings.......... |  | 32,100 |  | 10,000 |
| Motor vans................ |  | 20,000 |  | 3,000 |
|  |  | 52,100 |  | 13,000 |
| Curent Assets |  |  |  |  |
| Stock...................... | 10,700 |  | 6,000 |  |
| Debtors................... | 7,600 |  | 3,000 |  |
| Cash ..................... | 5,200 |  | 700 |  |
|  | 23,500 |  | 9,700 |  |
| Current Liabilities |  |  |  |  |
| Trade creditors.............. | 7,000 |  | 3,200 |  |
| Working capital............... |  | 16,500 |  | 6,500 |
|  |  | 68,600 |  | 19,500 |
| Financed by: |  |  |  |  |
| Capital....................... |  | 68,600 |  | 19,500 |

On 1 January 19X8 Sharpner purchased all of the assets, except cash, and liabilities of Pencil for £29,000 cash. The current values of Pencil's assets were:

|  | £ |
| --- | --- |
| Land and buildings................ | 15,000 |
| Motor van....................... | 2,700 |
| Stock........................... | 5,800 |

To finance the acquisition, Sharpner took out a loan of £25,000 repayable in 10 years time.

*Required:*
Prepare the balance sheet of Sharpner on 1 January 19X8 after the acquisition of Pencil's business has been completed.

## Question 8.4

The balance sheet of the business owned by I. Sellup at 31 December 19X2 was as follows:

*Balance Sheet*

| | £ | | £ | |
|---|---|---|---|---|
| Capital................. | 28,694 | Fixed Assets | | |
| Trade creditors........... | 7,462 | Freehold land and | | |
| Bank overdraft........... | 1,893 | buildings.............. | 22,100 | |
| | | Motor vans............. | 1,975 | |
| | | | | 24,075 |
| | | Current Assets | | |
| | | Stock........ 8,992 | | |
| | | Debtors...... 4,982 | | |
| | | | | 13,974 |
| | 38,049 | | | 38,049 |

Mr. Buyit agrees to purchase Sellup's business on 1 January 19X3 for £40,000 cash. He sells some investments and opens a business bank account with a deposit of £50,000 and immediately pays from it the sum due to Sellup. Buyit did not take over the debtors or liabilities, and accepted no responsibility for Sellup's bank overdraft. He did agree to collect the debts and to account to Sellup for the amount collected. Land and buildings, the van and stocks were taken over and were recorded in the books of Buyit at the values reported above.

The following balances were extracted from Buyit's books, maintained strictly in accordance with double entry principles, as at 31 December 19X3:

| | |
|---|---|
| Sales revenue........................... | 92,968 |
| Cost of sales............................ | 71,034 |
| Expenses............................... | 13,168 |
| Collected from Sellup's debtors............ | 2,740 |
| Paid to Sellup........................... | 2,610 |
| Debtors................................ | 6,949 |
| Creditors for supplies.................... | 4,972 |
| Stock in trade.......................... | 15,594 |
| Creditors for expenses.................... | 192 |

Depreciation on the van is to be charged at 20% per annum on the takeover price.

*Required:*
(a) A summary of Buyit's bank account for 19X3
(b) The trading and profit and loss account of Buyit's business for 19X3 and a balance sheet at 31 December 19X3.

## Question 8.5
The following is the balance sheet of Purlin at 30 June 19X5:

|  | £ | £ |  |  | £ |
|---|---|---|---|---|---|
| Capital | | 50,000 | Fixed Assets: | | |
| Trade creditors | 10,000 | | Premises | | 27,000 |
| Overdraft | 3,000 | | Equipment | | 5,000 |
| | | 13,000 | Motor car | | 2,000 |
| | | | | | 34,000 |
| | | | Stocks and Debtors | | 29,000 |
| | | 63,000 | | | 63,000 |

Lintel Ltd acquired the business of Purlin on 1 July 19X5 for £50,000, with the exceptions of the equipment, motor car and overdraft. Purlin sold the equipment separately for £4,000 cash and took the car over at book value for his own use.

*Required:*
Prepare the Realisation Account, Equipment Account, Cash Account and Capital Account to record the dissolution of the firm as they appear in the books of Purlin.

## Question 8.6
The premises of Advance & Co. suffered a fire during the night of 18 February 19X4 which destroyed a quantity of stock together with the stock records. The stock was insured against fire and the company wishes to submit a claim. The following information is available:
(a) The company's accounting date is 31 December, and the balance sheet at that date in 19X3 showed stock in trade of £66,000, debtors of £54,000 and creditors for purchases of £42,000.

(b) During the period 1 January to 18 February 19X4, the following transactions took place:

|                                      | £      |
| ------------------------------------ | ------ |
| Cash collected from debtors          | 97,000 |
| Discounts allowed                    | 1,000  |
| Cash paid to creditors               | 68,000 |
| Discounts received                   | 400    |
| Cash sales                           | 36,000 |
| Stock drawings by owner at cost      | 600    |

(c) The company's ledger shows that on 18 February 19X4 debtors owed £57,000 and creditors were owed £39,000.

(d) A stock take, carried out immediately after the fire, showed the value of undamaged stock to be £18,000.

(e) The company makes a gross profit of 25% on the selling price of its goods.

*Required:*
A calculation of the cost of stock lost in the fire.

# CHAPTER 9

# Partnerships

## 9.1 INTRODUCTION

Partnerships use the same basic accountancy techniques as those described so far in this book in the context of the sole trader, although some modifications are required in their application to suit the different constitution of the partnership. There is no legal requirement for partnerships to prepare annual accounts, but the need to share profits between the partners, and for partners to submit tax returns, makes their routine production essential if the conduct of the partnership is to proceed smoothly. As with sole traders, there is no requirement for the contents of partnership accounts to be made public even though they may relate to significant economic entities; this contrasts with the disclosure requirements imposed on limited companies described in chapter 10.

The legal background is provided by the *Partnership Act 1890* which defines a partnership as 'the relation which subsists between persons carrying on a business in common with a view of profit'. There is no formal legal procedure necessary to create a partnership; it can be deemed to exist because people are trading in a way which brings them within the definition. It is very important to determine whether a person is a partner, as the liability of each partner for all of the firm's debts is unlimited; if the firm cannot pay, then each partner becomes personally liable to the extent of the entire debt. (The *Limited Partnership Act 1907* makes special provision for a partnership to have limited partners whose liability is restricted to the value of their capital investment, provided there is at least one general partner who accepts full liability for all of the firm's debts. This provision is not widely used).

The most common reasons for forming a partnership are to raise the necessary finance to fund planned operations, and to pool together complementary skills: for example, an engineer who is very capable at developing new products may well need the services of a salesman to market them.

The number of partners allowed to combine in a partnership is restricted to 20, although some specific exemptions are granted, for example, firms of Chartered Accountants can have any number of partners. If a firm which is restricted to 20 partners wishes to seek funds from a larger group, then incorporation as a limited company is first necessary (see chapter 10).


## 9.2 THE PARTNERSHIP AGREEMENT

The owners of a partnership (the partners) also manage it, and each partner can enter into contracts on behalf of the firm which are binding on the partnership as a whole. In these circumstances, the partners must have a great deal of mutual trust, but in any case it is best for the arrangements under which the partnership is to be conducted to be formally set out in a legally binding Partnership Agreement. This should be signed by all of the partners. Examples of the matters to be covered by such an agreement are:

(a) The purpose for which the partnership is formed.
(b) The amount of capital each partner is to contribute.
(c) How profits and losses are to be divided between the partners. (See section 3 of this chapter).
(d) Whether separate capital and current accounts are to be maintained. (See section 4 of this chapter).
(e) The extent to which partners can make drawings.
(f) The frequency with which accounts are to be prepared and whether they are to be subjected to an independent audit.
(g) Regulations to be observed when: a partner retires; a new partner is admitted; the profit sharing ratio changes; or the partnership is dissolved. (See section 5 of this chapter).


Where no formal agreement exists, the terms of the partnership may be concluded from past behaviour, for example, if profits have always been divided between two partners in the ratio 2:1, without dissent from either partner, then this is presumed to be the agreed ratio. The *Partnership Act 1890* provides a 'safety net' of regulations which apply when there is no agreement, either formal or informal, to the contrary. Among the major of these provisions are:

(a) All profits and losses are to be shared equally among the partners.

(b)   No interest on capital, or remuneration for conducting the partnership business, is payable to any partner.

(c)   A partner is entitled to 5% per annum interest on any loans to the partnership in excess of his agreed capital contribution.

(d)   Every partner is authorised to take part in the firm's management.

(e)   All existing partners must agree to the admission of a new partner.


## 9.3   THE DIVISION OF PROFIT

The net profit of a partnership is calculated in the usual way, and is then transferred to the Appropriation Account where it is divided between the partners in the agreed manner. The agreement may provide for a straightforward allocation in accordance with a specific ratio, such as 3:2; alternatively, precise adjustments may be made to take account of the following factors:

(a)   The partners may provide different amounts of capital; this involves sacrificing different amounts of interest which could have been earned by, for example, putting the money in a bank deposit account. Compensation for this can be achieved by allowing a deduction to be made in the appropriation account for interest on partner's capital. The rate of interest may be fixed in the agreement or, because rates of interest fluctuate, it could be tied to some external indicator, such as the rate paid on long-term deposit accounts by banks. In whichever way the rate is determined, the greater the amount of capital a partner has invested in the firm, the greater is the interest received.

(b)   By deciding to join a partnership, each partner foregoes potential earnings as an employee of another firm. The sacrifice of alternative income may not be the same for each partner, for example, one may contribute more valuable skills. This can be recognised by giving each partner a salary related to potential 'outside earnings'. Such salaries are also deducted from profit in the appropriation account.

(c)   Partners make drawings from the firm which reduce the amount of their investment, and it may be decided to recognise this by charging partners interest on their drawings. This interest is then added to the profit to be shared between the partners.

(d)   After any interest and salaries have been deducted, there must be agreement on how to divide the residual profit or loss. The ratio in which it is shared may be designed to reflect the partner's seniority, or some other basis, such as equality, may be adopted.

The steps necessary to carry out the division of partnership profit are:
1. Determine the manner in which profit is to be divided.
2. Determine the value of profit or loss to be shared. The value found takes no account of any payments to the partners, for example in the form of salaries, and is transferred to the appropriation account.
3. Add to profit any interest charged on drawings made by the partners.
4. Deduct from profit any interest allowed on capital account balances and any salaries payable to partners.
5. Split the residual profit or loss in the agreed ratio.

Steps 3 to 5 are recorded in the firm's books with the following entries:

| Debit | Credit | With |
|---|---|---|
| Capital Account* | Profit and Loss Appropriation Account | Interest Charged on Drawings |
| Profit and Loss Appropriation Account | Capital Account* | Interest Allowed on Capital, Salaries and Share of Profit |
| Capital Account* | Profit and Loss Appropriation Account | Share of Losses |

*These entries are instead made in the current accounts of partners where such accounts are maintained (see section 4 of this chapter).

The division of profit in the appropriation account is illustrated in Example 9.1.

**Example 9.1**
Oak and Tree are in partnership and prepare their accounts on a calendar year basis. They have agreed that profits are to be shared as follows:

1. Oak is to receive an annual salary of £5,000 and Tree one of £10,000.
2. 10% per annum interest is to be paid on each partner's capital account balance as on 1 January.
3. Residual profits and losses are to be shared equally.

On 1 January 19X6 the balance on Oak's capital account was £64,000 and on Tree's it was £30,000

*Required:*

Prepare the partnership's appropriation account on the alternative assumptions that the profit for 19X6 was:
   (a) £30,000
   (b) £20,000

## Solution

(a)

### Appropriation Account

| | | £ | | £ |
|---|---|---|---|---|
| Salary: | Oak................. | 5,000 | Profit......... | 30,000 |
| | Tree................. | 10,000 | | |
| Interest: | Oak................. | 6,400 | | |
| | Tree................. | 3,000 | | |
| Residue: | Oak................. | 2,800 | | |
| | Tree................. | 2,800 | | |
| | | 30,000 | | 30,000 |

(b)

### Appropriation Account

| | | £ | | £ |
|---|---|---|---|---|
| Salary: | Oak................. | 5,000 | Profit......... | 20,000 |
| | Tree................. | 10,000 | Share of loss: | |
| Interest: | Oak................. | 6,400 | Oak......... | 2,200 |
| | Tree................. | 3,000 | Tree......... | 2,200 |
| | | 24,400 | | 24,400 |

If there was no agreement, the profits in the above example would have been divided between the partners in accordance with the terms of the 1890 Partnership Act. Each would have received an equal share, namely, £15,000 in (a), and £10,000 in (b).

Readers should now work Question 9.1, which extends the above example to three partners and includes interest charged on drawings, and Question 9.2, both of which are at the end of this chapter.

## 9.4 CAPITAL AND CURRENT ACCOUNTS

The capital which each partner invests in the business can be divided into two elements:

(a) The part which is permanently required to finance the ability of the firm to trade. It is invested in fixed assets and working capital and cannot be withdrawn without reducing the capacity of the business.

(b) The part which can be withdrawn by the partners as drawings.

The permanent capital of each partner is entered in a 'Capital Account'. The partnership agreement usually stipulates the amount of permanent capital invested by each partner, and the balances remain constant until the partners agree to a change. Routine transactions between partners and the firm are entered in a 'Current Account'. The current account balance fluctuates as it is credited with each partner's share of profits, in the form of interest, salary and share of residue, and is debited with drawings and interest on drawings. To prevent partners withdrawing more than their entitlement, the partnership agreement should state that no current account is allowed to have a debit balance without the consent of the other partners.

## Example 9.2

Disk and Drive trade in partnership. The following information relates to 19X7:

|  | Disk £ | Drive £ |
|---|---|---|
| Current account credit balance 1 January 19X7.. | 9,130 | 8,790 |
| Interest allowed on capital................... | 1,000 | 1,500 |
| Interest charged on drawings................. | 150 | 390 |
| Salary..................................... | 5,000 | 3,000 |
| Share of residual profit..................... | 6,250 | 6,250 |
| Cash drawings............................. | 7,160 | 8,240 |
| Stock drawings............................. | 120 | 80 |

## Required:

Prepare the current accounts of Disk and Drive for 19X7. For each entry indicate clearly the location of its corresponding double entry.

## Solution

*Current Accounts*

| | Disk £ | Drive £ | | Disk £ | Drive £ |
|---|---|---|---|---|---|
| Appropriation | | | Balance b/d.... | 9,130 | 8,790 |
| Account: | | | Appropriation | | |
| Interest......... | 150 | 390 | Account: | | |
| Drawings: | | | Interest...... | 1,000 | 1,500 |
| Cash account.... | 7,160 | 8,240 | Salary....... | 5,000 | 3,000 |
| Purchases A/c... | 120 | 80 | Residue...... | 6,250 | 6,250 |
| Balance c/d....... | 13,950 | 10,830 | | | |
| | 21,380 | 19,540 | | 21,380 | 19,540 |

It is possible for substantial balances to accumulate in the current accounts where partners consistently withdraw less then their share of the profits. The funds represented by these balances may have been invested in trading assets, and so have taken on the aspect of permanent capital, that is, they are not available for quick withdrawal. This position is shown in Illustration 9.1.

## Illustration 9.1

The following is the summarised balance sheet of Paper and Clip at 31 December 19X9:

| | £000 |
|---|---|
| Fixed assets............................... | 75 |
| Working capital............................ | 25 |
| | 100 |

| | Paper £000 | Clip £000 | Total £000 |
|---|---|---|---|
| Capital accounts.......................... | 20 | 20 | 40 |
| Current accounts.......................... | 30 | 30 | 60 |
| | 50 | 50 | 100 |

It is clear that the current account balances could not be withdrawn without reducing the size of the business, since a large proportion of these balances has been invested in fixed assets which would have to be sold to release cash. This is unlikely to happen, and so to bring the balance sheet into line with economic reality, the partners may agree that each of them should transfer, say, £25,000 from current to capital account. The transfer is entered in the books by a debit in each current account and a corresponding credit in each capital account. This increase in capital account balances does not provide the firm with any additional funds, but simply recognises that the partners have invested funds previously available as drawings in the permanent structure of the undertaking. When *additional* capital funds are required by a partnership, they must be introduced by the partners and credited to their capital accounts.

Readers should now work Question 9.3 at the end of this chapter.

## 9.5 PARTNERSHIP ACCOUNTS

The value of profit calculated in the conventional profit and loss account of a going concern contains only realised profits. For example, the increase in value of a piece of land held as a fixed asset is only recognised when it is sold and the profit realised, even though at any particular date its actual value may be greatly in excess of its book value at historical cost. Occasions arise when it is necessary to bring into account changes in asset values which have not been recorded in the books; these are dealt with in sections 5.1 and 5.2 of this chapter. All changes in value must also be taken into account when the firm comes to the end of its life and is dissolved; the accounting procedures related to this eventuality are described in section 5.3 of this chapter.

### 9.5.1 Changes in Membership
The partnership business, unlike a limited company, is not recognised in law as a separate *legal* entity, and so a change in the ownership creates a new business. For accounting purposes, the firm is treated as a continuing entity and the same set of books usually remains in use when a new partner joins or an existing one retires, but entries must be made in the books to give effect to any financial adjustments which are needed.

Each partner is entitled to his share of the profits, or losses, which have accrued during the period of time for which he has been a partner. Adjustment must be made, when a partner retires or joins, for any increase in value not yet recognised in the accounts, otherwise the retiring partner is not credited with the full amount due and the incoming partner is credited with a share of the assets at below their current value. This is demonstrated in Example 9.3.

### Example 9.3
The following is the summarised balance sheet of Lamp and Bulb,

who share profits in the ratio 3:2 respectively, at 31 December 19X5:

| Capital Accounts: | £ | | £ |
|---|---|---|---|
| Lamp ............... | 1,000 | Net Assets............... | 2,000 |
| Bulb ................ | 1,000 | | |
| | 2,000 | | 2,000 |

It is agreed that:
1. Bulb is to retire on 1 January 19X6
2. The net assets have a current value of £3,000
3. Bulb is to be paid the sum due to him in cash immediately
4. Socket is to be admitted as a partner on 1 January 19X6
5. Socket and Lamp agree to share future profits and losses equally
6. Socket agrees to introduce cash equal to the value of Lamp's capital after the assets have been adjusted to current values
7. Current accounts shall not be maintained

*Required:*
(a) Calculate the amount due to Bulb on his retirement.
(b) Calculate the amount of capital to be introduced by Socket.
(c) Prepare the opening balance sheet of the Lamp and Socket partnership.
(d) Comment on the consequences of *not* adjusting the assets to current values.

## Solution

(a)

| | £ | £ |
|---|---|---|
| Current value of net assets......................... | | 3,000 |
| Historical cost of net assets........................ | | 2,000 |
| Increase in value.................................. | | 1,000 |
| Share of increase: Lamp........................... | 600 | |
| Bulb............................ | 400 | |
| | | 1,000 |
| Amount due to Bulb: | | |
| Capital...................................... | | 1,000 |
| Revaluation surplus............................. | | 400 |
| Total due....................................... | | 1,400 |

(b) Lamp and Socket have agreed to share profits equally and the amount which Socket should therefore introduce as capital is the same as the balance on Lamp's capital account:

1,000(balance) + 600(revaluation surplus) = £1,600

(c)

### Balance Sheet of Lamp and Socket

| | £ | | £ |
|---|---|---|---|
| Capital Accounts: | | | |
| Lamp................ | 1,600 | Net Assets.............. | 3,200* |
| Socket............... | 1,600 | | |
| | 3,200 | | 3,200 |

*2,000(original value) + 1,000(revaluation) - 1,400(paid to Bulb) + 1,600(cash from Socket) = £3,200

(d) Without the revaluation, Bulb would withdraw only the balance on his capital account, ie, £1,000; he therefore leaves £400 in the business which has accrued under his ownership. Socket would introduce only £1,000, the same as the balance on Lamp's capital account, but would be buying a half share in assets with a current value of £3,000.

We will now examine how these matters are recorded in the books of the partnership. A revaluation of assets is recorded in the books by means of a revaluation account in which the following entries are made:

| Debit | Credit | With |
|---|---|---|
| Revaluation Account | Asset Account | Reduction in asset value |
| Asset Account | Revaluation Account | Increase in asset value |

The revaluation account contains all the increases and decreases in value, and its balance, the net surplus or deficit, is shared between the partners in the agreed ratio. Each partner's share of the net adjustment is entered in his capital account as it is permanent in nature. The revaluation account and capital accounts of Lamp, Bulb and Socket, from Example 9.3, would contain the following information:

*Revaluation Account*

| | £ | | £ |
|---|---|---|---|
| Surplus shared: | | Increase in value | |
| Lamp - capital...... | 600 | of net assets.......... | 1,000 |
| Bulb - capital....... | 400 | | |
| | 1,000 | | 1,000 |

*Capital Accounts*

| | Lamp £ | Bulb £ | Socket £ | | Lamp £ | Bulb £ | Socket £ |
|---|---|---|---|---|---|---|---|
| Cash...... | | 1,400 | | Balance | | | |
| Balance | | | | b/d........ | 1,000 | 1,000 | |
| c/d......... | 1,600 | | 1,600 | Revaluation . | 600 | 400 | |
| | | | | Cash....... | | | 1,600 |
| | 1,600 | 1,400 | 1,600 | | 1,600 | 1,400 | 1,600 |

As well as adjusting the values of tangible assets included in the balance sheet, it is also usually necessary to create a balance for goodwill, since the partners are also entitled to share in the value of this intangible asset. The appropriate share of goodwill created during his period of ownership is due to a retiring partner, and an incoming partner must expect to pay for a share of existing goodwill.

The partners in the new firm may decide to record the assets taken over at their revalued figures; alternatively they may choose to restate some, or all, of the assets at their pre-revaluation amounts. If the latter course is adopted, the adjustment must be shared between the partners in the new firm in accordance with their agreed profit sharing ratio. Usually, the revised figures for tangible assets are accepted and goodwill is written off.

## Example 9.4

Bill, Ben and Flo are in partnership together and share profits and losses in the ratio of 2:2:1 respectively. The balance sheet of the partnership at 31 December 19X0 was as follows:

| | £000 | £000 | | £000 | £000 |
|---|---|---|---|---|---|
| Capital Accounts | | | Fixed Assets | | |
| Bill................. | | 90 | Land and buildings.... | | 50 |
| Ben................. | | 80 | Plant and equipment... | | 175 |
| Flo................. | | 70 | | | —— |
| | | —— | | | 225 |
| | | 240 | Current Assets | | |
| Current Accounts | | | Stock............... | 80 | |
| Bill................. | 10 | | Debtors............. | 90 | |
| Ben................. | 25 | | Cash............... | 5 | |
| Flo................. | 15 | | | — | 175 |
| | —— | 50 | | | |
| | | —— | | | |
| | | 290 | | | |
| Trade Creditors....... | | 110 | | | |
| | | —— | | | —— |
| | | 400 | | | 400 |

The following information is relevant:
A. Bill decides to retire on 31 December 19X0, while Ben and Flo intend to continue trading, sharing profits and losses equally.
B. To determine the amount due to Bill, the partners agree that the assets should be revalued as follows:

| | £000 |
|---|---|
| Land and buildings......................................... | 165 |
| Plant and equipment........................................ | 180 |
| Stock....................................................... | 75 |
| Debtors..................................................... | 85 |
| Goodwill................................................... | 100 |

C. After the retirement of Bill, the assets are to be left in the books at their revalued amounts, with the exception of Goodwill, which is to be written off. All adjustments are to be made through the partner's capital accounts.
D. All sums due to Bill are to be transferred to a loan account.

*Required:*
Prepare the partnership Balance Sheet for Ben and Flo after all the

above adjustments have been put into effect. Show clearly your calculation of the balances on Ben's and Flo's capital accounts and the amount due to Bill.

## Solution

### Ben and Flo Balance Sheet

| | £000 | £000 | | £000 | £000 |
|---|---|---|---|---|---|
| *Capital Accounts* | | | *Fixed Assets* | | |
| Ben.................. | | 114 | Land and buildings.... | | 165 |
| Flo................... | | 62 | Plant and equipment... | | 180 |
| | | 176 | | | 345 |
| *Current Accounts* | | | *Current Assets* | | |
| Ben.................. | 25 | | Stock................ | 75 | |
| Flo................... | 15 | | Debtors.............. | 85 | |
| | | 40 | Cash................. | 5 | |
| | | 216 | | | 165 |
| Loan from Bill........ | | 184 | | | |
| Trade creditors........ | | 110 | | | |
| | | 510 | | | 510 |

## Notes to Solution

### Revaluation Account

| | £000 | | £000 |
|---|---|---|---|
| Stock.................... | 5 | Goodwill................ | 100 |
| Debtors................. | 5 | Land and buildings....... | 115 |
| SURPLUS: | | Plant and equipment...... | 5 |
| Bill (loan a/c)........... | 84 | | |
| Ben: Capital account...... | 84 | | |
| Flo: Capital account...... | 42 | | |
| | 210 | | |
| | 220 | | 220 |

### Capital Accounts

| | Ben £000 | Flo £000 | | Ben £000 | Flo £000 |
|---|---|---|---|---|---|
| Goodwill............. | 50 | 50 | Balance b/d.......... | 80 | 70 |
| Balance c/d.......... | 114 | 62 | Surplus.............. | 84 | 42 |
| | 164 | 112 | | 164 | 112 |

*Amount due to Bill*

|  | £000 |
|---|---|
| Balance:Capital account.................................... | 90 |
| Current account................................. | 10 |
| Surplus.......................................... | 84 |
|  | 184 |

*Note* that all sums due to the retired partner are shown as a loan rather than as capital as he is no longer a partner.

Readers should now work Question 9.4 at the end of this chapter.

**9.5.2 Change in Profit Sharing Ratio**    It is necessary to revalue the assets when there is an alteration in the ratio in which profits are split so that changes in value up to that time are shared in the ratio which prevailed while they accrued; subsequent changes are shared in the new ratio. Failure to adopt this approach means that all value changes would be shared in the new ratio, even though this did not apply while some of the changes took place. Some assets may have increased in value while others have lost value, and a value should be assigned to goodwill. The necessary adjustments to values are again made through a revaluation account, the balance on which is shared between the partners in the old profit sharing ratio. If the original values of any assets are to be reinstated, the adjustments are also made through the revaluation account, the balance on which is transferred to the partners' capital accounts in accordance with the new ratio.

**Example 9.5**
Cut and Hack are in partnership sharing profits and losses equally. The firm's summarised balance sheet at 30 June 19X7 was:

|  |  | £ |  | £ |
|---|---|---|---|---|
| Capital: | Cut .............. | 5,000 | Fixed assets................. | 7,000 |
|  | Hack ............. | 5,000 | Working capital............. | 3,000 |
|  |  | 10,000 |  | 10,000 |

Hack decides to reduce the amount of time he spends working for the business, and it is agreed that from 1 July 19X7 profits should be shared between Cut and Hack in the ratio 2:1 respectively.

The partners consider that fair current values for the assets on 30 June 19X7 are:

|  | £ |
|---|---|
| Fixed assets........................................... | 10,000 |
| Working capital....................................... | 3,500 |
| Goodwill............................................. | 5,500 |

The assets are to be recorded in the books at their original values, after the necessary adjustments consequent upon the change in the profit sharing ratio have been effected.

## Required:

(a) Prepare the revaluation account of the partnership to record all the adjustments made to asset values.

(b) Prepare the partners' capital accounts showing clearly the balances after all adjustments have been made.

(c) Prepare the revised balance sheet of Cut and Hack.

## Solution

(a)

### Revaluation Account

| | £ | | £ |
|---|---|---|---|
| Surplus: Cut............... | 4,500 | Fixed assets.................. | 3,000 |
| Hack.............. | 4,500 | Working capital............. | 500 |
| | | Goodwill................... | 5,500 |
| | 9,000 | | 9,000 |
| Fixed assets................. | 3,000 | Written off: | |
| Working capital............. | 500 | Cut........................ | 6,000 |
| Goodwill................... | 5,500 | Hack...................... | 3,000 |
| | 9,000 | | 9,000 |

(b)

### Capital Accounts

| | Cut | Hack | | Cut | Hack |
|---|---|---|---|---|---|
| | £ | £ | | £ | £ |
| Revaluation account... | 6,000 | 3,000 | Opening balance...... | 5,000 | 5,000 |
| Balance c/d.......... | 3,500 | 6,500 | Revaluation account... | 4,500 | 4,500 |
| | 9,500 | 9,500 | | 9,500 | 9,500 |

(c)

*Revised Balance Sheet*

| Capital: | | £ | | £ |
|---|---|---|---|---|
| | Cut ........... | 3,500 | Fixed assets.............. | 7,000 |
| | Hack ......... | 6,500 | Working capital.......... | 3,000 |
| | | 10,000 | | 10,000 |

## 9.5.3 Dissolution of Partnerships

When a partnership comes to the end of its life, perhaps because the partners decide to sell up and retire, the firm is dissolved. In these circumstances, the assets are sold, the liabilities settled and the business ceases to exist. The *Partnership Act 1890* requires that the money raised from the sale of assets must be applied in the following order:

1. To settle all the firm's debts, other than those to the partners.
2. To repay any *loans* owed to partners.
3. To settle amounts due to partners on their capital and current accounts.

If, after all the assets have been sold, debts settled and loans repaid, any partner has a net debit balance on his combined capital and current accounts, he must introduce cash to cover the deficiency. If he cannot pay, the deficiency is allocated to the other partners on the basis of the balances on their capital accounts.

A realisation account, similar to that used for the sole trader and described in section 4.3 of chapter 8, is used to record the dissolution of the partnership. The following entries are made in it:

| Debit | Credit | With |
|---|---|---|
| Realisation Account | Sundry Asset Accounts | Book Values of Assets |
| Cash Account | Realisation Account | Receipts from Sale of Assets |
| Realisation Account | Cash | Expenses of Realisation |
| Capital Account | Realisation Account | Assets taken over by Partners at Valuation |
| Creditor Accounts | Realisation Account | Any gains (eg discounts) on Settlement |
| Realisation Account | Capital Accounts | Share of Profit on Realisation |
| Capital Accounts | Realisation Account | Share of Loss on Realisation |

## Example 9.6
Tape and Ribbon trade in partnership and share profits and losses equally. The firm's summarised balance sheet at 31 December 19X8 is:

| | | £ | | £ |
|---|---|---|---|---|
| Capital: | Tape............. | 15,000 | Fixed assets................. | 20,000 |
| | Ribbon........... | 12,500 | Current assets.............. | 12,500 |
| | | 27,500 | | |
| Overdraft.................. | | 1,000 | | |
| Sundry creditors........... | | 4,000 | | |
| | | 32,500 | | 32,500 |

The partners agree to dissolve the firm. Tape is to take over some of the fixed assets at a valuation of £14,000. The remaining fixed assets are sold for £20,000 and the current assets realise £15,000.

The expenses of realisation are £1,000 and a prompt payment discount of £200 is received from the creditors.

*Required:*
  (a)  The firm's Realisation Account
  (b)  The partners' Capital Accounts
  (c)  The firm's Cash Account

## Solution
(a)

*Realisation Account*

| | £ | | £ |
|---|---|---|---|
| Fixed assets................. | 20,000 | Tape (Fixed assets)........... | 14,000 |
| Current assets.............. | 12,500 | Cash (Fixed assets)........... | 20,000 |
| Cash (Expenses)............. | 1,000 | Cash (Current Assets)........ | 15,000 |
| Tape...................... | 7,850 | Discount Received........... | 200 |
| Ribbon................... | 7,850 | | |
| | 49,200 | | 49,200 |

(b)

### Capital Accounts

|  | Tape £ | Ribbon £ |  | Tape £ | Ribbon £ |
|---|---|---|---|---|---|
| Realisation A/c....... | 14,000 | – | Balance b/d.......... | 15,000 | 12,500 |
| Cash ............... | 8,850 | 20,350 | Realisation A/c....... | 7,850 | 7,850 |
|  | 22,850 | 20,350 |  | 22,850 | 20,350 |

(c)

### Cash Account

|  | £ |  | £ |
|---|---|---|---|
| Realisation Account: |  | Balance b/d............... | 1,000 |
| Fixed assets.............. | 20,000 | Realisation expenses......... | 1,000 |
| Current assets............ | 15,000 | Sundry creditors............ | 3,800 |
|  |  | Tape ..................... | 8,850 |
|  |  | Ribbon .................. | 20,350 |
|  | 35,000 |  | 35,000 |

Readers should now work Question 9.5 at the end of this chapter.

## 9.6 QUESTIONS
Questions 9.1 to 9.5 test individual aspects of partnership accounts specifically dealt with in this chapter; questions 9.6 and 9.7 deal with the preparation of a full set of partnership accounts.

### Question 9.1
Jack, Jill and Jane trade together in partnership, and they have agreed to share profits and losses on the following basis:
1. Annual salaries of £10,000, £7,500 and £5,000 are to be paid to Jack, Jill and Jane respectively.
2. Interest of 12% is to be allowed on the average balance of each partner's capital account for the year.
3. Interest of 12% is to be charged on drawings.
4. Residual profits and losses are to be shared: Jack 40%; Jill 40%; and Jane 20%.

You are given the following additional information:
1. On 1 January 19X2, the balances on the partners' capital accounts were:

|  | £ |
|---|---|
| Jack | 30,000 |
| Jill | 20,000 |
| Jane | 40,000 |

On 30 June 19X2, Jill introduced further capital of £5,000

2. The charges for interest on drawings for 19X2 are:

|  | £ |
|---|---|
| Jack | 600 |
| Jill | 450 |
| Jane | 400 |

3. The firm made a profit of £42,000 in 19X2.

*Required:*
Prepare the partnership appropriation account for 19X2.

## Question 9.2
*Required:*
(a) Prepare the partnership appropriation account of the Jack, Jill and Jane partnership using the information given in question 9.1 above and assuming that no partnership agreement exists.
(b) Explain the basis on which you have divided the profit in part (a).

## Question 9.3
Ice and Cube are in partnership, sharing profits and losses equally. The balances on their capital and current accounts at 1 January 19X4 are:

|  | Capital | Current |
|---|---|---|
|  | £ | £ |
| Ice............................................ | 50,000 | 30,000 |
| Cube........................................ | 60,000 | 20,000 |

The trading profit for 19X4 was £45,000, and during the year the cash drawings of Ice were £12,500 and of Cube £14,000. In addition, Ice took over one of the firm's cars at its book value of £1,500 to give to his daughter as an eighteenth birthday present.

The partners review the accounts for 19X4 and decide that, as some of their current account balances have been invested in the expansion of the firm, Ice should transfer £20,000 and Cube £10,000 from current to capital account.

*Required:*
Prepare the partners' current and capital accounts for 19X4.

## Question 9.4

Bush and Shrub are in partnership and share profits and losses in the ratio 1:2 respectively. The firm's balance sheet at 31 December 19X4 was:

|  | £ |  | £ |
|---|---|---|---|
| Capital: Bush............. | 10,000 | Fixed assets.............. | 15,000 |
| Shrub.......... | 20,000 | Working capital.......... | 15,000 |
|  | 30,000 |  | 30,000 |

It is agreed:
1. Flower is to join the firm as a partner on 1 January 19X5.
2. After 1 January 19X5 the partners are to share profits and losses equally.
3. Flower is to introduce cash of £14,000 as capital.
4. The assets are to be revalued:

|  | £ |
|---|---|
| Fixed assets.......................................... | 20,000 |
| Working capital...................................... | 13,000 |
| Goodwill............................................ | 9,000 |

5. The original asset values are to be reinstated after the adjustments resulting from Flower's joining have been made, and goodwill is to be written off.

*Required:*
(a) Prepare the revaluation account of the partnership.
(b) Prepare the partners' capital accounts.
(c) Prepare the partnership balance sheet on 1 January 19X5 after Flower has been admitted and all the consequent adjustments made.

## Question 9.5
Hex, Why and Zed trade in partnership and have always shared profits equally. The following is the firm's summarised balance sheet at 31 March 19X6:

|  | £ | £ |
|---|---|---|
| Fixed Assets at Written Down Value................ |  | 30,000 |
| Current Assets: |  |  |
| Stock...................................... | 21,000 |  |
| Debtors..................................... | 7,200 |  |
| Cash ....................................... | 3,250 |  |
|  | 31,450 |  |
| Less: Current Liabilities........................ | 12,370 |  |
|  |  | 19,080 |
|  |  | 49,080 |
| Capital Accounts: |  |  |
| Hex........................................ |  | 17,360 |
| Why ....................................... |  | 15,760 |
| Zed........................................ |  | 15,960 |
|  |  | 49,080 |

The partners decided to dissolve the partnership on 31 March 19X6, and the following transactions took place on 1 April 19X6:
1. Costs of dissolution of £1,000 paid in cash.
2. Hex took over most of the fixed assets at an agreed value of £35,000 and Why took stock valued at £1,500.
3. The rest of the fixed assets were sold for £6,000 cash and the remainder of the stock for £22,000 cash.
4. Creditors were paid in full and £6,850 received from debtors; the rest of the debts were bad.

*Required:*
(a) Prepare the realisation account of the partnership.
(b) Prepare the firm's cash account to record the dissolution.
(c) Prepare and close off the partners' capital accounts.
*Note:* All the partners are solvent and able to pay any amounts due to the partnership arising from the dissolution.

## Question 9.6

Second and Minute started trading as retail grocers in partnership on 1 January 19X4, but did not keep a set of double entry books. The firm's bank account, for 19X4, prepared from the record of cheques issued and cash paid into the bank, was:

| | £ | | £ |
|---|---|---|---|
| Capital introduced: | | Purchases............... | 160,000 |
| Second............... | 20,000 | Wages.................. | 17,000 |
| Minute............... | 20,000 | Rent and rates........... | 3,500 |
| Sales receipts banked...... | 200,000 | Light and heat........... | 1,260 |
| | | Delivery van............. | 19,000 |
| | | Drawings: Second........ | 18,000 |
| | | Minute....... | 16,000 |
| | | Balance c/d............. | 5,240 |
| | 240,000 | | 240,000 |

*Notes:*

1. The following payments were made directly from cash sales receipts:

| | £ |
|---|---|
| Petrol for van.................................... | 2,000 |
| Maintenance..................................... | 1,000 |
| Advertising...................................... | 900 |
| Purchases....................................... | 2,500 |
| | 6,400 |

2. The van, purchased on 1 January 19X4, is expected to have a life of 5 years, at the end of which its scrap value will be £3,000
3. The partners agree that separate capital and current accounts are to be kept and all profits and losses are to be shared equally.
4. At 31 December 19X4:

| | £ |
|---|---|
| Debtors...................................... | 5,460 |
| Trade creditors................................ | 3,800 |
| Prepaid rent.................................. | 100 |
| Light and heat accrued......................... | 140 |
| Stock........................................ | 9,200 |

5. During 19X4 both Second and Minute took groceries for personal use at cost price as follows:

| | £ |
|---|---|
| Second.......................................... | 1,000 |
| Minute.......................................... | 1,260 |
| | 2,260 |

*Required:*
Prepare the Trading and Profit and Loss Account for the year to 31
December 19X4 and the Balance Sheet at that date.

**Question 9.7**
The following is the trial balance of Bean and Stalk, who trade in
partnership, at 31 March 19X3:

| | £ | £ |
|---|---|---|
| Capital Account Balances 1 April 19X2: | | |
| Bean........................................ | | 30,000 |
| Stalk........................................ | | 10,000 |
| Current Account Balances 1 April 19X2: | | |
| Bean........................................ | | 3,000 |
| Stalk........................................ | | 5,000 |
| Sales........................................ | | 150,000 |
| Stock 1 April 19X2........................... | 30,000 | |
| Wages....................................... | 14,500 | |
| Rent........................................ | 5,000 | |
| Expenses.................................... | 3,000 | |
| Heat and light............................... | 1,200 | |
| Debtors/creditors............................ | 14,000 | 11,500 |
| Delivery costs............................... | 5,300 | |
| Drawings: | | |
| Bean........................................ | 7,000 | |
| Stalk........................................ | 9,000 | |
| Cash........................................ | 4,500 | |
| Fixed assets................................. | 6,000 | |
| Purchases................................... | 110,000 | |
| | 209,500 | 209,500 |

*Notes:*
1. Stock at 31 March 19X3 was valued at £40,000.
2. Depreciation of £1,500 is to be written off the Fixed Assets for
   the year to 31 March 19X3.
3. At 31 March 19X3 wages accrued amounted to £500 and rent of
   £1,000 was prepaid.
4. On 1 February 19X3 the firm ordered and paid for goods costing
   £700. These were recorded as purchases but were never received
   as they were lost by the carrier responsible for their delivery. The
   carrier accepted liability for the loss during March 19X3 and
   paid full compensation of £700 in April 19X3. No entries had
   been made in the books in respect of the loss or claim.
5. Bean took goods which had cost the firm £340 for his own use

during the year. No entry had been made in the books to record this.

6. The partnership agreement provided that profits and losses should be shared equally between the partners after:

    (a) allowing annual salaries of £2,000 to Bean and £4,000 to Stalk;

    (b) allowing interest of 5% per annum on the balance of each partner's capital account; and

    (c) charging Bean £200 and Stalk £300 interest in drawings.

7. The balances on the Capital Accounts shall remain unchanged, all adjustments being recorded in the Current Accounts.

*Required:*

Prepare the Trading, Profit and Loss and Appropriation Accounts for the Bean and Stalk partnership for the year to 31 March 19X3 and the Balance Sheet at that date.

# CHAPTER 10

# Company Accounts

The three main ways in which business activity is structured within the private sector were outlined in chapter 1; these are the sole trader, the partnership and the limited company. The accounting practices of sole traders and partnerships have been examined in earlier chapters and here we turn our attention to the form and content of the accounts of limited companies.

## 10.1 FORMATION OF 'REGISTERED' COMPANIES

A limited company is formed by registering under the Companies Act 1985, hence the term 'registered' company. Registration is a fairly simple process, but certain formalities must be complied with. It is possible for the individuals wishing to form a limited company to do the work themselves; alternatively they may choose to employ a specialist company registration agent who charges a fee in the region of £150. The following information must be filed with the Registrar of Companies at, or soon after, the registration date:

1. The names and addresses of the first directors.
2. A statement showing the amount of the company's authorised share capital (see section 6 of this chapter).
3. The address of the company's registered offfice.
4. The company's memorandum of association and articles of association.

A company must have at least two shareholders whose names and addresses appear in the memorandum to demonstrate the fact that this requirement has been fulfilled. The memorandum also gives the company's name and the nature of its proposed operations which are contained in the 'objects' clause(s). The purpose of the objects clause is to provide an element of protection for shareholders and creditors by ensuring that money invested and credit advanced is used for the expected purpose. For instance, if the company's object is to drill for oil in the North Sea, money invested for this purpose should not be used to acquire a chain of fish and chip shops in West

Yorkshire, however good the food may be. Where the directors enter into an *ultra vires* transaction, i.e.outside the scope of the powers specified in the objects clause, any debt which results is unenforceable against the company. In practice the protection provided by the *ultra vires* rule is more illusory than real; the full future range of business activities is rarely known when the company is formed, and the normal practice is to file objects clauses which cover not only transactions to be undertaken initially, but also all incidental activities and other areas of business into which the company may conceivably wish to expand at some future date.

The articles of association set out the internal rules and regulations of the company which must be observed by both shareholders and management; they deal with such matters as the voting rights of shareholders, the appointment and powers of directors and the borrowing powers of the company. The Companies Act contains a model set of articles which apply to any limited company not filing articles of its own. The specimen articles also apply to the extent that they are not specifically modified or excluded by any articles which the company files. The model articles are rarely entirely suitable and articles 'tailor made' to the company's individual requirements are usually prepared.

## 10.2 TYPES OF COMPANY
There are a number of different types of registered company (see Figure 10.1) and the option chosen will depend on the nature and scale of expected business operations.

**Figure 10.1**
*Types of Registered Company*

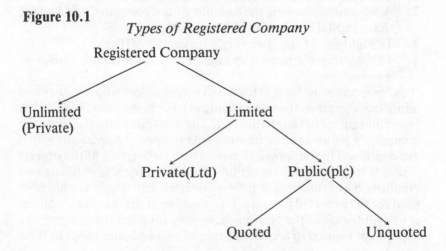

It is first necessary to decide whether the company is to be registered with limited liability or unlimited liability. Usually the main reason for forming a company is to obtain the protection of limited liability for business activities which, by their very nature, are likely to involve a significant element of risk. For this reason unlimited companies are few and far between, and we do not therefore need to consider them further.

There are two basic categories of limited company: the public company and the private company. The public company must include the designatory letters plc after its name, and must have a minimum issued share capital (see section 6 of this chapter) of £50,000, of which at least one quarter must be collected at the outset. Private companies must use the designatory letters Ltd and are not allowed to make an issue of shares or debentures (see section 10 of this chapter) to the general public. For both types of company the minimum number of shareholders is two and there is no maximum. Public companies are able to increase the marketability of their shares and debentures by making arrangements for these securities to be quoted on the Stock Exchange, but this is a feasible exercise only for very large concerns.

## 10.3 SEPARATION OF OWNERSHIP AND MANAGEMENT

The registered company was first created by the Companies Act 1844 so that business activity could be financed by raising capital from the general public. This type of business organisation eventually helped to transform completely the structure of British industry. The economy had previously been characterised by a very large number of small business units; sole traders and partnerships dominated, with the same individuals providing the bulk of the finance and taking all the major managerial decisions, i.e. ownership and management were in the same hands. The essential feature of the registered company is that it has the facility to raise a large quantity of capital by attracting finance in small amounts from many individuals. These 'share' holders do not necessarily play any part in running the concern since this job is often delegated to professional managers, called the Board of Directors. These circumstances produce a separation of the ownership group from the management group.

The extent of the separation varies tremendously, however, depending on the type of company involved. The small family firm, which previously traded as a partnership, may register as a private limited company simply to obtain the protection of limited liability. No other organisational changes need necessarily occur and the owners may continue to manage. In many private companies there is a looser connection between ownership and management, e.g. many of the shareholders may be members of the family interested in the business only as a source of unearned income, acquaintances of the family or business contacts, and play no part in management. In these circumstances, however, the members of the Board are likely to hold a significant proportion of the total shares issued. It is in the public limited company, whose shares are quoted on the Stock Exchange, that the separation between ownership and management is likely to be most marked; there may well be thousands of shareholders, with only a minute fraction of the issued share capital owned by members of the Board. Details of the shareholdings in Thorn EMI plc are given in Figure 10.2.

## Figure 10.2

### Analysis of Shareholdings in Thorn EMI plc

| Bands of Shareholdings at 28 June 1984 | Number of Shareholders | Total Ordinary Shares held |
|---|---|---|
| 1 to 500 | 39,605 | 6,907,751 |
| 501 to 2,500 | 11,157 | 10,756,281 |
| 2,501 to 5,000 | 796 | 2,849,383 |
| 5,001 to 10,000 | 354 | 2,591,338 |
| 10,001 and above | 887 | 151,810,176 |
| | 52,799 | 174,914,929 |

| Analysis of Shareholders as at 28 June 1984 | Total Shares held | Percentage of Ordinary Shares |
|---|---|---|
| Individuals | 22,068,552 | 12.61 |
| Banks and Nominees | 80,207,196 | 45.85 |
| Insurance Companies | 35,677,182 | 20.40 |
| Pension Funds | 26,072,484 | 14.91 |
| Other Corporate Bodies | 10,889,515 | 6.23 |
| | 174,914,929 | 100.00 |

At 31 March 1984 the directors' interests totalled 35,818 ordinary shares which was less than one quarter of one per cent of the company's issued ordinary share capital.

The separation of ownership and management puts the shareholder in a potentially vulnerable position. He has invested his money in a company and must rely on management to use the resources wisely. Naturally he wishes to know what progress has been made, and it is for this reason that directors are legally required to publish a profit and loss account and balance sheet at least once a year (The Stock Exchange requires quoted companies also to publish half yearly results).

## 10.4  CREDITORS' RISK

The introduction of limited liability shifted much of the financial risk associated with business activity from the owner to the creditor because, in the event of failure, the creditor could no longer claim against the owner's personal assets. Therefore, a careful assessment of the credit-worthiness of a potential customer became a greater priority. A thorough examination of the company's financial standing, as exhibited in its balance sheet, is therefore a sensible precaution, particularly before it is decided to grant credit to a first time customer. For this reason Company Law has taken steps to ensure that this information is publicly available at Companies House (see section 5.1 of this chapter).

## 10.5  REGULATIONS.

**10.5.1 Legal Regulations** The affairs of registered companies are regulated by the Companies Act 1985.

At Stage 1, students are not required to prepare accounts in accordance with the detailed disclosure requirements of the Act; this is Stage 2 material. However, answers should be presented in good form and, for this purpose, a specimen layout is given in Figure 10.3 which complies broadly with legal requirements.

# Figure 10.3     *Specimen Accounts for a Limited Company*

*Balance Sheet*

| | £ | £ |
|---|---|---|
| *Fixed Assets* | | |
| Intangible asset: Goodwill | | xxx |
| Tangible assets: Land and buildings | xxx | |
|                 Plant and machinery | xxx | |
|                 Fixtures and fittings | xxx | xxx |
| Investments | | xxx |
| | | xxx |
| | | |
| *Current Assets* | | |
| Stocks | xxx | |
| Trade debtors | xxx | |
| Prepayments | xxx | |
| Temporary investments | xxx | |
| Cash at bank | xxx | |
| | xxx | |
| *Less: Current Liabilities* | | |
| Debenture loans repayable within one year | xxx | |
| Unsecured loans repayable within one year | xxx | |
| Bank loans and overdrafts | xxx | |
| Trade creditors | xxx | |
| Taxation | xxx | |
| Dividends payable | xxx | |
| Accruals | xxx | |
| Net Current Assets (Working Capital) | | xxx |
| Total Assets less Current Liabilities | | xxx |
| *Less: Non-Current Liabilities* | | |
| Debentures | xxx | |
| Unsecured loans | xxx | |
| Taxation | xxx | xxx |
| | | xxx |
| | | |
| *Financed by:* | | |
| Share capital: Authorised | | xxx |
|                 Issued | | xxx |
| Share premium account | | xxx |
| Revaluation reserve | | xxx |
| General reserve | | xxx |
| Retained profit | | xxx |
| | | xxx |

*Specimen Accounts for a Limited Company*
*Trading, Profit and Loss and Appropriation Account*

|  | £ | £ |
|---|---|---|
| Turnover |  | xxx |
| Less: Cost of sales |  | xxx |
| Gross profit |  | xxx |
| Less: Distribution costs | xxx |  |
| Administration expenses | xxx | xxx |
| Net profit before tax |  | xxx |
| Less: Corporation tax |  | xxx |
| Net profit after tax |  | xxx |
| Less: Dividends | xxx |  |
| Transfer to reserves | xxx | xxx |
| Retained profit for the year |  | xxx |
| Retained profit at beginning of year |  | xxx |
| Retained profit at end of year |  | xxx |

*Notes:*
1. In the case of fixed assets, figures for original cost (or revalued amount) and accumulated depreciation should be provided.
2. The statements need amendment to take account of the particular circumstances of each case.

Copies of the profit and loss account and balance sheet must be sent to every shareholder and debenture holder at least twenty-one days before the annual general meeting (AGM). Other interested parties are able to discover the content of a company's annual accounts by taking advantage of the requirement for a copy to be filed with the Registrar of Companies as part of the annual return. These copies are available for public inspection at Companies House in London and in Cardiff. A payment of £1 must be made for each company's file inspected, and the customer is allowed to take away microfiche copies of the documents filed when the company was registered and the last few years' published accounts. The accounts filed with the Registrar are abridged versions of the shareholders' accounts in the case of 'small' and 'medium' sized companies as defined by the Act. The reason for this concession is to allow what are, in many cases, small family businesses a measure of confidentiality. A drawback regarding the information available at Companies House is that accounts need not be filed until nine months after the end of the accounting period to which they relate, and many companies even fail to keep to this generous timetable; hence the material is often hopelessly out of date.

**10.5.2 Other Regulations** The accounting profession issues additional instructions regarding the form and content of published accounts. The instructions are called Statements of Standard Accounting Practice (SSAPs) and they are formally issued by the Accounting Standards Committee on behalf of the accounting profession. Their main purpose is to improve the quality and comparability of published accounts by encouraging companies to employ procedures considered to represent best accounting practice. For example, SSAP 9 is entitled 'Stocks and Work in Progress', and this favours the total cost basis for valuing stocks for external reporting purposes. To date (August 1985) twenty-three SSAPs have been issued. A number of these are examined at Stage 2 but they are outside the Stage 1 syllabus. A final source of regulations is the instructions issued by the Stock Exchange which apply only to public quoted companies.

The remainder of this chapter examines a number of important respects in which limited company accounts differ from those prepared for sole traders and partnerships.

## 10.6   SHARE CAPITAL

The memorandum of association contains details of the share capital with which the company is to be initially registered and the division of that share capital into shares of a fixed amount. The figure for the company's registered share capital is described as the *authorised* share capital, and the face value of each share is called the 'nominal' or 'par' value. A company may be registered, for example, with an authorised share capital of £500,000 divided into 500,000 shares of £1 each. There is no fixed rule regarding the nominal value of each share, though £1 is often used.

There are a number of different categories of share capital; the two most common are *ordinary* or (equity) shares and *preference* shares. As the name implies, preference shares are given priority over ordinary shares as regards both payment of the annual dividend and repayment of capital on liquidation.

*Dividends* The annual dividend payable on preference shares is fixed, at say 8% per annum, and the dividend is usually paid if profits are sufficient. If profits are insufficient the dividend is lost, unless cumulative preference shares have been issued in which case any arrears must be paid, when trading results improve, before any dividend is paid to the ordinary shareholders. The dividend payable on ordinary shares is entirely at the discretion of the directors; if profits are low and/or the directors wish to retain all profits earned within the company, they may decide to pay no dividend whatsoever.

*Capital repayment* On liquidation of the company, business assets are applied first to settle outstanding liabilities and secondly to repay the preference shareholders the nominal value of their investment. Any balance which then remains is paid out to the ordinary shareholders as they possess the equity interest in the concern. Because creditors must be repaid first, often nothing is left over for shareholders in circumstances where the company is forced into liquidation by financial difficulties.

The directors do not necessarily issue the company's entire authorised share capital at the outset. The figure initially registered represents the total amount the directors expect the company to need over perhaps the next ten years. To begin with, however, the scale of activity may be relatively modest and the volume of shares issued should be restricted accordingly. The way in which the shares are issued depends, in particular, on whether the company is private or public. It is likely that the issued share capital of private companies will be acquired entirely by members of the first board of directors, and perhaps also their families and friends; in the case of a public company, an invitation may be made to the general public to acquire some, if not the whole, of the share capital which the directors plan to issue. In the latter case the shares are advertised in a document, known as the prospectus, the content of which is regulated by company law and, in the case of listed companies, also by the Stock Exchange rules.

Shareholders are not necessarily required to pay immediately the full nominal value of shares acquired. The nominal value may be paid in a number of stages; for example, in the case of a £1 share issued at par, 15p may be payable when the shares are applied for, a further 25p when the shares are issued (called the allotment) and two further instalments, designated 'calls', of 30p each at some future date. Where shares are offered to the general public, it is extremely unlikely for applications to match exactly the number of shares available for issue. If the issue is fifty per cent over-subscribed, one way of dealing with the problem is to issue each subscriber with two thirds of the shares applied for. If the issue is undersubscribed it is likely to fail unless the company has taken the precaution of arranging for the issue to be underwritten. The function of the underwriter, often a finance house or an insurance company, is to guarantee the success of an issue by undertaking to subscribe for a new issue of shares to the extent that it is not taken up by the general public. The transaction is in the nature of a speculation; if the issue is popular the underwriter receives his commission and does nothing, but if it fails to attract the required number of subscriptions the underwriter is obliged to acquire shares for which there is little demand and whose price, initially, is likely to fall.

**Example 10.1**
Griffin Ltd., a newly established private company, is registered with a share capital of £1,000,000 divided into 1,000,000 ordinary shares with a nominal value of £1 each. On 1 January 19X1 400,000 shares are issued at par to members of the board of directors and paid for immediately in cash.

*Required:*
Prepare the capital section of Griffin's balance sheet as at 1 January 19X1.

**Solution**

*Extracts from the Balance Sheet of Griffin Ltd. as at 1 January 19X1.*

|  | £ |
|---|---|
| Share Capital: | |
| *Authorised.* 1,000,000 ordinary shares of £1 each................ | 1,000,000 |
| *Issued.* 400,000 ordinary shares of £1 each fully paid............ | 400,000 |

The location of these items in a full balance sheet can be seen by referring back to Figure 10.3.

## 10.7 SHARE PREMIUM ACCOUNT

The initial issue of shares is normally made at par value and if, a few days later, one of the shareholders decides to sell his investment, he is likely to obtain a price not materially different from the issue price. The reason why there is unlikely to be a significant difference between the issue price and the resale price, at this stage, is because the prospects of the company have not materially altered during the short space of time which has elapsed since the company was formed. As time goes by the position changes and, assuming the company is successful, the demand for its shares is likely to rise with the result that the original shareholders are able to demand a price in excess of the nominal value when selling their shares to new investors. The nominal value of each share may be £1 but, depending on the success of the company, its market price may rise to, say, £1.50. It must be recognised, however, that any rise or fall in the market price of the company's shares has no effect on the finances of the company itself, and the shares continue to be reported in the balance sheet at their nominal value of £1.

The directors may decide, at some later stage, to make a further issue of shares to help finance an expansion of the company's scale of operations. This additional issue will be made, not at nominal value, but at the best price then obtainable. If the market value of the shares is £1.50, the issue price will be fixed at approximately that figure. An accounting problem arises because of a legal requirement that all share issues, not only the first, must be recorded in the share capital account at their nominal value. This problem is solved by recording any excess of the issue price over nominal value in a share premium account.

### Example 10.2

Assume the same facts as in Example 10.1, also that on 31 December 19X5 Griffin Ltd. issues, for cash, a further 200,000 ordinary shares at a price of £1.50 each.

*Required:*
Prepare the capital section of Griffin's balance sheet as at 31 December 19X5.

## Solution

*Extracts from the Balance Sheet of Griffin Ltd. as at 31 December 19X5.*

| Share Capital | £ |
|---|---|
| *Authorised.* 1,000,000 ordinary shares of £1 each................ | 1,000,000 |
| | |
| *Issued.* 600,000 ordinary shares of £1 each fully paid............. | 600,000 |
| Share premium account.................................... | 100,000 |

The balance on the share premium account must be treated in the same manner as share capital, which means that no part of it may be repaid to the shareholders except on liquidation or in the carefully controlled circumstances examined at Stage 2. There is, however, a limited range of uses to which the balance appearing to the credit of the share premium account may be put. These are:

1. To pay up any unissued shares for distribution to members as fully paid bonus shares (see section 14 of this chapter).
2. To write off (a) any preliminary expenses, such as solicitors' fees, incurred when the company was formed, or (b) any expenses of, or commission paid or discount allowed on, any issue of shares or debentures of the company.
3. To write off any premium payable on the redemption of debentures (see section 13 of this chapter) or shares (examined at Stage 2).

## 10.8  SHARE FORFEITURE

Sometimes a subscriber pays his application money but defaults either when required to pay the amount due on allotment or on one of the later calls. This may happen because he is short of money or because he feels that the shares are no longer a good buy. Since he has contracted to acquire the shares it is possible for the company to sue for the balance due but, even where the defaulting shareholder is perfectly solvent, this course of action is unlikely to be followed. The directors are more likely to exercise their right, under the company's articles, to consider the shares forfeited. The directors then endeavour to find another investor who is willing to acquire the shares at a price at least equal to the balance outstanding. Any excess received is credited to share premium account.

### Example 10.3

Thatchers Ltd is registered with a share capital of £500,000 divided into 1,000,000 ordinary shares with a nominal value of £0.50 each. On 1 January 19X2 600,000 shares are issued with the agreement that £0.30 is paid immediately and the balance outstanding on 31 March 19X2. The appropriate amounts are received on the dates due, except that Broke, who acquired 500 shares on 1 January, defaults on the payment of the final call. On 1 June the shares are forfeited and reissued to Wealthy for £0.45 each.

*Required:*
Appropriate balance sheet extracts from the capital section of Thatchers Ltd's balance sheet at:
(i)   1 January, after the shares have been issued.
(ii)  1 June, after Broke's shares have been forfeited and reissued to Wealthy.

**Solution.**

(i)  *Extracts from the Balance Sheet of Thatchers Ltd as at 1 January 19X2*

| | £ |
|---|---|
| Share Capital: | |
| *Authorised.* 1,000,000 ordinary shares of £0.50 each . . . . . . . . . . . . . . . . . . . . . | 500,000 |
| | |
| *Issued.* 600,000 ordinary shares of £0.50, £0.30 paid . . . . . . . . . . . . . . . . . . . . . | 180,000 |

(ii)  *Extracts from the Balance Sheet of Thatchers Ltd as at 1 June 19X2*

| | £ |
|---|---|
| Share Capital: | |
| *Authorised.* 1,000,000 ordinary shares of £0.50 each . . . . . . . . . . . . . . . . . . . . . | 500,000 |
| | |
| *Issued.* 600,000 ordinary shares of £0.50 each, fully paid . . . . . . . . . . . . . . . . . . | 300,000 |
| Share premium account . . . . . . . . . . . . . . . . . . . . . . . . . . . . . . . . . . . . . . . . . | 125* |

| | £ |
|---|---|
| *Collected from: Broke, 500 x £0.30 . . . . . . . . . . . . . . . . . . . . . . . . . . . . . . . . . . | 150 |
| Wealthy, 500 x £0.45 . . . . . . . . . . . . . . . . . . . . . . . . . . . . . | 225 |
| | |
| Total collected . . . . . . . . . . . . . . . . . . . . . . . . . . . . . . . . . . . . . . . . . . . . . . . | 375 |
| Less: Nominal value of shares issued, 500 x £0.50 . . . . . . . . . . . . . . . . . . . . . . . | 250 |
| | |
| Surplus to share premium account . . . . . . . . . . . . . . . . . . . . . . . . . . . . . . . . . . | 125 |

## 10.9   THE RIGHTS ISSUE

A rights issue occurs where a company requires additional capital and the shares are offered to existing shareholders on a pro rata basis according to their existing holdings. If the share issue described in Example 10.2 was a right issue, it would mean that the existing shareholders of Griffin Ltd were offered one new share at

£1.50 each for every two shares presently held. Public companies are legally required to raise additional share capital by way of a rights issue, unless this course of action is impracticable, in which case an invitation to subscribe may be made to the general public. A particular attraction to the company of the rights issue is that it is an inexpensive method of raising funds as the formalities associated with the issue are kept to a minimum, e.g. a full prospectus need not be issued. From the shareholders' point of view an advantage of this procedure is that control of the company remains in the same hands.

## 10.10  LOAN CAPITAL AND DEBENTURES

A company's memorandum usually authorises the directors to raise finance by borrowing money as well as by issuing shares. Such loans may be secured or unsecured. A secured loan normally takes the form of a 'debenture' which may be defined as the 'written acknowledgement of a debt usually made under seal'. The security for the loan may take the form of either a fixed charge or a floating charge on the company's assets. A fixed charge exists where the asset on which the loan is secured is specified in the debenture deed. Ideally the asset should be one which is likely to appreciate rather than depreciate in value over time, such as land and buildings. As a further protection the company is prevented from selling the charged asset without the debenture holder's express approval. A floating charge exists where the debenture is secured on particular categories of assets, for example stocks and debtors, or the assets of the company generally. This form of debenture gives the company greater flexibility, since it is allowed to trade in the assets subject to the floating charge, and their composition may well change on a daily basis.

Debentures are usually issued for a specified period of time, after which they are redeemed. The debenture deed will, however, provide for early repayment in certain circumstances. For example, should the company default on an interest payment, a receiver may be appointed by the debenture holders to take control of the secured assets, sell them, and repay the amount owed. The main differences between debentures, unsecured loans and share capital are summarised below:

1.  Debentures and unsecured loans carry interest at a fixed rate which is payable regardless of profit levels. Dividends, even on preference shares, are payable only if profits are sufficient,

and the directors decide to make a distribution which is approved by the shareholders attending the AGM.

2. Interest is an allowable expense in calculating taxable profit; dividends are not an allowable expense.

3. Interest is debited to the profit and loss account; dividends are debited to the appropriation account (see section 11 of this chapter).

4. Debentures and unsecured loans are almost always redeemable; share capital is redeemable only in certain circumstances (examined at Stage 2).

5. Debentures enjoy priority of repayment on liquidation. Unsecured loans rank alongside other unsecured creditors, such as trade creditors. Share capital is repaid, on liquidation, only if resources remain after all liabilities have been satisfied.

6. A company may at any time purchase its own debentures in the market; these then remain available for re-issue until cancelled. In certain circumstances (examined at Stage 2) a company may purchase its own shares, but these must be cancelled immediately.

7. Unsecured loans and debentures are reported in the balance sheet as a non-current liability and deducted from the balance of total assets less current liabilities (see Figure 10.3). Each year, of course, loans and debentures get closer to their redemption date, and they are eventually re-classified as a current liability when repayable during the forthcoming accounting period. Share capital is reported as part of the shareholders' equity.

## 10.11 THE APPROPRIATION ACCOUNT

Profit is calculated in the trading and profit and loss account; the way in which profit is applied is dealt with in the appropriation account. The basic procedure to be followed was demonstrated for partnerships in chapter 9; in sections 11.1 to 11.3 of this chapter, we examine the entries made to take account of the particular circumstances of the limited company.

**10.11.1 Corporation Tax**  Sole traders and partnerships pay income tax on the profits arising from their business activities, whereas the profits of limited companies are subject to corporation tax. The rate of corporation tax differs, depending on the level of profits, and is fixed in the budget. For example, the March 1984 budget fixed the rate of corporation tax on profits arising during the year to 31 March 1984 at 30% on profits up to £100,000 and 50% on profits over £½ million; a sliding scale of rates applies where profits are between £100,000 and £½ million. In the case of a profitable company corporation tax may well represent the largest single cash outflow during an accounting period, and it is therefore of considerable importance.

Corporation tax is levied on taxable profits, and a basic fact which students must grasp is that the figure for taxable profits is rarely the same as the profit figure reported in the company's accounts, which is called accounting profit. The reason for this is that the accountant and the Government have different priorities when measuring profit. A good illustration concerns the treatment of capital expenditure. The aim of the accountant is to produce a profit figure which fairly represents the results of the firm for the year. For example, if it is estimated that an item of plant will last five years and then be worthless, the accountant would consider it appropriate to spread the cost over that period and a depreciation charge of 20% might be made each year (see section 3 of chapter 7). A major priority of the Government is to ensure equity between taxpayers, and it is for this reason that they replace the depreciation charge, which may vary considerably from one company to another, with fixed rates of capital allowance which are also laid down in the budget. For example, the rate of capital allowance on plant and machinery purchased during the year ended 31 March 1985 was fixed as follows: 75% of cost written off in the year of acquisition and the remaining balance written off, on the reducing balance basis, at 25% per annum.

There are many other adjustments which produce less marked differences between accounting profit and taxable profit. For instance, the cost of entertainment, other than for overseas customers, is disallowed for tax purposes but would be treated as a business cost when accounting profit is computed.

Corporation tax is payable, by companies formed since 5 April 1965, nine months after the end of the accounting period to which it relates. The corporation tax charge is disclosed in the profit and loss appropriation account as a deduction from net profit; in the balance sheet the amount payable appears as a current liability. The aspect of taxation examined in this section is technically described as 'Mainstream' Corporation Tax; the complications of 'Advance' Corporation Tax and Deferred Tax are examined at Stage 2.

**Example 10.4**

Swan Ltd was incorporated on 1 January 19X1, issued 150,000 ordinary shares of £1 each for cash, and commenced business on the same day. Plant, purchased at a cost of £130,000, was expected to possess a four year life and be worth £10,000 at the end of that time. The company reported a profit of £90,000 for 19X1, after charging depreciation of £30,000 (£130,000 - £10,000 ÷ 4).

*Required:*
(a) A calculation of corporation tax payable for 19X1. For this purpose a first year capital allowance of 75% and a corporation tax rate of 30% are to be assumed.
(b) The appropriation account for 19X1.

**Solution**

(a)

|  | £ |
|---|---|
| Accounting profit | 90,000 |
| Add: Depreciation charge disallowed | 30,000 |
|  | 120,000 |
| Less: Capital allowance (£130,000 x 75%)* | 97,500 |
| Taxable profit | 22,500 |

Corporation tax payable, £22,500 x 30% = £6,750

*The remaining balance is carried forward and claimed against profits in future years.

(b)

*Profit and Loss Appropriation Account for 19X1*

|  | £ |
|---|---|
| Net profit before tax | 90,000 |
| Less: Corporation tax | 6,750 |
| Net profit after tax | 83,250 |

*Note.* At this level students are not expected to make calculations of taxable profit; this information will be given in the question, as will rates of corporation tax which the Government regularly changes.

**10.11.2 Dividends**   It is the job of the directors to decide how additional resources, generated as the result of profitable trading, are to be employed. There are two options: the money may be either distributed as dividends or retained in the business.

Investors are willing to finance business activity because they expect that, at some future date, the cash returns to them will exceed their initial investment by an amount sufficient to compensate for risk and loss of liquidity. The shareholder of a limited company expects to receive cash returns in two forms, namely dividends and the sales proceeds which arise when the security is eventually sold. Under UK law it is for management to decide how much the firm can afford to pay in the form of a dividend. The shareholders have no power to increase the dividend, but they can choose to accept a lesser amount. The rationale underlying this rule is that the directors are in the best position to judge how much the company can afford, and the shareholders are prevented from insisting on higher payouts which might undermine the financial position of the concern and thereby prejudice the claims of creditors. Dividends, which are expressed in terms of pence per share, appear as a deduction in the appropriation account. The final dividend is usually paid some months after the end of the financial year, the amount payable being decided upon when the results for the year are known. Where the directors are fairly confident that results will be satisfactory, it is common practice to pay an interim dividend during the financial year.

The directors rarely pay out the entire profits in the form of dividends, and shareholders are usually willing to accept a decision to retain resources within the company because, although they forego immediate income, the expectation is that reinvestment will produce greater future returns. Management usually aims for a reasonable balance between distributions and retentions, although in relatively good years the proportion distributed may be rather lower than in poor years when the bulk of the reported profits may be paid out as dividends to demonstrate management's confidence in the future viability of the concern.

Where the current year's profit is insufficient, dividends can be either partly or wholly paid out of undistributed profits brought forward. Where there are accumulated losses brought forward, these must first be made good before a dividend is paid out of the current year's profit.

**Example 10.5**
Hanbury Ltd. has an authorised and issued share capital of £400,000 divided into 800,000 ordinary shares of 50p each. The company made a net profit of £200,000 during 19X1 and, in July of

that year, the directors paid an interim dividend of 3p per share. The directors decide to recommend a final dividend of 7p per share, making a total of 10p per share for the year. The retained profit at 1 January 19X1 amounted to £94,000. A provision for corporation tax of £75,000 is to be made on the profits for the year.

*Required:*
The profit and loss appropriation account of Hanbury for 19X1.

**Solution**

*Profit and Loss Appropriation Account of Hanbury Ltd. for 19X1.*

|  | £ | £ |
|---|---|---|
| Net profit before tax........................ | | 200,000 |
| Less: Corporation tax..................... | | 75,000 |
| Net profit after tax......................... | | 125,000 |
| Less: Dividends: Paid...................... | 24,000 | |
| Proposed ................. | 56,000 | 80,000 |
| Retained profit for 19X1..................... | | 45,000 |
| Retained profit at 1 January 19X1............. | | 94,000 |
| Retained profit at 31 December 19X1.......... | | 139,000 |

*Note:* Total profit retained and re-invested in the company since it was formed amounts to £139,000, of which £45,000 was retained in the current accounting period.

**10.11.3 Provisions and Reserves** A *Provision* is legally defined as any amount written off or retained by way of providing for depreciation, renewals or diminution in the value of assets or retained by way of providing for any known liability of which the amount cannot be determined with substantial accuracy. This definition covers three basic adjustments:

1. The amount written off fixed assets by way of depreciation.
2. The amount written off current assets or investments to reflect the fact that book value exceeds the amount which is ultimately expected to be recoverable. Examples are a provision for bad debts or any provision necessary to reduce stock to net realisable value.
3. The amount set aside to meet a known liability, the amount of which cannot be accurately estimated. This may arise where a company is in breach of contract with an employee,

but the amount of damages payable is yet to be decided. A second example is a provision for taxation.

A *Reserve* is a transfer made out of profits at the directors' discretion. The reason for retaining profits, as reserves, may be to help finance expansion, to enable dividends to be declared in a future year when profits are low, to earmark funds for the redemption of share capital or debentures (see section 13 of this chapter) or to meet contingencies unknown at the date of the accounts.

The distinction between provisions and reserves is very important because it affects the measurement of profit and the way financial information is presented in the annual accounts. A provision is a cost of carrying on business activity whereas a transfer to reserves is not. Provisions are therefore charged *above the line* (in the profit and loss account) and affect reported profits, whereas transfers to reserves are made *below the line* (in the appropriation account) and leave reported profit unaffected. Clearly it is important for management to identify accurately whether a particular item is in the nature of a provision or a reserve. Equally important, care must be taken when the amount of a provision is estimated, since any under or over provision will directly affect the accuracy of the reported profit figure.

**Example 10.6**
A company is sued by an employee for unfair dismissal. The company expects the court to allow its former employee damages amounting to £6,000. A provision for this amount is made when computing the reported profit, of £50,000, for 19X1. Assuming the court subsequently awards damages of £15,000 it is clear that the company's liabilities, at 31 December 19X1, have been understated by £9,000 and that profits, for 19X1, have been overstated by a similar figure. If the directors had succeeded in forecasting accurately the damages payable, a profit of £41,000 would have been reported for 19X1.

In the balance sheet provisions are either:
1. deducted from the value of the asset to which they relate, e.g. depreciation of fixed assets, or
2. included as a current liability e.g. provision for taxation.

Reserves, on the other hand, remain part of the shareholders' interest and are listed after issued share capital and any balance on share premium account on the face of the balance sheet (see Figure 10.3).

Most of the matters discussed so far in this chapter are contained in Example 10.7 which students should work before looking at the solution.

## Example 10.7

Miskin Ltd commenced business on 1 January 19X2 and the following trial balance was extracted as at 31 December 19X2.

|  | £ | £ |
|---|---|---|
| Share capital............................... |  | 380,000 |
| 8% debentures repayable 19X9............... |  | 100,000 |
| 10% unsecured loan repayable 30 June 19X3.... |  | 20,000 |
| Tangible fixed assets at cost.................. | 480,000 |  |
| Gross profit............................... |  | 152,000 |
| Trade debtors............................. | 61,500 |  |
| Trade creditors............................ |  | 37,870 |
| Bank balance.............................. | 7,400 |  |
| Bad debts written off....................... | 320 |  |
| Administration and selling expenses........... | 63,200 |  |
| Interest paid, 30 June 19X2.................. | 5,000 |  |
| Interim dividend paid....................... | 12,000 |  |
| Stock in trade at 31 December 19X2............ | 60,450 |  |
|  | 689,870 | 689,870 |

The following additional information is provided:
1.  The authorised share capital is £500,000 divided into ordinary shares of £1. The balance on the share capital account represents the proceeds from issuing 300,000 shares.
2.  A provision for doubtful debts is to be made of 2% on outstanding trade debtors.
3.  Depreciation is to be charged on fixed assets at the rate of 4% on cost.
4.  The directors propose to recommend a final dividend of 5p per share.
5.  Corporation tax of £18,000 is to be provided on the profits for 19X2
6.  A transfer of £10,000 is to be made to dividend equalisation reserve.

*Required:*
   (a)  A profit and loss account and an appropriation account for 19X2
   (b)  A balance sheet at 31 December 19X2.

# Solution

*Profit and Loss Account and Appropriation Account for 19X2.*

|  | £ | £ |
|---|---|---|
| Gross profit.................................... |  | 152,000 |
| Less: Administration and selling expenses ............. | 63,200 |  |
| Bad and doubtful debts, £320 + (2% of £61,500)... | 1,550 |  |
| Interest, £5,000 + £5,000 (1 July-31 Dec. 19X2) . . . | 10,000 |  |
| Provision for depreciation (4% of £480,000) ... .. | 19,200 | 93,950 |
| Net profit before tax ............................. |  | 58,050 |
| Less: Corporation tax............................. |  | 18,000 |
| Net profit after tax ............................. |  | 40,050 |
| Less: Dividends: Paid............................. | 12,000 |  |
| Proposed (5p x 300,000) ............. | 15,000 |  |
| Transfer to dividend equialisation reserve ........ | 10,000 | 37,000 |
| Retained profit for 19X2 |  | 3,050 |

*Balance Sheet at 31 December 19X2*

| *Fixed Assets.* | £ | £ |
|---|---|---|
| Tangible assets at cost...................... | | 480,000 |
| Less: Accumulated depreciation............. | | 19,200 |
| | | 460,800 |
| *Current Assets* | | |
| Stocks.................................. | 60,450 | |
| Trade debtors (£61,500 - £1,230)............. | 60,270 | |
| Bank................................... | 7,400 | |
| | 128,120 | |
| *Less: Current Liabilities* | | |
| Unsecured loan repayable 30 June 19X3........ | 20,000 | |
| Trade creditors............................ | 37,870 | |
| Taxation due 30 September 19X3............. | 18,000 | |
| Dividend payable.......................... | 15,000 | |
| Accrual for interest owed................... | 5,000 | |
| | 95,870 | |
| Working capital........................... | | 32,250 |
| Total Assets less Current Liabilities........... | | 493,050 |
| *Less: Non-Current Liabilities* | | |
| 8% debentures repayable 19X9.............. | | 100,000 |
| | | 393,050 |
| *Financed by:* | | |
| Share Capital: | | |
| *Authorised.* 500,000 ordinary shares of £1 each................................... | | 500,000 |
| *Issued.* 300,000 ordinary shares of £1 each...... | | 300,000 |
| Share premium account (£380,000 - £300,000)... | | 80,000 |
| Dividend equalisation reserve................ | | 10,000 |
| Retained profit............................ | | 3,050 |
| | | 393,050 |

Students should now work Questions 10.1 and 10.2 at the end of this chapter.

## 10.12 REVALUATION RESERVE

The revaluation reserve is an exception to the general rule that reserves are created as the result of transfers from reported profit. Despite determined efforts on the part of successive governments to control inflation, prices have risen almost continuously since 1940. This process has had a significant effect on the usefulness of accounting statements based on the historical cost concept. The major balance sheet items, fixed assets and stocks, are reported at their original cost less, where appropriate, depreciation to comply with this concept. However, fixed assets may have been aquired many years ago when prices were much lower than is the case today; therefore these assets are reported at figures far removed from their current value to the concern. This discrepancy has caused many individuals to question the usefulness of the balance sheet as a statement of a company's financial position, and uneasiness increased with the acceleration in the rate of inflation during the 1970s. The revaluation reserve was developed as a means of restoring an acceptable measure of reality to the corporate balance sheet. The adjustment is quite straightforward:

1.  The book value of the fixed asset is increased from historical cost less depreciation to the revalued figure.
2.  The surplus arising on revaluation is credited to revaluation reserve which is reported as part of the shareholders' equity in the balance sheet (see Figure 10.3).

The adjustment is entered in the books as follows:

| Debit | Credit | With |
|---|---|---|
| Revaluation account | Fixed asset at cost account | Historical cost of fixed asset |
| Provision for depreciation account | Revaluation account | Accumulated depreciation |
| Fixed asset at revaluation account | Revaluation account | New valuation |
| Revaluation account | Revaluation reserve | Surplus arising on revaluation |

Today, many large companies supplement their historical cost based accounting reports with financial statements adjusted to take account of the effect of changing price levels. This was the outcome of the inflation accounting debate which raged throughout the 1970s and it is an important development in corporate reporting techniques which is examined at Stage 2.

## 10.13 REDEMPTION OF DEBENTURES

It is essential that the directors plan a company's finances carefully and, in particular, ensure that a proper balance between short-term, medium-term and long-term funds is achieved. Both share capital and loan capital fall into the category of long-term finance, but share capital may be redeemable and loan capital will invariably be redeemable at some future date. It is management's job to ensure that the long-term capital base is not eroded as a result of the redemption. Indeed, in the case of share capital, the directors are under a strict legal obligation to ensure that this does not happen (share capital maintenance is examined at Stage 2).

Company law imposes no conditions regarding the redemption of debentures. Debenture holders are treated in law as creditors rather than as providers of permanent capital, consequently there exists no requirement that the company should take steps to replace the resources which are paid out when redemption occurs. However, such obligations may either be imposed by the company's articles of association or be assumed voluntarily by the directors. Debentures may be repayable gradually over a period of years or, at the other extreme, the total amount borrowed may be repayable at a single future date. The effect on the company's finances will be less marked in the former situation, and it is often possible to make the necessary repayments out of funds generated from trading operations. In these circumstances the directors may transfer a sum, equal to the value of debentures redeemed, from profits to a debenture redemption reserve in order to acknowledge the fact that resources have been used in this way.

### Example 10.8

The debentures of Arches Ltd are repayable by ten equal annual instalments of £10,000 commencing 31 December 19X1. The relevant balance sheet extracts, immediately before the first repayment are as follows:

*Extracts from Balance Sheet of Arches Ltd. as at 31 December 19X1*

|  | £ |
|---|---|
| Issued ordinary share capital | 200,000 |
| Profit and loss account balance | 50,000 |
| Shareholders equity | 250,000 |
| Debentures redeemable by ten equal instalments, 19X1-19Y0 | 100,000 |

The company redeems one tenth of the debentures on 31 December 19X1, at par, and transfers a similar amount to debenture redemption reserve.

*Required:*

Revised extracts from the balance sheet of Arches after the first redemption has taken place.

**Solution**

*Revised Extracts from Balance Sheet of Arches Ltd., 31 December 19X1*

|  | £ |
|---|---|
| Issued ordinary share capital.................... | 200,000 |
| Debenture redemption reserve................... | 10,000 |
| Profit and loss account (£50,000−£10,000)......... | 40,000 |
| | |
| Shareholders' equity.......................... | 250,000 |
| Debentures redeemable by nine equal | |
| instalments, 19X2-19Y0....................... | 90,000 |

Where the total amount of debentures raised are to be repaid on a single date, transfers to the debenture redemption reserve may be made over a number of years in anticipation of this event. Additional action must be taken, of course, to ensure that the necessary amount of cash is available to finance repayment when it falls due. One approach is to invest separately, each year, an amount of cash equal to the figure transferred to the debenture redemption reserve. These investments may be described, in the balance sheet, as 'debenture redemption investment fund', and the balance on this account appears as a separate item amongst the current assets of the company. The investments are sold, when the redemption date approaches, and the debentures redeemed out of the proceeds. The debenture redemption investment fund is seldom employed today.

The balance to the credit of the debenture redemption reserve remains legally available for distribution but, in reality, it forms part of the company's permanent capital. To acknowledge this fact, a further transfer may be made from debenture redemption reserve to a non-distributable capital redemption reserve after the redemption has taken place; a second alternative is to capitalise the credit balance on debenture redemption reserve by making a bonus isssue (see section 14 of this chapter).

Students should now attempt Question 10.3 at the end of this chapter.

## 10.14 BONUS (CAPITALISATION, SCRIP) ISSUE OF SHARES

The following is a typical balance sheet of a manufacturing company which has traded successfully for a number of years and financed a great deal of its expansion out of retained profits.

### Illustration 10.1

*Balance Sheet of Star plc as at 31 December 19X1*

|  | £ | £ |
|---|---:|---:|
| *Fixed Assets* | | |
| Plant and machinery at cost...................... | | 850,000 |
| Less: Accumulated depreciation................... | | 360,000 |
| | | 490,000 |
| *Current Assets* | | |
| Stock and work in progress....................... | 426,000 | |
| Trade debtors and prepayments................... | 250,000 | |
| Cash in hand.................................... | 2,000 | |
| | 678,000 | |
| *Less: Current Liabilities* | | |
| Trade creditors and accruals...................... | 207,000 | |
| Bank overdraft................................. | 136,000 | |
| | 343,000 | |
| Working capital................................ | | 335,000 |
| | | 825,000 |
| *Financed by* | | |
| Share capital (£1 ordinary shares).................. | | 250,000 |
| Reserves....................................... | | 575,000 |
| | | 825,000 |

Over the years Star has generated and retained profits amounting to £575,000 and the whole of this amount is legally available for distribution to the shareholders of the company. An examination of the information contained in the above balance sheet clearly shows that, in practice, the company is in no position to pay any dividend whatsoever. The company has a cash balance of just £2,000 to meet day to day cash outgoings and there is a bank overdraft of £136,000. Clearly all the profits retained in the company, although initially in the form of cash, have since been reinvested in business assets. Consequently, although these profits remain legally available for distribution, in practice the company is not capable of distributing them.

It is argued that, for this reason, the equity section of the balance sheet does not fairly represent the financial position of Star. The balance sheet reports distributable reserves of £575,000 but a dividend of this amount could be paid only by selling some and perhaps all the company's assets. This finding is proof of the fact that resources which arose initially in the form of profits have since become part of the permanent capital of Star and cannot be distributed without significantly undermining the company's financial viability. The directors can acknowledge this fact by transferring a major part of the balance on reserves to share capital. The procedure followed is to issue shareholders with additional shares in proportion to their existing holdings, and to make necessary adjustments to the relevant ledger accounts. The process is described as a capitalisation of profits and the share issue to existing investors is called a bonus issue or a scrip issue. The adjustment is entered in the books as follows:

| Debit | Credit | With |
|-------|--------|------|
| Retained profit | Share capital | The amount of the bonus issue |

Assuming the directors of Star make a bonus issue of two shares for every one share presently held, the capital section of the balance sheet is revised as follows:

*Extract from the Balance Sheet of Star plc as at 31 December 19X1*

| Financed by: | £ |
|--------------|---|
| Share capital (£1 shares)........................ | 750,000 |
| Reserves..................................... | 75,000 |
| | 825,000 |

The term bonus issue is misleading. The implication is that the shareholder has received some additional financial benefit which he did not previously enjoy. This is not the case. It is true that after the issue has taken place each shareholder holds three times as many shares, but the company receives nothing extra and its profit-earning potential remains unchanged. This can be demonstrated by examining the net asset value per share both before and after the bonus issue.

Net asset value per share.

| | | |
|---|---|---|
| Before | $\dfrac{£825,000}{250,000}$ | = £3.30 |
| After | $\dfrac{£825,000}{750,000}$ | = £1.10 |

A person who initially owned 100 shares had a total interest in the book value of the company's net assets of 100 x £3.30 = £330. After the bonus issue he owns 300 shares, but their underlying asset value has fallen to £1.10 each and the total book value of his interest remains unchanged at £330 (300 x £1.10). The market price of the share falls in a similar manner to reflect the larger number of shares in circulation.

It has been noted earlier that the source of a bonus issue of shares is not limited to distributable profits; in particular, balances on the share premium account, revaluation reserve, debenture redemption reserve and capital redemption reserve may be applied in this way.

Students should now attempt Questions 10.4 to 10.6 at the end of this chapter.

## 10.15 QUESTIONS
### Question 10.1
(i)   Define provisions and reserves and give two examples of each.

(ii)  Describe how provisions and reserves are (a) accounted for in the profit and loss account and (b) reported in the balance sheet.

### Question 10.2
The following information is provided in respect of the affairs of Newton Ltd., a trading company, for 19X0 and 19X1.

*Draft Profit and Loss Account, Year to 31 December.*

|  | 19X0 | 19X1 |
|---|---|---|
|  | £000 | £000 |
| Administration expenses........................... | 1,620 | 1,809 |
| Selling costs..................................... | 520 | 572 |
| Distribution costs............................... | 140 | 164 |
| Transfer to general reserve....................... | — | 500 |
| Depreciation charge............................. | 250 | 300 |
| Proposed dividend............................... | 100 | 200 |
| Balance of profit................................ | 300 | 60 |
|  | 2,930 | 3,605 |

*Draft Balance Sheet, 31 December*

|  | 19X0 | 19X1 |
|---|---|---|
| Debit balances: | £000 | £000 |
| Stock........................................ | 724 | 771 |
| Debtors...................................... | 570 | 524 |
| Plant and machinery at cost..................... | 1,840 | 2,650 |
| Cash at bank................................. | 92 | 305 |
|  | 3,226 | 4,250 |
| Credit balances: |  |  |
| Trade creditors............................... | 416 | 480 |
| Provision for depreciation...................... | 520 | 820 |
| General reserve............................... | — | 500 |
| Dividend..................................... | 100 | 200 |
| Share capital (£1 shares)....................... | 1,600 | 1,600 |
| Profit and loss account........................ | 590 | 650 |
|  | 3,226 | 4,250 |

## Required:

(a) Re-draft the above accounts in order to make them more informative. The profit and loss account should show figures for gross profit, net profit and retained profit; the balance sheet should include an appropriate classification of assets and liabilities.

(b) Comment on the view expressed by one of Newton Ltd.'s directors that the company should not pay the proposed increased dividend because profits have declined.

## Question 10.3

The following trial balance was extracted from the books of Medway plc as at 31 December 19X9:

|  | £ | £ |
|---|---|---|
| Share capital authorised and issued, 700,000 |  |  |
| Ordinary shares of £1 each......................... |  | 700,000 |
| 15% Debentures repayable 19Y5 (issued 1 Jan. 19X5) ... |  | 250,000 |
| Freehold properties at cost ........................ | 850,000 |  |
| Motor vans: |  |  |
| Balance 1 Jan. 19X9 at cost...................... | 225,000 |  |
| Additions (at cost) less proceeds of sale (note c.)...... | 24,000 |  |
| Provision for depreciation of motor |  |  |
| vans to 1 Jan. 19X9............................ |  | 101,200 |
| Stock in trade 1 Jan 19X9......................... | 206,300 |  |
| Balance at bank................................. | 96,900 |  |
| Bad debts...................................... | 15,700 |  |
| Debenture redemption reserve..................... |  | 100,000 |
| Trade debtors.................................. | 166,500 |  |
| Trade creditors................................. |  | 159,800 |
| Directors' remuneration.......................... | 60,000 |  |
| Wages and salaries.............................. | 198,700 |  |
| Motor expenses................................. | 42,300 |  |
| Rates.......................................... | 10,500 |  |
| Purchases...................................... | 1,650,000 |  |
| Sales.......................................... |  | 2,350,000 |
| Legal expenses................................. | 9,100 |  |
| General expenses............................... | 86,000 |  |
| Debenture interest.............................. | 37,500 |  |
| Profit and loss acount: Balance at 1 Jan. 19X9........ |  | 17,500 |
|  | 3,678,500 | 3,678,500 |

You are given the following information:
(a)   Stock in trade at 31 December 19X9, £217,800.
(b)   Rates paid in advance, 31 December 19X9 £2,000
(c)   On 1 January 19X9 a motor van which had cost £10,000 was sold for £1,000. Depreciation provided for this van up to 31 December 19X8 was £8,250.
(d)   Provide for depreciation of motor vans (including additions) at 20% of cost.
(e)   The figure for legal expenses includes £7,900 in connection with the purchase of a freehold property.
(f)   It is the directors' policy to make an annual transfer of £25,000 to the debenture redemption reserve.
(g)   A provision for corporation tax of £90,000 should be made on the profit for the year.
(h)   The directors propose to pay a dividend of 12p per share.

*Required:*

  (a)  A trading and profit and loss and appropriation account for the year 19X9 and a balance sheet at 31 December 19X9, each presented in vertical format.
  (b)  Explain the purpose of the annual transfer to debenture redemption reserve.

*Note:* Ignore depreciation of freehold properties.

## Question 10.4

The following trial balance was extracted from the books of Porchester Ltd. on 31 March 19X6.

|  | £ | £ |
|---|---|---|
| Ordinary share capital (£1 shares) .................... |  | 500,000 |
| Retained profit to 1 April 19X5..................... |  | 1,039,000 |
| 10% Debentures repayable 19X9.................... |  | 300,000 |
| Freehold land and buildings at cost.................. | 400,000 |  |
| Plant and machinery at cost....................... | 1,300,000 |  |
| Provision for depreciation on plant and machinery at 1 April 19X5............... |  | 512,000 |
| Debtors and prepayments (including Trade debtors, £360,000)........................ | 370,080 |  |
| Stock and work in progress at 31 March 19X6.......... | 984,020 |  |
| Bank balance..................................... | 268,000 |  |
| Provision for doubtful debts at 31 March 19X6 ........ |  | 15,000 |
| Creditors and accrued expenses..................... |  | 351,500 |
| Gross profit for the year........................... |  | 1,020,800 |
| Administration expenses........................... | 216,900 |  |
| Selling expenses.................................. | 150,400 |  |
| Bad debts written off.............................. | 8,700 |  |
| General repairs and maintenance.................... | 25,200 |  |
| Debenture interest to 30 September 19X5............. | 15,000 |  |
|  | 3,738,300 | 3,738,300 |

Additional information is provided as follows:

  1.  The company's freehold property was revalued at £900,000 on 1 October 19X5. The directors have decided to use this figure for the purpose of the accounts.
  2.  The company made a bonus issue of two ordinary shares, fully paid, for each share held on 1 October 19X5. No entry has been made in the books in respect of the issue.
  3.  The directors propose to pay a dividend of 5% on the nominal value of the ordinary share capital at 31 March 19X6.
  4.  The company purchased additional plant costing £120,000 on 31 March 19X6. The plant was delivered to the company's

premises on that date together with the purchase invoice to be paid within 7 days, but no entry has been make in the books in respect of the transaction.

5. Depreciation is to be provided at 25%, reducing balance, on all plant and machinery owned by the company at the year end, except the plant referred to under 4 above. Ignore depreciation of freehold property.

6. Corporation tax of £150,000, due for payment on 1 January 19X7, is to be provided out of the trading profit for the year.

7. The company's authorised share capital is £2,000,000 divided into ordinary shares of £1 each.

*Required:*
The profit and loss account and profit and loss appropriation account of Porchester Ltd. for the year ended 31 March 19X6, together with the balance sheet at that date. Particular attention should be given to layout, although the accounts need not necessarily be in a form appropriate for publication.

**Question 10.5**
What is the purpose of a bonus issue of shares? Using the information prepared in your answer to question 10.4, consider whether the issue was reasonable in amount.

**Question 10.6**
The trial balance of Southgate plc at 31 December 19X9 was as follows:

| | £ | £ |
|---|---|---|
| Ordinary share capital (shares £1 each)............... | | 500,000 |
| Freehold property at cost......................... | 500,000 | |
| Furniture and equipment at cost.................... | 375,000 | |
| Provision for depreciation of furniture and equipment, 1 January 19X9.................. | | 59,500 |
| Debtors and prepayments......................... | 105,000 | |
| Stock and work in progress at 31 December 19X9....... | 104,200 | |
| Creditors and accruals............................ | | 85,300 |
| Balance at bank................................. | 72,000 | |
| Gross profit on trading........................... | | 416,500 |
| Rent and rates ................................. | 30,000 | |
| Office salaries.................................. | 142,600 | |
| Advertising costs................................ | 21,000 | |
| Transport costs................................. | 23,600 | |
| Profit and loss account balance, 1 Jan. 19X9.......... | | 278,500 |
| Taxation due 1 Jan. 19Y0 on 19X8 profits............. | | 103,600 |
| Deposit on new equipment........................ | 10,000 | |
| Temporary investment........................... | 60,000 | |
| | 1,443,400 | 1,443,400 |

You are given the following additional information:

1. The company has contracted to purchase new equipment at a cost of £50,000. A deposit of £10,000 was paid during December 19X9 and the remainder will be paid during January when delivery is expected.

2. Depreciation is to be provided on furniture and equipment, other than the new equipment referred to under 1., at the rate of 10% on cost.

3. The figure for rent and rates in the above trial balance covers the fifteen months to 31 March 19Y0.

4. During December 19X9 the company used part of the profit and loss account balance at 1 January 19X9 to make a bonus issue of 1 new share for every five shares already held. The issue was made at par but has not yet been written into the books.

5. During November 19X9 the company's freehold premises were valued at £650,000 by a firm of professional valuers. The company's directors have decided to write the revaluation into the 19X9 accounts and credit the surplus arising to revaluation reserve.

6. Taxation is to be provided at 50% on the company's net profit from trading operations.

*Required:*
(a) The profit and loss account of Southgate for 19X9 and balance sheet at 31 December 19X9. Each accounting statement should be presented in vertical format.
(b) Your comments on the suggestion, from one director, that the company should pay a dividend of 10p per share on the issued share capital in view of the large bank balance and the fact that no dividend was paid for 19X8.

*Note:* Ignore depreciation of freehold property.

# CHAPTER 11

# Decision Making

## 11.1 INTRODUCTION

The accounting process has many aspects, and, so far, this book's emphasis has been on recording and reporting the financial consequences of past economic activity. The essence of this approach is that it is a 'post-fact' exercise and concentrates on events which have already taken place. An important application of accounting techniques is to provide a basis on which decisions can be taken. Appropriate information is needed by management to direct the entity's future activity; this may be in the form of either past results or forecasts of the likely future financial consequences of different courses of action.

This chapter:
1. Reviews the manner in which post-fact reports can be presented to assist management (section 2);
2. Introduces students to the study and interpretation of cost behaviour which must be understood in order to prepare forecasts (sections 3 and 4); and
3. Examines the forecast of cash flows and trading results (section 5).

## 11.2 ANALYSED ACCOUNTING REPORTS

Management needs to know how well each section of the business is performing, and accounting statements can be prepared to report the progress and position of each of the various activities which together make up the company. For example, a business may have a number of separate departments or branches and trade in a number of products; management must know which of these are performing well and which poorly so that areas of weakness can be strengthened and successful activities built upon. In these circumstances, the costs and revenues should be identified in a way which makes them controllable, so that if, for example, a company has separate branches, then each branch should be monitored, and if it trades in a number of distinct product lines, then the results of each of these should also be measured. The activities for which reports are prepared are known as cost centres.

The production of detailed accounting statements relies upon the careful analysis of the flows of expense and revenue at the time of their initial recording in the day books. Where possible, costs should be *allocated*, that is, recorded as belonging directly to a particular cost centre. For example, the wages of an employee who works in a particular department can be allocated directly to that department. However, there are some costs which cannot be allocated, and these have to be *apportioned* in the manner described in section 2 of chapter 8. Costs which are apportioned can alternatively be described as 'joint costs' as they give benefit to more than one cost centre, and the benefit itself is not divisible. For example, rent has to be paid for the occupation of a building and relates to all of the departments it contains; each department therefore has to contribute towards the cost of rent, but does not make its own direct payment in respect of the charge.

It is usual to present analysed accounting reports in columnar format as this makes comprehension easier and facilitates comparison between the separate units, or departments, to which the report relates. In columnar presentation, the results of each separate unit are entered in a column alongside the results of the other units. This technique is illustrated in Example 11.1.

## Example 11.1
The following list of balances was extracted from the books of Bucket Ltd in respect of the year to 31 March 19X9:

|  | £ | £ |
|---|---|---|
| Sales: Department X | 68,000 | |
| Y | 54,000 | |
| Z | 41,000 | 163,000 |
| | | |
| Purchases: Department X | 44,880 | |
| Y | 37.060 | |
| Z | 29,060 | 111,000 |
| | | |
| Lighting and heating | | 3,570 |
| Delivery expenses | | 1,956 |
| Commission paid | | 3,260 |
| Printing and stationery | | 750 |
| Salaries and wages | | 27,000 |
| General expenses | | 6,900 |
| | | |
| Opening stock: Department X | | 12,410 |
| Y | | 9,550 |
| Z | | 7,750 |
| | | |
| Closing stock: Department X | | 10,540 |
| Y | | 7,350 |
| Z | | 8,280 |

Expenses are to be apportioned between the departments as follows:

a. Delivery expenses in proportion to sales
b. Commission at 2% of sales
c. Printing and stationery and wages and salaries in the proportion 6:4:5
d. Other expenses equally

## Required:

A columnar trading and profit and loss account for the year ended 31 March 19X9.

## Solution

Departmental Trading and Profit and Loss Account
for the Year to 31 March 19X9

|  | X £ | Y £ | Z £ | Total £ |
|---|---|---|---|---|
| Sales.......................... | 68,000 | 54,000 | 41,000 | 163,000 |
| Less: |  |  |  |  |
| Opening stock................. | 12,410 | 9,550 | 7,750 | 29,710 |
| Purchases..................... | 44,880 | 37,060 | 29,060 | 111,000 |
| Closing stock................. | (10,540) | (7,350) | (8,280) | (26,170) |
| Cost of goods sold............. | 46,750 | 39,260 | 28,530 | 114,540 |
| Gross profit................... | 21,250 | 14,740 | 12,470 | 48,460 |
| Less: |  |  |  |  |
| Delivery expenses.............. | 816 | 648 | 492 | 1,956 |
| Commission................... | 1,360 | 1,080 | 820 | 3,260 |
| Printing and stationery.......... | 300 | 200 | 250 | 750 |
| Salaries and wages............. | 10,800 | 7,200 | 9,000 | 27,000 |
| Lighting and heating............ | 1,190 | 1,190 | 1,190 | 3,570 |
| General expenses.............. | 2,300 | 2,300 | 2,300 | 6,900 |
| Total expenses................. | 16,766 | 12,618 | 14,052 | 43,436 |
| Net Profit (Loss).............. | 4,484 | 2,122 | (1,582) | 5,024 |

Readers should now work Question 11.1 at the end of this chapter.


## 11.3  COST BEHAVIOUR

The decisions which management must take include:
1.  Whether existing activity should be expanded or reduced;
2.  Whether a new product should be introduced;
3.  How existing production techniques could be improved;
4.  Whether new products should be manufactured or purchased ready made;
5.  The manufacturing techniques to be used for new products.

In the attempt to maximise profit, all decisions must be viewed according to their impact on profit, and management must be satisfied, before resources are committed, that any proposed activity, or change in existing activity, will add to overall profit. Therefore, when any decisions, such as those outlined above, are under consideration, financial forecasts are needed to show the likely outcomes of alternative courses of action so that the most profitable ones can be adopted. The preparation of forecasts involves an understanding of cost behaviour so that the level of costs likely to result from different actions can be predicted.

The manner in which production or trading activity is organised sets the capacity of the undertaking. For example, the acquisition of a particular machine sets the maximum output which can be achieved before an additional machine must be bought; similarly, the size of premises used by a shop determines the maximum number of product lines which can be displayed and stored; above a certain level, further space is needed. Therefore, the capacity of the business sets the upper level of activity. The output of a firm is the extent to which the available capacity is utilised; the lowest level is zero, and the greatest is the largest amount permitted by available capacity. Management must decide what the likely output will be and arrange capacity accordingly, bearing in mind that growth may take place. In the long run it may prove cheaper to acquire at the start of the project the additional capacity likely to be needed so as to take advantage of the economies of scale which can result from the use of capital intensive techniques.

**11.3.1 Fixed and Variable Costs**   Business costs may be classified according to how they behave in response to changes in output:

*Fixed Costs.*   These remain constant over a range of output and include such items as rent and depreciation. For example, the rent for premises or a straight line depreciation charge related to a machine are constant irrespective of whether these assets are being used at full capacity or well below. However, if an output in excess of the existing full capacity is contemplated, then an additional set of fixed costs must be incurred to provide additional capacity.

*Variable Costs.*   These vary in direct proportion to output, and include the costs of raw material and manufacturing wages. For example, if no production takes place, then no raw materials have to be purchased, while, at full capacity, the total cost of materials is the number of units produced times the material cost per unit.

Forecast output is unlikely to be achieved exactly in practice, and calculations of the profit expected at different levels of output are helpful in making a decision about whether a new project should be undertaken. This is shown in Example 11.2.

## Example 11.2

The management of Glass Ltd. is considering the possibility of manufacturing a new product which will sell at £15 per unit. Existing capacity is fully utilised, and so a new factory would have to be rented and plant, with a life of 10 years, purchased. The expected costs are:

|  | £ |
|---|---|
| Annual factory rent | 10,000 |
| Purchase price of plant | 75,000 |
| Raw material cost per unit | 2.10 |
| Labour cost per unit | 1.50 |
| Other variable costs per unit | 1.00 |
| Fixed costs (excluding rent and depreciation) | 6,500 |

*Note:* The company depreciates plant on the straight line basis assuming a zero residual value.

*Required:*
Forecast the profit which will be made from sales of the new product at the alternative annual rates of:

    (a)   2,500 units
    (b)   5,000 units

## Solution

*Profit Forecasts at Different Sales Levels*

|  | (a) £ | (a) £ | (a) £ | (b) £ | (b) £ | (b) £ |
|---|---|---|---|---|---|---|
| Sales |  |  | 37,500 |  |  | 75,000 |
| Fixed costs: |  |  |  |  |  |  |
|   Rent | 10,000 |  |  | 10,000 |  |  |
|   Depreciation | 7,500 |  |  | 7,500 |  |  |
|   Other | 6,500 |  |  | 6,500 |  |  |
|  |  | 24,000 |  |  | 24,000 |  |
| Variable costs: |  |  |  |  |  |  |
|   Raw materials | 5,250 |  |  | 10,500 |  |  |
|   Labour | 3,750 |  |  | 7,500 |  |  |
|   Other | 2,500 |  |  | 5,000 |  |  |
|  |  | 11,500 |  |  | 23,000 |  |
|  |  |  | 35,500 |  |  | 47,000 |
| Profit |  |  | 2,000 |  |  | 28,000 |

Output has doubled, but profit has increased fourteen times. This result is examined further in sections 3.4 and 3.5 of this chapter.

Another use of forecasts, of the type prepared in Example 11.2 above, is to help decide the method of production; the choice often lies between 'capital intensive' and 'labour intensive' techniques. Capital intensive production uses automatic machines, such as the 'robots' seen on car production lines, and requires a· large investment in plant with a consequent high level of fixed costs; variable costs are lower as each additional unit produced requires only a small labour input. Additional potential benefits from capital intensive methods are that raw materials are used more efficiently, and therefore cost less per unit, and there is a lower rejection rate at the stage of inspecting the finished product. Labour intensive methods use relatively little plant and have low fixed costs, but high variable costs per unit as each additional item produced requires a large input of labour.

## Example 11.3
The directors of Hasard Ltd are sure that 10,000 units a year of a newly developed product can be sold at £90 each. They are undecided about how to produce it. The alternatives are:

| | Method 1 | Method 2 |
|---|---|---|
| | £ | £ |
| Investment in plant with a 10 year life................. | 125,000 | 750,000 |
| Fixed costs (excluding depreciation)................. | 185,000 | 200,000 |
| Variable cost per unit: | | |
| Raw materials................................ | 35 | 30 |
| Labour....................................... | 20 | 5 |
| Other........................................ | 6 | 2 |

*Note*: The company calculates depreciation on the straight line basis assuming a zero scrap value.

*Required:*
Prepare financial statements to show the likely profit from each of the two methods at the expected level of sales.

## Solution.

### Forecast Trading Results

| | Method 1 | | | Method 2 | | |
|---|---|---|---|---|---|---|
| | £ | £ | £ | £ | £ | £ |
| Sales.................. | | | 900,000 | | | 900,000 |
| Fixed costs: | | | | | | |
| Depreciation.......... | 12,500 | | | 75,000 | | |
| Other................ | 185,000 | | | 200,000 | | |
| | | 197,500 | | | 275,000 | |
| Variable Costs: | | | | | | |
| Raw materials......... | 350,000 | | | 300,000 | | |
| Labour.............. | 200,000 | | | 50,000 | | |
| Other................ | 60,000 | | | 20,000 | | |
| | | 610,000 | | | 370,000 | |
| | | | 807,500 | | | 645,000 |
| Profit................. | | | 92,500 | | | 255,000 |

Readers should now work Question 11.2 at the end of this chapter.

Some costs are neither completely fixed nor fully variable; they are termed 'semi-variable'. Although semi-variable costs respond to volume changes, they do not change in direct proportion to them. It is possible for semi-variable costs to remain constant over a relatively small range of activity, and each successive set of costs may differ in price from its predecessor. For example, an increase in manufacturing output creates additional work in the accounts department. The initial load may be carried by an accountant who alone performs all the necessary activities; when his capacity is exceeded, a book keeper may be added to the staff, and then a clerk. Each additional employee, hired to increase the capacity of the accounts department in response to an increase in manufacturing output, adds relatively less to costs as an accountant is paid more than a book keeper, who in turn earns more than a clerk. This type of response to changes in output occurs in the case of General Expenses in Question 11.3 at the end of this chapter, which should now be worked.

**11.3.2 Direct and Indirect Costs**   Direct costs are those which can be traced in full to an individual costing unit; indirect costs are those which relate only partially to a particular costing unit and must be apportioned to it. Care has to be taken when interpreting results based on apportioned (joint) costs as they have to be met in full irrespective of whether activity in a particular department continues or is discontinued. An initial examination of results may produce the conclusion that a department or branch is making a loss and so should be closed, but it must be remembered that its share of apportioned costs will then have to be met by the remaining cost centres.

**Example 11.4**
The business of Bits & Co. is divided into three departments of equal size: A, B, and C. The departmental results for 19X7 were (£000):

*Departmental Trading Results*

|  | Department | | | Total |
|---|---|---|---|---|
|  | A | B | C |  |
| Sales........................... | 50 | 120 | 180 | 350 |
| Cost of goods sold.................. | 25 | 60 | 90 | 175 |
| Gross profit....................... | 25 | 60 | 90 | 175 |
| Departmental wages................ | 10 | 20 | 30 | 60 |
|  | 15 | 40 | 60 | 115 |
| Rent (shared equally)................ | 20 | 20 | 20 | 60 |
| Profit (Loss)...................... | (5) | 20 | 40 | 55 |

Mr.Bits is considering closing Department A because it is making a loss. He says it is better to leave the floor space empty than to use it to lose money.

*Required:*
Prepare a statement to show Mr.Bits the effect on total profit if Department A is closed.

## Solution (£000)

### Revised Departmental Trading Results

|  | Department | | Total |
|---|---|---|---|
|  | B | C |  |
| Sales................................. | 120 | 180 | 300 |
| Cost of goods sold..................... | 60 | 90 | 150 |
| Gross profit........................ | 60 | 90 | 150 |
| Departmental wages.................. | 20 | 30 | 50 |
|  | 40 | 60 | 100 |
| Share of rent*....................... | 30 | 30 | 60 |
| Profit (Loss)........................ | 10 | 30 | 40 |

*Rent and rates shared equally between the remaining departments

Department A should be kept open as it meets 75% of its share of apportioned costs. Total profit is reduced by £15,000 if it is closed. The revised departmental trading results show that the plan of Mr.Bits to close department A is based on his failure to appreciate the difference between direct and indirect costs.

It is sometimes argued that, because the accounting information which results can lead to wrong decisions, the apportionment of indirect costs should not be made. If indirect costs are not apportioned, the departmental trading results of Bits & Co. would be presented as follows (£000):

|  | Department | | | Total |
|---|---|---|---|---|
|  | A | B | C |  |
| Sales...................... | 50 | 120 | 180 | 350 |
| Cost of goods sold................ | 25 | 60 | 90 | 175 |
| Gross Profit.................. | 25 | 60 | 90 | 175 |
| Departmental wages.............. | 10 | 20 | 30 | 60 |
| Departmental surplus............. | 15 | 40 | 60 | 115 |
| Rent...................... |  |  |  | 60 |
| Profit..................... |  |  |  | 55 |

The above presentation highlights the fact that all departments are making a surplus or *contribution* to general overhead costs which are not controllable at the departmental level.

The nature of a cost, that is whether it is direct or indirect, has to be decided in accordance with the costing unit under examination. For example, if the costing unit is a manufacturing department, then the depreciation of machines located in it and the salary of the departmental supervisor are direct costs. However, if the costing unit is a single item of output, then the depreciation and supervisor's salary are indirect costs as they also relate to the rest of the output. Raw materials and manufacturing wages are examples of direct costs where the costing unit is a single item of output.

**11.3.3 Contribution Costing** A useful technique to apply when examining the way in which fixed and variable costs respond to changes in the level of activity, is to calculate the *contribution* which each unit sold makes towards fixed costs. Analysis based on this approach assumes that the revenue from each unit is applied first to meet its related variable costs, and any surplus, the contribution, is then set against total fixed costs. Once the fixed costs have been completely recovered, the contribution of each additional unit sold adds to profit. The contribution of each unit is calculated by the formula:

$$\text{Contribution} = \frac{\text{Selling Price}}{\text{per Unit}} - \frac{\text{Variable Cost}}{\text{per Unit}}$$

**Example 11.5**
Product Z incurs the following variable costs per unit:

|  | £ |
|---|---|
| Materials | 5.00 |
| Wages | 4.50 |
| Expenses | 1.25 |

*Required:*
Calculate the contribution of product Z if its selling price per unit is:
   (a)   £12
   (b)   £15

## Solution

The total variable cost is:

|  | £ |
|---|---|
| Materials ........................... | 5.00 |
| Wages .............................. | 4.50 |
| Expenses ........................... | 1.25 |
| Total .............................. | 10.75 |

(a)   Contribution = £12 − £10.75 = £1.25
(b)   Contribution = £15 − £10.75 = £4.25

The technique of contribution costing is used in break-even analysis and target profit calculations which are dealt with in sections 3.4 and 3.5 of this chapter.

**11.3.4 Break-even Analysis**   A forecast of sales should be prepared as part of the appraisal of whether a particular project should be undertaken. The volume of anticipated sales sets the capacity which has to be provided and also determines the total value of variable costs. Forecasts cannot be wholly accurate, and so it is usual to examine results based on a number of alternative outcomes. A particularly useful piece of information to have is the volume of sales needed to achieve break-even, which occurs where total costs equal total revenues and neither a profit nor loss is made. Looked at another way, a company breaks even when the contribution from sales is exactly equal to fixed costs. The break-even point is calculated with the formula:

$$\text{Break-even point, measured in units sold} = \frac{\text{Fixed Costs}}{\text{Contribution per unit}}$$

The break even point in terms of the value of sales can be calculated by multiplying the number of units by the selling price per unit.

The importance of the break-even point is that, below it, a loss is suffered, and above it a profit is earned. It is, therefore, very important that management selects projects which are likely to achieve at least enough sales to break even.

# Example 11.6

The directors of Cumberland Ltd are considering an investment project which is expected to involve the following costs and revenues:

|  | £ |
|---|---|
| Annual fixed costs.............. | 100,000 |
| Selling price per unit............ | 10 |
| Variable cost per unit........... | 7.50 |

*Required:*
  (a)  Calculate the number of units which have to be sold for the project to break-even.
  (b)  Calculate the profit or loss which would occur if sales are:
  (i)  1,000 units greater than those needed to break even, and
  (ii)  1,000 less than those needed to break even.

## Solution.

(a)   Contribution = £10 − £7.50 = £2.50
      Break-even point = $\dfrac{£100,000}{£2.50}$ = 40,000 units

(b)

|  | (i) 1,000 less | (ii) 1,000 more |
|---|---|---|
| Sales in units............................ | 39,000 | 41,000 |
|  | £ | £ |
| Contribution (unit sales x 2.5).............. | 97,500 | 102,500 |
| Fixed costs............................ | 100,000 | 100,000 |
| Profit (Loss)............................ | (2,500) | 2,500 |

*Note:* An alternative way to calculate the effect of changes in the level of sales on profit is to calculate the increase, or decrease, in the contribution. In this case, the starting profit is zero, and the contribution from sales of 1,000 units = 1,000 x £2.50 = £2,500. Therefore, an increase in sales of 1,000 units gives a profit of £2,500, and a decrease of 1,000 units gives a loss of £2,500.

The certainty with which sales can be forecast may influence the choice of production method and also affect decisions about which products to trade in. Where there is great uncertainty, production methods and products with low break-even points may be chosen to minimise the risk of losses. However, the choice of a method or product with a low break-even point may restrict the total profits which can be earned if high sales are achieved.

## Example 11.7

The directors of Trestle Ltd are considering the following alternative methods of manufacturing a new product:

|  | Method 1 | Method 2 |
|---|---|---|
|  | £ | £ |
| Plant with a life of 10 years.................. | 50,000 | 150,000 |
| Other annual fixed costs.................... | 3,000 | 3,000 |
| Variable cost per unit...................... | 7 | 6.50 |
| Selling price per unit...................... | 8 | 8 |

The plant is expected to have a zero scrap value at the end of its life, and the company uses the straight line method of depreciation.

Method 2 has a lower variable cost because it uses less labour and has lower wastage rates for raw materials.

*Required:*
(a) Calculate the break-even point for each method of production.
(b) Calculate the profit or loss for each method which results from sales levels of 10,000 units, 20,000 units and 30,000 units.
(c) What is the greatest loss which might be suffered under each method.
(d) Advise management on which method should be adopted.

## Solution

|  | Method 1 | Method 2 |
|---|---|---|
|  | £ | £ |
| (a) |  |  |
| Fixed Costs: |  |  |
| Depreciation ............... | 5,000 | 15,000 |
| Other..................... | 3,000 | 3,000 |
|  | 8,000 | 18,000 |
| Contribution | £8 − £7 = £1 | £8 − £6.50 = £1.50 |
| Break-even point | $\frac{8,000}{1}$ = 8,000 units | $\frac{18,000}{1.50}$ = 12,000 units |

(b)

*10,000 units*

| | | |
|---|---|---|
| Contribution . . . . . . . . . . . . . . . . . . | 10,000 | 15,000 |
| Fixed Costs . . . . . . . . . . . . . . . . . . . | 8,000 | 18,000 |
| | | |
| Profit (Loss) . . . . . . . . . . . . . . . . . . | 2,000 | (3,000) |

*20,000 units*

| | | |
|---|---|---|
| Contribution . . . . . . . . . . . . . . . . . . | 20,000 | 30,000 |
| Fixed Costs . . . . . . . . . . . . . . . . . . . | 8,000 | 18,000 |
| | | |
| Profit | 12,000 | 12,000 |

*30,000 units*

| | | |
|---|---|---|
| Contribution . . . . . . . . . . . . . . . . . . | 30,000 | 45,000 |
| Fixed Costs . . . . . . . . . . . . . . . . . . . | 8,000 | 18,000 |
| | | |
| Profit . . . . . . . . . . . . . . . . . . . . . . | 22,000 | 27,000 |

(c) The greatest loss occurs when there is no contribution (i.e. zero output), and is equal to the fixed costs. Therefore, the maximum loss of Method 1 is £8,000 and of Method 2 is £18,000.

(d) Once method 2 breaks even, £1.50 is added to profit by every additional unit sold, while method 1 adds only £1. However, method 1 breaks even at a lower level of sales. Both methods make the same profit at sales of 20,000 units.

The decision about which method to select therefore rests on expected sales. If 20,000 is the maximum level of expected sales, then Method 1 is better; if sales are expected easily to exceed that level, then Method 2 is better.

Readers should now work Question 11.4 at the end of this chapter.

**11.3.5 Target Profit Calculation**   Once the contribution is known, it is also possible to calculate the level of sales needed, in terms of either value or quantity, to earn a given amount of profit. First, sales have to be sufficient to earn a total contribution equal to fixed costs, and then sufficient additional sales must be made to give the required profit. The formula to calculate the sales, in units, for a particular profit is:

$$\text{Sales in units} = \frac{\text{Fixed Costs} + \text{Required Profit}}{\text{Contribution per unit}}$$

The value of sales can then be calculated by multiplying the number of units by the selling price per unit.

## Example 11.8

The directors of Carp Ltd. are considering the manufacture of a new product which sells at £16 per unit. Its manufacture would involve annual fixed costs of £147,500 and a variable cost per unit of £9.50. The directors are only willing to undertake the project if a profit of £80,000 can be made.

*Required:*
Calculate the sales required, in terms of both quantity and value, to produce the desired profit.

**Solution.**

|  | £ |
|---|---|
| Selling price per unit............... | 16.00 |
| Variable cost per unit............... | 9.50 |
| Contribution per unit.............. | 6.50 |

$$\text{Required sales} = \frac{£147,500 + £80,000}{£6.50}$$

$$= 35,000 \text{ units OR}$$
$$35,000 \times £16 = £560,000$$

Readers should now work Question 11.5 at the end of this chapter.

## 11.4   PROFIT RATIOS

The study of break-even analysis in section 3.4 of this chapter shows that the amount of profit depends on the level of sales. It is useful for management, when assessing performance, to examine not only the absolute figure for profit, but also the relative profitability of different options. This is done by calculating the gross profit and net profit ratios. These ratios are used either to interpret past results or to assist the process of making decisions where the choice lies between a number of alternatives.

**11.4.1 Gross Profit Margin (Ratio)**   This ratio compares gross profit with sales. It is calculated, as a percentage, using the formula:

$$\text{Gross Profit Margin} = \frac{\text{Gross Profit}}{\text{Sales}} \times 100$$

In the case of a trader, who buys and sells goods without processing them further, the ratio is expected to remain constant when sales levels change as the entire cost of goods sold is a variable cost.

## Example 11.9

The sales, cost of goods sold and gross profit of Printer Ltd for 19X4 and 19X5 were:

|  | 19X4 £ | 19X5 £ |
|---|---|---|
| Sales | 162,000 | 196,000 |
| Cost of goods sold | 121,500 | 147,000 |
| Gross profit | 40,500 | 49,000 |

### Required:

Calculate the gross profit margin for each year.

### Solution

The gross profit margin for each year is:

$$
\begin{array}{cc}
19X4 & 19X5 \\
\dfrac{40,500}{162,000} \times 100 & \dfrac{49,000}{196,000} \times 100 \\
= 25\% & = 25\%
\end{array}
$$

The constant gross profit margin results from the fact that for each additional unit sold, an extra unit is purchased, and prices, both for buying and selling, are unchanged. In practice, the margin does not always remain stable for reasons which include the following:

1.  Increased purchases may enable bulk purchase discounts to be obtained. This gives a lower average unit cost and therefore increases the gross profit margin.
2.  Prices may be reduced to enable more units to be sold. This reduces the gross profit margin, but, provided sufficient extra units are sold, total gross profit may still increase.

The gross profit margin of *manufacturers* varies with changes in the level of activity even where there are no price changes. This is because manufacturing expenses include some fixed costs and, as production increases, the fixed costs are spread over a greater number of units with the result that the total cost per unit falls.

## Example 11.10

Yale Ltd. incurs annual fixed manufacturing costs of £75,000 and a variable manufacturing cost per unit of £5. Each unit sells for £10.

20,000 units were produced and sold in 19X1 and 25,000 in 19X2. There were no opening or closing stocks in either year.

*Required*:
(a) Calculate the average fixed manufacturing cost per unit.
(b) Calculate the company's total gross profit and gross profit margin for each year.
(c) Comment on the results prepared in answer to parts (a) and (b).

## Solution

(a)

|  | 19X1 | | 19X2 | |
|---|---|---|---|---|
| Average fixed manufacturing cost per unit | $\dfrac{£75,000}{20,000}$ | = £3.75 | $\dfrac{£75,000}{25,000}$ | = £3 |

(b)

|  | £ | £ | £ | £ |
|---|---|---|---|---|
| Sales......................... |  | 200,000 |  | 250,000 |
| Fixed costs.................... | 75,000 |  | 75,000 |  |
| Variable cost.................. | 100,000 |  | 125,000 |  |
|  |  | 175,000 |  | 200,000 |
| Gross profit................... |  | 25,000 |  | 50,000 |
| Gross profit margin............ | $\dfrac{£25,000}{£200,000}$ x 100 | | $\dfrac{£50,000}{£250,000}$ x 100 | |
|  | = 12.5% | | = 20% | |

(c) An increase in sales of 25% has resulted in an increase in gross profit of 100% and in the gross profit margin of 60%. This is because the average fixed cost per unit has fallen from £3.75 to £3.00.

The interpretation of the gross profit margin of a manufacturer is also affected by the possibility of changes in purchase or selling prices which accompany a change in the rate of activity as described above for traders. Other unit cost changes may result from increased activity, for example, overtime, which is paid at a higher rate, may have to be worked.

**11.4.2 Net Profit Percentage (Ratio)** The net profit percentage compares net profit with sales and is expressed as a percentage. It is calculated by the formula:

$$\text{Net Profit Percentage} = \frac{\text{Net Profit}}{\text{Sales}} \times 100$$

The expenses charged against gross profit to calculate the net profit can be either fixed or variable with respect to sales. For example, interest paid on debentures is fixed provided that no further loans are taken out, while delivery costs are likely to respond to changes in the level of sales. Therefore, the net profit percentage of both traders and manufacturers changes as a result of an increase or decrease in sales. It is anticipated that increased sales, which spread the fixed costs over a greater output, will be accompanied by an increase in the net profit percentage, while decreased sales will be reflected by a fall in the percentage. Both the gross profit and net profit percentages may be affected by changes in prices unrelated to the level of sales, for example, if the price of raw material rises, the effect on the percentages depends on the extent to which the increase can be passed on to the firm's customers.

## Example 11.11
Crackle is a trader who buys and sells goods. His trading results for 19X6 and 19X7 were:

*Summarised Trading Results*

|  | 19X6 £ | 19X7 £ |
|---|---|---|
| Sales | 80,000 | 100,000 |
| Cost of goods sold | 60,000 | 75,000 |
| Gross profit | 20,000 | 25,000 |
| Expenses | 10,000 | 12,000 |
| Net profit | 10,000 | 13,000 |

There were no opening or closing stocks in either year. The cost of goods which Crackle sells rose by 10% on 1 January 19X7.

*Required:*
(a) Calculate Crackle's gross profit margin and net profit percentage for 19X6 and 19X7.
(b) Comment on the changes in the percentages calculated in part (a).

## Solution.

(a)

|  | 19X6 | 19X7 |
|---|---|---|
| Gross profit margin | $\frac{20,000}{80,000}$ x 100 = 25% | $\frac{25,000}{100,000}$ x 100 = 25% |
| Net profit percentage | $\frac{10,000}{80,000}$ x 100 = 12.5% | $\frac{13,000}{100,000}$ x 100 = 13% |

(b)   The gross profit margin has remained constant at 25%, and so Crackle has been able to pass on the 10% increase in costs to his customers. The growth in the value of sales is due not only to the price rise, but also to an increase in the volume of sales. If sales had simply risen in line with the price rise, they would have been only £80,000 + 10% = £88,000

   The value of sales has grown by 25%, while expenses have increased by only 20% (perhaps some of them are fixed costs). As a result, the net profit percentage has increased from 12.5% to 13%.

Changes in the gross profit margin also affect the net profit percentage, and, to examine the relative impact of items charged in the profit and loss account, it is useful to express them all as a percentage of sales.

## Example 11.12

Stamp Ltd, a trading company, did not increase its selling prices between 19X6 and 19X7, but the cost of the goods it sells rose 1.25% on 1 January 19X7. Its trading and profit and loss accounts for 19X6 and 19X7 were:

*Summarised Trading and Profit and Loss Accounts*

|  | 19X6 | 19X7 |
|---|---|---|
|  | £ | £ |
| Sales.......................................... | 50,000 | 60,000 |
| Cost of goods sold.............................. | 40,000 | 48,600 |
| Gross profit................................... | 10,000 | 11,400 |
| Rent.......................................... | 1,200 | 1,200 |
| Other expenses................................. | 2,000 | 2,400 |
|  | 3,200 | 3,600 |
| Net profit..................................... | 6,800 | 7,800 |

*Required:*

  (a)   Prepare statements for 19X6 and 19X7 in which all costs, the net profit and the gross profit are expressed as percentages of sales.

  (b)   Comment on the results shown in the statement prepared in part (a).

## Solution

(a)

|  | 19X6 | 19X7 |
|---|---|---|
|  | % | % |
| Sales........................................... | 100.0 | 100.0 |
| Cost of goods sold............................... | 80.0 | 81.0 |
| Gross profit.................................... | 20.0 | 19.0 |
| Rent........................................... | 2.4 | 2.0 |
| Other expenses................................. | 4.0 | 4.0 |
|  | 6.4 | 6.0 |
| Net profit...................................... | 13.6 | 13.0 |

(b) The gross profit has risen, but the gross profit margin has fallen by 1% as a result of the rise in the cost of goods it sells (if this had not risen, cost of goods sold would have been £48,000; 1.25% x 48,000 = 600 is the price rise). Rent is a fixed cost, and its impact has fallen from 2.4% to 2% and other expenses have remained constant at 4%; the net result is a fall in the total profit and loss account costs from 6.4% to 6%. The overall impact is a fall in the net profit percentage of 0.6%, although the amount of net profit has risen. If the gross profit margin could have been maintained by passing on the price rise to customers, the net profit percentage would also have risen.

Readers should now work Question 11.6 at the end of this chapter.

## 11.5 FORECAST RESULTS
Management is often faced with a number of alternative courses of action, especially when it is considering the long-term development of the company. It is of great assistance to management to prepare forecasts which predict the likely outcome of alternatives so that choices are based on the best information possibly available.

Forecasts cannot be completely accurate, as many of the factors which influence actual results, such as the cost of raw materials and the actual demand for the product, are outside the control of management. However, this does not invalidate the exercise of preparing forecasts since the alternative is to make decisions without evaluating the outcome of management's expectations. To prepare forecasts, management must answer such vital questions as: how many units do you expect to sell; what will be the selling price per unit; how much labour, at what cost, will it take to produce each unit? Forecasts bring together the answers to all these questions in accounting statements, and show the expected impact of alternatives on key financial magnitudes such as cash, profit and working capital. Cash forecasts are considered in section 5.1 of this chapter; the forecast trading and profit and loss account and balance sheet are dealt with in section 5.2.

**11.5.1 Cash Forecasts** Management must ensure that the company can afford any new project which is under consideration, i.e. that the company will not run out of cash if a particular plan is followed. Additional external finance, such as a bank overdraft, can be sought if the company's own cash resources are insufficient, but lenders will only be willing to provide funds which are likely to be repaid. The impact of plans on the cash resources of a company can be predicted using a cash forecast, and this is also of great interest to any person or organisation, such as a bank, which is approached for funds. If cash forecasts are not prepared, a company may suddenly find itself short of cash or holding unproductive surplus funds in its bank account. A cash forecast enables a company to foresee a deficit, for which appropriate funding can be sought, or a surplus for which uses can be prepared in advance.

The preparation of a monthly cash forecast involves the identification of the cash flows expected to take place in each month and the calculation of the forecast cash position at the end of each month. The following techniques are used to predict cash transactions:
1.  Sales. Cash sales are entered in the forecast as receipts for the month in which they take place. The time lag has to be taken into account for credit sales, for example, cash from March sales may be received in April.
2.  Purchases. Cash purchases are entered in the month in which they take place. The time lag has to be taken into account for credit purchases, for example, cash for October purchases may be paid in November.
3.  Regular payments are entered in the appropriate month, possibly with adjustment for a lag between the date when the expense is incurred and when it is paid.
4.  Irregular items, such as the purchase of fixed assets or the payment of tax, are also entered according to their incidence.

**Example 11.13**
Hamel runs a shop which makes all of its sales for cash. Forecasts for the first half of 19X6 are:

Sales:................. January to March - £25,000 per month
April to June - £30,000 per month

Purchases:.............. A gross margin of 20% on selling prices is made
Every item sold is immediately replaced
Suppliers are paid in the month following delivery

Payments:.............. Wages and other expenses £4,000 per month
Drawings £1,000 per month
Delivery van cost £7,000; delivered on 1 January and paid
for in February

Opening Balances:........ Owed to suppliers £16,000
Cash £1,000

Ignore interest on any overdraft which may arise.

## Required:

(a) Calculate the value of monthly purchases.
(b) Prepare a cash forecast for Hamel for the first six months of 19X6 which shows the cash balance at the end of each month.
(c) Comment on the position shown by the forecast.

## Solution.

(a)

|  | Sales | Purchases (sales – 20%) |
|---|---|---|
|  | £000 | £000 |
| January | 25 | 20 |
| February | 25 | 20 |
| March | 25 | 20 |
| April | 30 | 24 |
| May | 30 | 24 |
| June | 30 | 24 |

(b)

|  | Jan £ | Feb £ | March £ | April £ | May £ | June £ | Total £ |
|---|---|---|---|---|---|---|---|
| CASH IN: |  |  |  |  |  |  |  |
| Sales.............. | 25,000 | 25,000 | 25,000 | 30,000 | 30,000 | 30,000 | 165,000 |
| CASH OUT: |  |  |  |  |  |  |  |
| Purchases........... | 16,000 | 20,000 | 20,000 | 20,000 | 24,000 | 24,000 | 124,000 |
| Wages and other expenses..... | 4,000 | 4,000 | 4,000 | 4,000 | 4,000 | 4,000 | 24,000 |
| Drawings........... | 1,000 | 1,000 | 1,000 | 1,000 | 1,000 | 1,000 | 6,000 |
| Delivery Van........ |  | 7,000 |  |  |  |  | 7,000 |
|  | 21,000 | 32,000 | 25,000 | 25,000 | 29,000 | 29,000 | 161,000 |
| Opening balance..... | 1,000 | 5,000 | (2,000) | (2,000) | 3,000 | 4,000 | 1,000 |
| + Cash In........... | 25,000 | 25,000 | 25,000 | 30,000 | 30,000 | 30,000 | 165,000 |
| – Cash Out.......... | 21,000 | 32,000 | 25,000 | 25,000 | 29,000 | 29,000 | 161,000 |
| Closing Balance...... | 5,000 | (2,000) | (2,000) | 3,000 | 4,000 | 5,000 | 5,000 |

(c)  The purchase of the van creates a cash deficit in February and March, but this is made good from trading cash inflows by April. The bank should be approached for a temporary loan; an overdraft would be best. By the end of June the business is accumulating a cash surplus which will continue to increase if trade stays at the same level. Thought should be given to how any permanently spare cash is to be used.

Note the columnar layout of the solution to part (b) of the example. The use of this presentation is recommended because:

1.  It saves time as the descriptions of cash flows do not have to be repeated for each month.

2.  Errors are less likely to occur as any inconsistent entries are more easily identified.

3.  It aids comparison throughout the period covered by the forecast of the individual elements of cash flow.

Readers should now work Question 11.7 at the end of this chapter.

**11.5.2 Forecast Trading and Profit and Loss Account and Balance Sheet**  The preparation of a trading and profit and loss account and balance sheet from the cash account, and opening and closing values for assets and liabilities, was explained in chapter 3 in the context of past results. Once the cash forecast has been prepared, the same techniques may be applied to prepare a forecast trading and profit and loss account and balance sheet.

# Example 11.14

The balance sheet of Hamel at 31 December 19X5 was:

*Balance Sheet*

| | £ | £ |
|---|---|---|
| FIXED ASSETS | | |
| Premises............................................. | | 10,000 |
| CURRENT ASSETS | | |
| Stock............................................ | 18,500 | |
| Cash............................................ | 1,000 | |
| | 19,500 | |
| CURRENT LIABILITIES | | |
| Trade creditors.................................. | 16,000 | |
| | | 3,500 |
| | | 13,500 |
| CAPITAL........................................ | | 13,500 |

Hamel expects to undertake the transactions given in Example 11.13 above during the first six months of 19X6. You may assume that the monthly cash forecast has been prepared which gives a summary of cash transactions in the 'Total' column.

The van is expected to have a life of five years and a zero scrap value at the end of that time. Hamel uses the straight line method to calculate depreciation.

## Required:

Prepare Hamel's forecast trading and profit and loss account for the six months to 30 June 19X6 and a balance sheet at that date.

## Solution.

*Forecast Trading and Profit and Loss Account*

| | £ | £ |
|---|---|---|
| Sales........................................... | | 165,000 |
| Less: cost of goods sold (Working)................. | | 132,000 |
| Gross profit.................................... | | 33,000 |
| Wages......................................... | 24,000 | |
| Depreciation (0.5 x 7,000/5)..................... | 700 | |
| | | 24,700 |
| Net Profit...................................... | | 8,300 |

*Balance Sheet*

|                                    | £      | £      |
|------------------------------------|--------|--------|
| **FIXED ASSETS**                   |        |        |
| Premises.......................................... |        | 10,000 |
| Van........................................... | 7,000  |        |
| Less: Depreciation............................. | 700    |        |
|                                    |        | 6,300  |
|                                    |        | 16,300 |
| **CURRENT ASSETS**                 |        |        |
| Stock......................................... | 18,500 |        |
| Cash ......................................... | 5,000  |        |
|                                    | 23,500 |        |
| **CURRENT LIABILITIES**            |        |        |
| Trade creditors (June purchases)................... | 24,000 |        |
|                                    |        | (500)  |
|                                    |        | 15,800 |
| **CAPITAL**                        |        |        |
| Opening balance.............................. |        | 13,500 |
| Plus: profit.................................. |        | 8,300  |
|                                    |        | 21,800 |
| Less: drawings................................ |        | (6,000) |
|                                    |        | 15,800 |

**Working:**

Purchases  =  Payments  –  opening  creditors  +  closing  creditors
Purchases = 124,000 – 16,000 + 24,000 (June purchases) = 132,000

The level of stock has remained unchanged, and so purchases and cost of goods sold have the same value.

Readers should now work Question 11.8 at the end of this chapter.

## 11.6   QUESTIONS
### Question 11.1
Calc Ltd. has a head office and three branches. The company's results for 19X6 were:

|  |  | £000 | £000 |
|---|---|---:|---:|
| Sales:............................ | Branch 1.......... | 250 | |
| | Branch 2.......... | 300 | |
| | Branch 3.......... | 175 | |
| | | | 725 |
| Cost of goods sold:................ | Branch 1.......... | 125 | |
| | Branch 2.......... | 160 | |
| | Branch 3.......... | 67 | |
| | | | 352 |
| Gross profit...................... | | | 373 |
| Running costs:................... | Branch 1.......... | 60 | |
| | Branch 2.......... | 85 | |
| | Branch 3.......... | 47 | |
| | | | 192 |
| | | | 181 |
| Head Office costs.................. | | | 90 |
| Profit........................... | | | 91 |

*Required:*
Re-draft the accounts to show the results achieved by each branch.


## Question 11.2
Rock Ltd manufactures a single product which passes through two separate processes, designated X and Y, in two separate factories; all products must pass through both processes before they are ready for sale.

Rock's summary revenue account for 19X5 is as follows:

|  |  | £ |
|---|---|---:|
| Process X |  |  |
| Raw materials.................... |  | 20,000 |
| Wages.......................... |  | 30,000 |
| Depreciation .................... |  | 12,000 |
| Rent .......................... |  | 8,000 |
|  |  |  |
| Transfer to process Y............... |  | 70,000 |
| Process Y |  |  |
| Raw materials.................... |  | 10,000 |
| Wages.......................... |  | 40,000 |
| Depreciation .................... |  | 12,000 |
| Rent .......................... |  | 8,000 |
|  |  |  |
| Cost of production............... |  | 140,000 |
| General expenses................. |  | 36,000 |
| Net profit....................... |  | 24,000 |
|  |  |  |
| Sales (100,000 units).............. |  | 200,000 |

There are no stocks of any type at the beginning or at the end of the year.

There is a heavy demand for the product. Production costs and selling price are to be maintained at the same level as in 19X5.

Consideration is being given to three proposals for increasing production as follows:

(i)   The expansion of manufacturing capacity at both factories. The cost of rent and the depreciation charge will in both cases be double that for 19X5; materials consumed and wage rates would continue for both factories at the same unit cost as for 19X5.

(ii)  The purchase of the additional Process X components from an outside source at a price of 80p. per unit. Expansion of manufacturing capacity at factory Y on the same terms and the same cost as for proposal (i).

(iii) The purchase of the additional finished goods from an outside source at 180p per unit and their sale at 200p per unit. No additional capacity would be required.

General expenses will increase in all cases at the rate of £2,000 per additional 25,000 units sold.

*Required:*

Prepare a financial statement for management which shows the forecast *additional* profit under each of the three proposals if outputs and sales increase by (a) 25,000 units and (b) 50,000 units.

**Question 11.3**

Glen Eagles is the proprietor of a small but long-established manufacturing business which has consistently made an annual profit of £20,000. The financial results of the business have shown little change in recent years, and the financial position has been very stable, supported by the fact that annual drawings have generally been lower than the profit. The expectation is that there will be little change over the next few years and that the level of profit will be maintained.

Eagles has recently been invited by Troon Ltd. to increase his production to meet an export demand in a market where the prospects of development and increased sales are very substantial. Additional plant with a life of 10 years, and a zero residual value at the end of that period, will be needed for such an expansion. Machines which will produce 46,000 items per annum are available at a cost of £36,000 each.

The selling price per item is £1, and the variable costs of manufacture for the export market will be 55p. per item. Additional general expenses will amount to £10,000 for the first £46,000 increase in sales, but will fall to £4,000 for each £46,000 block of additional sales above the first £46,000.

Eagles has no private resources. The existing liquid resources of the business would cover any additional working capital required, and also provide £10,000 towards the capital cost of the new project. A bank is willing to lend up to £100,000 to Eagles at an interest rate of 15% per annum.

An alternative proposal is made to Eagles. Troon Ltd offers him £120,000 in cash for his entire business and is prepared to retain his services as a manager on a 10 year contract at a salary of £14,000 per annum plus an additional £3,000 per annum for each £46,000 increase in turnover.

Eagles can expect to invest the proceeds of the sale of his business to earn interest of 10% per annum

*Required:*
(a) Statements reporting on the profit likely to be received from overseas sales at the rate of £46,000, £92,000 and £138,000 per annum respectively.

(b) Prepare a report to Eagles which shows the results of the alternative courses of action open to him.

## Question 11.4

During 19X4 Feather Ltd. sold 60,000 units of a product and made a net profit of £20,000. The contribution to fixed costs and profit per unit was £2, and the selling price was £5 per unit. The variable costs are expected to increase by £0.10 for 19X5 and fixed costs in 19X5 are expected to be £4,500 greater than in 19X4; apart from these changes, trading conditions are expected to remain the same.

*Required:*
(a) Prepare the summary profit and loss account for 19X4, showing sales, variable costs, fixed costs, and profit.
(b) Calculate the break even level of sales for 19X4 in terms of units and £'s.
(c) Calculate the break even level of sales for 19X5 in terms of both units and £'s.

## Question 11.5

The summarised profit and loss account of Latchmere Ltd. for 19X6 is as follows:

|  | £ |  | £ |
|---|---|---|---|
| Raw materials........... | 50,000 | Sales(100,000 units |  |
| Wages.................. | 100,000 | at £2 each)............ | 200,000 |
| Depreciation ............ | 10,000 |  |  |
| Gross profit............. | 40,000 |  |  |
|  | 200,000 |  | 200,000 |
| General expenses......... | 20,000 | Gross profit.......... | 40,000 |
| Net profit............... | 20,000 |  |  |
|  | 40,000 |  | 40,000 |

The company's plant has now reached its maximum level of production and the directors are considering proposals for expansion.

Two plans have been suggested:
1. The purchase of additional plant of the same type and capacity as that in use at present, and which will operate at exactly the same raw materials and wages costs per unit as the existing plant, in the expectation of doubling the level of sales. It is

thought that a market exists at the current selling price of £2 per unit. The plant will cost £100,000.

2. The purchase of additional plant, at a cost of £200,000, capable of manufacturing a similar product with the same raw material content as the current product, but for which the wages cost will be reduced to 15% of the expected selling price of £2 per unit.

Under both plans, *additional* general expenses amounting to £5,000 will be incurred for any increase in turnover up to £100,000 (total sales £300,000) and a further £10,000 will be incurred for any increase in turnover above £100,000 and up to £200,000 (total sales £400,000). The cost of production and the selling price per unit of the first £200,000 of sales will be the same as for 19X6, and the profit on those sales will be unchanged.

For both plans, the life of the new plant will be 10 years at the end of which it will have a zero scrap value. The purchase will be financed by a fixed term 10 year loan at 10% per annum.

*Required:*
 (a) Prepare a trading and profit and loss account of Latchmere Ltd for 19X7 assuming that plan 1 is implemented and that the expected sales increase of £200,000 is achieved.
 (b) Calculate the minimum increase in sales needed under plan 2 to ensure that the net profit after charging interest is equal to the profit which it is calculated will be produced under plan 1.
 (c) Calculate the sales necessary in 19X7 under plan 2 which give the company as a whole the same net profit, after interest, as was earned in 19X6, that is, £20,000.

## Question 11.6
The summarised profit and loss account of Sanoy Ltd for 19X5 is as follows:

| | £ | | £ |
|---|---|---|---|
| Expenses............... | 50,400 | Sales.................. | 56,000 |
| Net profit.............. | 5,600 | | |
| | 56,000 | | 56,000 |

Two alternative plans for 19X6 have been prepared and they are under consideration. The plans are:

|                                                                  | £       |
| ---------------------------------------------------------------- | ------- |
| **PLAN 1**                                                       |         |
| An investment in plant costing                                   | 16,000  |
| Sales expected to increase to                                    | 84,000  |
| Anticipated total expenses (including depreciation)              | 76,440  |
| **PLAN 2**                                                       |         |
| An investment in plant costing                                   | 36,000  |
| Sales expected to increase to                                    | 112,500 |
| Anticipated total expenses (including depreciation)              | 103,500 |

*Required:*

(a) Summary profit and loss accounts for 19X6 showing the results of Plan 1 and Plan 2 as they would appear if the forecasts are exactly achieved.

(b) A comparison of the financial results to be expected under each of the two plans, both between themselves and with respect to the results of 19X5, including calculations of the net profit percentages.

## Question 11.7

Grant commences business on 1 January 19X6 and introduces £20,000 cash as capital. He also borrows £8,000 from his brother at 10% per annum interest, payable half yearly in June and December. He makes the following estimates about the first six months of 19X6:

| | |
| --- | --- |
| Fixed assets | £20,000 purchased for cash in January |
| Sales | £12,000 per month. Two months' credit to be given to customers |
| Purchases | £16,000 in January and £8,000 per month thereafter. Suppliers will allow one month's credit |
| Expenses | £800 per month average, excluding interest, payable in the month in which they are incurred |
| Drawings | £200 per month |

*Required:*

Prepare a cash forecast for the business of Grant for the first six months of 19X6 which shows the cash balance at the end of each month.

## Question 11.8
*Required:*

Use the information in Question 11.7 to prepare Grant's forecast

Trading and Profit and Loss Account for the six months to 30 June 19X6 and his balance sheet at that date.

The fixed assets are to be depreciated at the rate of 20% per annum on cost, and Grant calculates selling prices of goods by adding 50% to their cost price.

Grant expects that the interest on the forecast overdraft will cost £300 and be paid in July.

# CHAPTER 12

# Performance Assessment

## 12.1 THE NEED FOR PROFIT AND CASH

It is widely accepted that the maximisation of profit is a major business objective, and it is part of management's job to devise an effective means of achieving this aim. The link between growth in output and profitability was established in section 3 of chapter 11, and it is because sales and profit usually increase together that management often follows a policy of expansion. Management must, however, recognise that there exists an effective constraint on the rate of expansion, and this limitation is the quantity of cash available at any point in time. If management pursues a policy of expansion without first taking steps to ensure that sufficient cash is available for this purpose, the consequence will be, at the very least, financial embarrassment and, at worst, bankruptcy or liquidation.

It is therefore important for management to plan carefully future business developments, and this planning process should concentrate attention on two separate, but related, areas:
1. Profitability
2. Financial stability

Each area is of equal importance, and any tendency to emphasise one aspect to the exclusion of the other is likely to produce unfavourable repercussions. For instance, pre-occcupation with financial stability is likely to discourage innovation. Constant changes in consumer demand are a fact of business life, and the failure of management to anticipate, or at least respond to, these changes will result in a decline in the demand for the company's products to a level where the business is no longer viable. On the other hand, investment in a project which promises high profits in the near future, without first attempting to assess whether the company can afford the project, is equally ill advised. Recognition of the importance of financial stability should not cause management to ignore the need for profit, but it will cause management to follow a policy of long run rather than short run profit maximisation.

A proper assessment of business performance must therefore focus attention on the adequacy of both profit and cash. The way in which this is done is examined in this chapter.

## 12.2 RETURN ON CAPITAL EMPLOYED (ROCE)*

The amount of profit earned by a business is important but, in order to assess the relative performance of a number of businesses, or even the performance of the same business over a number of years, it is necessary to examine the figure for profit in relation to the amount of money invested (capital employed) in the business.

### Example 12.1

The following information is provided for 19X1.

|  | Company A | Company B |
|---|---|---|
|  | £ | £ |
| Net profit | 100,000 | 150,000 |
| Capital employed | 500,000 | 1,500,000 |

Company A has reported a profit of £100,000 whereas company B has reported a profit of £150,000. Company B has therefore generated 50% more profit than company A but, before any rational conclusions can be reached concerning the relative success of the two companies, it is necessary to relate these profit figures to the amount invested in each business using the following accounting ratio:

$$\text{Return on Capital Employed} = \frac{\text{Net Profit}}{\text{Capital Employed}} \times 100$$

This ratio is now calculated for each of the two companies.

$$\text{Company A} = \frac{£100,000}{£500,000} \times 100 = 20\%$$

$$\text{Company B} = \frac{£150,000}{£1,500,000} \times 100 = 10\%$$

It is therefore clear that, contrary to the initial impression, company A is the better proposition for, say, a prospective investor. Company B earns a profit which is 50% higher but, to achieve this,

* Tax complications are ignored throughout section 2 of this chapter.

three times the level of investment is required. When profit is related to the amount invested we find that company A earns a return of 20% compared with 10% by company B, i.e. on every £1 invested in company A, a return of 20p is earned whereas, on every £1 invested in company B, a return of 10p is earned.

**12.2.1 Calculation of Capital Employed** Capital employed is the amount of money invested in the business. The two most common methods of calculating capital employed are as follows:

*Owners' capital employed (net assets).* This is the amount invested by the owner or owners. It is the balance on the sole trader's capital account; the aggregate of the balances on the partners' capital and current accounts or, in the case of a limited company, the ordinary shareholders' capital plus share premium account, retained profits and any balances on reserve accounts. Using an asset-based approach, owners' capital employed is alternatively calculated by taking total assets and deducting non-ownership liabilities.

*Total capital employed (gross assets).* This is found by adding together all sources of finance i.e. capital, non-current liabilities and current liabilities. The alternative asset-based calculation adds together the balance for each category of asset belonging to the business.

**Example 12.2**
The following balances were extracted from the books of Compass Ltd. at 31 December 19X2.

|  | £ |
|---|---|
| Fixed assets | 130,000 |
| Ordinary share capital | 100,000 |
| Share premium account | 20,000 |
| 10% loan repayable 19X8 | 50,000 |
| Trade creditors | 25,000 |
| Current assets | 105,000 |
| Revaluation reserve | 12,000 |
| Proposed dividend | 10,000 |
| Retained profit | 18,000 |

*Required:*
(a) The balance sheet of Compass Ltd. at 31 December 19X2, presented in horizontal format.

(b)   The figures for:   (i)   Owners'capital employed
                         (ii)  Total capital employed

## Solution

(a)

*Balance Sheet of Compass Ltd at 31 December 19X2*

| | £ | | £ |
|---|---|---|---|
| Ordinary share capital....... | 100,000 | Fixed assets................ | 130,000 |
| Share premium account...... | 20,000 | Current assets.............. | 105,000 |
| Revaluation reserve......... | 12,000 | | |
| Retained profit............. | 18,000 | | |
| | 150,000 | | |
| 10% Loan repayable 19X8... | 50,000 | | |
| | 200,000 | | |
| *Current Liabilities* | | | |
| Trade creditors............. | 25,000 | | |
| Proposed dividend.......... | 10,000 | | |
| | 235,000 | | 235,000 |

(b)
(i)   Owners' capital employed, £150,000.
(ii)  Total capital employed, £235,000.

## 12.2.2 Matching Profit with Capital Employed  The profit figure
used for the purpose of calculating ROCE will differ depending on
the version of capital employed under consideration.

Owners' capital employed -   Use net profit reported in the
                             accounts.
Total capital employed -     Use net profit *before* deducting
                             any interest charges, including
                             interest on any bank overdraft.

The different purposes of these calculations are that the former
calculation measures the return earned for investors, while the latter
calculation directs attention to the efficiency with which
management utilises the total resources at its disposal.

**Example 12.3**

Assume the same facts as for Example 12.2. In addition, the summarised profit and loss account of Compass Ltd for 19X2 is as follows:

*Profit and Loss Account of Compass Ltd for 19X2*

|  | £ | £ |
|---|---|---|
| Gross profit | | 100,000 |
| Less: Administrative costs | 54,000 | |
| Selling and distribution costs | 17,000 | |
| Interest on long term loan | 5,000 | 76,000 |
| | | |
| Net profit | | 24,000 |
| Less: Dividends | | 10,000 |
| | | |
| Retained profit for 19X2 | | 14,000 |
| Retained profit at 1 January 19X2 | | 4,000 |
| | | |
| Retained profit at 31 December 19X2 | | 18,000 |

*Required:*

Calculations of the return on:
(i)   Owners'capital employed
(ii)  Total capital employed

**Solution**

(i)  Owners'capital employed.

$$\text{Return} = \frac{24,000}{150,000} \times 100 = 16\%$$

(ii)  Total capital employed.

$$\text{Return} = \frac{29,000^*}{235,000} \times 100 = 12.3\%$$

\* £24,000 (net profit) + £5,000 (interest charges)

The rate of return earned on total capital employed is 12.3%; looked at another way, the directors of Compass have managed to achieve a return of 12.3% on the total resources at their disposal. The return earned on the owners' capital employed is significantly higher, at 16%. There are two reasons for this:

1.  Compass benefits from 'free' finance amounting to £35,000, consisting of the dividend not yet due (£10,000) and trade credit (£25,000), and it is for this reason that businessmen usually take the maximum amount of finance offered by suppliers.

2.   The directors have raised some loan capital at a favourable rate of interest, i.e. the £50,000 loan repayable in 19X8 attracts interest at the rate of 10% per annum and, because the return earned on total capital employed is higher, the surplus accrues to the ordinary shareholders who are, as a result, better off. This will not always happen; if the return on total capital employed is *below* 10%, the providers of loan finance must still be paid their 10%, and the 'loss' is suffered by the ordinary shareholders. Management should therefore raise loan capital only if it is reasonably confident that the return earned will exceed that payable to loan creditors.

The rates of return, calculated in this section, are based on capital employed at the *year end*. Profit arises throughout the twelve month period, however, and a more precise calculation is made by using *average* capital employed during the year. Because the information needed to calculate average capital employed is rarely provided, and because absolute accuracy is not a priority, it is perfectly acceptable to use the year end figure which usually produces a close approximation.

Students should now work Question 12.1 at the end of this chapter.

## 12.3   WORKING CAPITAL

A business must be able to meet its debts as they fall due if it is to maintain its credit-worthiness and continue as a going concern. Section 3 of chapter 2 drew attention to the fact that a business must have an adequate balance of working capital for this desirable state of affairs to exist, and a secure financial position is illustrated in Example 12.4.

### Example 12.4

The following balances were extracted from the books of Campion Ltd. as at 31 December 19X1.

|  | £ |
|---|---|
| Share capital | 100,000 |
| Reserves | 75,000 |
| Taxation due 30 September 19X2 | 10,000 |
| Trade creditors | 15,000 |
| Balance of cash at bank | 5,000 |
| Fixed assets at cost less depreciation | 150,000 |
| Stock | 22,000 |
| Trade debtors | 23,000 |

*Required:*
A calculation of Campion's working capital balance at 31 December 19X1.

## Solution

Calculation of working capital:

|  |  |  | £ | £ |
|---|---|---|---:|---:|
| Current assets: | Stock | | | 22,000 |
| | Trade debtors | | | 23,000 |
| | Bank balance | | | 5,000 |
| | | | | 50,000 |
| Less: | Current Liabilities: | Trade creditors | 15,000 | |
| | | Taxation payable | 10,000 | 25,000 |
| Working capital | | | | 25,000 |

The above calculation shows that Campion is able to pay its current liabilities out of resources made available by the conversion of current assets into cash and, in addition, it shows that £25,000 will remain after the necessary payments have been made. The fact that business activity is continuous means that additional purchases will be made during January 19X2 and more sales will also occur, consequently the £25,000 surplus will never actually arise in a single lump sum. Nevertheless, the working capital calculation provides a useful indication of the company's ability to meet its short-term debts as they fall due for payment, i.e. it focuses attention on the solvency position of the firm.

**12.3.1 Working Capital Ratio**  The significance which can be attached, in isolation, to the balance for working capital is, however, limited. A figure of £25,000 suggests financial stability in the case of a small business, such as Campion, but probably not in a much larger enterprise. In another company, the deduction of current liabilities amounting to, say, £975,000 from current assets of £1,000,000 would also show a working capital balance of £25,000 but, in view of the much larger scale of short-term commitments, it would probably be regarded as a totally inadequate financial 'cushion'. It is for this reason that users of accounting statements pay more attention to the working capital (or current) *ratio,* which examines the proportional relationship between current assets and current liabilities. It is calculated as follows:

$$\text{Working capital ratio} = \frac{\text{Current Assets}}{\text{Current liabilities}} :1$$

The working capital ratio of Campion is as follows:

$$\text{Working capital ratio} = \frac{£50,000}{£25,000} :1$$

$$= 2:1$$

The purpose of the working capital ratio is to help assess the solvency position of a business, and the question which therefore naturally arises is 'What is an acceptable ratio?' Unfortunately it is not possible to be dogmatic, since much depends on the nature of the trade in which the company is engaged. It may be assumed, for the purpose of illustration, that Campion is a trading company which purchases and sells goods on credit, also that the company receives from suppliers the same period of credit that it allows to customers; thirty days is the normal credit period, although the exact duration is unimportant because, provided a company allows customers, on average, the same period of credit as is granted by its suppliers, the amount of money due from customers will be received in time for the creditors to be paid as their debts fall due. Because Campion sells goods on credit, however, none of the money presently tied up in stock will be converted into cash in time to pay the existing current liabilities as they mature. It is true that some stock will be sold in the next few days, but it will be at least a further thirty days before the cash is collected from the customer. It will be even longer before the remaining stock is converted into cash. The conclusion which arises from this analysis is that the working capital ratio must be sufficiently high to accommodate the inclusion of stock amongst the current assets. If stock comprises no more than 50% of total current assets, as is the case at Campion, an adequate ratio of current assets to current liabilities is in the region of 2:1.

In practice a ratio of 2:1 is conventionally regarded as the acceptable norm. It cannot be emphasised too strongly, however, that this is a broad generalisation which should be treated with great caution. For example, companies in certain sectors of the economy turn stock into cash very quickly and, for them, a ratio of well below 2:1 may be quite acceptable. This state of affairs usually exists in the retail trade where sales are made mainly for cash. In circumstances where resources are tied up in stock for a much longer time period, as happens in the construction industry, a working capital ratio of perhaps 4:1 may be regarded as essential.

## 12.3.2 Working Capital Requirements and Dividend Policy

Dividends are declared on the basis of profits earned, but a payment can be made only if cash is available for this purpose. When deciding whether a dividend should be paid and, if so, how much, the directors take account of the company's current financial position and future commitments. Their aim is to ensure that, as far as possible, the shareholders receive an adequate return on their investment; also that the financial position is not undermined as a result of the payment made.

### Example 12.5

The balance sheets of Galston Ltd. as at 31 December 19X5 and 19X6 are as follows:

|  | 19X5 | | 19X6 | |
| --- | --- | --- | --- | --- |
|  | £ | £ | £ | £ |
| Fixed assets at cost.............. |  | 303,000 |  | 367,500 |
| Less: Accumulated depreciation |  | 124,500 |  | 157,500 |
|  |  | 178,500 |  | 210,000 |
| *Current Assets:* |  |  |  |  |
| Stock........................ | 37,500 |  | 75,000 |  |
| Debtors...................... | 34,500 |  | 43,500 |  |
| Bank........................ | 18,000 |  | 1,500 |  |
|  |  | 90,000 |  | 120,000 |
|  |  | 268,500 |  | 330,000 |
| Share capital................... |  | 150,000 |  | 150,000 |
| Retained profit at 31 Dec. 19X5... |  | 73,500 |  | 73,500 |
| Profit for 19X6............... |  | - |  | 51,000 |
|  |  | 223,500 |  | 274,500 |
| Current Liabilities............. |  | 45,000 |  | 55,500 |
|  |  | 268,500 |  | 330,000 |

The figure of current liabilities as at 31 December 19X5 includes a proposed dividend of £7,500 for the year to that date. No decision has been taken yet about the dividend to be paid for 19X6, and nothing is included in the 19X6 balance sheet for such a dividend.

The directors are considering the dividend that should be paid for 19X6 in the light of the excellent results for that year.

*Required:*
(a) Calculations of Galston's working capital and working capital ratio as at 31 December 19X5 and 31 December 19X6.
(b) A calculation of the maximum dividend that should be declared for 19X6 if the working capital ratio at 31 December 19X6 is to be the same as at 31 December 19X5.
(c) A brief discussion of the financial policy pursued by the directors of Galston Ltd. in 19X6.

**Solution**

(a) *31 December:*

|  | 19X5 | 19X6 |
|---|---|---|
|  | £ | £ |
| Current assets..................................... | 90,000 | 120,000 |
| Less: Current liabilities........................... | 45,000 | 55,500 |
| Working capital.................................... | 45,000 | 64,500 |
| Working capital ratio.............................. | 2:1 | 2.16:1 |

(b) *31 December 19X6:*

|  | £ |
|---|---|
| Current assets per balance sheet....·.................... | 120,000 |
| Current liabilities, assuming a working capital ratio of 2:1 | 60,000 |
| Current liabilities per balance sheet.................... | 55,000 |
| Maximum permissible dividend...................... | 4,500 |

(c) The directors have made an additional net investment of £31,500 in fixed assets, but this is amply covered by the retained profits of £46,500 (£51,000 - dividend of £4,500) and the working capital ratio has been maintained at 2:1. The financial policy pursued by the directors appears a little less sound when we look at the cash position. The heavy investment in stock has been at the expense of cash; debtors have also increased but at a rate which is not unreasonable in relation to the other changes.

## 12.4 LIQUIDITY RATIO

The purpose of the liquidity ratio is similar to the working capital ratio, in that it is designed to assess the ability of a business to meet its debts as they fall due. The calculation is as follows:

$$\text{Liquidity ratio} = \frac{\text{Liquid assets}}{\text{Current liabilities}} :1$$

It is a more rigorous test of solvency than the working capital ratio, because it omits the current assets which are unlikely to be converted into cash in time to meet liabilities falling due in the near future. The ratio is for this reason sometimes described as the 'acid test' of solvency. Non-liquid current assets which must therefore be left out of the calculation include stock (unless sales are made on the cash basis, in which case stock is also a liquid asset) and any trade debts not receivable in the near future, because customers have been allowed an extended period of credit.

The liquidity ratio of Campion (Example 12.4) is as follows:

$$\text{Liquidity ratio} = \frac{\pounds 23,000 + \pounds 5,000}{\pounds 25,000} : 1$$
$$= 1.1 : 1$$

This calculation shows that Campion Ltd. has sufficient liquid assets to cover its current liabilities. A ratio of 1:1 is generally considered desirable in practice and, on the whole, this is a fair test. However, students should be aware of the fact that the conventional method of calculation can understate the short-term financial position of the firm because, although current assets are carefully examined and less liquid items excluded, the same distinction is not made in the case of current liabilities. Normally all current liabilities are included despite the fact that some of the amounts outstanding, particularly taxation, may not be payable for a number of months. In Campion's case, current liabilities include taxation which is not due for payment until 30 September 19X2, nine months after the balance sheet date. A more realistic calculation of the liquidity ratio should therefore exclude taxation as well as stock.

$$\text{Liquidity ratio} = \frac{\pounds 23,000 + \pounds 5,000}{\pounds 15,000} : 1$$
$$= 1.9 : 1$$

The conventional approach to the calculation of the liquidity ratio, which includes all current liabilities, is consistent with the accounting concept of 'prudence' but may, in certain circumstances, be a little misleading.

Readers should now work Question 12.2 at the end of the chapter.

## 12.5   THE STATEMENT OF SOURCES AND APPLICATIONS OF FUNDS

For very many years, companies have been legally obliged to publish annually both a balance sheet and a profit and loss account. During the 1960s, a number of companies voluntarily adopted the practice of supplementing these two documents with a third financial statement, called the 'statement of sources and applications of funds', often abbreviated to 'statement of funds'. This voluntary development reflected management's recognition of an important gap in the information made available to external users of accounting reports. The balance sheet sets out the financial state of a business at a particular point in time whereas the profit and loss account reports the financial effects of those transactions which occur during the year and directly impinge upon the calculation of profit i.e. revenues, and expenditures. Other transactions involving flows of resources, such as an issue of shares or debentures, or the purchase of a fixed asset are not reported in the profit and loss account since they are *capital* as opposed to *revenue* transactions. Gradually the view developed that these events, which often involve significant amounts of money, were of interest to investors and should be reported to them. Consequently the statement of funds was devised to provide this information.

*Definition.* The statement of funds sets out, in an orderly manner, the sources of finance which have been raised and generated by a business during the year and the ways in which those funds have been applied.

*Objective.* The purpose of the statement of funds is to provide some insights into the financial policy pursued by management during the year, and the likely effect of that policy on the financial position of the company.

The various sources of finance available to businesses, and the ways in which they are employed, are examined in the next two sections. The construction of the statement is then examined in section 5.3 of this chapter.

### 12.5.1   Sources of Funds

It is management's job to ensure that there is a satisfactory balance between long, medium and short-term finance. The main sources of finance and the periods for which they are available are listed below.

1. *Owners Capital.* This is the amount invested by the owner(s) in the business and is long term finance.
2. *Debentures and loans.* In the case of debentures, the advance is normally made on a long-term basis, for between ten and forty years. The duration for which loans are made depends on the terms of the agreement between the borrower and the lender.
3. *Hire purchase and extended credit.* These are useful ways for a company to spread the heavy cost of a new fixed asset. The finance is either short-term, where the instalments are all payable within one year, or a mixture of short- and medium-term where they extend beyond a twelve month period.
4. *Trade credit from suppliers.* This is short-term finance, although new creditors will replace those currently paid, thus ensuring a more or less permanent source of finance in this form.
5. *Taxation and dividends payable.* These are liabilities but, until the payment is made, the cash may be used by the company. They are therefore short-term finance.
6. *Bank overdraft.* This is, in theory, a short-term source of finance, although in practice it is employed on a long-term basis by many businesses.
7. *Sale of fixed assets.* The cash inflow from the sale of fixed assets is available for management to invest on a long-term basis.
8. *Funds generated from operations.* During the course of trading activity a company generates revenue, principally in the form of sales receipts, and incurs expenditure comprising a wide range of different outlays some of which result in an outflow of funds in the current accounting period and others which do not. Most outlays fall into the first category, e.g. expenditure on purchases of materials, wages, salaries and rent. There are, however, a small number of items, the most important of which is depreciation, which are charged against profit but do not result in a current outflow of funds.

The purpose of the depreciation charge is to reflect the fact that sales revenue has benefitted, during the period under review, from the acquisition of fixed assets which occurred in a previous accounting period. The effect of making the charge is to reduce reported profit and ensure that an equivalent amount of cash is retained within the business, which may be used, in due course, to help finance replacement of the asset when it is worn out. It is therefore necessary to add back the depreciation charge to the reported profit figure to identify total funds generated from operations, i.e.

$$\text{Funds generated from operations} = \text{Profit} + \text{Depreciation}$$

Some of the profit is usually paid out in the form of taxation and dividends, of course, but the remainder is retained and is available for investment on a long-term basis.

Students often find it difficult to grasp the fact that the depreciation charge is *represented* by an equivalent *inflow* of cash. The link is demonstrated in Example 12.6.

## Example 12.6

The balance sheet of Pencil Ltd., which purchases and sells goods for cash, is as follows at 31 December 19X1.

*Balance Sheet at 31 December 19X1*

| | £ | | £ | £ |
|---|---|---|---|---|
| Share capital............. | 1,000 | Fixed assets at cost..... | | 1,800 |
| Retained profit........... | 360 | Less: Depreciation... | | 540 |
| | 1,360 | | | 1,260 |
| 10% loan repayable 19X7... | 500 | *Current Assets* | | |
| | | Stock................ | 400 | |
| | | Cash................ | 200 | 600 |
| | 1,860 | | | 1,860 |

During 19X2 cash sales and cash purchases amounted respectively to £4,000 and £2,500. The stock level remained unchanged during the year and £600 was *paid out* for wages and other operating expenses. In addition, loan interest was paid on 31 December 19X2, and depreciation of £240 was charged on fixed assets.

*Required:*
(a)  The cash account for 19X2.
(b)  The trading and profit and loss account for 19X2.
(c)  The balance sheet at 31 December 19X2.
(d)  A calculation of funds generated from operations during 19X2, i.e. profit + depreciation.

# Solution.

(a)

### Cash Account for 19X2

| | £ | | £ |
|---|---|---|---|
| Opening balance............ | 200 | Purchases............ | 2,500 |
| Sales..................... | 4,000 | Wages etc............ | 600 |
| | | Interest.............. | 50 |
| | | Closing balance....... | 1,050 |
| | 4,200 | | 4,200 |

(b)

### Trading and Profit and Loss Account for 19X2

| | £ | | £ |
|---|---|---|---|
| Opening stock.............. | 400 | Sales................. | 4,000 |
| Purchases.................. | 2,500 | | |
| Less: Closing stock......... | (400) | | |
| Cost of goods sold........... | 2,500 | | |
| Gross profit................ | 1,500 | | |
| | 4,000 | | 4,000 |
| Wages etc.................. | 600 | Gross profit.......... | 1,500 |
| Interest.................... | 50 | | |
| Depreciation ............... | 240 | | |
| | 890 | | |
| Net profit.................. | 610 | | |
| | 1,500 | | 1,500 |

(c)

### Balance Sheet at 31 December 19X2

| | £ | | £ | £ |
|---|---|---|---|---|
| Share capital.............. | 1,000 | Fixed assets at cost..... | | 1,800 |
| Retained profit | | Less: Depreciation..... | | 780 |
| (360 + 610).............. | 970 | | | 1,020 |
| | 1,970 | | | |
| 10% loan repayable 19X7... | 500 | Current Assets | | |
| | | Stock................ | 400 | |
| | | Cash................ | 1,050 | 1,450 |
| | 2,470 | | | 2,470 |

(d)   Funds generated from operations:

|                          | £    |
|--------------------------|------|
| Profit.................... | 610  |
| Depreciation............. | 240  |
| Funds from operations...... | 850  |

The cash balance has increased from £200 to £1,050 and the cash account shows, in detail, how this increase of £850 has been brought about. The profit and loss account shows a profit figure of £610, and this is less than the increase in the cash balance because a 'non-cash' item of expenditure, i.e. depreciation £240, has been debited to the profit and loss acount. It therefore follows that to reconcile the opening cash balance with the closing cash balance it is necessary to add the figure for 'funds generated from operations', profit + depreciation, to the opening cash figure.

|                                              | £     |
|----------------------------------------------|-------|
| Opening cash balance......................... | 200   |
| Add:   Funds generated from operations......... | 850   |
| Closing cash balance......................... | 1,050 |

In practice, the change in the cash balance is rarely entirely due to funds generated from operations. There are numerous other transactions which cause it to change, e.g. new plant is purchased or additional shares issued.

*A note of warning.* A common misconception is that the depreciation charge *produces* an inflow of cash, and that cash inflows can be increased by raising the amount of the charge. This is entirely wrong. Cash is generated from trading transactions, and the depreciation charge is merely a 'book entry' which earmarks a proportion of funds generated from operations for retention within the business. If the depreciation charge, in the above example, is increased from £240 to £400, profit falls from £610 to £450 and funds generated from operations remain unchanged at £850 (depreciation £400 + profit £450). An effect of raising the charge is, however, to earmark a *larger* quantity of funds for retention within the business in the current year; although later in the asset's life, charges and retentions will be correspondingly lower because the balance which remains to be written off at 31 December 19X2 is reduced by £240.

## Example 12.7

Assume the same facts as appear in the solution to Example 12.6.

*Required:*

Calculate the closing cash balance of Pencil, on 1 January 19X3, in each of the following circumstances:

(a)   The entire profit of £610 is paid out as dividends on 1 January 19X3.

(b)   The depreciation charge is amended to £400 and the entire profit of £450 is paid out as dividends on 1 January 19X3.

*Note:* No other transactions occur on 1 January 19X3.

## Solution.

|  | (a) | (b) |
|---|---|---|
|  | £ | £ |
| Cash balance at 31 December 19X2...................... | 1,050 | 1,050 |
| Less:   Dividends ..................................... | 610 | 450 |
| Cash balance at 1 January 19X3......................... | 440 | 600 |

*Note*: The increase in the depreciation charge, under (b), reduces the maximum dividend payable by £160 and, as a result, the balance of cash which remains is £160 higher, at £600.

**12.5.2   Applications of Funds**   The sources of funds, described in the previous section, may be applied in the following ways:

1.   *Purchase of fixed assets.* This is a long-term investment.

2.   *Repayment of loan capital.* To maintain a secure base of long term finance, the loan repaid will usually be replaced by a new issue of either long-term loans or shares; alternatively the repayment may be financed out of profits earned and retained in the business, provided they have not already been used for another purpose. (A company may also redeem or purchase its own shares in certain circumstances; these options are examined at Stage 2).

3.   *Payment of tax and dividends.* These payments are claims against profit earned during the year.

4.   *Investment in stocks.* This is a short-term investment in the sense that the stock is sold after a relatively short interval, although it will then probably be replaced by new purchases.

5.   *Cedit allowed to customers.* Again a short-term investment, but
where new debts replace those currently paid.

The main sources and applications of funds, discussed above, are
summarised in Figure 12.1.

**Figure 12.1**

*Checklist of Sources and Applications of Funds*

|  | Sources | Applications |
|---|:---:|:---:|
| Capital and loans raised ............................. | ✔ | |
| Capital and loans repaid ............................. | | ✔ |
| Increase in current asset balances........................ | | |
| (e.g. stock, debtors, bank) ............................ | | ✔ |
| Decrease in current asset balances ...................... | ✔ | |
| Increase in current liability balances .................... | | |
| (e.g. creditors, overdraft, dividends and tax payable) ..... | ✔ | |
| Decrease in current liability balances.................... | | ✔ |
| Funds generated from operations....................... | | |
| (positive) ................................... | ✔ | |
| (negative)................................... | | ✔ |
| Provisions for tax and dividends ....................... | | ✔ |

**12.5.3   Constructing a Statement of Funds**   The statement was
defined, in section 5 of this chapter, as one which sets out the
sources of finance which have been raised and generated by a
business during the year and the ways in which those funds have
been applied. Since the balance sheet shows the accumulated
sources of finance and the way in which that money has been spent,
up to a particular point in time, most of the information required to
prepare a statement of funds can be obtained by deducting the
balances appearing in the opening balance sheet from those
appearing in the closing balance sheet.

## Illustration 12.1

The following information is provided for Ruler Ltd:

| | Balance Sheets 31 December | | | | Differences | |
| | 19X3 | | 19X4 | | Source | Application |
| Fixed Assets: | £000 | £000 | £000 | £000 | £000 | £000 |
| Machinery at cost......... | | 320 | | 470 | | 150 |
| Less: Accumulated depreciation........ | | 150 | | 192 | 42 | |
| | | 170 | | 278 | | |
| Current Assets: | | | | | | |
| Stock................... | 86 | | 107 | | | 21 |
| Trade debtors........... | 53 | | 75 | | | 22 |
| Bank.................. | 12 | | 64 | | | 52* |
| | 151 | | 246 | | | |
| Less:Current Liabilities: | | | | | | |
| Trade creditors........... | 46 | | 61 | | 15 | |
| Working capital.......... | | 105 | | 185 | | |
| | | 275 | | 463 | | |
| Financed by: | | | | | | |
| Share capital............. | | 200 | | 220 | 20 | |
| Retained profit........... | | 75 | | 103 | 28 | |
| | | 275 | | 323 | | |
| 12% loan repayable 19X9.. | | - | | 140 | 140 | |
| | | 275 | | 463 | 245 | 245 |

\* The increase in the cash balance is shown as an application because it represents extra cash made available during the year which has not yet been invested in business assets or used for any other purpose.

The above 'work sheet' shows sources of funds, totalling £245,000, and the ways in which those funds have been applied. The statement of source and application of funds (see below) arranges these items in two groups.

1. Sources and applications of funds which *cause* working capital to increase or decrease. These are further divided into (i) Funds generated from operations, and (ii) Funds from other sources.
2. Changes in the various items which make up working capital i.e. in this example, stocks, debtors, cash and trade creditors.

*Statement of Sources and Applications of Funds for 19X4*

| | £000 | £000 |
|---|---|---|
| SOURCES OF FUNDS | | |
| Profit . . . . . . . . . . . . . . . . . . . . . . . . . . . . . . . . . . . . . . . . . . . . . | | 28 |
| Add:  Item not involving an outflow of funds | | |
| Depreciation . . . . . . . . . . . . . . . . . . . . . . . . . . . . . . . . | | 42 |
| | | |
| Funds generated from operations . . . . . . . . . . . . . . . . . . . . . . . | | 70 |
| Funds from other sources: | | |
| Share issue . . . . . . . . . . . . . . . . . . . . . . . . . . . . . . . . . . . . . . . | 20 | |
| Loan . . . . . . . . . . . . . . . . . . . . . . . . . . . . . . . . . . . . . . . . . . . | 140 | 160 |
| | | |
| | | 230 |
| APPLICATIONS OF FUNDS | | |
| Purchase of machinery . . . . . . . . . . . . . . . . . . . . . . . . . . . . . | | 150 |
| | | |
| INCREASE IN WORKING CAPITAL | | 80 |
| CHANGES IN WORKING CAPITAL ITEMS | | |
| Decrease in working capital (Sources) | | |
| Trade creditors . . . . . . . . . . . . . . . . . . . . . . . . . . . . . . . . . . | (15) | |
| Increases in working capital (Applications) | | |
| Stock . . . . . . . . . . . . . . . . . . . . . . . . . . . . . . . . . . . . . . . . . . | 21 | |
| Trade debtors . . . . . . . . . . . . . . . . . . . . . . . . . . . . . . . . . . . . | 22 | |
| Bank . . . . . . . . . . . . . . . . . . . . . . . . . . . . . . . . . . . . . . . . . . . | 52 | 80 |

The above statement shows that Ruler raised and generated long term finance amounting to £230,000 during 19X4; funds from operations contributed £70,000 and other sources £160,000. £150,000 of the total amount made available was invested long-term, in new machinery, and the surplus, of £80,000, increased working capital from £105,000 to £185,000 (see balance sheet figures). The second part of the statement gives details of changes in the various items which make up the balance of working capital. Current assets have increased, in total, by £95,000 (21,000 + £22,000 + £52,000). This has been partly financed by additional credit from suppliers, £15,000, with the remaining £80,000 provided from longer-term sources.

Readers should now work Questions 12.3 and 12.4 at the end of this chapter.

Ruler Ltd is a simplified illustration, and it is normally necessary to take account of information contained in the profit and loss account and notes to the accounts to build up some of the figures for inclusion in the statement of funds. For example, assume that we are now told that the directors of Ruler paid an interim dividend of £15,000 during July 19X4. The profit for 19X4 becomes:

|                                   | £000 |
|-----------------------------------|------|
| Retained profit for 19X4.......... | 28   |
| Add:   Interim dividend .......... | 15   |
| Total profit from operations 19X4. | 43   |

In the statement of funds, profit of £43,000 should be shown as a source of funds and the dividend paid, of £15,000, as an application of funds.

A second common complication occurs when a company sells *and* purchases fixed assets during the year. In these circumstances the work sheet shows only the 'net' change and it is useful to build up a fixed asset schedule which shows gross changes during the year.

**Example 12.8**
The following information is extracted from the balance sheet of Pencil Ltd. at 31 December.

| *Fixed Assets*                     | 19X0    | 19X1    |
|------------------------------------|---------|---------|
| Motor vehicles at cost ........... | £40,000 | £57,500 |
| Less:   Accumulated depreciation.. | 22,700  | 31,600  |
|                                    | 17,300  | 25,900  |

On 1 July 19X1, Staple sold a motor vehicle for £750. The machine had cost £6,000 some years ago, and accumulated depreciation at 31 December 19X0 was £4,900. The company's policy is to charge a full year's depreciation in the year of purchase and none in the year a vehicle is sold.

*Required:*
(a) Calculations of the net changes in the balances for motor vehicles and accumulated depreciation during the year.
(b) Calculations of additions during the year and depreciation charged.
(c) Prepare the following ledger accounts for 19X1: motor vehicles at cost, accumulated depreciation and disposal of motor vehicle.
(d) Details to be included in the statement of funds concerning the motor vehicles.

# Solution.

**(a)**

| Fixed Assets | 19X0 | 19X1 | Differences | |
|---|---|---|---|---|
| | | | Source | Application |
| Motor vehicles at cost | £40,000 | £57,500 | | £17,500 |
| Less:Accumulated depreciation | 22,700 | 31,600 | £8,900 | |

**(b)**

| | Cost | Depreciation |
|---|---|---|
| | £ | £ |
| Net increases.................................. | 17,500 | 8,900 |
| Add: Sales.................................... | 6 000 | 4 900 |
| Additions/Charge for the year | 23,500 | 13,800 |

**(c)**

### Motor Vehicles at Cost

| | £ | | £ |
|---|---|---|---|
| 1.1.X1 Balance b/d.......... | 40,000 | 1.7.X1 Disposal account......... | 6,000 |
| 31.12.X1 Additions.......... | 23,500 | 31.12.X1 Balance c/d.......... | 57,500 |
| | 63,500 | | 63,500 |

### Accumulated Depreciation

| | £ | | £ |
|---|---|---|---|
| 1.7.X1 Disposal account...... | 4,900 | 1.1.X1 Balance b/d............. | 22,700 |
| 31.12.X1 Balance c/d....... | 31,600 | 31.12.X1 Profit and loss A/c..... | 13,800 |
| | 36,500 | | 36,500 |

### Disposal of motor vehicle

| | £ | | £ |
|---|---|---|---|
| 1.7.X1 Motor vehicle A/c..... | 6,000 | 1.7.X1 Cash................... | 750 |
| | | 1.7.X1 Acc. depreciation........ | 4,900 |
| | | 31.12.X1 Profit and loss A/c..... | 350 |
| | 6,000 | | 6,000 |

**(d) Sources:**

| | |
|---|---|
| Depreciation charged.............................. | £13,800 |
| Loss on sale of vehicle............................. | 350* |
| Sales proceeds..................................... | 750 |

| | |
|---|---|
| Applications: Purchase of motor vehicles........................... | 23,500 |

---

\* The loss on sale, of £350, is debited to the profit and loss account to make up for the fact that insufficient depreciation has been charged. Like depreciation, the loss on sale is a non-cash expense and must be added back to profit to produce the figure for funds generated from operations. Any profit on sale, credited to the profit and loss account, must likewise be deducted from profit, as the entire sales proceeds appear in the statement under the heading 'funds from other sources'.

## 12.6 FINANCIAL POLICY

Section 5 of this chapter draws attention to the fact that the purpose of the statement of funds is to provide some insights into the financial policy pursued by management during the year, and the effect of that policy on the financial position of the company. To interpret the information contained in the statement, the analyst should bear in mind the matters discussed, below, in sections 6.1 and 6.2 of this chapter.

**12.6.1 Financing Long-Term Investment** It is management's job to ensure that sources and applications of funds are properly matched i.e. short-term finance should only be committed for a short period of time while long-term investment must be paid for out of long-term finance. For example, the purchase of a fixed asset should be paid for by raising a long-term loan, or shares, or by retaining profits permanently within the business. The reason for this is that a company is likely to suffer acute financial embarrassment if it attempts to finance the purchase of, for example, factory premises, using a short-term source of funds such as a bank overdraft. The new acquisition is expected to generate sufficient revenue to cover its cost and produce an adequate balance of profit, but this process will probably take a number of years and short-term finance will have to be repaid long before it is complete.

**12.6.2 Over-Trading** Over-trading is a condition which arises when a company attempts to do too much too quickly and, as a result, fails to maintain a satisfactory balance between profit maximisation and financial stability. Usually it occurs when a company rapidly expands its scale of business activities but fails first to make available sufficient long-term finance for this purpose. Where a company has over-traded, some or all of the following financial consequences will be apparent from an examination of consecutive balance sheets.

1. A sharp increase in expenditure on fixed assets.
2. A decrease in the balance of cash, and perhaps the emergence of a bank overdraft.
3. The structure of the current assets becomes less liquid, probably because the proportion of current assets 'tied up' in stock increases dramatically.
4. A sharp increase in creditors caused by the company's inability to pay debts as they fall due.

5.    The working capital and liquidity ratios decline to inadequate levels.

The actual *causes* of over-trading are clearly demonstrated in the statement of funds which shows how much long-term finance has been made available during the year, the extent to which it covers long-term applications, and the effect of developments on the working capital of the business.

### Example 12.9

Madoc is confused and worried and has come to you for advice. He tells you that, although he made a bigger profit in 19X7 than in 19X6, and has also made less drawings, he does not seem to be any better off and is finding difficulty in paying his creditors.

The balance sheets of Madoc's business at the end of 19X6 and 19X7 are shown below:

*Balance Sheets at 31 December*

|  | 19X6 £ | 19X7 £ |  | 19X6 £ | 19X7 £ |
|---|---|---|---|---|---|
| Opening capital....... | 12,000 | 11,000 | Machines at cost....... | 10,000 | 20,500 |
| Add: Net profit....... | 5,000 | 7,000 | Less:  Depreciation... | 3,000 | 5,500 |
| Less: Drawings........ | (6,000) | (4,000) |  | | |
|  | | | | 7,000 | 15,000 |
| Closing capital........ | 11,000 | 14,000 | | | |
|  | | | Stock............... | 1,700 | 4,900 |
| Creditors ........... | 3,000 | 10,000 | Debtors............. | 1,800 | 3,700 |
|  | | | Bank............... | 3,500 | 400 |
|  | 14,000 | 24,000 |  | 14,000 | 24,000 |

*Required:*

Explain to Madoc what has happened, and support your explanation with an appropriate numerical statement. Briefly advise Madoc on future policy.

(Students should first prepare a 'work sheet', although this can be omitted with practice, as is done in this case).

# Solution

## Statement of Funds for 19X7

| SOURCES OF FUNDS | £ | £ |
|---|---:|---:|
| Net profit.......................................... | | 7,000 |
| Add:  Depreciation (5,500-3,000)..................... | | 2,500 |
| | | |
| Funds generated from operations....................... | | 9,500 |
| APPLICATIONS OF FUNDS | | |
| Drawings ......................................... | 4,000 | |
| Purchase of fixed assets............................. | 10,500 | 14,500 |
| | | |
| REDUCTION IN WORKING CAPITAL.................. | | (5,000) |
| CHANGES IN WORKING CAPITAL ITEMS | | |
| Increases in working capital: | | |
| Increase in stocks.................................... | 3,200 | |
| Increase in debtors................................... | 1,900 | |
| Decreases in working capital: | | |
| Increase in creditors................................. | (7,000) | |
| Decrease in bank balance............................. | (3,100) | (5,000) |

The cause of Madoc's confusion is that he mistakenly believes that profit produces an equivalent increase in the bank balance. This may happen, in certain circumstances, but only if no additional investment takes place. The above statement of funds shows that Madoc has invested heavily in additional fixed assets, and there have also been substantial increases in stocks and debtors. In total, these outlays significantly exceed funds generated from operations; the result is that the bank balance has fallen dramatically and the amount owed to creditors has more than trebled.

Madoc is in a very difficult financial position, as a result of *over-trading,* and it is important that he undertakes no further investment at this stage. He should also keep drawings to a minimum and use future profits to reduce his firm's reliance on short-term credit.

Readers should now work Question 12.6 at the end of this chapter.

## 12.7  LINKING TOGETHER FUNDS FLOW ANALYSIS AND RATIO ANALYSIS

Accounting ratios, such as the gross profit percentage, net profit percentage and the return on capital employed can be used to assess the profit performance of a company during an accounting period. Comparisons with earlier years and the performance of other businesses provide useful yardsticks for assessing whether or not an improvement has occured and for gauging whether or not results are as good as they could be. Additional ratios may be calculated as a basis for assessing the company's solvency position at particular points in time; the most useful ratios for this purpose are the working capital ratio and the liquidity ratio. The statement of funds complements these calculations by helping to explain how improvements in a company's financial position have been brought about or why a deterioration has occurred. Example 12.10 illustrates how the two forms of financial analysis may be employed, alongside one another, to gain an understanding of the financial performance and position of a business enterprise. In addition, it shows how the annual accounts, although relating to a *past* time period, may be used as a basis for estimating likely future prospects.

**Example 12.10**
Expansion Ltd. is a private company which has carried on copper mining activities for a number of years. At the beginning of 19X2 the company purchased a small established tin mine at a cost of £350,000; production commenced at once. Tin extracted from the new mine in 19X2 amounted to 600 tons; this is expected to increase to 900 tons by 19X8 and then decline gradually. Finance for the new mine was partly provided by a 2 year loan of £300,000 repayable by equal monthly instalments.

The summarised Balance Sheets for 19X1 and 19X2 are as follows:

| ASSETS | 19X1 | | 19X2 | |
|---|---|---|---|---|
| *Fixed Assets* | £ | £ | £ | £ |
| Mines at cost................. | 465,000 | | 815,000 | |
| Less:  Depreciation........... | 150,000 | 315,000 | 190,000 | 625,000 |
| | | | | |
| Plant and equipment at cost...... | 213,250 | | 263,250 | |
| Less:  Depreciation........... | 56,200 | 157,050 | 75,200 | 188,050 |
| | | 472,050 | | 813,050 |
| *Current Assets* | | | | |
| Stocks of tin and copper......... | 143,100 | | 169,000 | |
| Debtors...................... | 86,250 | | 118,250 | |
| Cash at bank.................. | 44,100 | 273,450 | 1,800 | 289,050 |
| | | 745,500 | | 1,102,100 |
| | | | | |
| CAPITAL AND LIABILITIES | | | | |
| Share capital.................. | | 500,000 | | 500,000 |
| Profit and loss account......... | | 182,500 | | 314,000 |
| | | 682,500 | | 814,000 |
| *Current Liabilities* | | | | |
| Trade creditors and | | | | |
| accrued expenses.............. | | 63,000 | | 138,100 |
| Short-term loan............... | | – | | 150,000 |
| | | 745,500 | | 1,102,100 |

The net profit earned during 19X2 was £181,500 (19X1 £103,000) of which £50,000 (19X1 £25,000) was paid out in dividends. Turnover increased from £1,060,000 in 19X1 to £1,500,000 in 19X2.

*Required:*
Examine the financial policies pursued by the directors of Expansion Ltd. during 19X2 and comment on proposals to develop further by acquiring an additional site in the early months of 19X3. You should use a statement of funds and relevant accounting ratios to suppport your analysis.

## Solution.
### Examination of Solvency

*Statement of Funds for 19X2*

| SOURCES OF FUNDS | £ | £ |
|---|---|---|
| Profit | | 181,500 |
| Add: Depreciation: Mine | | 40,000 |
| Plant | | 19,000 |
| | | |
| Funds generated from operations | | 240,500 |
| APPLICATIONS OF FUNDS | | |
| Purchases: Mine | 350,000 | |
| Plant | 50,000 | |
| Dividend | 50,000 | 450,000 |
| | | |
| DECREASE IN WORKING CAPITAL | | (209,500) |
| CHANGES IN WORKING CAPITAL ITEMS | | |
| Decreases in working capital | | |
| Bank | ( 42,300) | |
| Trade creditors | ( 75,100) | |
| Short term loan | (150,000) | |
| Increases in working capital | | |
| Stocks | 25,900 | |
| Debtors | 32,000 | (209,500) |

*Ratios*

| | 19X1 | 19X2 |
|---|---|---|
| Working capital ratio | 4.3:1 | 1:1 |
| Liquidity ratio | 2.1:1 | 0.4:1 |

The company had surplus funds at the end of 19X1 and so decided to expand. It financed the remainder of the expansion with a two year loan to be repaid out of funds generated from operations. The financial position at the end of 19X2 is weak due to the failure to raise sufficient long-term finance to meet the cost of the investment programme.

### Examination of Profitability
*Ratios*

| | 19X1 | 19X2 |
|---|---|---|
| Net profit percentage | 9.7% | 12.1% |
| Return on total capital employed | 13.8% | 16.5% |
| Return on owners equity | 15.1% | 22.3% |

A significant improvement in profitability has occurred which might be expected to continue with further increases in output from the new mine. The company has paid a good dividend.

## Conclusions and Prospects

Expansion has been funded out of short-term finance and the financial position at the end of 19X2 is weak. This is risky and an element of over-trading has undoubtedly occured. However the project is profitable and it seems that the company will recover on the basis of funds generated from operations which, in 19X2 amounted to £240,500. Further expansion appears undesirable at present; there should be a delay of a year to 18 months. If this is not possible, the company should raise medium/long-term finance to cover the cost of the additional site.

Readers should now work Questions 12.7 and 12.8 at the end of the chapter.

## 12.8 QUESTIONS
### Question 12.1

The summarised trading and profit and loss account of Rubber Ltd. for 19X1 and its summarised balance sheet at 31 December 19X1 are as follows:

*Trading and Profit and Loss Account for 19X1*

| | £ | | £ |
|---|---|---|---|
| Cost of sales (variable)........ | 126,000 | Sales ............... | 180,000 |
| Gross profit............... | 54,000 | | |
| | 180,000 | | 180,000 |
| Expenses (fixed)............ | 39,000 | Gross profit.......... | 54,000 |
| Net profit................ | 15,000 | | |
| | 54,000 | | 54,000 |

*Note:* A dividend of £10,000 is proposed for 19X1.

*Balance Sheet as at 31 December 19X1*

| | £ | | £ |
|---|---|---|---|
| Share capital............... | 100,000 | Fixed assets.......... | 113,000 |
| Retained profit............. | 50,000 | Current assets........ | 70,000 |
| | 150,000 | | |
| *Current Liabilities:* | | | |
| General £23,000 | | | |
| Dividend 10,000 | 33,000 | | |
| | 183,000 | | 183,000 |

The company could expand production to a sales level of £255,000 with no increase in fixed expenses and the cost of sales would remain the same percentage of sales as for 19X1.

*Required:*
(a) Calculate the gross profit margin, net profit as a percentage of sales and the return on capital employed for 19X1.
(b) A calculation of the additional sales that would have been necessary to increase the return on capital employed by $2\frac{1}{2}\%$.

*Note:* For the purpose of the answer, capital employed is to be interpreted as issued capital plus retained profit on 31 December.

**Question 12.2**
The following information has been extracted from the accounts of Lock Ltd., a wholesale trading company.

*Balances at 31 December*

|  | 19X1 | 19X2 |
|---|---|---|
|  | £000 | £000 |
| Fixed assets | 500 | 550 |
| Trade debtors | 125 | 150 |
| Cash at bank | 25 | - |
| Proposed dividend | 20 | 60 |
| Overdraft | - | 20 |
| Trade creditors | 80 | 100 |
| Stocks | 150 | 200 |

*Results for the year to 31 December*

|  | 19X1 | 19X2 |
|---|---|---|
|  | £000 | £000 |
| Sales | 2,000 | 3,000 |
| Cost of sales | 1,000 | 1,450 |
| Overhead costs | 800 | 1,300 |

*Required:*
(a) A statement showing the return on capital employed, the value of working capital, the working capital ratio and the liquidity ratio. Your answer should be presented in the following form.

|  | 19X1 | 19X2 |
|---|---|---|
| Return on Capital Employed | — | — |
| Working Capital | — | — |
| Working Capital Ratio | — | — |
| Liquidity Ratio | — | — |

(b) A brief discussion of the implications of the information calculated above.

*Note:* For the purpose of your calculations, capital employed is defined as shareholders' equity.

## Question 12.3

The following are the balance sheets of Dividers Ltd. as at 31 December 19X2 and 19X3.

| | 19X2 £ | 19X3 £ | | 19X2 £ | 19X3 £ |
|---|---|---|---|---|---|
| Share capital.......... | 20,000 | 20,000 | Fixed assets at cost........... | 25,000 | 30,000 |
| Reserves (profit & loss account)........ | 10,000 | 15,000 | Less: Accumulated depreciation.. | 5,000 | 6,500 |
| | | | | 20,000 | 23,500 |
| Debentures, 19X9..... | 1,000 | 800 | Stock............. | 11,000 | 17,000 |
| Trade creditors........ | 6,000 | 7,500 | Debtors........... | 5,000 | 6,000 |
| Overdraft............ | — | 3,200 | Cash at Bank...... | 1,000 | — |
| | 37,000 | 46,500 | | 37,000 | 46,500 |

There were no disposals of fixed assets during 19X3, and no dividends were paid.

*Required:*
(a) A statement showing the value of current assets, current liabilities and working capital together with the working capital ratio at 31 December 19X2 and 19X3. Your answer should be presented in the following form:

| | 19X2 | 19X3 |
|---|---|---|
| Current assets.................................... | — | — |
| Current liabilities................................ | — | — |
| Working capital.................................. | — | — |
| Working capital ratio............................ | — | — |

(b) A funds flow statement for 19X3.
(c) Comment briefly on the changes that have taken place in Dividers Ltd.'s working capital during 19X3.

## Question 12.4
The balance sheets of Southall Ltd at 31 December 19X1 and 31 December 19X2 are as follows:

|  | 19X1 | | 19X2 | |
|---|---|---|---|---|
| *Fixed Assets:* | £ | £ | £ | £ |
| Plant at cost................... | 52,000 | | 70,000 | |
| Less: Depreciation.............. | 16,500 | 35,500 | 22,700 | 47,300 |
| Transport at cost............... | 10,000 | | 10,000 | |
| Less: Depreciation.............. | 3,600 | 6,400 | 4,800 | 5,200 |
|  | | 41,900 | | 52,500 |
| *Current Assets:* | | | | |
| Stock......................... | 10,200 | | 12,600 | |
| Debtors....................... | 8,300 | | 13,700 | |
| Bank ......................... | 4,900 | | – | |
|  | 23,400 | | 26,300 | |
| *Less: Current Liabilities*: | | | | |
| Trade creditors................ | 5,100 | | 5,800 | |
| Bank overdraft................ | — | | 1,300 | |
|  | 5,100 | | 7,100 | |
| Working capital............... | | 18,300 | | 19,200 |
|  | | 60,200 | | 71,700 |
| Financed by: | | | | |
| Share capital................... | | 50,000 | | 54,000 |
| Profit and loss account......... | | 10,200 | | 17,700 |
|  | | 60,200 | | 71,700 |

*Required:*
A statement of funds for 19X2.

# Question 12.5

The following balances relate to the affairs of Tufton Ltd. as at 31 March 19X0 and 31 March 19X1.

|  | 19X0 £ | 19X1 £ |
|---|---|---|
| Share capital | 500,000 | 600,000 |
| Retained profit | 395,800 | 427,100 |
| 10% Debentures | 200,000 | 300,000 |
| Creditors | 179,800 | 207,500 |
| Proposed Dividend | 50,000 | 60,000 |
| Bank Overdraft | — | 36,900 |
|  | 1,325,600 | 1,631,500 |
| Plant at cost | 658,300 | 796,900 |
| Less: Depreciation | 263,500 | 371,600 |
|  | 394,800 | 425,300 |
| Freehold property at cost | 300,000 | 350,000 |
| Stock | 327,100 | 608,300 |
| Debtors | 265,700 | 247,900 |
| Cash at Bank | 38,000 | — |
|  | 1,325,600 | 1,631,500 |

You are given the following information:

(i)   During the year to March 19X1, plant with a written down value of £202,500 was sold for £169,500. This plant had originally cost £390,000.

(ii)   A bonus issue of one ordinary share for every five held was made out of retained profit on 1 June 19X0.

*Required:*

A statement of source and application of funds for the year to 31 March 19X1. You should prepare a work sheet and show the build up of your figures for profit, purchases of plant and equipment and depreciation charged.

## Question 12.6

The following information is provided for Sharpener Ltd:

### Balance Sheets 31 December

|                                      | 19X4 £ | 19X4 £  | 19X5 £ | 19X5 £  |
|--------------------------------------|--------|---------|--------|---------|
| *Fixed Assets:*                      |        |         |        |         |
| Cost.........................        |        | 650,000 |        | 680,000 |
| Less:   Accumulated depreciation     |        | 176,500 |        | 203,700 |
|                                      |        | 473,500 |        | 476,300 |
| *Current Assets*                     |        |         |        |         |
| Stock........................        | 126,400|         | 127,500|         |
| Trade debtors.................       | 97,700 |         | 95,000 |         |
| Bank  balance.................       | 23,600 |         | —      |         |
|                                      | 247,700|         | 222,500|         |
| *Less: Current Liabilities*          |        |         |        |         |
| Trade creditors................      | 72,900 |         | 87,100 |         |
| Proposed dividend.............       | 44,000 |         | 44,000 |         |
| Bank overdraft................       | -      |         | 37,900 |         |
|                                      | 116,900|         | 169,000|         |
| Working capital...............       |        | 130,800 |        | 53,500  |
|                                      |        | 604,300 |        | 529,800 |
| Share capital..................      |        | 400,000 |        | 400,000 |
| Retained profit................      |        | 104,300 |        | 109,800 |
|                                      |        | 504,300 |        | 509,800 |
| 6% Debentures repayable 19X9...      |        | 100,000 |        | 20,000  |
|                                      |        | 604,300 |        | 529,800 |

During 19X5 the directors offered to repay the debentures, and this invitation was accepted by the majority of the debenture holders.

*Required:*
(a)   A statement of funds for 19X5.
(b)   A brief explanation for the decline in the bank balance based on the information contained in the statement.

# Question 12.7

The following information relates to the affairs of General Engineering plc.

### Balance Sheets at 31 December

| | 19X7 | | 19X8 | |
|---|---|---|---|---|
| | £000 | £000 | £000 | £000 |
| Plant at cost less depreciation..... | | 2,600 | | 2,760 |
| Property at cost less depreciation.. | | 800 | | 700 |
| Investments at cost............. | | 300 | | 250 |
| | | 3,700 | | 3,710 |
| *Current Assets:* | | | | |
| Stock & work-in-progress...... | 900 | | 2,120 | |
| Debtors.................... | 660 | | 700 | |
| Short term loans & | | | | |
| deposits at bank........... | 290 | | 620 | |
| | 1,850 | | 3,440 | |
| *Current Liabilities:* | | | | |
| Creditors .................. | 520 | | 720 | |
| Proposed final dividend....... | 400 | | 400 | |
| | 920 | | 1,120 | |
| Working capital............... | | 930 | | 2,320 |
| | | 4,630 | | 6,030 |
| Financed by: | | | | |
| Issued share capital.......... | | 2,000 | | 2,500 |
| Share premium account....... | | — | | 200 |
| Retained profit.............. | | 2,630 | | 3,030 |
| | | 4,630 | | 5,730 |
| Long term loan (12%)........ | | — | | 300 |
| | | 4,630 | | 6,030 |

*Extracts from the profit and Loss Account for 19X8*

|  | £000 |
|---|---|
| Trading profit for the year after charging all costs, including depreciation of plant, £250,000 and depreciation of property, £100,000 | 700 |
| Interest and dividends received, less interest paid | 20 |
| Net profit from ordinary activities | 720 |
| Add: Profit from the sale of an investment | 80 |
|  | 800 |
| Less: Proposed dividend | 400 |
| Retained profit for the year | 400 |
| Retained profit at 1 January, 19X8 | 2,630 |
| Retained profit at 31 December, 19X8 | 3,030 |

During 19X8 investments which had cost £50,000 some years earlier were sold for £130,000.

*Required:*

(a)  A statement of funds for the year to 31 December 19X8.

(b)  A discussion of the change in the financial position of General Engineering between the end of 19X7 and the end of 19X8. You are not required to examine the profitability of the firm, but should use the working capital and liquidity ratios to help assess financial developments.

*Note:*  Ignore taxation.

## Question 12.8

The following information is obtained in connection with the affairs of two companies, manufacturing specialised metal products, in respect of the year ended 31 December 19X5.

|  | Metalmax Ltd £000 | Precision ProductsLtd £000 |
|---|---|---|
| Sales | 800 | 950 |
| Administration expenses | 30 | 30 |
| Selling expenses (including promotional costs) | 45 | 60 |
| Plant and machinery at cost | 360 | 360 |
| Depreciation to 31 December 19X4 | 110 | 110 |
| Current assets | 240 | 400 |
| Trade creditors | 120 | 320 |
| Share capital (£1 ordinary shares) | 200 | 200 |

It is also established that both companies incur variable costs of sales, excluding depreciation, of 80% on sales. Depreciation should be charged at 15% on the cost of machinery. Reserves may be treated as the balancing figure in the balance sheets.

*Required:*
(a)  Summary trading and profit and loss accounts for the year ended 31 December 19X5 and balance sheets at that date for each company in vertical format to facilitate comparison.
(b)  A comparison of the profitability of the two companies during 19X5 and of their respective financial positions at the end of the year. Relevant accounting ratios should be used to support the discussion.

*Notes:*
1.   Within the current asset totals are included balances in respect of stocks and work-in-progress as follows:

| | |
|---|---|
| Metalmax Ltd. | £120,000 |
| Precision Products Ltd. | £200,000 |

2.   Ignore taxation.

## CHAPTER 13

# Revision Questions

Chapter 13 contains 30 revision questions which should be worked; the solutions are contained in the Appendix. The order of the questions broadly follows the sequence of earlier chapters, although this is not always the case because some questions involve matters dealt with in more than one chapter. For example, Question 13.3 (Leyton and Woodford) involves:
  (a)  the calculation of profit by capital changes (chapter 2 material);
  (b)  the preparation of final accounts from cash records (chapter 3 material);
  (c)  a partnership (chapter 9 material).

As was mentioned in chapter 10, the published accounts of limited companies, presented in the horizontal format, *must* show assets on the left and liabilities on the right. Published accounts are outside the Stage 1 syllabus but, as a preparation for Stage 2, limited company balance sheets in this chapter (and the solutions) are presented that way round where the horizontal format is used.

**Question 13.1**
The summarised balance sheet of Fence Ltd. at 31 March, 19X4 was as follows:

|  | £(000) |  | £(000) |
|---|---|---|---|
| Fixed Assets: |  | Share capital: |  |
| At cost | 80 | Ordinary shares of £1 each | 60 |
| Less: Accumulated depreciation | 35 | Profit and loss account | 8 |
|  | 45 | Trade creditors | 10 |
| Stocks | 27 | Bank overdraft | 7 |
| Debtors | 13 |  |  |
|  | 85 |  | 85 |

On 1 April, 19X4 the following transactions took place:
(i) Collected cash from debtors £6,000.
(ii) Bought stock on credit for £2,000.
(iii) Sold goods on credit for £5,000; these goods had cost £3,000.
(iv) Purchased a fixed asset for £10,000 cash.
(v) Paid cash to creditors £1,000.
(vi) Raised a long-term loan of £18,000; the cash was received and banked on 1 April, 19X4.

*Required:*
(a) State the values, at 31 March 19X4, of the company's:
(i) Current assets
(ii) Current liabilities
(iii) Working capital
(b) Prepare the balance sheet of Fence, in vertical format, at the close of business on 1 April 19X4.

*Note:*
The calculation of each figure in your answer should be clearly shown.

**Question 13.2**
Ray Glastonbury runs a shop known as Glastonbury Gadgets, and on 1 January 19X3 his total assets and liabilities, including both personal and business items, were as follows:

|  | £ |
|---|---|
| Business premises | 12,000 |
| House | 36,000 |
| Delivery van | 2,600 |
| Cash in till | 70 |
| Trading stock | 4,350 |
| Balance in personal bank account | 1,810 |
| Business bank overdraft | 290 |
| Shop fittings | 3,000 |
| House furniture | 7,210 |
| Personal clothes | 1,350 |
| Premium bonds | 50 |
| Motor boat | 600 |
| Garden greenhouse | 320 |
| Garden shed | 400 |
| Watch | 50 |
| Creditors for stock purchases | 2,380 |
| Domestic electricity owing | 90 |
| Business electricity owing | 240 |

The business bank account for the year to 31 December 19X3 is:

| Receipts | £ | Payments | £ |
|---|---|---|---|
| Cash from sales | 57,390 | Balance brought down | 290 |
| | | Wages | 9,480 |
| | | Electricity | 1,020 |
| | | Motor expenses | 920 |
| | | Purchases | 31,270 |
| | | Drawings | 11,480 |
| | | Additional shop fittings | 2,000 |
| | | Balance carried down | 930 |
| | 57,390 | | 57,390 |

You are given the following additional information:
  (i)   The value of shop fittings at 31 December 19X3 was £4,500 and the van was considered to be worth £1,950.
  (ii)  At 31 December 19X3 creditors for purchases of stock were £1,780 and £150 was owed for business electricity.
  (iii) At 31 December 19X3 a cash float of £110 was held in the till, and trading stock was valued at £5,220.

*Required:*
  (a)   The balance sheet of Glastonbury Gadgets at 1 January 19X3 to show clearly the capital which Ray Glastonbury has invested in his business.
  (b)   The trading and profit and loss account of Glastonbury Gadgets for the year to 31 December 19X3 and a balance sheet at that date. The cost of goods sold and gross profit should be identified in the trading account.

*Note:*
Ignore depreciation of business premises.

**Question 13.3**
Leyton and Woodford were in partnership sharing profits equally. The partnership was commenced on 1 January 19X0 and each partner contributed £4,000 as his capital. The partners' drawings during 19X0 were Leyton £1,712, and Woodford £1,529. The following additional information is provided:

*Total bank account for 19X1.*

| | £ | | £ |
|---|---|---|---|
| Opening balance | 1,121 | Cash paid to suppliers | 30,886 |
| Cash received from | | Rent and rates | 1,200 |
| credit customers | 48,123 | Insurances | 211 |
| | | General expenses | 9,746 |
| | | Drawings: | |
| | | Leyton | 1,924 |
| | | Woodford | 1,863 |
| | | Closing balance | 3,414 |
| | 49,244 | | 49,244 |

| *Balances at 31 December:* | *19X0* | *19X1* |
|---|---|---|
| | £ | £ |
| Stock | 2,836 | 3,249 |
| Debtors | 3,121 | 3,211 |
| Creditors for: | | |
| Purchases | 1,811 | 2,162 |
| Rates | 62 | 71 |
| Insurance paid in advance | 26 | 29 |

Second hand motor vans which cost £3,600 on 1 January 19X0 are still in use and are to be written down by an annual depreciation charge of 25% on cost.

*Required:*
(a) Calculations of (i) the profit earned during 19X0 and (ii) the balance on the partners' capital accounts at 31 December 19X0 (i.e. separate current accounts are not maintained).
(b) The firm's trading account, profit and loss account, and appropriation account for 19X1, and balance sheet as at 31 December 19X1.

## Question 13.4
The summarised balance sheet of the Cathays Social Club at 31 December 19X4 was as follows:

| | £ | £ | | £ |
|---|---|---|---|---|
| Accumulated Fund | | 49,690 | Investments at cost | 27,400 |
| Creditors: | | | Furniture and equipment | |
| Bar purchases | 2,710 | | at cost less depreciation | 16,300 |
| Expenses | 150 | 2,860 | Bar stocks | 5,100 |
| | | | Bank balance | 3,750 |
| | | 52,550 | | 52,550 |

A summary of the Club's bank account for 19X5 is as follows:

| | £ | | £ |
|---|---|---|---|
| Balance at 1 January | 3,750 | Bar purchases | 38,870 |
| Subscriptions received | 7,700 | Wages and salaries (bar) | 11,250 |
| Bar sales | 62,100 | Rent and rates | 3,600 |
| Interest on investments | 3,180 | General expenses | 3,790 |
| | | Cost of new investments | 15,000 |
| | | Balance at 31 December | 4,220 |
| | 76,730 | | 76,730 |

On 31 December 19X5, bar stocks were valued at £6,250 and £2,810 was owing for bar supplies; £130 was owing for expenses.

The club occupies part of a building which the owner proposes to sell for £100,000; he has offered it to the trustees of the club and they are considering the proposal.

The investments held by the club could be sold for £35,000 and a member of the club has offered to lend £10,000 at 10% per annum, for five years. The secretary of the club has approached the bank to negotiate an overdraft for the balance needed to complete the purchase of the building; the bank has asked to see the 19X5 accounts and wishes to have an estimate of the amount that is likely to be available annually for repayment.

Part of the building is occupied by the local scout troop which pays its own rates and from which an annual rent of £200 is receivable. The club will remain liable for the rates on the part of the building it occupies amounting to £900 per annum.

There are no subscriptions in arrears or in advance; depreciation should be charged on the furniture and equipment at the rate of 10% per annum on the opening value.

*Required:*

   (a)  A bar trading account and an income and expenditure account for 19X5 and a balance sheet at the end of that year.

   (b)  A calculation showing:

      (i)  the amount to be borrowed on overdraft, as at 1 January 19X6, to meet the cost of the building;

      (ii)  the annual surplus that will be available to meet the interest on the overdraft and for repayment on the assumption that the 19X5 results are repeated in each of the following five years.

## Question 13.5

Rover Ltd maintains control accounts for its sales and purchases ledgers. Balances at 31 December 19X0 are:

|  | Debit £ | Credit £ |
|---|---|---|
| Sales ledger | 74,090 | 667 |
| Purchases ledger | 461 | 58,487 |

Details of transactions during 19X1 are as follows:

|  | £ |
|---|---|
| Sales on credit | 633,772 |
| Cash sales | 511,604 |
| Purchases on credit | 454,406 |
| Cash purchases | 1,089 |
| Returns from credit customers | 3,740 |
| Returns to credit suppliers | 4,120 |
| Receipts from credit customers | 605,107 |
| Payments to suppliers for goods purchased on credit | 438,734 |
| Bad debts written off | 4,173 |
| Provision for doubtful debts to be increased by | 672 |

There were credit balances on the sales ledger at 31 December 19X1 amounting to £798. There were no debit balances on the purchases ledger at that date.

## Question 13.6

The draft balance sheet of I Notrite at 31 December 19X2 was as follows:

| Capital | £ | £ | Fixed Assets | £ |
|---|---|---|---|---|
| 1 January 19X2 |  | 45,750 | at book value | 37,500 |
| Profit for 19X2 |  | 22,500 |  |  |
|  |  | 68,250 | Stock | 18,750 |
| Drawings |  |  | Trade debtors | 15,000 |
| during 19X2 |  | (15,000) | Cash | 750 |
| 31 December 19X2 |  | 53,250 |  |  |
| Creditors | 15,750 |  |  |  |
| Overdraft | 4,500 |  | Suspense account | 1,500 |
|  |  | 20,250 |  |  |
|  |  | 73,500 |  | 73,500 |

The balance sheet did not balance and the difference was placed in the Suspense Account. Investigations revealed the following errors:

    (a)    I Notrite had withdrawn stock for his private use which cost £450. No entry had been made in the books in respect of this.

    (b)    The figure for trade debtors had been extracted from the books wrongly when the trial balance was prepared. The correct value is £17,250.

    (c)    No entry had been made in the books for goods purchased on credit from B. Baker for £1,350 which were received on 30 December 19X2. These goods had been included in the stock figure shown in the above balance sheet.

    (d)    An accrual of £750 for rent owed to I Left at 31 December 19X2, although correctly dealt with in the profit and loss account, was omitted from the balance sheet.

    (e)    No entry had been made in the accounts in respect of insurance prepaid at 31 December 19X2 to the value of £60.

*Required:*
    (a)    Prepare the revised balance sheet of I Notrite as at 31 December 19X2 in which the above errors have been corrected.

    (b)    Write up the suspense account, showing how the debit balance is eliminated.

## Question 13.7 Part (a)

An inexperienced book-keeper, who did not maintain control accounts, has drawn up the following Trial Balance as at 31 December 19X4:

|  | £ | £ |
|---|---|---|
| Capital............................................. |  | 48,642 |
| Debtors (from sales ledger)....................... | 11,131 |  |
| Creditors (from purchases ledger)................ |  | 7,283 |
| Stock 1 January 19X4........................... | 14,169 |  |
| Premises at Cost................................ | 25,000 |  |
| Vans at cost.................................... | 10,000 |  |
| Sales........................................... |  | 122,488 |
| Purchases...................................... | 89,952 |  |
| Rent and rates................................. | 2,460 |  |
| Light and heat.................................. | 841 |  |
| Salaries and wages.............................. | 14,865 |  |
| General expenses................................ |  | 1,861 |
| Bad debts...................................... | 622 |  |
| Doubtful debts provision at 1 January 19X4........ | 862 |  |
| Provision for van depreciation at 1 January 19X4............................. |  | 6,000 |
| Motor expenses................................ | 1,326 |  |
| Drawings...................................... | 7,146 |  |
| Bank overdraft................................. | 4,302 |  |
| Discounts received.............................. | 501 |  |
| Discounts allowed.............................. |  | 1,738 |
| Office equipment............................... | 2,000 |  |
| Provision for depreciation of office equipment at 1 January 19X4.................. | 400 |  |
|  | 185,577 | 188,012 |

*Required:*
Prepare a corrected trial balance. Any remaining difference should be inserted as a debit or credit balance in a suspense account.

## Question 13.7 Part (b)

Investigation of the ledger accounts listed above reveals the following ledger posting errors:

  (a)  Goods bought on credit from a supplier for £13 had been posted to his account as £73. The posting to the Purchases Account was correct.

  (b)  Office equipment which had cost £293 had been debited to the General Expenses Account.

(c)   An invoice from a supplier for £372 had been entered in the Purchases Day Book and posted to the supplier's account in the Purchases Ledger, but not to the Purchases Account.

(d)   Sales on credit to a customer for £1,750 had been posted to the Sales Account but not to the Sales Ledger.

(e)   The balance on the Capital Account had been incorrectly copied. The correct balance is £43,642.

(f)   A payment of £256 received from a debtor in settlement of his account had been entered in the Cash Book as a cash sale.

(g)   Discounts Allowed had been undertotalled in the cash book by £185.

*Required:*

(i)   Prepare a list of the adjustments to correct the errors. Show for each error the name of the balance affected, whether the adjustment is a debit or a credit, and the amount of the adjustment.

(ii)   Prepare a trial balance in which the errors have been corrected.

**Question 13.8**

On 2 January 19X2, Lyn Ltd bought a machine from Cutter Ltd on the following hire purchase terms:

|  | £ |
|---|---|
| Cash price | 4,185 |
| Deposit paid 2 January | 1,200 |
| Three annual payments, to be paid on 31 December each year, commencing 31 December 19X2 | 1,200 |
| The interest charge for each year is: | |
| 19X2 | 298 |
| 19X3 | 208 |
| 19X4 | 109 |

*Required:*

Prepare the relevant accounts in the ledger of Lyn Ltd for the calendar years 19X2, 19X3 and 19X4.

**Question 13.9**

Arno Ltd. and Garland Ltd. are two companies which were incorporated on 1 January 19X6 and commenced trading on that date. They continued in business until December 19Y0 when they were both taken over by a large public company.

Both companies traded in an identical product and their trading activities, which were identical throughout the five year period, were as follows:

| | Units Purchased | Units Sold | Purchase Price (per unit) | Sales Price (per unit) |
|---|---|---|---|---|
| | | | £ | £ |
| 19X6 | 4,000 | 2,000 | 14 | 20 |
| 19X7 | 6,000 | 4,000 | 16 | 23 |
| 19X8 | 8,000 | 6,000 | 18 | 27 |
| 19X9 | 8,000 | 6,000 | 20 | 29 |
| 19Y0 | 8,000 | 16,000 | 22 | 30 |

Arno Ltd. matches purchases with sales on the basis of first-in-first-out (FIFO), Garland on the basis of last-in-first-out (LIFO).

*Required:*

(a)   Arno's trading account for each of the years 19X6 to 19Y0 in columnar form.

(b)   Garland's trading account for each of the years 19X6 to 19Y0 in columnar form.

(c)   Calculate the total gross profit of each company over the five year period.

(d)   Comment on the results of your calculations under (a) to (c) above.

**Question 13.10.**
Andrew Holland manufactures a new type of dish washer. The following information has been extracted from the books of the company relating to 19X0.

| | £000 |
|---|---|
| Stocks of raw materials, 1 January 19X0 | 30,000 |
| Stocks of raw materials, 31 December 19X0 | 35,000 |
| Stocks of finished goods, 1 January 19X0 (300 dishwashers) | 90,000 |
| Purchases of raw materials | 175,000 |
| Manufacturing wages | 110,000 |
| Factory indirect expenses | 20,000 |
| Sales | 525,000 |
| Office expenses | 82,000 |
| Selling and distribution expenses | 15,000 |

You are given the following additional information:

|  |  | No. |
|---|---|---|
| (i) | Dishwashers manufactured | 1,000 |
|  | Dishwashers sold | 950 |

(ii) Manufacturing costs were incurred at an even rate during 19X0.

(iii) Finished stock is valued on the basis of total manufacturing cost per unit.

*Required:*

The manufacturing, trading and profit and loss account of Andrew Holland for 19X0. You should show your calculations of the finished stock at 31 December 19X0.

*Note:* There was no work in progress at either the beginning or the end of the year.

**Question 13.11**

Birchwood Ltd., which was established and started trading on 1 January 19X0, prepares its accounts on the calendar year basis. Its purchases and disposals of fixed assets, during the first three years in business, were as follows:

| Asset | Date of Purchase | Cost £ |
|---|---|---|
| A | 1 January 19X0............. | 5,000 |
| B | 1 January 19X0............. | 2,500 |
| C | 1 January 19X2............. | 7,000 |

|  | Date of Disposal | Proceeds on Disposal £ |
|---|---|---|
| B | 1 January 19X2............. | 900 |

The company charges depreciation of 20% per annum calculated on the straight line basis; this assumes that the fixed assets will possess a zero residual value at the end of their five year useful life.

*Required:*
(a)    Prepare the following accounts as they would appear in the books of Birchwood Ltd. for each of the years 19X0, 19X1 and 19X2:
    (i)    Fixed assets at cost account.
    (ii)   Provision for depreciation account.
    (iii)  Disposal of fixed asset account.
(b)    Assuming the company instead charges depreciation at the rate of 30% per annum on the *reducing balance basis*, show your calculation of:
    (i)    The depreciation charge for the years 19X0, 19X1 and 19X2.
    (ii)   The profit or loss on the disposal of asset B.
(c)    Discuss the purpose of charging depreciation when preparing a set of accounts and indicate on what basis the choice of method should be made.

## Question 13.12

Hadstock, a retailer of a specialised type of camera, has been in business for a number of years. Shortly before the end of 19X6 he forecast his sales and expenses for the remainder of the year and prepared a forecast of the profit and loss account to 31 December 19X6 as follows:

*Profit and Loss Account for 19X6*

| | £ | | £ |
|---|---|---|---|
| Variable cost of sales.......... | 160,000 | Sales (cash) 5,000 units | |
| Administration expenses....... | 20,000 | at £40 each.................. | 200,000 |
| Profit...................... | 20,000 | | |
| | 200,000 | | 200,000 |

Hadstock feels that his business is now well established, that demand for the product is strong, and that the expected results for 19X6 justify expansion. He considers two alternatives plans:

(a)  A hire purchase section might be added to the business. The existing rate of cash sales (5,000 units at the 19X6 selling price), at the same gross profit margin, would continue unchanged. In addition, 2,500 units would be sold on hire purchase terms at £50 per unit, payable in five half-yearly instalments of £10 each, with the first instalment due on the day of sale. All hire purchase sales for a particular year would be made on 1 January; the second and third instalments would be due on 30 June and 31 December respectively in the year of sale, and the remaining instalments on the same dates in the following year. The variable cost per unit would be the same as for cash sales. The profit on the hire purchase sales would be divided between the two years in the ratio of 3:2 (i.e. 3/5 will be taken in the year of sale and 2/5 in the year in which payment is completed).

(b)  The rate of cash sales would be doubled to 10,000 units, but it would be necessary to reduce the selling price of all units to £39.50. The variable cost per unit of sales would remain unchanged. There would be no hire purchase sales under this plan.

Under either plan the administration expenses would rise to £36,000 per annum. Hadstock has arranged to borrow £100,000 for a ten year term at 10% per annum interest, and this loan will be necessary irrespective of the plan chosen.

*Required:*
A brief report for Hadstock, advising him which plan he should select, giving reasons for your proposals. Your report should be supported by annual profit and loss accounts (prepared for each plan separately) which will indicate to Hadstock the prospective long term financial results of the choice he makes.

*Note*: Assume that the level of sales referred to under the two plans will remain unchanged for at least ten years.

## Question 13.13

The following information is extracted from the books and records of Trout Ltd., a manufacturing company, in respect of the year ended 31 December 19X4:

|  | £ |
|---|---|
| Retained profit 1 January 19X4 | 168,100 |
| Stock: raw materials 1 January 19X4 | 52,200 |
| Stock: raw materials 31 December 19X4 | 57,500 |
| Stock: manufactured goods 1 January 19X4 | 76,200 |
| Stock: manufactured goods 31 December 19X4 | 69,000 |
| Purchases of raw materials | 427,500 |
| Sundry factory indirect expenses | 43,600 |
| Plant and machinery at cost | 320,000 |
| Fixtures and fittings at cost | 90,000 |
| Rent and rates | 12,000 |
| Direct manufacturing wages | 432,400 |
| Sales | 1,350,000 |
| General administration expenses | 118,100 |
| Salesmens' salaries | 22,400 |
| Other selling expenses | 43,700 |
| Work in progress 1 January 19X4 | 71,800 |
| Work in progress 31 December 19X4 | 81,600 |
| Returns inwards | 13,100 |
| Discounts received | 4,500 |
| Discounts allowed | 10,300 |
| Lighting and heating | 23,100 |
| Proposed divided for 19X4 | 100,000 |

The following additional information is provided:
1. After the above figures were extracted, invoices relating to 19X4 were received in respect of administration expenses. These invoices amounted, in total, to £1,600.
2. The fixed assets were all purchased on 1 January 19X1. The plant and machinery is thought to possess an 8 year life and the fixtures and fittings will last 10 years. For the purposes of calculating depreciation, a nil residual value is assumed.
3. Costs incurred in respect of 'rent and rates' and 'lighting and heating' are considered to relate to the factory, two-thirds, and office accommodation, one-third.
4. Work in progress and finished goods have been valued on the basis of total factory cost.

*Required*
Prepare the manufacturing, trading and profit and loss accounts of Trout Ltd for 19X4.

## Question 13.14

Jones owns a newsagents which was managed for him by an employee until 31 December 19X4, at which date the manager left. Jones suspects that cash has been misappropriated during 19X4 and the following information relating to that year is extracted from the firm's records:

| (i) | Assets and liabilities at | 1 January £ | 31 December £ |
|---|---|---|---|
| | Stock | 60,600 | 73,160 |
| | Debtors | 34,400 | 42,820 |
| | Balance at bank | 20,200 | 28,580 |
| | Creditors | 23,600 | 38,840 |

(ii) The sales and cost of goods sold figures appearing in the firm's trading account for 19X4 were £480,000 and £300,000 respectively.

(iii) Payments for wages and expenses during 19X4 amounted to £96,920, and, in addition, fixed assets costing £20,000 were purchased and paid for.

(iv) Jones' cash drawings for 19X4 were £24,000.

*Required*

Use the figures given above to construct a cash account and thereby calculate the amount of any cash discrepancy.

## Question 13.15

Lacton Ltd has been trading for some years. From 1 January 19X7 it commenced selling on hire purchase terms, and also to rent out equipment to householders. The following information was available at the end of 19X7:

(i) Hire purchase sales:

| | £ |
|---|---|
| Total selling price | 60,000 |
| Cost price of goods sold | 42,000 |
| Cash received from customers during 19X7 | 15,000 |

*Note:* Profit in respect of hire purchase sales is to be credited to the trading account each year on the basis of that proportion of the total selling price received in cash during the year.

(ii) The following table shows the rents received, in 19X7 (in monthly instalments), from customers for goods rented from the given dates. It also gives the cost price of the goods rented out on both dates:

| | Rents Received £ | Cost Price of Goods £ |
|---|---|---|
| Goods rented from: | | |
| 1 January | 24,000 | 48,000 |
| 1 July | 37,200 | 144,000 |

It is estimated that the goods will be worthless when the renting contract has run for four years, and it is the policy of the company to write off the cost price of the goods over that period on a straight line basis.

(iii) Cash sales............................................... £55,200

(iv) *Credit sales:* £

Cash received from customers........................... 42,600

Opening debtors...................................... 9,600

Closing debtors...................................... 16,800

*Note:* The closing debtors figure includes one item of £600 which is to be written off as a bad debt.

(v) Cost of goods sold for cash and on credit................... £80,400

(vi) A van, which cost £12,000 was purchased on 1 January 19X7 and depreciation is to be charged at the rate of 20% per annum on cost.

(vii) Administration expenses................................ £36,720

## Required:
Lacton Ltd's trading and profit and loss account for 19X7.

## Question 13.16
The trial balance of Ludlow Ltd. at 31 December 19X9 is as follows:

|  | £000 | £000 |
| --- | --- | --- |
| Share capital......................................... |  | 600 |
| Profit and Loss Account 1 January 19X9................ |  | 260 |
| 10% Debentures, repayable 19Y8..................... |  | 500 |
| Land and buildings at cost (including land £50,000)........ | 620 |  |
| Plant and machinery at cost.......................... | 500 |  |
| Patents, copyrights and licences at book value............ | 63 |  |
| Provision for depreciation on plant and machinery, 1 January 19X9.................................... |  | 150 |
| Stock at 1 January 19X9............................. | 246 |  |
| Sales................................................ |  | 2,060 |
| Purchases........................................... | 1,350 |  |
| Debenture interest to 30 June 19X9..................... | 25 |  |
| Rent and insurance.................................. | 14 |  |
| Rates............................................... | 17 |  |
| Debtors............................................. | 120 |  |
| Salaries and wages................................... | 365 |  |
| Provision for doubtful debts, 1 January 19X9............ |  | 2 |
| Creditors ........................................... |  | 103 |
| Temporary investments.............................. | 300 |  |
| Cash at bank........................................ | 70 |  |
| Income from investments............................. |  | 15 |
|  | 3,690 | 3,690 |

You discover that:
1. The value of the stock at 31 December 19X9 is £286,000.
2. The debenture interest for the half year ended 31 December 19X9 has not yet been paid.
3. The plant and machinery was purchased on 1 January 19X6. It was decided to depreciate it by the straight line method. Its useful life was estimated to be ten years, at the end of which time the scrap value was forecast to be nil.
4. A provision of 5% of the balance on the debtors accounts is to be established in respect of doubtful debts.
5. £9,000 is to be written off patents, copyrights and licences.
6. The balance of share capital includes the entire proceeds from the issue of 100,000 £1 shares at £1.40 during the year.
7. The directors have decided to use a recent revaluation of the company's land and buildings, of £750,000, for the purpose of the accounts.
8. Corporation tax is to be provided of £76,000.
9. The directors plan to recommend a dividend of 20 pence per share to the annual general meeting.

*Required:*
The trading and profit and loss account of Ludlow Ltd. for the year to 31 December 19X9 and the balance sheet of Ludlow Ltd. at 31 December 19X9.

**Question 13.17**
The summarised balance sheet of Poslingford Ltd. as at 31 December, 19X0 was as follows:

| | £ | | £ |
|---|---|---|---|
| Fixed assets at cost.......... | 236,000 | Share capital: 150,000 shares | |
| Less: Accumulated | | of £1 each fully paid......... | 150,000 |
| depreciation........ | 40,200 | Retained profit............. | 89,700 |
| | 195,800 | | 239,700 |
| Current assets.............. | 97,500 | Current liabilities (including dividend for 19X0)....... | 53,600 |
| | 293,300 | | 293,300 |

The net profit and the dividends paid for each of the years to 31 December, 19X1, 19X2, 19X3 and 19X4, were as follows:

|      | Net profit £ | Dividend £ |
|------|--------------|------------|
| 19X1 | 31,200       | 13,500     |
| 19X2 | 47,300       | 15,000     |
| 19X3 | 58,400       | 16,500     |
| 19X4 | 77,800       | 36,000     |

New fixed assets, which cost £260,000, were purchased during the four years to 31 December 19X4, and the total depreciation written off during this period amounted to £125,300. All the fixed assets remained in use at the end of 19X4.

The current liabilities at 31 December, 19X4, including the proposed dividend for 19X4, were £77,400.

The directors of Poslingford Ltd. decided, in November, 19X4, to make a capitalisation issue, i.e. a bonus issue, of 150,000 fully paid shares of £1 each at par. On 31 December, 19X4 the necessary formalities were completed and the issue was made.

The directors also decided to issue for cash 60,000 £1 shares at a premium of 50p per share; the shares were issued and the full amount due was paid on 31 December, 19X4.

*Required:*
  (a)   A calculation of the current asset balance at 31 December 19X4 based on the flow of funds during 19X1-X4.
  (b)   The balance sheet of Poslingford Ltd. on 31 December, 19X4, after all the above matters had been completed.

**Question 13.18**
Getaround Holidays Ltd. provides holidays at resorts in France, Spain and Greece. Its profit and loss account for the year to 31 December 19X4 is as follows:

| | £ | | £ |
|---|---|---|---|
| Agents' commission...... | 85,400 | Sales of holidays......... | 854,000 |
| Hire of planes........... | 90,000 | Net loss for year.......... | 5,700 |
| Coaches from airports to hotels............... | 6,000 | | |
| Hotel accommodation.... | 547,800 | | |
| Salaries and expenses of resort representatives..... | 29,500 | | |
| Head office and other common costs.......... | 101,000 | | |
| | 859,700 | | 859,700 |

The managing director complains that this profit and loss account does not tell him where or why the net loss has been incurred. You are given the following information:

1. The public book their holidays with the company through local travel agents who are paid a commission of 10% of the gross price of the holiday.

2. Holidays were offered at six resorts:
   A and B in France
   C and D in Spain
   E and F in Greece

3. Only one hotel was used in each resort.

4. Flights were from Cardiff Airport to one airport in each country. Every flight carries passengers for both the resorts in the country of destination. The costs were:

|  | £ |
|---|---|
| France............................. | 25,000 |
| Spain.............................. | 35,000 |
| Greece............................. | 30,000 |

5. The following information shows the costs and revenues for each resort:

| Resort | Sales of holidays | Cost of coaches from airport to hotel | Cost of hotel accommo- | Cost of local representative |
|---|---|---|---|---|
|  | £ | £ | £ | £ |
| A..... | 452,000 | 900 | 300,600 | 4,600 |
| B..... | 230,000 | 700 | 147,600 | 4,100 |
| C..... | 26,000 | 1,200 | 17,000 | 5,500 |
| D..... | 59,000 | 1,000 | 39,800 | 5,100 |
| E..... | 23,000 | 1,500 | 4,600 | 5,300 |
| F..... | 64,000 | 700 | 38,200 | 4,900 |

*Required:*

(a) Prepare a revised profit and loss account which meets the objections of the managing director.

(b) Comment on the results revealed by the revised profit and loss account and advise management.

## Question 13.19

Downing Ltd. produces a single product called Blotto. The direct costs associated with the production of a single unit of Blotto are as follows:

|  | £ |
|---|---|
| Materials | 12.75 |
| Expenses | 2.75 |
| Labour | 5.00 |

The fixed expenses incurred by the company during 19X8, when 20,000 units were produced and sold, were:

|  | £ |
|---|---|
| Factory | 47,600 |
| Selling (including sales representatives' salaries) | 58,700 |
| Administration | 55,200 |

During 19X8, the factory did not operate at its full capacity and it is expected that results will decline further if the present selling methods continue. Management is of the view that a change in the system for remunerating sales representatives will increase sales significantly. At present, 5 representatives are each paid an annual salary of £10,000. The proposal is to reduce the annual salary to £6,000 and, in addition, pay them a commission of 3% on sales. Reorganisation is expected to reduce the fixed factory expenses by £13,500 and the fixed administration expenses by £2,000; other expenses will remain unchanged and the selling price will continue at the 19X8 price of £30 per unit.

Budgets for 19X9 show that the cost of materials is expected to rise to £13.25 per unit and the labour cost by 12%

*Required:*
   (a)   Prepare a statement to show the results of trading in 19X8.
   (b)   Calculate the level of sales required to break even in 19X9.
   (c)   Calculate the level of sales required during 19X9 to achieve the same profit as that of 19X8.

## Question 13.20

Potter Ltd. and Lenton Ltd., two independent businesses, both produce and sell two products, G and H. Neither company sells anything else. Potter has an issued share capital of 100,000 ordinary shares of £1 each and Lenton's issued share capital consists of 60,000 ordinary shares of £1 each. The following information was extracted from their financial books at the end of 19X9:

|  | Potter | Lenton |
|---|---|---|
|  | £ | £ |
| Sales for 19X9 - G. | 100,000 | 60,000 |
| Sales for 19X9 - H. | 60,000 | 100,000 |
| Cost of sales for 19X9 - G. | 90,000 | 54,000 |
| Cost of sales for 19X9 - H. | 45,000 | 75,000 |
| Stocks at 31 December 19X9 - G. | 20,000 | 8,000 |
| Stocks at 31 December 19X9 - H. | 12,000 | 15,000 |
| Debtors for sales at 31 December 19X9. | 18,000 | 16,000 |
| Creditors for supplies at 31 December 19X9. | 14,500 | 19,500 |
| General expenses for 19X9. | 15,000 | 12,000 |
| Fixed assets at cost. | 80,000 | 60,000 |
| Depreciation charge for 19X9 (included in cost of sales). | 8,000 | 6,000 |
| Total depreciation to end of 19X9. | 24,000 | 18,000 |
| Cash and bank balance. | 25,000 | 12,000 |

*Note:* There are no assets and no non-ownership external liabilities other than those recorded above.

*Required:*

(a) Summary trading and profit and loss accounts for each company for 19X9 which disclose the relative contribution of each product.

(b) The balance sheet of each company at 31 December 19X9.

(c) An explanation, based on accounting ratios, of the different financial performance of the two companies.

## Question 13.21

Bibble Ltd. manufactures four different products, called A, B, C and D, in a factory which is divided into four separate sections, one for each product. The products are all sold at a uniform price of £3 per unit. The factory belongs to the company; part of the building was sublet but is now vacant.

The following financial information relates to 19X8:

| Product | Sales £ | Variable Costs £ | Fixed Costs £ |
|---|---|---|---|
| A | 72,000 | 57,600 | 6,000 |
| B | 48,000 | 36,000 | 6,000 |
| C | 36,000 | 24,000 | 9,000 |
| D | 120,000 | 102,000 | 4,800 |

The directors have decided to expand. The vacant part of the building is large enough to allow an increase in production, and sales, of 36,000 units. However, the space is only large enough to enable one additional machine to be installed, and so the whole of the increased output must be concentrated on one of the four products.

The rate of variable cost for whichever product is chosen for expansion will be the same as in 19X8, but, depending on the product chosen, additional fixed costs will be incurred as follows:

| Product | £ |
|---|---|
| A | 8,400 |
| B | 9,600 |
| C | 15,000 |
| D | 6,000 |

It is expected that the selling price of all units, including the additional output, will remain unchanged at £3 per unit.

*Required:*

(a) Profit and loss accounts for 19X8 in columnar form showing the results for each product separately.

(b) Forecast profit and loss accounts for 19X9 showing for each product separately the net profit which may be expected in 19X9 from the additional sales if the estimates are fulfilled. (These accounts should be limited to the additional sales; it is not necessary to repeat the results from existing trade).

(c) Explain which product should be chosen for increased production.

## Question 13.22

Post Ltd. and Haste Ltd. both started trading on 1 January 19X4. They produce and sell the same single product, called Stampo, which sells for £20 per unit. The following information is relevant:

| | Post Ltd | Haste Ltd |
|---|---|---|
| Plant purchased 1 January 19X4.................... | £100,000 | £250,000 |
| Expected life of plant.............................. | 10 years | 10 years |
| Fixed costs (other than depreciation) per year.......... | £5,000 | £12,000 |
| Variable cost per unit of Stampo produced: | | |
| Labour....................................... | £6 | £2 |
| Materials..................................... | £10 | £10 |
| Maximum annual output (units).................... | 7,000 | 7,000 |

Both firms calculate depreciation on the straight line basis, assuming a zero residual value.

*Required:*

(a) Calculate the profit or loss which would be made by each company in 19X4 if it achieved an output and sales of:
   (i)   7,000 units
   (ii)  4,500 units
(b) Write a brief report comparing the results of Post Ltd. and Haste Ltd. This report should include a comment on, and explanation of, the variation in the results of the two companies at the different levels of output.

## Question 13.23

The summarised manufacturing and profit and loss account of Eraser Ltd for 19X2 was as follows:

| | £ |
|---|---|
| Manufacturing wages.............. | 120,000 |
| Raw materials consumed........... | 160,000 |
| General administration............. | 32,000 |
| Depreciation of plant.............. | 45,000 |
| Factory rent...................... | 20,000 |
| Factory administration............. | 30,000 |
| Net profit........................ | 43,000 |
| | 450,000 |
| Sales (10,000 units at £45 each)....... | 450,000 |

The selling price of each unit was reduced by 10% from 1 January 19X3, and this caused the volume of sales to increase by 50%. To meet the additional demand, extra accommodation and plant was acquired. The additional costs which resulted from this expansion were:

|                          |   £    |
|--------------------------|--------|
| Factory rent             | 12,000 |
| Depreciation of plant    | 22,000 |
| General administration   |  3,000 |
| Factory administration   | 11,000 |

The wage rates in 19X3 were the same as in 19X2, and the cost of raw materials and the labour time for the production of each unit remained unchanged.

*Required:*

(a) Calculate for 19X2 (that is, the year prior to expansion):

    (i)      The prime cost of production

    (ii)     The total cost of production

    (iii)    The total cost of Eraser Ltd's operations

    (iv)    The total variable cost of production

    (v)     The total fixed cost of production

    (vi)    The direct cost of production per unit

    (vii)   The average indirect cost of production per unit

(b) Prepare a statement to show Eraser's profit for 19X3.

(c) Comment on whether the expansion was worthwhile. Would your conclusion differ if the additional sales could have been achieved with no reduction in the selling price per unit?

## Question 13.24

The summarised accounts of Falkirk Ltd. for 19X8 are as follows:

*Profit and Loss Account for 19X8*

|  | £ |
|---|---|
| Sales | 224,000 |
| Expenses (including depreciation £24,000) | 201,600 |
| Net profit | 22,400 |

*Balance Sheet at 31 December 19X8*

|  | £ | £ |
|---|---|---|
| Fixed assets at cost | | 240,000 |
| less: depreciation | | 64,000 |
| | | 176,000 |
| Current assets | 49,600 | |
| less: current liabilities | 24,000 | |
| Working capital | | 25,600 |
| | | 201,600 |
| Share capital (issued 19X5) | | 128,000 |
| Retained profit | | 73,600 |
| | | 201,600 |

Two alternative plans for 19X9 have been prepared and they are under consideration. The essential features of each plan are:

| Plan 1 | | £ |
|---|---|---|
| | An investment in plant costing | 64,000 |
| | Turnover expected to increase to | 336,000 |
| | Expenses (including depreciation £30,400) | 305,760 |
| | Current liabilities at 31 December 19X9 | 36,000 |
| Plan 2 | | £ |
| | An investment in plant costing | 114,000 |
| | Turnover expected to increase to | 450,000 |
| | Expenses (including depreciation £38,400) | 414,000 |
| | Current liabilities at 31 December 19X9 | 44,000 |
| | Issue of new share capital on 1 January 19X9 | 40,000 |

*Required:*
(a) A summary profit and loss account for 19X9 and a balance sheet at 31 December 19X9, as they would appear under each of the alternative plans given above, assuming that the respective forecasts for the plans were achieved exactly.

(b) A comparison of the financial results to be expected under each of the two plans, including calculations showing net profit as a percentage of sales and as a percentage of capital employed.

*Notes:*
1. For the purposes of this question, capital employed is defined as the issued share capital plus retained profit on 1 January in the year in question. This includes any additional capital issued on 1 January.
2. For both 19X8 and 19X9 no dividends have been paid and none are proposed.
3. Current assets may be treated as the balancing item in the balance sheets prepared in answer to requirement (a) above.

## Question 13.25

Stargazer Ltd. commenced business on 1 January 19X3 and its accounts were prepared on the calendar year basis. The following figures were extracted from the company's books:

| | Sales | Purchases | Increase (+) or decrease (-) in stock during year | Selling expenses | Rent | General expenses |
|---|---|---|---|---|---|---|
| | £ | £ | £ | £ | £ | £ |
| 19X3 | 450,000 | 487,500 | + 150,000 | 11,250 | 37,500 | 56,250 |
| 19X4 | 675,000 | 468,750 | − 37,500 | 16,870 | 37,500 | 65,630 |
| 19X5 | 975,000 | 787,500 | + 56,250 | 24,370 | 37,500 | 75,000 |
| 19X6 | 1,500,000 | 1,350,000 | + 150,000 | 45,000 | 75,000 | 112,500 |
| 19X7 | 1,875,000 | 1,687,500 | + 187,500 | 65,630 | 75,000 | 140,620 |

*Required:*
(a) A statement showing the book value of stock on 31 December each year from 19X3 to 19X7 inclusive.

(b) Trading and profit and loss accounts in columnar form for each of the five years to 31 December 19X7.

(c) A discussion, based on relevant accounting ratios, of the implications of these figures and the inferences you would draw from them.

## Question 13.26

Greenleaf is employed by a large company as a marketing director at an annual salary of £8,000. He owns securities worth £50,000 comprising local authority bonds at 11%. He could withdraw the full amount immediately without suffering any penalty.

He is considering the following alternatives:

   (i)   He could invest £20,000 in a small well-run business which would produce a return of £5,000 per annum. He would be required to advise generally on selling policies and methods. His firm is prepared to release him for the necessary period but his salary would drop to £6,000 per annum.

   (ii)   He could invest £40,000 in a second business. He would be required to devote his full time to the business at a salary of £9,000 per annum and he could expect an annual dividend of 7% on the amount he invests in the business.

*Required:*

   (a)   Statements comparing the results of the different alternatives open to Greenleaf and your advice as to the course of action he should follow.

   (b)   Would your advice be affected if under alternative (ii) Greenleaf could expect that, in the second and all subsequent years, his salary would increase to £12,000 and the annual dividend on the £40,000 investment would rise to 12%? Prepare a statement to support your argument.

*Notes:*

   (1)   Assume that there will be no changes, other than those mentioned, for at least five years.

   (2)   Ignore taxation.

## Question 13.27

The summarised accounts of Hudson Ltd. for 19X3 are as follows:

*Profit and Loss Account for 19X3.*

| | £ | | £ |
|---|---|---|---|
| Cost of sales............ | 36,600 | Sales.................. | 50,000 |
| Administration expenses... | 4,400 | | |
| Depreciation ............ | 5,000 | | |
| | 46,000 | | |
| Net profit (all retained).... | 4,000 | | |
| | 50,000 | | 50,000 |

*Balance Sheet 31 December 19X3.*

| | £ | | £ |
|---|---|---|---|
| Fixed assets: | | Share capital............ | 30,000 |
| Cost................. | 50,000 | Profit and loss account.... | 14,000 |
| Less: Accumulated | | | |
| depreciation........... | 12,000 | | 44,000 |
| | | Creditors .............. | 6,400 |
| | 38,000 | | |
| Current assets............ | 12,400 | | |
| | 50,400 | | 50,400 |

Forecasts for 19X4 provide for:
  (a)  an increase in the percentage return on capital employed of 4%;
  (b)  a reduction in the net profit percentage of 1%;
  (c)  an increase of £1,000 in the administration expenses;
  (d)  the purchase of additional plant on 1 January, 19X4 at a cost of £6,000;
  (e)  a charge for depreciation at the rate of 10% of the cost of fixed assets;
  (f)  an increase in creditors of 50%.

*Required:*
  (a)  Draft profit and loss account for 19X4 and balance sheet at 31 December, 19X4 as they will appear if these forecasts are fulfilled. For the purpose of this requirement, insert current assets as the balancing figure.
  (b)  A reconciliation based on funds flow, of the current asset balance between the end of 19X3 and the end of 19X4.

*Note:* Capital employed is defined in this question as issued capital plus retained profit on 1 January in the year in question. No dividends have been paid and none are proposed.

## Question 13.28

Warton Ltd. commenced business on 1 January 19X0, with an authorised share capital of £600,000. The following information is given about the company:
  (i)   The company issued 300,000 shares of £1 each at par for cash on 1 January 19X0.
  (ii)  The company purchased for cash fixed assets on:
        1 January 19X0 at a cost of £240,000.
        31 December 19X1 at a cost of £160,000.
        Depreciation is charged at the rate of 10% per annum on the cost price of the fixed assets in use on 1 January in each of the relevant years.
  (iii) Current assets and current liabilities on 31 December in each of the relevant three years were:

|  | 19X0 | 19X1 | 19X2 |
| --- | --- | --- | --- |
|  | £ | £ | £ |
| Stocks and debtors................. | 135,000 | 171,000 | 210,800 |
| Bank |  |  |  |
| in hand....................... | 69,600 | — | 62,000 |
| overdrawn .................... | — | 45,000 | — |
| Trade creditors................... | 77,900 | 95,000 | 121,000 |

*Required:*
  (a)   Balance sheets in columnar form at 31 December of each year 19X0, 19X1 and 19X2, disclosing a separate figure for the working capital for each year, and for profit for the year.
  (b)   Calculate the funds generated from business operations separately for each of the three years.
  (c)   A brief discussion explaining the reason for the bank overdraft and the shortage of working capital in 19X1.

*Note:*
No dividends were paid in any of the years covered by the figures given above.

## Question 13.29

The summarised balance sheets of Black Ltd at 31 December, 19X1, and at 31 December, 19X4 are as follows:

### 31 December 19X1.

| Fixed Assets | £ | £ | | £ |
|---|---:|---:|---|---:|
| Plant at cost.......... | 120,400 | | Share capital....... | 90,000 |
| Less: Depreciation... | 45,600 | | Profit and loss | |
| | | | account.......... | 17,600 |
| | | 74,800 | | 107,600 |
| | | | | |
| Current Assets | | | Current Liabilities | |
| Stock............... | 26,740 | | Trade creditors..... | 21,400 |
| Debtors............. | 16,820 | | | |
| Cash............... | 10,640 | 54,200 | | |
| | | 129,000 | | 129,000 |

### 31 December 19X4.

| Fixed Assets | £ | £ | | £ |
|---|---:|---:|---|---:|
| Plant at cost.......... | 195,900 | | Share capital....... | 120,000 |
| Less: Depreciation... | 66,530 | | Profit and loss | |
| | | | account.......... | 46,400 |
| | | 129,370 | | 166,400 |
| | | | | |
| Current Assets. | | | Current Liabilities | |
| Stock............... | 40,120 | | Trade creditors..... | 29,000 |
| Debtors............. | 27,510 | 67,630 | Bank overdraft..... | 1,600 |
| | | 197,000 | | 197,000 |

Plant which cost £30,000, some years earlier, was scrapped in 19X2 and replaced by new plant in the same year; the written down value of the plant scrapped was £2,000. In addition, plant sold during the period 1 January 19X2 to 31 December, 19X4 realised £3,400; the accumulated depreciation to the date of sale amounted to £14,600 and a net loss on this sale of £1,000 resulted. There were no other changes in fixed assets during the three years in question.

*Required:*
(a) Calculations reconciling the figures for plant at cost and for accumulated depreciation in the two balance sheets.
(b) A statement of funds for the three years from 31 December, 19X1 to 31 December, 19X4.
(c) A brief discussion of the financial position and development of Black Ltd, during the period 19X2 to 19X4. Your analysis should include calculations of relevant solvency ratios.

*Note:*
Ignore dividends and taxation.

## Question 13.30

The balance sheets of Yellow Hammer Ltd. (a small private company owned by the two directors), as at 31 December 19X5 and 31 December 19X6 are given below:

*Balance Sheets of Yellow Hammer.*

| | 19X5 | | | 19X6 | |
|---|---|---|---|---|---|
| £ | £ | | £ | £ |
| | | *Fixed Assets* | | |
| | 28,000 | Buildings a cost............... | | 28,000 |
| | 31,400 | Plant at net book value.......... | | 62,100 |
| | 59,400 | | | 90,100 |
| | | *Current Assets* | | |
| 11,290 | | Stock........................ | 22,410 | |
| 7,020 | | Debtors...................... | 16,440 | |
| 6,210 | | Bank........................ | — | |
| 24,520 | | | 38,850 | |
| | | *Current Liabilities* | | |
| 11,720 | | Trade creditors................ | 26,740 | |
| 2,500 | | Dividends.................... | 2,500 | |
| — | | Bank overdraft................ | 15,110 | |
| 14,220 | | | 44,350 | |
| | 10,300 | Working capital............... | | (5,500) |
| | 69,700 | Total assets less current liabilities.. | | 84,600 |
| | — | Loan repayable 19Y5............ | | 10,000 |
| | 69,700 | | | 74,600 |
| | | Financed by: | | |
| | 50,000 | Share capital.................. | | 50,000 |
| | 19,700 | Retained profit................ | | 24,600 |
| | 69,700 | | | 74,600 |

## Details of plant are as follows:

|  | 19X5 £ | 19X6 £ |
|---|---|---|
| Cost.......................................... | 42,500 | 79,900 |
| Less depreciation to date........................... | 11,100 | 17,800 |
| Balance as above................................ | 31,400 | 62,100 |

Turnover has increased from £91,400 in 19X5 to £126,300 in 19X6. The net profit in 19X5 amounted to £6,610. Bad debts written off were £140 in 19X5 and £360, in 19X6.

### Required:
An assessment of the financial policy pursued by Yellow Hammer Ltd. in 19X6 and its effects on the financial position of the company as at 31 December 19X6.

### Note:
Ignore taxation.

# APPENDIX

# Solutions to Questions

## Solution 1.1
Business. Transactions (ii), (iii), (iv).
Personal. Transaction (i).
Part business/part personal. Transaction (v).


## Solution 1.2
(a)          *Balance Sheet of John's Business, 1 April 19X2*

| | £ | | £ |
|---|---|---|---|
| Capital................ | 4,000 | Cash at bank............ | 4,000 |

(b)          *Balance Sheet of John's Business, 2 April 19X2*

| | £ | | £ |
|---|---|---|---|
| Capital................ | 4,000 | Cash at bank............ | 4,600 |
| Loan from John's father... | 600 | | |
| | 4,600 | | 4,600 |

(c)          *Balance Sheet of John's Business, 4 April 19X2*

| | £ | | £ |
|---|---|---|---|
| Capital................ | 4,000 | Cash at bank............ | 4,600 |
| Loan from John's father... | 600 | Cash in hand............ | 150 |
| Loan from Peter........ | 150 | | |
| | 4,750 | | 4,750 |


## Solution 1.3
(a)          *Balance Sheet of Roger's Business, 1 September 19X3*

| | £ | | £ |
|---|---|---|---|
| Capital................ | 1,200 | Cash at bank............ | 1,200 |

(b)               *Balance Sheet of Roger's Business, 2 September 19X3*

| | £ | | £ |
|---|---|---|---|
| Capital............... | 1,200 | Machine............... | 750 |
| Endridge Local Authority.. | 1,000 | Bank (£1,200 + £1,000)... | 2,200 |
| Creditors.............. | 750 | | |
| | 2,950 | | 2,950 |


(c)               *Balance Sheet of Roger's Business, 3 September 19X3*

| | £ | | £ |
|---|---|---|---|
| Capital............... | 1,200 | Machines (£750 + £1,820). | 2,570 |
| Endridge Local Authority.. | 1,000 | Stock.................. | 420 |
| Creditors.............. | 750 | | |
| Bank overdraft | | | |
| (£2,200 − £1,820 − £420). | 40 | | |
| | 2,990 | | 2,990 |


(d)               *Balance Sheet of Roger's Business, 4 September 19X3*

| | £ | | £ |
|---|---|---|---|
| Capital............... | 1,200 | Machines.............. | 2,570 |
| Endridge Local Authority.. | 1,000 | Stock (£420 + £215)...... | 635 |
| Creditors (£750 + £215)... | 965 | | |
| Bank overdraft.......... | 40 | | |
| | 3,205 | | 3,205 |


# Solution 1.4

(a)               *Balance Sheet of Jeff's Business, 2 October 19X5*

| | £ | | £ |
|---|---|---|---|
| Capital............... | 5,300 | Machine............... | 2,200 |
| Add: Profit (£80 + £75)... | 155 | Stock (£2,870 − £360)..... | 2,510 |
| | 5,455 | Debtors (£800 + £315).... | 1,115 |
| Trade creditors.......... | 690 | Bank (£120 + £200)....... | 320 |
| | 6,145 | | 6,145 |

(b)　　　　　　　*Balance Sheet of Jeff's Business, 3 October 19X5*

| | £ | | £ |
|---|---|---|---|
| Capital................ | 5,455 | Machinery.............. | 2,200 |
| Trade creditors | | | |
| (£690 + £190)......... | 880 | Stock (£2,510 + £190)..... | 2,700 |
| | | Debtors (£1,115 − £150)... | 965 |
| | | Bank (£320 + £150)....... | 470 |
| | 6,335 | | 6,335 |

(c)　　　　　　　*Balance Sheet of Jeff's Business, 4 October 19X5*

| | £ | | £ |
|---|---|---|---|
| Capital................ | 5,455 | Machines (£2,200 + £600). | 2,800 |
| Trade creditors | | | |
| (£880 − £75)........... | 805 | Stock................... | 2,700 |
| Bank overdraft | | Debtors................. | 965 |
| (£470 − £75 − £600)..... | 205 | | |
| | 6,465 | | 6,465 |

# Solution 1.5

(a)　　　　　　*Balance Sheet of Daley at 31 December 19X1*

| | £ | | £ |
|---|---|---|---|
| Capital (balancing figure).. | 13,450 | Business premises........ | 9,000 |
| Loan from Weakly....... | 3,000 | Stock................... | 5,250 |
| Trade creditors.......... | 2,890 | Trade debtors........... | 3,340 |
| | | Cash................... | 1,750 |
| | 19,340 | | 19,340 |

(b)　　　　　　　*Balance Sheet of Daley at:*

| | Jan. 1 | Jan. 2 | Jan. 3 | Jan. 4 | Jan. 5 | Jan. 6 | Jan. 7 |
|---|---|---|---|---|---|---|---|
| SOURCES OF FINANCE | £ | £ | £ | £ | £ | £ | £ |
| Capital.......................... | 13,450 | 13,450 | 13,450 | 13,450 | 13,450 | 13,450 | 13,450 |
| Add: Profit...................... | | | | | 180 | 180 | 180 |
| Less: Drawings................... | | | | | | | (100) |
| | | | | | 13,630 | 13,630 | 13,530 |
| Loan from Weakly................. | 3,000 | 3,000 | 3,000 | 3,000 | 3,000 | 2,000 | 2,000 |
| Trade creditors................... | 3,390 | 3,390 | 2,720 | 2,980 | 2,980 | 2,980 | 2,980 |
| | 19,840 | 19,840 | 19,170 | 19,430 | 19,610 | 18,610 | 18,510 |
| | | | | | | | |
| ASSETS | | | | | | | |
| Business premises................. | 9,000 | 9,000 | 9,000 | 9,000 | 9,000 | 9,000 | 9,000 |
| Typewriter....................... | 500 | 500 | 500 | 500 | 500 | 500 | 500 |
| Stocks........................... | 5,250 | 5,250 | 5,250 | 5,510 | 5,160 | 5,160 | 5,060 |
| Trade debtors..................... | 3,340 | 3,150 | 3,150 | 3,150 | 3,150 | 3,150 | 3,150 |
| Cash............................ | 1,750 | 1,940 | 1,270 | 1,270 | 1,800 | 800 | 800 |
| | 19,840 | 19,840 | 19,170 | 19,430 | 19,610 | 18,610 | 18,510 |

## Solution 1.6

| TRANSACTION | CAPITAL | + LIABILITIES | = ASSETS |
|---|---|---|---|
| | £ | £ | £ |
| 1 | +2,000 | 0 | = +2,000 |
| 2 | 0 | 0 | = +3,000 |
| | | | −3,000 |
| 3 | 0 | +800 | = +800 |
| 4 | 0 | +5,000 | = +5,000 |
| 5 | 0 | 0 | = −750 |
| | | | +750 |
| 6 | +400 | 0 | = −1,000 |
| | | | +1,400 |
| 7 | 0 | −220 | = −220 |
| 8 | 0 | 0 | = +350 |
| | | | −350 |
| 9 | 0 | +60 | = +60 |
| 10 | −100 | 0 | = −100 |

## Solution 1.7

### Balance Sheet at 31 December 19X1

| | A | B | C | D | E | F |
|---|---|---|---|---|---|---|
| SOURCES OF FINANCE | £ | £ | £ | £ | £ | £ |
| Capital at 1 January 19X1........... | 2,500 | 2,000 | 3,000 | 4,000 | 3,800 | 7,400 |
| Add: Profit..................... | 1,000 | 3,200 | 1,400 | 5,700 | 2,300 | 7,000 |
| Less: Drawings.................. | (800) | (3,000) | (1,000) | (4,900) | (2,500) | (4,500) |
| | 2,700 | 2,200 | 3,400 | 4,800 | 3,600 | 9,900 |
| Current Liabilities............... | 750 | 400 | 600 | 1,300 | 1,700 | 2,100 |
| | 3,450 | 2,600 | 4,000 | 6,100 | 5,300 | 12,000 |
| ASSETS | £ | £ | £ | £ | £ | £ |
| Fixed assets..................... | 1,800 | 1,750 | 2,800 | 4,200 | 3,700 | 8,500 |
| Current assets................... | 1,650 | 850 | 1,200 | 1,900 | 1,600 | 3,500 |
| | 3,450 | 2,600 | 4,000 | 6,100 | 5,300 | 12,000 |

## Solution 1.8

(i) *Accountancy*. This is a system for recording and reporting business transactions, in financial terms, to interested parties who use this information as the basis for decision-making and performance assessment.

(ii) *Entity concept*. It is assumed, for accounting purposes, that the business entity has an existence separate and distinct from owners, managers and other individuals with whom it comes into contact during the course of its trading activities.

The assumption requires business transactions to be separated from personal transactions and accounting statements to concentrate upon the financial position of the firm and its relationship with outsiders.

(iii) *Balance sheet*. This is a financial statement which shows, on the one hand, the sources from which a business has raised finance and, on the other, the ways in which those monetary resources are employed. The balance sheet sets out the financial position at a particular moment in time and has been colourfully described as an instantaneous financial photograph of a business.

(iv) *Realisation concept*. This assumes that profit is earned or realised when the sale takes place. The justification for this treatment is that a sale results in the replacement of stock by either cash or a legally enforeable debt due from the customer.

(v) *Trade credit*. This is the period of time which elapses between the dates goods are supplied and paid for.

(vi) *Trading cycle, credit transactions*. This is a series of transactions which begins with the delivery of stock from suppliers. The stock is then sold and delivered to customers resulting in a profit being realised or a loss incurred. Next, cash is collected from customers and the cycle is completed by paying suppliers the amount due.

(vii) $C + L = A$. This formula expresses the balance sheet relationship between sources of finance and assets where—

$$C = \text{Capital invested by the owners, including retained profits.}$$
$$L = \text{Liabilities.}$$
$$A = \text{Assets.}$$

The balance sheet must always balance because all assets appearing on the right hand side of the balance sheet must be financed, and the various sources employed appear on the left.

(viii) *Owner's capital*. This is the amount of the initial investment in the concern, to which is added any further injections of capital plus profit earned, and from which is deducted drawings made by the owner for personal use.

(ix) *Money measurement concept*. Assets are reported in the balance sheet only if the benefit they provide can be measured or quantified, in money terms, with a reasonable degree of precision.

(x)   *Fixed assets*. These are purchased and retained to help carry on the business. Fixed assets are not sold in the normal course of business and their disposal will usually occur only when they are worn out e.g. machinery.

(xi)  *Current assets*. These are assets which are held for resale or conversion into cash e.g. stock-in-trade and trade debtors.

(xii) *Current liabilities*. These are debts payable within twelve months of the balance sheet date e.g. trade creditors and a bank overdraft.

(xiii) *Gross assets*. These are the total assets belonging to a business entity and therefore include both fixed assets and current assets.


## Solution 1.9

Current liabilities: (iv) (ix)
Current assets: (ii) (vii)
Fixed assets: (i) (iii)
Items not indicated:

(v)    Capital investment. This is reported in the capital section, i.e. the first item on the sources of finance side of the balance sheet.

(vi)   Pearl knecklace and gold wristwatch. These are the personal belongings of Mrs Greasy and must be excluded from the balance sheet.

(viii) Loan. This is a non-current liability and is reported between the capital and current liability sections of the balance sheet.

(x)    Shop. This must be excluded from the balance sheet since it belongs to the property company.

# Solution 1.10

### Balance Sheet of C. Forest at 31 Dec. 19X3

| | £ | £ | | £ | £ |
|---|---|---|---|---|---|
| Opening capital...... | | 52,380 | *Fixed Assets* | | |
| Add: Profit......... | | 12,600 | Leasehold premises.. | | 25,000 |
| Less: Drawings...... | | (10,950) | Plant and machinery.. | | 26,500 |
| | | | | | |
| | | 54,030 | | | 51,500 |
| Loan repayable 19X9. | | 9,000 | | | |
| | | | *Current Assets* | | |
| *Current Liabilities* | | | Stock-in-trade....... | 14,200 | |
| Loan repayable 19X4. | 2,500 | | Trade debtors....... | 14,100 | |
| Trade creditors...... | 10,600 | | Cash-in-hand ....... | 270 | 28,570 |
| Bank overdraft...... | 3,940 | 17,040 | | | |
| | | | | | |
| | | 80,070 | | | 80,070 |

# Solution 2.1

(a) Gross assets, £6,700.

Net assets, £6,500 (gross assets £6,700 – liabilities £200).

Working capital, £4,500 (current assets £4,700 – current liabilities £200).

(b)

| Transaction | Profit £ | Net Assets £ | Gross Assets £ | Working Capital £ |
|---|---|---|---|---|
| 1 | NIL | NIL | NIL | NIL |
| 2 | NIL | Increase, £500 | Increase, £500 | Increase, £500 |
| 3 | Decrease, £100 | Decrease, £100 | Decrease, £100 | Decrease, £100 |
| 4 | NIL | Decrease, £50 | Decrease, £50 | Decrease, £50 |
| 5 | NIL | NIL | Increase, £150 | NIL |
| 6 | NIL | NIL | NIL | Decrease, £700 |

# Solution 2.2

(a) Calculation of capital by deducting liabilities from assets:

*Statement of Assets, Liabilities and Capital at 30 June 19X4*

|  | £ | £ |
|---|---|---|
| *Assets* | | |
| Stocks.......................................... | | 9,850 |
| Debtors......................................... | | 4,270 |
| Cash at bank.................................... | | 1,450 |
| Cash in hand.................................... | | 570 |
| | | 30 |
| | | 16,170 |
| *Less: Liabilities* | | |
| Loan........................................... | 3,000 | |
| Trade creditors................................. | 1,890 | 4,890 |
| Capital......................................... | | 11,280 |

(b) Calculation of profit on the basis of the increase in capital:

|  | £ |
|---|---|
| Closing capital................................. | 11,280 |
| Less: Opening capital............................ | 10,330 |
| Profit.......................................... | 950 |

(c)                  *Balance Sheet at 30 June 19X4*

|  | £ | £ |
|---|---|---|
| Fixed Assets.................................... | | 9,850 |
| *Current Assets* | | |
| Stocks.......................................... | 4,270 | |
| Debtors......................................... | 1,450 | |
| Cash at bank.................................... | 570 | |
| Cash in hand.................................... | 30 | |
| | 6,320 | |
| *Less: Current Liabilities* | | |
| Trade creditors................................. | 1,890 | |
| Working capital................................. | | 4,430 |
| | | 14,280 |
| Financed by: | | |
| Opening capital................................. | | 10,330 |
| Add: Net profit................................. | | 950 |
| Closing capital................................. | | 11,280 |
| Loan........................................... | | 3,000 |
| | | 14,280 |

# Solution 2.3

(a) Calculation of capital by deducting liabilities from assets.

*Statement of Assets, Liabilities and Capital at 31 Dec. 19X8*

|  | £ | £ |
|---|---|---|
| *Assets* | | |
| Fixed assets..................................... | | 15,930 |
| Stock.......................................... | | 6,536 |
| Debtors........................................ | | 4,864 |
| | | 27,330 |
| *Less: Liabilities* | | |
| Bank overdraft................................. | 2,492 | |
| Creditors: Goods............................... | 4,236 | |
| Expenses............................. | 168 | 6,896 |
| Capital........................................ | | 20,434 |

(b) Calculation of profit.

|  | £ |
|---|---|
| Closing capital................................ | 20,434 |
| Less: Opening capital........................... | 23,496 |
| Reduction in capital............................ | (3,062) |
| Add: Drawings................................. | 10,800 |
| Profit......................................... | 7,738 |

*Note:* Drawings have exceeded profit by £3,062 (£10,800 − £7,738) and capital has therefore fallen by this amount.

(c)                      *Balance Sheet at 31 Dec. 19X8*

| | £ | £ |
|---|---|---|
| Fixed assets. . . . . . . . . . . . . . . . . . . . . . . . . . . . . . . . . . . . . . . . | | 15,930 |
| *Current Assets:* | | |
| Stock. . . . . . . . . . . . . . . . . . . . . . . . . . . . . . . . . . . . . . . . . . | 6,536 | |
| Debtors. . . . . . . . . . . . . . . . . . . . . . . . . . . . . . . . . . . . . . . . | 4,864 | |
| | 11,400 | |
| *Less: Current Liabilities* | | |
| Creditors: Goods. . . . . . . . . . . . . . . . . . . . . . . . . . . . . . . | 4,236 | |
| Expenses. . . . . . . . . . . . . . . . . . . . . . . . . . . | 168 | |
| Bank overdraft. . . . . . . . . . . . . . . . . . . . . . . . . . . . . . . . . . | 2,492 | |
| | 6,896 | |
| Working capital. . . . . . . . . . . . . . . . . . . . . . . . . . . . . . . . . . | | 4,504 |
| | | 20,434 |
| Financed by: | | |
| Opening capital. . . . . . . . . . . . . . . . . . . . . . . . . . . . . . . . . | | 23,496 |
| Add: Profit. . . . . . . . . . . . . . . . . . . . . . . . . . . . . . . . . . . . . | | 7,738 |
| | | 31,234 |
| Less: Drawings. . . . . . . . . . . . . . . . . . . . . . . . . . . . . . . . . . | | 10,800 |
| Closing capital. . . . . . . . . . . . . . . . . . . . . . . . . . . . . . . . . | | 20,434 |

# Solution 2.4

(a)  Calculation of capital

*Statement of Assets, Liabilities and Capital at 31 December*

| | | 19X3 | | 19X4 |
|---|---|---|---|---|
| | £ | £ | £ | £ |
| *Gross Assets* | | | | |
| Fixed assets. . . . . . . . . . . . . . . . . . . | | 9,000 | | 12,144(1) |
| Stocks. . . . . . . . . . . . . . . . . . . . . . . | | 2,650 | | 3,710 |
| Trade debtors. . . . . . . . . . . . . . . . . | | 5,200 | | 5,600 |
| Bank balance. . . . . . . . . . . . . . . . . | | — | | 50 |
| | | 16,850 | | 21,504 |
| *Less: Liabilities* | | | | |
| Trade creditors. . . . . . . . . . . . . . . . | 1,710 | | 1,210 | |
| Bank overdraft. . . . . . . . . . . . . . . . | 360 | 2,070 | — | 1,210 |
| Capital. . . . . . . . . . . . . . . . . . . . . . | | 14,780 | | 20,294 |

£

Calculation of profit

| | £ |
|---|---|
| Closing capital................ | 20,294 |
| Less: Opening capital.......... | 14,780 |
| Increase in capital............. | 5,514 |
| Add: Drawings................. | 8,100(2) |
| Less: Capital introduced........ | (600) |
| Profit ....................... | 13,014 |

Workings:
(1) £9,000 + £3,144 = £12,144
(2) (£150 × 52) + £300 = £8,100

(b)                     *Balance Sheet at 31 Dec. 19X4*

| | £ | £ | | £ | £ |
|---|---|---|---|---|---|
| Opening capital...... | | 14,780 | Fixed assets......... | | 12,144 |
| Add: Net Profit...... | | 13,014 | | | |
| Additional capital | | | | | |
| investment...... | | 600 | | | |
| | | 28,394 | *Current Assets:* | | |
| | | | Stocks ............. | 3,710 | |
| Less: Drawings-cash.. | 7,800 | | Trade debtors....... | 5,600 | |
| -stock. | 300 | 8,100 | Bank balance........ | 50 | 9,360 |
| | | 20,294 | | | |
| *Current Liabilities* | | | | | |
| Trade creditors...... | | 1,210 | | | |
| | | 21,504 | | | 21,504 |

## Solution 3.1

(a)                     *Balance Sheet at 31 Dec. 19X4*

| | £ | | £ | £ |
|---|---|---|---|---|
| Capital (A – L) | 3,190 | *Fixed Assets:* | | |
| *Current Liabilities* | | Furniture and fittings at | | |
| Trade creditors.......... | 1,630 | cost less depreciation...... | | 400 |
| | | *Current Assets:* | | |
| | | Stock.................. | 2,040 | |
| | | Debtors................ | 1,900 | |
| | | Bank .................. | 480 | 4,420 |
| | 4,820 | | | 4,820 |

(b) *Workings*: Convert cash flows to flows of goods.

|  |  | £ |
|---|---|---|
| (1) Purchases: Payments to suppliers | | 24,800 |
| Less: Opening creditors | | (1,630) |
| Add: Closing creditors | | 1,930 |
| | | 25,100 |
| (2) Sales: Received from debtors | | 31,560 |
| Less: Opening debtors | | (1,900) |
| Add: Closing debtors | | 2,344 |
| | | 32,004 |

*Trading and Profit and Loss Account of Stoll for 19X5*

| | £ | £ |
|---|---|---|
| Sales | | 32,004(2) |
| Less: Purchases | 25,100(1) | |
| Add: Opening stock | 2,040 | |
| Less: Closing stock | (1,848) | |
| Cost of goods sold | | 25,292 |
| Gross profit | | 6,712 |
| Less: General expenses | 2,524 | |
| Rent | 300 | |
| Depreciation | 40 | 2,864 |
| Net profit | | 3,848 |

*Balance Sheet of Stoll at 31 Dec. 19X5*

|  | £ | £ |
|---|---|---|
| *Fixed Assets* |  |  |
| Furniture at cost less depreciation................... |  | 360 |
| *Current Assets*................................. | 1,848 |  |
| Stock......................................... | 2,344 |  |
| Bank......................................... | 816 |  |
|  | 5,008 |  |
| *Less: Current Liabilities* |  |  |
| Trade creditors................................ | 1,930 |  |
| Working capital................................ |  | 3,078 |
|  |  | 3,438 |
| Financed by: |  |  |
| Opening capital................................ |  | 3,190 |
| Add: Net profit................................ |  | 3,848 |
| Less: Drawings................................ |  | (3,600) |
|  |  | 3,438 |

## Solution 3.2

*Workings*

| (1) *Sales* | £ |
|---|---|
| Proceeds from: credit sales..... | 7,560 |
| cash sales...... | 32,100 |
|  | 39,660 |
| Less: Opening debtors......... | (1,060) |
| Add: Closing debtors.......... | 1,840 |
|  | 40,440 |

| (2) *Purchases* |  |
|---|---|
| Payments to suppliers.......... | 20,850 |
| Less: Opening creditors........ | (850) |
| Add: Closing creditors......... | 1,140 |
|  | 21,140 |

| (3) *General expenses* |  |
|---|---|
| Payments.................... | 7,560 |
| Add: Opening prepayments..... | 400 |
| Less: Opening accruals......... | (260) |
| Less: Closing prepayments..... | (520) |
| Add: Closing accruals......... | 310 |
|  | 7,490 |

| (4) *Vehicles* | £ |
|---|---|
| Balance at 1 January........... | 10,000 |
| Add: Purchases............... | 4,000 |
|  | 14,000 |

| (5) *Vehicles: Accum. dep.* |  |
|---|---|
| Balance at 1 January........... | 2,000 |
| Add: Charge for year.......... | 2,800* |
|  | 4,800 |

| (6) *Bank overdraft* |  |
|---|---|
| Opening balance.............. | 2,030 |
| Add: Payments............... | 44,910 |
| Less: Receipts............... | (42,310) |
|  | 4,630 |

*£14,000 (cost of vehicles owned at year end) × 20% = £2,800

*Trading and Profit and Loss Account for 19X1*

|  | £ | £ |
|---|---|---|
| Sales . . . . . . . . . . . . . . . . . . . . . . . . . . . . . . . . . . . . . . . . . . . . |  | 40,440(1) |
| Less: Purchases. . . . . . . . . . . . . . . . . . . . . . . . . . . . . . . | 21,140(2) |  |
| Add: Opening stock . . . . . . . . . . . . . . . . . . . . . . . . | 3,750 |  |
| Less: Closing stock . . . . . . . . . . . . . . . . . . . . . . . . | (4,600) |  |
| Cost of goods sold . . . . . . . . . . . . . . . . . . . . . . . . . . |  | 20,290 |
| Gross profit . . . . . . . . . . . . . . . . . . . . . . . . . . . . . . . . . . . . |  | 20,150 |
| Add: Bank interest received . . . . . . . . . . . . . . . . . . . . . . . |  | 50 |
|  |  | 20,200 |
| Less: General expenses . . . . . . . . . . . . . . . . . . . . . . . . . . | 7,490(3) |  |
| Depreciation . . . . . . . . . . . . . . . . . . . . . . . . . . . . . . | 2,800 |  |
| Loan interest (£2,000 × 15%) . . . . . . . . . . . . . . . . . | 300 | 10,590 |
| Net profit . . . . . . . . . . . . . . . . . . . . . . . . . . . . . . . . . . . . . |  | 9,610 |

*Balance Sheet at 31 December 19X1*

|  | £ | £ |
|---|---|---|
| *Fixed Assets.* Motor vehicles at cost . . . . . . . . . . . . . . . . . |  | 14,000(4) |
| Less: Accumulated depreciation . . . . . . . . . |  | 4,800(5) |
|  |  | 9,200 |
| *Current Assets* |  |  |
| Stock . . . . . . . . . . . . . . . . . . . . . . . . . . . . . . . . . . . . . . . | 4,600 |  |
| Debtors . . . . . . . . . . . . . . . . . . . . . . . . . . . . . . . . . . . . . | 1,840 |  |
| Bank deposit account (£650 + £50) . . . . . . . . . . . . . . . | 700 |  |
| Prepaid expenses . . . . . . . . . . . . . . . . . . . . . . . . . . . . . | 520 |  |
|  | 7,660 |  |
| *Less: Current Liabilities* |  |  |
| Creditors . . . . . . . . . . . . . . . . . . . . . . . . . . . . . . . . . . . . | 1,140 |  |
| Loan interest . . . . . . . . . . . . . . . . . . . . . . . . . . . . . . . . | 300 |  |
| Accruals . . . . . . . . . . . . . . . . . . . . . . . . . . . . . . . . . . . . | 310 |  |
| Bank overdraft . . . . . . . . . . . . . . . . . . . . . . . . . . . . . . . | 4,630(6) |  |
|  | 6,380 |  |
| Working capital . . . . . . . . . . . . . . . . . . . . . . . . . . . . . . |  | 1,280 |
|  |  | 10,480 |

Financed by:

| | |
|---|---:|
| Opening capital................................. | 8,720 |
| Add: Capital injection-legacy...................... | 2,650 |
| Net profit................................ | 9,610 |
| Less: Drawings.................................. | (12,500) |
| | 8,480 |
| Loan at 15%.................................... | 2,000 |
| | 10,480 |

## Solution 3.3

(a)

*Balance Sheet of Stondon at 31 Dec. 19X3*

| | £ | £ | | £ | £ |
|---|---:|---:|---|---:|---:|
| Capital (A − L)...... | | 9,947 | *Fixed Assets* | | |
| *Current Liabilities* | | | Furniture and | | |
| Trade creditors...... | 3,586 | | fittings............. | | 800 |
| Bank overdraft...... | 782 | 4,368 | Motor van at cost | | |
| | | | less depreciation..... | | 2,500 |
| | | | | | 3,300 |
| | | | *Current Assets*: | | |
| | | | Stock.............. | 6,891 | |
| | | | Trade debtors....... | 4,124 | 11,015 |
| | | 14,315 | | | 14,315 |

(b)

| | £ |
|---|---:|
| Capital at 31 December 19X3............................. | 9,947 |
| Less: Capital at 31 December 19X2......................... | 7,940 |
| Increase in capital....................................... | 2,007 |
| Add: Drawings........................................... | 12,840 |
| | 14,847 |
| Less: Capital introduced.................................. | 4,200 |
| Net profit for 19X3...................................... | 10,647 |

*Trading and Profit and Loss Account for 19X3*

|  | £ | £ |
|---|---|---|
| Sales (25,067 × 4)......................... |  | 100,268(4) |
| Less: Purchases (by difference).............. | 76,708 (8) |  |
|        Add: Opening stock................... | 5,384 (7) |  |
|        Less: Closing stock.................... | (6,891)(6) |  |
| Cost of goods sold.................... |  | 75,201(5) |
| Gross profit............................. |  | 25,067(3) |
| Less: Running expenses..................... |  | 14,420(2) |
| Net profit............................... |  | 10,647(1) |

*Note:* The numbers, in brackets, indicate the order in which the trading and profit and loss account is reconstructed.

## Solution 3.4

*Workings:*

(1)                 *Balance Sheet at 1 January 19X8*

|  | £ |  | £ |
|---|---|---|---|
| Accumulated fund (A − L).... | 96,840 | Furniture.................. | 30,400 |
| Creditors: supplies........... | 4,080 | Investments................ | 49,200 |
|          expenses.......... | 160 | Stocks..................... | 8,200 |
|  |  | Bank...................... | 13,280 |
|  | 101,080 |  | 101,080 |

(2) *Purchases*

|  | £ |
|---|---|
| Payments for purchases..................................... | 80,760 |
| Less: Opening creditors.................................... | (4,080) |
| Add: Closing creditors..................................... | 4,568 |
|  | 81,248 |

(3) *General expenses*

|  | £ |
|---|---|
| Payments for general expenses............................. | 5,360 |
| Less: Opening creditors.................................... | (160) |
| Add: Closing creditors..................................... | 248 |
|  | 5,448 |

(4) *Depreciation*: £30,400 × 10% = £3,040

(a)                          *Bar Trading Account for 19X8*

|  | £ |  | £ |
|---|---|---|---|
| Opening stock.............. | 8,200 | Sales...................... | 107,600 |
| Add: Purchases............. | 81,248(2) |  |  |
| Less: Closing stock.......... | (11,936) |  |  |
| Cost of goods sold........... | 77,512 |  |  |
| Gross profit................ | 30,088 |  |  |
|  | 107,600 |  | 107,600 |

(b)                    *Income and Expenditure Account for 19X8*

|  | £ |  | £ |
|---|---|---|---|
| Rent...................... | 2,800 | Bar profit.................. | 30,088 |
| Rates..................... | 2,000 | Subscriptions............... | 12,400 |
| General expenses............ | 5,448(3) | Interest.................... | 4,160 |
| Depreciation ............... | 3,040(4) |  |  |
| Salaries.................... | 16,840 |  |  |
| Surplus.................... | 16,520 |  |  |
|  | 46,648 |  | 46,648 |

(c)                       *Balance Sheet at 31 December 19X8*

| | £ | £ | | £ | £ |
|---|---|---|---|---|---|
| Accumulated fund... | | 96,840(1) | *Fixed Assets* | | |
| Add: Surplus....... | | 16,520 | Furniture........... | | 30,400 |
| | | | Less: Depreciation... | | 3,040 |
| | | 113,360 | | | 27,360 |
| *Current Liabilities* | | | | | |
| Creditors: supplies... | 4,568 | | *Current Assets* | | |
| expenses.. | 248 | | Investments........ | 75,200 | |
| | | 4,816 | Stocks ............. | 11,936 | |
| | | | Bank .............. | 3,680 | |
| | | | | | 90,816 |
| | | 118,176 | | | 118,176 |

## Solution 3.5

*Workings:*

| (1) *Accumulated fund* | £ |
|---|---|
| Assets | |
| Clubhouse . . . . . . . . . . . . . . . . | 38,000 |
| Tennis courts. . . . . . . . . . . . . : . . | 24,000 |
| Furniture and equipment. . . . . | 5,000 |
| Bar stocks. . . . . . . . . . . . . . . . | 4,400 |
| Bank balance. . . . . . . . . . . . . . | 1,500 |
| | 72,900 |
| Less: Liabilities | |
| Creditors £3,720 + £500. . . . . . | 4,220 |
| | 68,680 |

| (2)*Tennis section*. . . . . . . . . . . | |
|---|---|
| Tournament fees. . . . . . . . . . . | 240 |
| 10 year subscriptions. . . . . . . . | 1,200* |
| Other subscriptions. . . . . . . . . | 6,400 |
| Court fees. . . . . . . . . . . . . . . . | 5,700 |
| | 13,540 |

| Less: Repairs | £2,520 | |
|---|---|---|
| Prizes | 140 | |
| Depreciation | 4,800** . . | 7,460 |
| Surplus. . . . . . . . . . . . . . . . . . | | 6,080 |

| (3) *Rugby secton* | | £ |
|---|---|---|
| Subscriptions. . . . . . . . . . . . . . | | 1,300 |
| Collections. . . . . . . . . . . . . . : . . | | 180 |
| | | 1,480 |
| Less: Kit. . . . . . . . . . . | £900 | |
| Rental. . . . . . . . . | £400 | 1,300 |
| Surplus. . . . . . . . . . . . . . . . . . | | 180 |

| (4) *Bar purchases* | |
|---|---|
| Payments. . . . . . . . . . . . . . . . . | 48,400 |
| Less: Opening creditors. . . . . . . | (3,720) |
| Add: Closing creditors. . . . . . . | 4,300 |
| | 48,980 |

| (5) *General expenses* | |
|---|---|
| Payments. . . . . . . . . . . . . . . . . | 17,300 |
| Less: Opening creditors. . . . . . . | (500) |
| Add: Closing creditors. . . . . . . | 640 |
| | 17,440 |

* One tenth of the 10 year tennis membership subscriptions is credited to the income and expenditure account; the remainder is reported in the balance sheet as subscriptions received in advance. The ten year subscription might alternatively have been credited, in full, direct to the accumulated fund.

** (£40,000 × 10%) + (£16,000 × 10% × 0.5)

(a)   *Bar Trading Account and General Income and Expenditure Account for 19X1*

| | £ | | £ |
|---|---|---|---|
| Opening stock............... | 4,400 | Sales...................... | 69,660 |
| Purchases.................. | 48,980(4) | | |
| Closing stock............... | (5,280) | | |
| | | | |
| Cost of goods sold........... | 48,100 | | |
| Wages..................... | 7,800 | | |
| | 55,900 | | |
| Bar profit.................. | 13,760 | | |
| | 69,660 | | 69,660 |
| | | | |
| General expenses............ | 17,440(5) | Bar profit.................. | 13,760 |
| Rates...................... | 1,100 | Tennis surplus.............. | 6,080(2) |
| Depreciation of furniture..... | 500 | Rugby surplus.............. | 180(3) |
| | 19,040 | | |
| Surplus.................... | 980 | | |
| | 20,020 | | 20,020 |

(b)                    *Balance Sheet at 31 December 19X1*

| | £ | | £ | £ |
|---|---|---|---|---|
| Accumulated fund at 1 Jan.... | 68,680(1) | *Fixed Assets* | | |
| Add: Surplus.............. | 980 | Clubhouse at cost... | | 38,000 |
| | 69,660 | Tennis courts at cost | | |
| Subscriptions in advance...... | 10,800 | less depreciation... | | 35,200 |
| *Current Liabilities* | | Furniture and equip- | | |
| | | ment at book | | |
| Creditors: Bar purchases...... | 4,300 | value........... | | 4,500 |
| General expenses... | 640 | | | 77,700 |
| | | *Current Assets* | | |
| | | Bar stocks......... | 5,280 | |
| | | Bank balance...... | 2,420 | 7,700 |
| | 85,400 | | | 85,400 |

## Solution 4.1

*Cash Account*

| January | | £ | January | | £ |
|---|---|---|---|---|---|
| 1 | Capital introduced....... | 5,000 | 2 | Van.................... | 4,000 |
| 1-31 | Cash Sales.............. | 2,250 | 3 | Rent ................... | 100 |
| 1-31 | Debtors ................ | 450 | 1-31 | Creditors .............. | 2,500 |
| | | | 15 | Drawings .............. | 110 |
| | | | 30 | Insurance.............. | 120 |
| | | | 31 | Balance c/d............. | 870 |
| | | 7,700 | | | 7,700 |
| February | | | | | |
| 1 | Balance b/d............. | 870 | | | |

## Solution 4.2

(i)

*Cash Account*

| 19X1 | | £ | 19X1 | | £ |
|---|---|---|---|---|---|
| 30 June | Balance b/d........... | 1,296 | 30 June | Rent................. | 500 |
| | Debtor................ | 160 | | Returned cheque...... | 200* |
| | | | | Bank charges......... | 175 |
| | | | | Balance c/d......... | 581 |
| | | 1,456 | | | 1,456 |
| | Balance b/d......... | 581 | | | |

\* This entry cancels the previously recorded receipt; the amount now appears on both sides of the account. The company should take steps to recover the amount due.

(ii)

*Bank reconciliation at 30 June 19X1*

| | | | £ |
|---|---|---|---|
| | | Balance per cash book................... | 581 |
| | Add: | Cheques not yet presented............... | 682 |
| | Less: | Lodgements not yet recorded............. | (1,350) |
| | | Balance per bank statement............. | (87) |

## Solution 4.3

### Double Column Cash Book

| | Cash £ | Bank £ | | Cash £ | Bank £ |
|---|---|---|---|---|---|
| Capital........... | | 10,000 | Premises.......... | | 8,000 |
| Loan.............. | 5,000 | | Equipment........ | | 2,750 |
| Cash.............. | | 750 | Van.............. | 4,000 | |
| Sales.............. | 5,500 | | Bank.............. | | 750 |
| Cash.............. | | 4,250 | Purchases......... | 1,000 | 3,000 |
| | | | Wages............ | 100 | |
| | | | Drawings......... | 150 | |
| | | | Rates............ | | 250 |
| | | | Bank.............. | 4,250 | |
| | | | Balance c/d....... | 250 | 1,000 |
| | 10,500 | 15,000 | | 10,500 | 15,000 |
| Balance b/d....... | 250 | 1,000 | | | |

## Solution 4.4

### Analysed Cash Book

| Day | Detail | Total £ | Sales £ | Sundry £ | Day | Detail | Total £ | Purchases £ | Wages £ | Sundry £ |
|---|---|---|---|---|---|---|---|---|---|---|
| 1 | Sales....... | 1,790 | 1,790 | | 1 | Balance b/d | 6,510 | | | |
| 2 | Sales....... | 2,190 | 2,190 | | 1 | Purchases... | 2,250 | 2,250 | | |
| 3 | Sales....... | 1,250 | 1,250 | | 2 | Wages...... | 380 | | 380 | |
| | Sale of Fixed | | | | 4 | Interest..... | 400 | | | 400 |
| | Asset..... | 1,000 | | 1,000 | 5 | Purchases... | 3,140 | 3,140 | | |
| 4 | Sales....... | 3,720 | 3,720 | | 6 | Wages...... | 450 | | 450 | |
| 5 | Sales....... | 1,540 | 1,540 | | 6 | Balance c/d | 1,070 | | | |
| 6 | Sales....... | 2,710 | 2,710 | | | | | | | |
| | | 14,200 | 13,200 | 1,000 | | | 14,200 | 5,390 | 830 | 400 |
| 6 | Balance b/d | 1,070 | | | | | | | | |

*Note* that, to agree the cross-cast of the payments columns, the opening and closing balances have to be subtracted from the total column as they do not have a corresponding entry in the analysis columns.

## Solution 4.5

(a)

*Petty Cash Account*

| Date | Detail | £ | Date | Voucher No. | Total £ | Stationery £ | Post £ | Travel £ |
|------|--------|---|------|-------------|---------|--------------|--------|----------|
| Dec | | | Dec | | | | | |
| 1 | Balance b/d.... | 14 | 2 | 37 | 5 | 5 | | |
| | Bank.......... | 86 | 2 | 38 | 7 | | 7 | |
| | | | 3 | 39 | 22 | | | 22 |
| | | | 4 | 40 | 19 | 19 | | |
| | | | 5 | 41 | 13 | | | 13 |
| | | | 5 | 42 | 5 | | 5 | |
| | | | 6 | 43 | 12 | | | 12 |
| | | | | | 83 | 24 | 12 | 47 |
| | | | | Balance | 17 | | | |
| | | 100 | | | 100 | | | |

(b)   The value of vouchers 37 to 43 is £83. Therefore £83 has to be drawn from the bank to make the float up to £100 when added to the cash in hand of £17.

## Solution 4.6

*Sales Day Book*

| Day | Detail | Total £ | Typewriters £ | Stationery £ | Repairs £ |
|-----|--------|---------|---------------|--------------|-----------|
| 1 | Gum Ltd...... | 375 | 300 | 75 | |
| | Glue Ltd...... | 100 | | | 100 |
| 2 | Stick Ltd...... | 70 | | 70 | |
| 3 | Fast Ltd....... | 450 | 450 | | |
| | Stick Ltd...... | 50 | | | 50 |
| | | 1,045 | 750 | 145 | 150 |

## Solution 5.1

|  | Debit £ | Credit £ |
|---|---|---|
| Capital.............................................. |  | 8,500 |
| Current liabilities.................................... |  | 4,600 |
| Plant and machinery................................. | 4,500 |  |
| Stock............................................... | 2,700 |  |
| Debtors............................................. | 5,200 |  |
| Cash............................................... | 700 |  |
|  | 13,100 | 13,100 |

## Solution 5.2

### Sales Day Book (SDB)

| Customer | £ |
|---|---|
| Vision............................................... | 7,000 |
| Sister............................................... | 4,000 |
| Batty............................................... | 2,700 |
| Flat................................................. | 200 |
| Broke............................................... | 300 |
|  | 14,200 |

### Purchases Day Book (PDB)

| Supplier | Total £ | Goods for Resale £ | Motor Expenses £ | Office Expenses £ |
|---|---|---|---|---|
| Tele.............. | 3,000 | 3,000 |  |  |
| Trany............ | 2,000 | 2,000 |  |  |
| Valve............ | 2,400 | 2,400 |  |  |
| Garage........... | 100 |  | 100 |  |
| Paper............ | 50 |  |  | 50 |
|  | 7,550 | 7,400 | 100 | 50 |

### Returns Inwards Day Book (RIDB)

| Customer | £ |
|---|---|
| Vision................................................. | 300 |
| Batty................................................. | 200 |
|  | 500 |

### Returns Outwards Day Book (RODB)

| Supplier | £ |
|---|---|
| Trany................................................... | 100 |
| Valve................................................... | 150 |
| | 250 |

### Cash Book (CB) Receipts (debit)

| Detail | Discount £ | Cash £ | Debtors £ | Sundry £ |
|---|---|---|---|---|
| Balance b/d....... | | 700 | | |
| Vision............ | 50 | 6,350 | 6,350 | |
| Sister............ | 40 | 3,500 | 3,500 | |
| Batty............. | 25 | 2,600 | 2,600 | |
| Scrap............. | | 100 | | 100 |
| | 115 | 13,250 | 12,450 | 100 |

### Cash Book (CB) Payments (credit)

| Detail | Discount £ | Cash £ | Creditors £ | Wages £ | Motor Expenses £ | Sundry £ |
|---|---|---|---|---|---|---|
| Tele........... | 55 | 2,950 | 2,950 | | | |
| Trany......... | 35 | 1,950 | 1,950 | | | |
| Valve.......... | 20 | 2,200 | 2,200 | | | |
| Plantmax...... | | 1,000 | | | | 1,000 |
| Wages........ | | 1,500 | | 1,500 | | |
| Accom ........ | | 600 | | | | 600 |
| Supplies ....... | | 250 | | | | 250 |
| Garage ........ | | 300 | | | 300 | |
| | 110 | 10,750 | 7,100 | 1,500 | 300 | 1,850 |
| Balance c/d.... | | 2,500 | | | | |
| | | 13,250 | | | | |

# Solution 5.3

### Capital

| | £ | | £ |
|---|---|---|---|
| | | Journal................. | 8,500 |

### Purchase Ledger Control Account

| | | £ | | | £ |
|---|---|---|---|---|---|
| January | RODB............ | 250 | January | Journal......... | 4,600 |
| | CB Discounts...... | 110 | | PDB ........... | 7,550 |
| | CB Cash.......... | 7,100 | | | |
| | Balance c/d....... | 4,690 | | | |
| | | 12,150 | | | 12,150 |

### Plant and Machinery

| | | £ | | | £ |
|---|---|---|---|---|---|
| January | Journal........... | 4,500 | January | Balance c/d..... | 5,500 |
| | CB............... | 1,000 | | | |
| | | 5,500 | | | 5,500 |

### Stock

| | | £ | | £ |
|---|---|---|---|---|
| January | Journal........... | 2,700 | | |

### Sales Ledger Control Account

| | | £ | | | £ |
|---|---|---|---|---|---|
| January | Journal........ | 5,200 | January | RIDB........ | 500 |
| | SDB........... | 14,200 | | CB Discounts.. | 115 |
| | | | | CB Cash...... | 12,450 |
| | | | | Balance c/d... | 6,335 |
| | | 19,400 | | | 19,400 |

### Sales

| | | £ | | | £ |
|---|---|---|---|---|---|
| January | RIDB . . . . . . . . | 500 | January | SDB . . . | 14,200 |
| | Balance c/d . . . . | 13,700 | | | |
| | | 14,200 | | | 14,200 |

### Purchases

| | | £ | | | £ |
|---|---|---|---|---|---|
| January | PDB . . . . . . . . . . . . | 7,400 | January | RODB . . . . . . . . | 250 |
| | | | | Balance c/d . . . | 7,150 |
| | | 7,400 | | | 7,400 |

### Motor Expenses

| | | £ | | | £ |
|---|---|---|---|---|---|
| January | PDB . . . . . . . . . . . . | 100 | January | Balance c/d . . . . | 400 |
| | CB . . . . . . . . . . . . . . | 300 | | | |
| | | 400 | | | 400 |

### Office Expenses

| | | £ | | | £ |
|---|---|---|---|---|---|
| January | PDB . . . . . . . . . . . . | 50 | January | Balance c/d . . | 300 |
| | CB . . . . . . . . . . . . . . | 250 | | | |
| | | 300 | | | 300 |

### Discounts Allowed

| | | £ | | £ |
|---|---|---|---|---|
| January | CB . . . . . . . . . . . . . . | 115 | | |

### Discounts Received

|  | £ |  |  | £ |
|---|---|---|---|---|
|  |  | January | CB.......... | 110 |

### Sale of Fixed Assets

|  |  | £ |  | £ |
|---|---|---|---|---|
| January | CB.............. | 100 |  |  |

### Wages

|  |  | £ |  | £ |
|---|---|---|---|---|
| January | CB.............. | 1,500 |  |  |

### Rent

|  |  | £ |  | £ |
|---|---|---|---|---|
| January | CB.............. | 600 |  |  |

## Solution 5.4

### Sales Ledger

#### Vision

|  |  | £ |  |  | £ |
|---|---|---|---|---|---|
| January | Balance b/d....... | 2,500 | January | RIDB .......... | 300 |
|  | SDB.............. | 7,000 |  | CB Discounts.... | 50 |
|  |  |  |  | CB Cash........ | 6,350 |
|  |  |  |  | Balance c/d..... | 2,800 |
|  |  | 9,500 |  |  | 9,500 |

#### Sister

|  |  | £ |  |  | £ |
|---|---|---|---|---|---|
| January | Balance b/d....... | 1,500 | January | CB Discounts... | 40 |
|  | SDB.............. | 4,000 |  | CB Cash........ | 3,500 |
|  |  |  |  | Balance c/d..... | 1,960 |
|  |  | 5,500 |  |  | 5,500 |

## Batty

| January | | £ | January | | £ |
|---|---|---|---|---|---|
| | Balance b/d...... | 1,200 | | RIDB....... | 200 |
| | SDB.............. | 2,700 | | CB Discounts. | 25 |
| | | | | CB Cash..... | 2,600 |
| | | | | Balance c/d.. | 1,075 |
| | | 3,900 | | | 3,900 |

## Flat

| January | | £ | | | £ |
|---|---|---|---|---|---|
| | SDB.............. | 200 | | | |

## Broke

| January | | £ | | | £ |
|---|---|---|---|---|---|
| | SDB.............. | 300 | | | |

### *Purchases Ledger*

## Tele

| January | | £ | January | | £ |
|---|---|---|---|---|---|
| | CB Discounts...... | 55 | | Balance b/d...... | 2,300 |
| | CB Cash.......... | 2,950 | | PDB ........... | 3,000 |
| | Balance c/d....... | 2,295 | | | |
| | | 5,300 | | | 5,300 |

## Trany

| January | | £ | January | | £ |
|---|---|---|---|---|---|
| | RODB............ | 100 | | Balance b/d.. | 1,000 |
| | CB Discount....... | 35 | | PDB ........ | 2,000 |
| | CB Cash.......... | 1,950 | | | |
| | Balance c/d....... | 915 | | | |
| | | 3,000 | | | 3,000 |

Valve

| | | £ | | | £ |
|---|---|---|---|---|---|
| January | RODB............ | 150 | January | Balance c/d... | 1,300 |
| | CB Discount....... | 20 | | PDB ......... | 2,400 |
| | CB Cash.......... | 2,200 | | | |
| | Balance c/d....... | 1,330 | | | |
| | | 3,700 | | | 3,700 |

Garage

| | £ | | | £ |
|---|---|---|---|---|
| | | January | PDB ........ | 100 |

Paper

| | £ | | | £ |
|---|---|---|---|---|
| | | January | PDB ........ | 50 |

# Solution 5.5

*Sales Ledger*

| | £ |
|---|---|
| Vision................................................... | 2,800 |
| Sister.................................................... | 1,960 |
| Batty.................................................... | 1,075 |
| Flat...................................................... | 200 |
| Broke.................................................... | 300 |
| As per Control Account................................... | 6,335 |

*Purchase Ledger*

| | £ |
|---|---|
| Tele..................................................... | 2,295 |
| Trany.................................................... | 915 |
| Valve.................................................... | 1,330 |
| Garage................................................... | 100 |
| Paper.................................................... | 50 |
| As per Control Account................................... | 4,690 |

## Solution 5.6

|  | Debit £ | Credit £ |
|---|---|---|
| Cash | 2,500 | |
| Capital | | 8,500 |
| Creditors | | 4,690 |
| Plant and machinery | 5,500 | |
| Stock | 2,700 | |
| Debtors | 6,335 | |
| Sales | | 13,700 |
| Purchases | 7,150 | |
| Motor expenses | 400 | |
| Office expenses | 300 | |
| Discounts allowed | 115 | |
| Discounts received | | 110 |
| Wages | 1,500 | |
| Rent | 600 | |
| Sale of fixed asset | | 100 |
| | 27,100 | 27,100 |

## Solution 5.7

(a)

(i)  Real accounts represent assets, or items of property other than claims against external persons. Balances on real accounts are, in normal circumstances, assets, for example, when motor vehicles, furniture or plant and machinery are purchased, real accounts under those headings are debited.

(ii)  Personal accounts are those which show the relationship of the business with other persons or firms. A debit balance on a personal account is an asset and represents the right to receive money in the future. A credit balance is a liability.

(iii)  Nominal accounts are used to record items of income and expense. Debit balances are expenses and credit balances are income.

(b)    (i)    Fixed asset at cost £10,000 — Real Account
        (ii)   Wages £700 — Nominal Account
        (iii)  Discounts received £1,400 — Nominal Account
        (iv)  Balance due from Double Ltd £1,500 — Personal Account

## Solution 5.8

The accountant uses the trial balance:
- (a) To check the accuracy of the entries in the ledger, but note that some of the errors are not revealed.
- (b) As the basis for preparing the trading and profit and loss accounts and balance sheet.

## Solution 5.9

*Sales Ledger Control Account*

| 19X4 | | £ | 19X4 | | £ |
|---|---|---|---|---|---|
| 1 October | Balance b/d.... | 102,300 | 1 October | Balance b/d.... | 340 |
| | Sales.......... | 630,800 | | Cash.......... | 498,660 |
| | | | | Returns........ | 2,700 |
| | | | | Discounts...... | 11,790 |
| | | | | Purchase Ledger | |
| | | | | Contras........ | 5,200 |
| | | | | Bad debts...... | 3,950 |
| 19X5 | | | 19X5 | | |
| 30 September | Balance c/d.... | 510 | 30 September | Balance c/d.... | 210,970 |
| | | 733,610 | | | 733,610 |

*Note:* Items 4, 6 and 8 do not belong in the Sales Ledger Control Account.

## Solution 5.10

(i)

*Error Co. Ltd. — Journal*

| | | Dr | Cr |
|---|---|---|---|
| | | £ | £ |
| (a) | Suspense Account.............................. | 1,000 | |
| | Creditors Control Account........................ | | 1,000 |

Sum due to Zed omitted from Control Account

| | | Dr | Cr |
|---|---|---|---|
| | | £ | £ |
| (b) | Debtors Control Account........................ | 2,400 | |
| | Sales Account.................................. | | 2,400 |

Correction of undercast sales day book

| | | | |
|---|---|---|---|
| (c) | Discounts Allowed Account....................... | 4,890 | |
| | Suspense Account.............................. | | 4,890 |

Discounts for June not posted to Nominal Ledger

(d)    Purchases Account.............................    24,100
       Accruals.........................................            24,100

---

Invoice for goods in stock not invoiced at 30 June 19X2

---

(e)    Sales Account...................................    1,920
       Debtors Control Account..........................            1,920

---

Correction of wrong posting

---

(ii)    *Effect on Profit for Year*

|  |  | £ |
|---|---|---:|
| Decreases in Profit: | | |
| Discounts allowed (c)................ | | 4,890 |
| Purchases omitted (d)................ | | 24,100 |
| Cash posted to sales account in error (e) | | 1,920 |
| | | 30,910 |
| Increase in Profit: | | |
| Undercast sales day book (b)........... | | 2,400 |
| Reduction in Profit...................... | | 28,510 |

(iii)    *Calculation of Suspense Account Balance*

Suspense Account

| | £ | | £ |
|---|---:|---|---:|
| Creditors Control Account (a).............. | 1,000 | Discounts Allowed (c)...... | 4,890 |
| Original balance*.......... | 3,890 | | |
| | 4,890 | | 4,890 |

\* Balancing figure.

## Solution 6.1

(a)

| Item | Location | Comment |
|------|----------|---------|
| Sales | Trading Account | Revenue |
| Returns Inwards | Trading Account | Reduces the value of sales |
| Stock 1 January | Trading Account | Charged against sales |
| Returns outwards | Trading Account | Reduces purchases |
| Purchaes | Trading Account | Expense |
| Capital | Balance Sheet | Liability to ownership |
| Cash at bank | Balance Sheet | Asset |
| Debtors | Balance Sheet | Asset |
| Creditors | Balance Sheet | Liability |
| Premises | Balance Sheet | Asset |
| Wages | Profit and Loss Account | Expense |
| Discounts received | Profit and Loss Account | Sundry revenue |
| Rent and rates | Profit and Loss Account | Expense |
| Delivery costs | Profit and Loss Account | Expense |
| Cash withdrawn | Balance Sheet | Reduces capital |
| Heat and light | Profit and Loss Account | Expense |
| Sundry expenses | Profit and Loss Account | Expenses |

*Trading and Profit and Loss Account for the Year to
31 December, 19X4*

|  | £ | £ |
|--|--:|--:|
| Sales............................................ |  | 130,000 |
| Less: Returns inwards............................ |  | 250 |
|  |  | 129,750 |
| Opening Stock................................... | 15,000 |  |
| Purchases....................................... | 80,000 |  |
| Less:  Returns outwards.......................... | (150) |  |
| Closing stock............................ | (17,750) |  |
| Cost of goods sold.............................. |  | 77,100 |
| Gross profit.................................... |  | 52,650 |
| Discounts received.............................. |  | 300 |
|  |  | 52,950 |
| Wages.......................................... | 17,300 |  |
| Rent and rates................................. | 3,000 |  |
| Delivery....................................... | 2,750 |  |
| Heat and light................................. | 3,500 |  |
| Sundry expenses................................ | 2,750 |  |
|  |  | 29,300 |
| Net Profit...................................... |  | 23,650 |

*Balance Sheet at 31 December, 19X4*

| | £ | | £ | £ |
|---|---|---|---|---|
| Capital, 1 January........ | 27,600 | Premises.............. | | 8,000 |
| Profit for year........... | 23,650 | Stock................. | 17,750 | |
| | 51,250 | Debtors............... | 15,400 | |
| Drawings .............. | (12,000) | Cash ................. | 3,100 | |
| Capital, 31 December..... | 39,250 | | | 36,250 |
| Creditors .............. | 5,000 | | | |
| | 44,250 | | | 44,250 |

# Solution 6.2

(a)

*Fixed Assets at Cost*

| | | £ | | | £ |
|---|---|---|---|---|---|
| 1.1.X1 | Asset A......... | 5,000 | 31.12.X1 | Balance c/d....... | 7,500 |
| | Asset B......... | 2,500 | | | |
| | | 7,500 | | | 7,500 |
| 1.1.X2 | Balance b/d..... | 7,500 | 1.1.X3 | Disposal of Asset B.. | 2,500 |
| 1.2.X3 | Asset C......... | 7,000 | | Balance c/d........ | 12,000 |
| | | 14,500 | | | 14,500 |

*Accumulated Depreciation*

| | | £ | | | £ |
|---|---|---|---|---|---|
| 31.12.X2 | Balance c/d.... | 3,000 | 31.12.X1 | Profit and Loss.... | 1,500 |
| | | | 31.12.X2 | Profit and Loss.... | 1,500 |
| | | 3,000 | | | 3,000 |
| 1.1.X3 | Disposal of Asset B....... | 1,000 | 1.1.X3 | Balance b/d...... | 3,000 |
| 31.12.X3 | Balance c/d.... | 4,400 | 31.12.X3 | Profit and Loss.... | 2,400 |
| | | 5,400 | | | 5,400 |

*Disposal of Fixed Assets*

| | | £ | | | £ |
|---|---|---|---|---|---|
| 1.1.X3 | Fixed Assets..... | 2,500 | 1.1.X3 | Depreciation........ | 1,000 |
| | | | | Proceeds.......... | 900 |
| | | | | Profit and Loss..... | 600 |
| | | 2,500 | | | 2,500 |

(b) *Balance Sheet Extracts:*

| | 31.12.X1 | 31.12.X2 | 31.12.X3 |
|---|---|---|---|
| | £ | £ | £ |
| Fixed Assets at Cost················ | 7,500 | 7,500 | 12,000 |
| less: Accumulated Depreciation.... | 1,500 | 3,000 | 4,400 |
| Written Down Value............... | 6,000 | 4,500 | 7,600 |

# Solution 6.3

*Trading and Profit and Loss Account*
*for the Year to 30 June 19X7*

| | £ | £ |
|---|---|---|
| Sales......................................... | | 108,920 |
| Opening stock................................. | 9,470 | |
| Purchases..................................... | 72,190 | |
| Closing stock................................. | (9,960) | |
| Cost of goods sold............................. | | 71,700 |
| *Gross Profit*.................................... | | 37,220 |
| Depreciation ................................. | 3,000 | |
| Rent......................................... | 1,000 | |
| Wages........................................ | 14,330 | |
| Other Costs................................... | 4,590 | |
| | | 22,920 |
| *Net Profit*...................................... | | 14,300 |

*Balance Sheet at 30 June 19X7*

|  | £ | £ |
|---|---|---|
| **FIXED ASSETS** | | |
| At Cost........................................ | | 35,000 |
| less: Accumulated depreciation | | |
| (12,500 + 3,000)........................... | | 15,500 |
| | | 19,500 |
| **CURRENT ASSETS** | | |
| Stock........................................ | 9,960 | |
| Debtors....................................... | 7,350 | |
| Cash......................................... | 1,710 | |
| | 19,020 | |
| **CURRENT LIABILITIES** | | |
| Creditors..................................... | 6,220 | |
| | | 12,800 |
| | | 32,300 |
| **CAPITAL** | | |
| At 1 July 19X6................................ | | 30,350 |
| Profit........................................ | | 14,300 |
| | | 44,650 |
| Drawings..................................... | | (12,350) |
| | | 32,300 |

# Solution 6.4

(a)

*Motor Vehicles at Cost Account*

| | £ | | £ |
|---|---|---|---|
| Balance per Trial Balance.. | 127,000 | Van scrapped (1)............ | 2,000 |
| Disposals—Trade in (2).... | 1,500 | Disposal—Car (2).......... | 5,000 |
| Disposal of Van (4)....... | 2,500 | Disposal—Car (3).......... | 4,000 |
| | | Disposal—Van (4).......... | 10,000 |
| | | Balance c/d............... | 110,000 |
| | 131,000 | | 131,000 |

### Motor Vehicles Depreciation Account

| | £ | | £ |
|---|---|---|---|
| Van Scrapped (1)......... | 2,000 | Balance per Trial Balance..... | 76,000 |
| Disposal—Car (2)........ | 3,000 | Profit and Loss | |
| Disposal—Car (3)(W1).... | 2,750 | Account—Charge for | |
| Disposal—Van(4)(W2).... | 6,750 | 19X3..................... | 25,000 |
| Balance c/d............. | 86,500 | | |
| | 101,000 | | 101,000 |

### Disposal of Motor Vehicles Account

| | £ | | £ |
|---|---|---|---|
| Car at cost (2)............ | 5,000 | Balance per Trial Balance..... | 1,600 |
| Car at cost (3)............ | 4,000 | Trade in allowance (2)........ | 1,500 |
| Van at cost (4)............ | 10,000 | Depreciation (2)............ | 3,000 |
| | | Depreciation (3)(W1)........ | 2,750 |
| | | Proceeds on sale of van (4).... | 2,500 |
| | | Depreciation (4)(W2)........ | 6,750 |
| | | Loss on disposal of vehicles | |
| | | transferred to profit and loss | |
| | | account................... | 900 |
| | 19,000 | | 19,000 |

*Workings*

W1. *Disposal of Car*
   Using the formula:
   Written down value = Cost − Accumulated Depreciation
   Then 1,250         = 4,000 − Accumulated Depreciation
   ∴Accumulated Depreciation = £2,750

W2. *Disposal of Delivery Van*
   Using the formula:
   Proceeds − (Cost − Accumulated Depreciation) = Profit (Loss) on disposal
   then 2,500 − (10,000 − Accumulated Depreciation) = (750)
   ∴Accumulated Depreciation = £6,750

b)   *Balance Sheet Extract at 31 December 19X3*

| | £ |
|---|---|
| Motor vehicles at cost..................................... | 110,000 |
| Less: Accumulated depreciation............................ | 86,500 |
| | 23,500 |

*Note* The number in brackets after some of the entries in the accounts refers to the number of the note given in the question on which the entry is based.

# Solution 6.5

*Insurance Account*

| 19X8 | | £ | 19X8 | | £ |
|---|---|---|---|---|---|
| 1 January | Balance b/d.......... | 450 | 31 December | Balance c/d..... | 510 |
| June | Cash................ | 1,020 | | Profit and Loss | |
| | | | | Account........ | 960 |
| | | 1,470 | | | 1,470 |

*Rates Account*

| 19X8 | | £ | 19X8 | | £ |
|---|---|---|---|---|---|
| 1 January | Balance b/d.......... | 290 | 31 December | Balance c/d..... | 390 |
| March | Cash................ | 780 | | Profit and Loss | |
| September | Cash................ | 780 | | Account........ | 1,460 |
| | | 1,850 | | | 1,850 |

*Gas Account*

| 19X8 | | £ | 19X8 | | £ |
|---|---|---|---|---|---|
| March | Cash.......... | 850 | 1 January | Balance b/d..... | 600 |
| June | Cash.......... | 840 | 31 December | Profit and Loss | |
| September | Cash.......... | 610 | | Account........ | 3,340 |
| December | Cash.......... | 960 | | | |
| 31 December | Balance    c/d... | 680 | | | |
| | | 3,940 | | | 3,940 |

*Electricity Account*

| 19X8 | | £ | 19X8 | | £ |
|---|---|---|---|---|---|
| February | Cash.......... | 900 | 1 January | Balance b/d..... | 300 |
| May | Cash.......... | 820 | 31 December | Profit and Loss | |
| August | Cash.......... | 690 | | Account........ | 3,050 |
| November | Cash.......... | 550 | | | |
| 31 December | Balance c/d..... | 390 | | | |
| | | 3,350 | | | 3,350 |

# Solution 6.6

(a)

### Sales Ledger Control Account

| | £ | | £ |
|---|---|---|---|
| Balance b/d............... | 156,937 | B.Clyde—bad debt....... | 560 |
| | | M.Poppins—bad debt..... | 227 |
| | | Balance c/d............. | 156,150 |
| | 156,937 | | 156,937 |

### Bad Debts Account

| | £ | | £ |
|---|---|---|---|
| Balance b/d............... | 750 | Profit and Loss Account... | 1,537 |
| Sales Ledger Control Account................. | 560 | | |
| Sales Ledger Control Account................. | 227 | | |
| | 1,537 | | 1,537 |

### Doubtful Debts Account

| | £ | | £ |
|---|---|---|---|
| Provision for Doubtful Debts Account.............. | 1,648 | Profit and Loss Account... | 1,648 |

### Provision for Doubtful Debts Account

| | £ | | £ |
|---|---|---|---|
| Balance c/d............... | 4,248 | Balance b/d............. | 2,600 |
| | | Doubtful Debts Account* | |
| | | S. Wars........... | 340 |
| | | M. Express........ | 78 |
| | | M. Ash........... | 80 |
| | | Increase in provision ......... | 1,150 |
| | 4,248 | | 4,248 |

\* Total value £1,648

(b) *Balance Sheet-Extract*

|  | £ |
|---|---|
| Debtors........................................................ | 156,150 |
| Less:Provision for doubtful debts............................ | 4,248 |
|  | 151,902 |

# Solution 6.7

*Trading and Profit and Loss Account for the*
*Year to 31 December 19X6*

|  | £ | £ |
|---|---|---|
| Sales........................................... |  | 234,481 |
| Stock 1 January................................ | 32,193 |  |
| Purchases...................................... | 164,770 |  |
|  | 196,963 |  |
| Less: Goods taken as drawings...................... | (1,250) |  |
| Stock 31 December......................... | (34,671) |  |
| Cost of goods sold.............................. |  | 161,042 |
| Gross Profit.................................... |  | 73,439 |
| Profit on sale of van............................. |  | 500 |
|  |  | 73,939 |
| Rent and rates (3,000 – 300)...................... | 2,700 |  |
| General expenses............................... | 7,263 |  |
| Wages (26,649 + 271)............................ | 26,920 |  |
| Bad debts (693 + 104)............................ | 797 |  |
| Depreciation................................... | 7,000 | 44,680 |
| Net Profit...................................... |  | 29,259 |

*Balance Sheet at 31 December 19X6*

|  | £ | £ | £ |
|---|---|---|---|
| *Fixed Assets* | | | |
| Freehold land and buildings........................ | | | 114,000 |
| Motor Vans at cost (37,500 | | | |
| − 2,500 + 1,500).............................. | | 36,500 | |
| Less: Depreciation (15,450 | | | |
| + 7,000 − 1,500).............................. | | 20,950 | |
| | | | 15,550 |
| | | | 129,550 |
| *Current Assets* | | | |
| Stock............................................. | | 34,671 | |
| Debtors.......................................... | 20,911 | | |
| Less: Provision for doubtful | | | |
| debts (876 + 104)........................... | 980 | | |
| | | 19,931 | |
| Prepaid rent and rates............................ | | 300 | |
| Cash............................................. | | 32,728 | |
| | | 87,630 | |
| *Less: Current Liabilities* | | | |
| Creditors........................................ | 13,006 | | |
| Accrued wages................................... | 271 | | |
| | | 13,277 | |
| Working Capital.................................. | | | 74,353 |
| | | | 203,903 |
| | | | |
| *Capital* | | | |
| At 1 January..................................... | | | 193,894 |
| Profit for 19X6.................................. | | | 29,259 |
| | | | 223,153 |
| Less: Drawings: Cash............................ | | 18,000 | |
| Stock............................ | | 1,250 | |
| | | | 19,250 |
| | | | 203,903 |

# Solution 6.8

(a)                                    *S. Top — Journal*

| | Debit £ | Credit £ |
|---|---|---|
| 1. Plant and machinery.......................... | 2,750 | |
| Repairs to machinery........................... | | 2,750 |
| Transfer of purchase of lathe wrongly recorded | | |
| | | |
| 2. Repairs....................................... | 350 | |
| Manufacturing wages........................... | | 350 |
| Transfer of repair costs wrongly recorded | | |
| | | |
| 3. Bad debts..................................... | 1,290 | |
| Debtors........................................ | | 1,290 |
| Irrecoverable debt due from J.Jones written off | | |
| | | |
| 4. Drawings..................................... | 200 | |
| Rates.......................................... | | 200 |
| Transfer of rates on S.Top's private house | | |
| | | |
| 5. Purchases.................................... | 1,500 | |
| Creditors...................................... | | 1,500 |
| Goods received but not recorded at year end | | |
| | | |
| 6. Provision for depreciation...................... | 1,000 | |
| Machinery..................................... | | 1,000 |
| Fully depreciated machine scrapped during year | | |
| | | |
| 7. Drawings..................................... | 150 | |
| Purchases..................................... | | 150 |
| Goods taken for S.Top's personal use | | |
| | | |
| 8. Delivery...................................... | 125 | |
| Purchases..................................... | | 125 |
| Transfer of delivery cost wrongly recorded | | |

(b)                    *Statement of Effect of Adjustments on Profit*

| | Decrease Profit £ | Increase Profit £ |
|---|---|---|
| 1. Expense capitalized............................ | | 2,750 |
| 3. Increase in bad debts........................... | 1,290 | |
| 4. Expense charged to owner....................... | | 200 |
| 5. Increase in purchases........................... | 1,500 | |
| 7. Purchases charged to owner...................... | | 150 |
| | 2,790 | 3,100 |
| | | 2,790 |
| Net increase in profit............................. | | 310 |

## Solution 7.1

The fundamental rule is that stock should be valued at the *lower* of cost and net realisable value, taking each item or groups of similar items separately.

Valuation of stock calculated as follows:

| Product | Cost | NRV | Lower of cost and NRV |
|---|---|---|---|
| A | 2,400 | 2,760 | 2,400 |
| B | 1,290 | 740 | 740 |
| C | 3,680 | 750 | 750 |
| D | 2,950 | 4,760 | 2,950 |
| E | 6,280 | 9,730 | 6,280 |
| Value of stock | | | 13,120 |

## Solution 7.2

Perpetual inventory: Stock records are written up on a regular basis to record receipts and issues of stock and the quantity on hand after each transaction. Sometimes the records are also maintained in terms of values and, where this is done, values for total issues (cost of goods sold) and closing stock are readily available under this system. Where values are not recorded, the cost of goods sold is obtained as the balancing item (see below).

Periodic stock-take. Stocks are physically counted and valued at the end of each accounting period. The figure for cost of goods sold is the balancing item obtained by applying the formula:
*Opening stock + Purchases − Closing stock = Cost of goods sold.*

## Solution 7.3

(a) Units of stock on hand: 235 − 155 = 80 (*workings*).
Valuation of stock:

|  |  | £ |
|---|---|---|
| (i) FIFO: | 75 units at £30 | 2,250 |
|  | 5 units at £25 | 125 |
|  | 80 | 2,375 |
| (ii) LIFO: | 80 units at £20 | 1,600 |
| (iii) AVCO: | 80 units at £24.47(£5,750 ÷ 235) | 1,958 |

(b) Calculation of cost of goods sold (balancing item):

|  | FIFO £ | LIFO £ | AVCO £ |
|---|---|---|---|
| Opening stock | 0 | 0 | 0 |
| Add: Purchases (*workings*) | 5,750 | 5,750 | 5,750 |
| Less: Closing stock | 2,375 | 1,600 | 1,958 |
| Cost of goods sold | 3,375 | 4,150 | 3,792 |

(c) Calculation of gross profit:

|  | FIFO £ | LIFO £ | AVCO £ |
|---|---|---|---|
| Sales (*workings*) | 6,260 | 6,260 | 6,260 |
| Less: Cost of goods sold | 3,375 | 4,150 | 3,792 |
| Gross profit | 2,885 | 2,110 | 2,468 |

*Workings:*

| Purchases | Units | Price | £ |
|---|---|---|---|
| January: 8 | 100 | 20 | 2,000 |
| 13 | 60 | 25 | 1,500 |
| 17 | 75 | 30 | 2,250 |
|  | 235 |  | 5,750 |

| Sales | | | |
|---|---|---|---|
| January: 14 | 125 | 40 | 5,000 |
| 22 | 30 | 42 | 1,260 |
|  | 155 |  | 6,260 |

## Solution 7.4

(a) (i) Down. LIFO uses older prices than FIFO and gives a higher value for the same volume of goods. Also net realisable value at 31 December 19X1 is lower than the FIFO value calculated on the basis of purchases immediately prior to the year end.

   (ii) Up. FIFO values stock at the most recent purchase price, and this is higher than the LIFO value.

(b)   LIFO. It gives the highest value for closing stock and hence the lowest value for cost of goods sold.

(c)   Lower of FIFO and Net Realisable Value. Cost of goods sold is calculated by applying the formula:
*Opening Stock + Purchases − Closing Stock.*
Cost of goods sold will be lowest, and hence profit highest, when closing stock is greater than opening stock, and the difference betwen them is maximised.

(d)     LIFO. This method gives the lowest stock value at 31 December 19X3, and hence the highest cost of goods sold figure for the three year period.

Answers (b) to (d) may alternatively be based on the following calculations:

|  | 19X1 | 19X2 | 19X3 | Totals |
|---|---|---|---|---|
| *LIFO* | £ | £ | £ | £ |
| Opening stock................ | — | 96,480 | 87,360 | — |
| Purchases..................... | 240,000 | 252,000 | 324,000 | 816,000 |
| Closing stock................. | (96,480) | (87,360) | (100,320) | (100,320) |
| Cost of goods sold............. | 143,520 | 261,120 | 311,040 | 715,680 |
| *FIFO* | | | | |
| Opening stock................ | — | 96,000 | 86,400 | — |
| Purchases..................... | 240,000 | 252,000 | 324,000 | 816,000 |
| Closing stock................. | (96,000) | (86,400) | (105,600) | (105,600) |
| Cost of goods sold............. | 144,000 | 261,600 | 304,800 | 710,400 |
| *Lower of FIFO and* | | | | |
| *Net Realisable Value.* | | | | |
| Opening stock................ | — | 88,800 | 81,600 | — |
| Purchases..................... | 240,000 | 252,000 | 324,000 | 816,000 |
| Closing stock................. | (88,800) | (81,600) | (105,600) | (105,600) |
| Cost of goods sold............. | 151,200 | 259,200 | 300,000 | 710,400 |

## Solution 7.5

(a) There are two main tests:
   (i) Expenditure which enhances the ability of the firm to earn profits is capital, whereas expenditure designed merely to maintain the existing level of operation is revenue.
   (ii) Capital expenditure is incurred on the purchase of assets which are expected to possess a useful life which extends over a number of accounting periods; moreover, it is not intended to sell these assets in the normal course of business. Revenue expenditure is incurred in aquiring goods and services which are consumed in a short space of time. A correct allocation is important, because otherwise profit and asset values are wrongly reported. For example the misallocation of capital to revenue causes both profit and gross assets to be understated.

(b)

(i) Revenue. This is a normal repair to make good wear and tear.

(ii) Capital. Hourly capacity is increased.

(iii) Capital. This is part of the cost of acquiring the new asset.

(iv) Capital. This increases the firm's productive capacity.

(v) Capital. This expenditure is needed to make the plant ready for use.

## Solution 7.6

(a)

*Bank account for 19X3.*

| | £ | | £ |
|---|---|---|---|
| Bank balance 1.1.19X3.... | 19,400 | General expenses......... | 2,500 |
| Receipts................ | 76,500 | Cost of properties........ | 85,250 |
| | | Legal expenses on purchases.............. | 2,550 |
| | | Legal expenses on sales.... | 1,250 |
| | | Improvements........... | 1,780 |
| | | Closing balance.......... | 2,570 |
| | 95,900 | | 95,900 |

(b)

*Profit and Loss Account for 19X3\**

| | | £ | £ |
|---|---|---|---|
| Sales | .............................. | | 107,750 |
| Less: Cost of properties sold: | | | |
| | No. 1.......................... | 30,250 | |
| | 3   36,250 + 1,000 + 260....... | 37,510 | |
| | 4   24,000 + 750 + 1,000....... | 25,750 | |
| | | 93,510 | |
| | Selling expenses.................. | 1,250 | |
| | General expenses................. | 2,500 | |
| Net profit | | | 97,260 |
| | | | 10,490 |

*Balance Sheet at 31 December 19X3*

| | £ | | | £ |
|---|---|---|---|---|
| Opening capital............ | 79,000 | Properties on hand: | | |
| Profit.................... | 10,490 | 2................... | | 29,350 |
| | | 5 25,000 + 800 + | | |
| | | 520............... | | 26,320 |
| | | | | 55,670 |
| | | Bank balance........... | | 2,570 |
| | | Debtors............... | | 31,250 |
| | 89,490 | | | 89,490 |

| | £ | £ |
|---|---|---|
| * An alternative presentation: | | |
| Sales...................................... | | 107,750 |
| Opening stock........................... | 59,600 | |
| Purchases (including legal expenses, on purchase, and improvements)........ | 89,580 | |
| Closing stock............................ | (55,670) | 93,510 |
| | | 14,240 |
| Gross profit............................. | | |
| Less: Legal expenses on sales................ | 1,250 | |
| General expenses..................... | 2,500 | 3,750 |
| Net Profit | | 10,490 |

# Solution 7.7

(a)

| | (i) Straight line | | (ii) Units of service | | (iii) Reducing balance | |
|---|---|---|---|---|---|---|
| Year | Charge | Book value | Charge | Book value | Charge | Book value |
| | £ | £ | £ | £ | £ | £ |
| 19X1 | 3,800 | 16,200 | 5,000 | 15,000 | 9,000 | 11,000 |
| 19X2 | 3,800 | 12,400 | 5,000 | 10,000 | 4,950 | 6,050 |
| 19X3 | 3,800 | 8,600 | 5,000 | 5,000 | 2,723 | 3,327 |
| 19X4 | 3,800 | 4,800 | 2,000 | 3,000 | 1,497 | 1,830 |
| 19X5 | 3.800 | 1,000 | 2,000 | 1,000 | 830 | 1,000 |
| | 19,000 | | 19,000 | | 19,000 | |

Calculations:
Straight line: (£20,000 − £1,000) ÷ 5 = £3,800.
Units of service: (£20,000 − £1,000) ÷ 76,000 = £0.25 per hour.
Reducing balance: 45% of net book value.

(b) Depreciation charge is lowest and reported profit highest using the following methods.
    19X1 – Straight line.
    19X2 – Straight line.
    19X3 – Reducing balance.
    19X4 – Reducing balance.
    19X5 – Reducing balance.

Over the entire 5 year period each method produces exactly the same effect on reported profit as the total charge amounts to £19,000.

## Solution 7.8

| | £ | £ |
|---|---:|---:|
| (a) Godwill: | | |
| Price paid................................... | | 120,000 |
| Less: Net assets acquired. | | |
| Fixed assets............................ | 71,500 | |
| Stocks................................... | 20,000 | |
| Debtors................................. | 10,000 | |
| | 101,500 | |
| Deduct trade creditors.................... | 5,000 | 96,500 |
| | | 23,500 |
| (b) Goodwill at cost............................. | | 23,500 |
| Less: Amount written off (£23,500 ÷ 5).......... | | 4,700 |
| | | 18,800 |

## Solution 7.9

Examples are:

(a)    Insurance premiums received before the period covered by the insurance; rents received before the rental period.

(b)    Cash sales of goods; sale of goods on credit where the cash is collected in the same accounting period.

(c)    Collection of customers' accounts in the period following the sale; receipt of interest after the period to which it relates.

(d)    Prepayment of insurance premiums or subscription fees.

(e)    Payments for office salaries and telephone charges in the period in which they are used (debit entry is to an expense account).

(f)    Payment of suppliers' accounts outstanding at the year end; payment for rent accrued at the year end.

# Solution 7.10

(a)
### Trading Account for 19X1

|  | £ | £ |
|---|---|---|
| Sales........................................... |  | 100,000 |
| Less: Opening stock.............................. | 10,000 |  |
| Purchases................................ | 80,000 |  |
| Closing stock............................ | (11,000) |  |
| Cost of goods sold.......................... |  | 79,000 |
| Gross profit.................................... |  | 21,000 |

(b) The effect of the revision is to reduce gross profit and, therefore, net profit by £3,000.

# Solution 8.1

### Manufacturing, Trading and Profit and Loss Account
### for the year to 31 March 19X6

|  | £ | £ | £ |
|---|---|---|---|
| Raw Materials: Opening stock............... |  | 12,000 |  |
| Purchases.................. |  | 40,000 |  |
|  |  | 52,000 |  |
| Closing stock............... |  | (14,000) |  |
| Consumed................. |  | 38,000 |  |
| Production wages......................... |  | 30,000 |  |
|  |  | 68,000 |  |
| Depreciation............................ |  | 7,000 |  |
| Rent...................................... |  | 4,800 |  |
| Light, heat and power....................... |  | 9,000 |  |
| Overheads............................... |  | 17,500 |  |
|  |  | 106,300 |  |
| Work in progress at 1.4.X5.................. |  | 2,000 |  |
|  |  | 108,300 |  |
| at 31.3.X6.................. |  | (7,000) |  |
| Manufacturing cost of goods completed........ |  | 101,300 |  |
| Manufacturing profit (15% of total cost)....... |  | 15,195 |  |
| Transfer to Trading Account................. |  | 116,495 |  |

|  | £ | £ | £ |
|---|---|---|---|
| Sales..................................... |  |  | 208,000 |
| Finished goods: Stock at 1.4.X5 |  | 11,500 |  |
| Transfers |  | 116,495 |  |
|  |  | 127,995 |  |
| Stock at 31.3.X6.............. |  | (13,800) |  |
|  |  |  | 114,195 |
| Gross profit on trading..................... |  |  | 93,805 |
| Manufacturing profit...................... |  |  | 15,195 |
|  |  |  | 109,000 |

Administration Expenses:

| Rent................................ | 1,600 |  |
|---|---|---|
| Light, heat and power.................. | 3,000 |  |
| Expenses............................ | 7,500 |  |
| Salaries............................. | 15,000 |  |
| Hire of equipment..................... | 7,000 |  |
| Postage and telephone.................. | 5,350 |  |
|  |  | 39,450 |

Finance Costs:

| Bank charges......................... | 1,250 |  |
|---|---|---|
| Loan interest......................... | 3,000 |  |
|  |  | 4,250 |

Delivery Costs:

| Van hire............................. | 2,000 |  |
|---|---|---|
| Wages.............................. | 7,000 |  |
| Petrol, etc........................... | 1,000 |  |
|  |  | 10,000 |
| Adjustment for unrealised profit (W1)......... | 300 |  |
|  |  | 54,000 |
| Net profit............................... |  | 55,000 |

*Balance Sheet at 31 March 19X6*

| | £ | £ | £ |
|---|---|---|---|
| Fixed assets at cost......................... | | | 70,000 |
| Less: Accumulated depreication.............. | | | 21,000 |
| | | | 49,000 |
| *Current Assets* | | | |
| Stocks: Raw materials..................... | | 14,000 | |
| Work in progress................... | | 7,000 | |
| Finished goods (W1)................ | | 12,000 | |
| | | 33,000 | |
| Debtors.................................. | | 20,000 | |
| | | 53,000 | |
| *Current Liabilities* | | | |
| Overdraft.............................. | 10,000 | | |
| Creditors .............................. | 5,000 | | |
| | | 15,000 | |
| Working Capital.......................... | | | 38,000 |
| | | | 87,000 |
| *Financed by:* | | | |
| Capital at 1 April 19X5..................... | | | 50,000 |
| Profit for year.......................... | | | 55,000 |
| | | | 105,000 |
| Less: Drawings............................ | | | 48,000 |
| Capital at 31 March 19X6................... | | | 57,000 |
| Loan.................................... | | | 30,000 |
| | | | 87,000 |

W1: The transfer price of stock is 115% of its cost. To convert it to cost, it must be multiplied by 100/115, ie:

$$£13,800 \times 100/115 = £12,000$$

The unrealised profit in closing stock is £13,800 − £12,000 = £1,800

The required adjustment to the provision is £1,800 − £1,500 (opening balance) = £300

## Solution 8.2

*Hire Purchase Trading and Profit and Loss Account for 19X5*

|  | £ | £ |
|---|---|---|
| Cash received........................ |  | 33,600 |
| Cost of sales: |  |  |
| VCs (250 x 96).................... | 24,000 |  |
| EPs (200 x 144)................... | 28,800 |  |
|  | 52,800 |  |
| Less: Stock held by HP debtors (W1)..... | 33,600 |  |
|  |  | 19,200 |
| Gross profit......................... |  | 14,400 |
| Expenses (1,980 + 460)............... | 2,440 |  |
| Bank interest....................... | 1,086 |  |
|  |  | 3,526 |
| Net profit........................... |  | 10,874 |

*Balance Sheet 31.12.19X5*

|  | £ |  |  | £ |
|---|---|---|---|---|
| Capital at start........... | 10,000 | Stock with H.P. Debtors... |  | 33,600(W1) |
| Add profit.............. | 10,874 | Stocks held |  |  |
|  | 20,874 | VCs..... | 4,800 |  |
| Less drawings........... | 3,500 | EPs..... | 7,200 | 12,000 |
|  | 17,374 |  |  |  |
| *Current liabilities* |  |  |  |  |
| VCs........ | 4,800 |  |  |  |
| Expenses.... | 460 |  |  |  |
| Bank |  |  |  |  |
| overdraft ... | 22,966 | 28,226 |  |  |
|  | 45,600 |  |  | 45,600 |

*Workings*

| | *Vacuum Cleaners* | *Electric Polishers* |
|---|---|---|
| W1 = Stock with H.P. Debtors | | |
| C = Cost of Goods Sold = | 24,000 | 28,800 |
| S = Total Selling Price = | $250 \times 168$ = 42,000 | $200 \times 252$ = 50,400 |
| Cash collected | 21,000 | 12,600 |
| I = Instalments due in future accounting periods | 21,000 | 37,800 |
| V = Stock out on HP = $\frac{I}{S} \times C$ = | $\frac{21,000}{42,000} \times 24,000 = \underline{12,000}$ | $\frac{37,800}{50,400} \times 28,800 = \underline{21,600}$ |

|  | *Total* |
|---|---|
| Vacuum Cleaners.................. | 12,000 |
| Electric Polishers.................. | 21,600 |
| | £33,600 |

# Solution 8.3

### *Balance Sheet of Sharpner at 1 January 19X8*

| | £ | £ |
|---|---|---|
| Fixed Assets | | |
| Land and buildings (32,100 + 15,000).............. | | 47,100 |
| Motor vans (20,000 + 2,700)..................... | | 22,700 |
| Goodwill (W1)................................. | | 5,700 |
| | | 75,500 |
| *Current Assets* | | |
| Stock (10,700 + 5,800)......................... | 16,500 | |
| Debtors (7,600 + 3,000)........................ | 10,600 | |
| Cash (W2)..................................... | 1,200 | |
| | 28,300 | |
| *Current Liabilities* | | |
| Trade creditors (7,000 + 3,200).................. | 10,200 | |
| *Working Capital*................................ | | 18,100 |
| | | 93,600 |
| *Financed by:* | | |
| Capital.......................................... | | 68,600 |
| Loan............................................ | | 25,000 |
| | | 93,600 |

## Workings

### W1. Goodwill

|  |  | £ | £ |
|---|---|---:|---:|
| Paid |  |  | 29,000 |
| Acquired: | Land and buildings............ | 15,000 |  |
|  | Motor van.................... | 2,700 |  |
|  | Stock....................... | 5,800 |  |
|  | Debtors..................... | 3,000 |  |
|  |  | 26,500 |  |
|  | Creditors.................... | 3,200 |  |
|  |  |  | 23,300 |
|  |  |  | 5,700 |

### W2. Cash

|  | £ |
|---|---:|
| Opening balance....................... | 5,200 |
| Loan raised........................... | 25,000 |
| Paid to Pencil........................ | (29,000) |
|  | 1,200 |

# Solution 8.4

(a)

### Bank Account

| | £ | | £ |
|---|---:|---|---:|
| Capital................. | 50,000 | Purchases (W2).......... | 72,664 |
| Sales (W1).............. | 86,019 | Expenses (W3)........... | 12,976 |
| Sellup's debtors.......... | 2,740 | Purchase of business...... | 40,000 |
| | | Paid to Sellup........... | 2,610 |
| | | Closing balance......... | 10,509 |
| | 138,759 | | 138,759 |

(b)

### Trading and Profit and Loss Account 19X3

|  | £ | £ |
|---|---:|---:|
| Sales............................................ |  | 92,968 |
| Cost of sales.................................... |  | 71,034 |
| Gross profit.................................... |  | 21,934 |
| Expenses....................................... | 13,168 |  |
| Depreciation ................................... | 395 |  |
|  |  | 13,563 |
| Net profit....................................... |  | 8,371 |

*Balance Sheet at 31 December 19X3*

|  | £ | £ | £ |
|---|---|---|---|
| **FIXED ASSETS** | | | |
| Freehold land and buildings.... | | | 22,100 |
| Motor vans................. | | 1,975 | |
| Less Depreciation.......... | | 395 | |
| | | | 1,580 |
| Goodwill (W4)............... | | | 6,933 |
| | | | 30,613 |
| **CURRENT ASSETS** | | | |
| Stock....................... | | 15,594 | |
| Debtors..................... | | 6,949 | |
| Bank....................... | | 10,509 | |
| | | 33,052 | |
| **CURRENT LIABILITIES** | | | |
| Purchases................... | 4,972 | | |
| Expenses.................... | 192 | | |
| Sellup  (2,740 – 2,610)........ | 130 | | |
| | | 5,294 | |
| **WORKING CAPITAL** | | | 27,758 |
| | | | 58,371 |
| Financed by: | | | |
| **CAPITAL** | | | |
| Balance at 1 January.......... | | | 50,000 |
| Profit ...................... | | | 8,371 |
| | | | 58,371 |

## Workings

*W1 Cash from Sales*

|  | £ |
|---|---|
| Sales....................... | 92,968 |
| Less closing debtors........... | 6,949 |
| | 86,019 |

*W2 Cash to Suppliers*

|  | £ |
|---|---|
| Cost of sales................. | 71,034 |
| Plus closing stock............. | 15,594 |
| Less opening stock............ | (8,992) |
| Purchases................... | 77,636 |
| Less closing creditors......... | 4,972 |
| | 72,664 |

*W3 Cash for Expenses*

|  | £ |
|---|---|
| Cost of expenses.............. | 13,168 |
| Less closing creditor.......... | 192 |
| | 12,976 |

*W4 Goodwill*

|  | £ | £ |
|---|---|---|
| Purchase price............... |  | 40,000 |
| Assets taken over: |  |  |
| Freehold land.............. | 22,100 |  |
| Motor van................. | 1,975 |  |
| Stock..................... | 8,992 |  |
|  |  | 33,067 |
|  |  | 6,933 |

# Solution 8.5

## *Realisation Account*

| | £ | | £ |
|---|---|---|---|
| Premises................... | 27,000 | Creditors ............. | 10,000 |
| Stock and debtors........... | 29,000 | Purchaser............. | 50,000 |
| Loss on equipment........... | 1,000 | | |
| Profit transferred to | | | |
| Capital Account............. | 3,000 | | |
| | 60,000 | | 60,000 |

## *Equipment Account*

| | £ | | £ |
|---|---|---|---|
| Balance b/d................ | 5,000 | Cash ................. | 4,000 |
| | | Loss transferred to | |
| | | Realisation Account.... | 1,000 |
| | 5,000 | | 5,000 |

## *Cash Account*

| | £ | | £ |
|---|---|---|---|
| Purchaser.................. | 50,000 | Balance b/d.......... | 3,000 |
| Equipment................. | 4,000 | Purlin—Capital........ | 51,000 |
| | 54,000 | | 54,000 |

*Capital Account*

| | £ | | £ |
|---|---|---|---|
| Motor car.................. | 2,000 | Balance b/d........... | 50,000 |
| Cash..................... | 51,000 | Profit on realisation.... | 3,000 |
| | 53,000 | | 53,000 |

# Solution 8.6

| | £ |
|---|---|
| Sales (W1)........................ | 137,000 |
| Gross profit (25% × 137,000)....... | 34,250 |
| Cost of goods sold................ | 102,750 |
| Opening stock.................... | 66,000 |
| Purchases (W2).................. | 64,800 |
| Closing stock (balancing figure)...... | (28,050) |
| | 102,750 |
| Theoretical closing stock............ | 28,050 |
| Undamaged stock................ | 18,000 |
| Stock lost....................... | 10,050 |

## *Workings*

| *W1 Sales* | £ | *W2 Purchases for Resale* | £ |
|---|---|---|---|
| Cash from debtors........... | 97,000 | Cash paid.............. | 68,000 |
| Discounts allowed........... | 1,000 | Discounts received....... | 400 |
| Closing debtors............. | 57,000 | Closing creditors......... | 39,000 |
| Opening debtors............ | (54,000) | Opening creditors........ | (42,000) |
| Cash sales................. | 36,000 | Drawings ............... | (600) |
| | 137,000 | | 64,800 |

## Solution 9.1

*Appropriation Account*

| | £ | £ | | £ | £ |
|---|---|---|---|---|---|
| Salaries: Jack......... | 10,000 | | Profit............ | | 42,000 |
| Jill.......... | 7,500 | | Interest on drawings: | | |
| Jane......... | 5,000 | | Jack............. | 600 | |
| | | 22,500 | Jill.............. | 450 | |
| Interest on Capital: | | | Jane............. | 400 | |
| Jack................ | 3,600 | | | | 1,450 |
| Jill (W1)............ | 2,700 | | | | |
| Jane................ | 4,800 | | | | |
| | | 11,100 | | | |
| Residue: Jack......... | 3,940 | | | | |
| Jill | 3,940 | | | | |
| Jane......... | 1,970 | | | | |
| | | 9,850 | | | |
| | | 43,450 | | | 43,450 |

*Workings*

W1. 12% × 20,000 (opening capital) + 12% × 5,000 × .5 (capital introduced half way through the year) = 2,700

## Solution 9.2

(a)

*Appropriation Account*

| | £ | | £ |
|---|---|---|---|
| Share of Profit: | | Profit.................. | 42,000 |
| Jack.................... | 14,000 | | |
| Jill..................... | 14,000 | | |
| Jane.................... | 14,000 | | |
| | 42,000 | | 42,000 |

(b) In the absence of an agreement to the contrary, the provisions of the Partnership Act 1890 apply. The profit is divided equally between the partners and there are no charges for salaries or interest.

# Solution 9.3

*Current Accounts*

|  | Ice £ | Cube £ |  | Ice £ | Cube £ |
|---|---|---|---|---|---|
| Drawings: |  |  | Balance b/d........ | 30,000 | 20,000 |
| Cash.............. | 12,500 | 14,000 | Share of profit...... | 22,500 | 22,500 |
| Car disposal a/c..... | 1,500 |  |  |  |  |
| Transfer to |  |  |  |  |  |
| capital account........ | 20,000 | 10,000 |  |  |  |
| Balance c/d.......... | 18,500 | 18,500 |  |  |  |
|  | 52,500 | 42,500 |  | 52,500 | 42,500 |

*Capital Accounts*

|  | Ice £ | Cube £ |  | Ice £ | Cube £ |
|---|---|---|---|---|---|
| Balance c/d.......... | 70,000 | 70,000 | Balance b/d........ | 50,000 | 60,000 |
|  |  |  | Transfer from |  |  |
|  |  |  | Current Account.... | 20,000 | 10,000 |
|  | 70,000 | 70,000 |  | 70,000 | 70,000 |

# Solution 9.4

(a)

*Revaluation Account*

|  | £ |  | £ |
|---|---|---|---|
| Working Capital............ | 2,000 | Fixed assets............ | 5,000 |
| Bush...................... | 4,000 | Goodwill.............. | 9,000 |
| Shrub.................... | 8,000 |  |  |
|  | 14,000 |  | 14,000 |
| Fixed assets................ | 5,000 | Working capital........ | 2,000 |
| Goodwill.................. | 9,000 | Bush.................. | 4,000 |
|  |  | Shrub................. | 4,000 |
|  |  | Flower................. | 4,000 |
|  | 14,000 |  | 14,000 |

(b)                                    *Capital Accounts*

|  | Bush £ | Shrub £ | Flower £ |  | Bush £ | Shrub £ | Flower £ |
|---|---|---|---|---|---|---|---|
| Revaluation |  |  |  | Balance b/d.. | 10,000 | 20,000 | — |
| Account...... | 4,000 | 4,000 | 4,000 | Cash | — | — | 14,000 |
| Balance c/d... | 10,000 | 24,000 | 10,000 | Revaluation |  |  |  |
|  |  |  |  | Account | 4,000 | 8,000 | — |
|  | 14,000 | 28,000 | 14,000 |  | 14,000 | 28,000 | 14,000 |

(c)                          *Balance Sheet at 1 January 19X5*

| Capital: | £ |  | £ |
|---|---|---|---|
| Bush...................... | 10,000 | Fixed assets.............. | 15,000 |
| Shrub..................... | 24,000 | Working capital.......... | 29,000* |
| Flower.................... | 10,000 |  |  |
|  | 44,000 |  | 44,000 |

*Includes the cash received from Flower

# Solution 9.5

(a)                              *Realisation Account*

| | £ | | £ |
|---|---|---|---|
| Fixed assets................. | 30,000 | Hex Capital Account..... | 35,000 |
| Stock...................... | 21,000 | Why Capital Account.... | 1,500 |
| Debtors.................... | 7,200 | Cash from fixed assets.... | 6,000 |
| Cash-dissolution costs........ | 1,000 | Cash from stock......... | 22,000 |
| Surplus shared: |  | Cash from debtors....... | 6,850 |
| Hex..................... | 4,050 |  |  |
| Why.................... | 4,050 |  |  |
| Zed.................... | 4,050 |  |  |
|  | 71,350 |  | 71,350 |

(b)                                 *Cash Account*

| | £ | | £ |
|---|---|---|---|
| Balance b/d................ | 3,250 | Dissolution costs........ | 1,000 |
| Realisation Account: |  | Creditors ............. | 12,370 |
| Fixed assets.............. | 6,000 | Capital Account Why.... | 18,310 |
| Stock................... | 22,000 | Capital Account Zed..... | 20,010 |
| Debtors................. | 6,850 |  |  |
| Capital Account Hex......... | 13,590 |  |  |
|  | 51,690 |  | 51,690 |

(c)

*Capital Accounts*

|  | Hex £ | Why £ | Zed £ |  | Hex £ | Why £ | Zed £ |
|---|---|---|---|---|---|---|---|
| Realisation Account...... | 35,000 | 1,500 | — | Balance..... | 17,360 | 15,760 | 15,960 |
|  |  |  |  | Surplus..... | 4,050 | 4,050 | 4,050 |
| Cash........ | — | 18,310 | 20,010 | Cash........ | 13,590 | — | — |
|  | 35,000 | 19,810 | 20,010 |  | 35,000 | 19,810 | 20,010 |

# Solution 9.6

*Trading and Profit and Loss Account*
*Year to 31 December 19X4*

|  | £ | £ |
|---|---|---|
| Sales (200,000 + 6,400 + 5,460)................... |  | 211,860 |
| Purchases:  160,000 (bank) |  |  |
| 2,500 (cash) |  |  |
| 3,800 (creditors) |  |  |
| − 2,260 (drawings) |  |  |
|  | 164,040 |  |
| Less: Closing stock............................. | 9,200 |  |
| Cost of goods sold............................. |  | 154,840 |
| Gross profit................................. |  | 57,020 |
| Less: |  |  |
| Rent and rates (3,500 − 100)..................... | 3,400 |  |
| Light and heat (1,260 + 140).................... | 1,400 |  |
| Depreciation  (19,000 − 3,000)/5................. | 3,200 |  |
| Wages....................................... | 17,000 |  |
| Petrol....................................... | 2,000 |  |
| Maintenance ................................. | 1,000 |  |
| Advertising.................................. | 900 |  |
|  |  | 28,900 |
| Net Profit....................................... |  | 28,120 |
| Appropriation: |  |  |
| Minute...................................... | 14,060 |  |
| Second ..................................... | 14,060 |  |
|  |  | 28,120 |

*Balance Sheet at 31 December 19X4*

| | £ | £ | £ |
|---|---|---|---|
| Van: Cost................................. | | | 19,000 |
| Depreciation.......................... | | | 3,200 |
| | | | 15,800 |
| Current Assets: | | | |
| Stock................................. | | 9,200 | |
| Debtors............................... | | 5,460 | |
| Prepaid rent........................... | | 100 | |
| Cash.................................. | | 5,240 | |
| | | 20,000 | |
| Current Liabilities: | | | |
| Trade creditors......................... | 3,800 | | |
| Accrued light and heat.................... | 140 | | |
| | | 3,940 | |
| Working Capital.......................... | | | 16,060 |
| | | | 31,860 |

| | Second | Minute | |
|---|---|---|---|
| Capital Accounts.......................... | 20,000 | 20,000 | 40,000 |
| Current Accounts: | | | |
| Profit................................. | 14,060 | 14,060 | |
| Drawings: Cash......................... | (18,000) | (16,000) | |
| Stock........................ | (1,000) | (1,260) | |
| | (4,940) | (3,200) | (8,140) |
| | | | 31,860 |

# Solution 9.7

*Trading and Profit and Loss Account*
*for the Year to 31 March 19X3*

|  | £ | £ |
|---|---:|---:|
| Sales | | 150,000 |
| Opening stock | 30,000 | |
| Purchases | 110,000 | |
| Goods lost | (700) | |
| Stock drawings | (340) | |
| Closing stock | (40,000) | |
| *Cost of goods sold* | | 98,960 |
| *Gross profit* | | 51,040 |
| Depreciation | 1,500 | |
| Wages (14,500 + 500) | 15,000 | |
| Rent  (5,000 – 1,000) | 4,000 | |
| Expenses | 3,000 | |
| Heat and light | 1,200 | |
| Delivery | 5,300 | |
| | | 30,000 |
| *Net Trading Profit* | | 21,040 |
| *Appropriation:* | | |
| Interest on drawings: | | |
| Bean | | 200 |
| Stalk | | 300 |
| | | 21,540 |
| Salaries: | | |
| Bean | 2,000 | |
| Stalk | 4,000 | |
| | | 6,000 |
| | | 15,540 |
| Interest: | | |
| Bean | 1,500 | |
| Stalk | 500 | |
| | | 2,000 |
| | | 13,540 |
| Residue: | | |
| Bean | 6,770 | |
| Stalk | 6,770 | |
| | | 13,540 |

*Balance Sheet at 31 March 19X3*

|  | £ | £ | £ |
|---|---|---|---|
| Fixed assets................................... |  |  | 6,000 |
| Less: Depreciation............................ |  |  | 1,500 |
|  |  |  | 4,500 |
| **Current Assets:** |  |  |  |
| Stock..................................... |  | 40,000 |  |
| Debtors................................... |  | 14,000 |  |
| Debtor for goods lost........................ |  | 700 |  |
| Prepaid rent.............................. |  | 1,000 |  |
| Cash..................................... |  | 4,500 |  |
|  |  | 60,200 |  |
| **Current Liabilities:** |  |  |  |
| Creditors................................. | 11,500 |  |  |
| Accured Wages............................ | 500 |  |  |
|  |  | 12,000 |  |
| Working Capital............................. |  |  | 48,200 |
|  |  |  | 52,700 |

|  | Bean | Stalk |  |
|---|---|---|---|
| Capital..................................... | 30,000 | 10,000 | 40,000 |
| **Current Accounts:** |  |  |  |
| Balance 1 April 19X2........................ | 3,000 | 5,000 |  |
| Interest on drawings........................ | (200) | (300) |  |
| Drawings: Cash............................ | (7,000) | (9,000) |  |
| Stock............................ | (340) | — |  |
| Interest on capital......................... | 1,500 | 500 |  |
| Salaries................................... | 2,000 | 4,000 |  |
| Share of residue........................... | 6,770 | 6,770 |  |
|  | 5,730 | 6,970 | 12,700 |
|  |  |  | 52,700 |

## Solution 10.1

(i)  *Provisions.* These are balances set aside to meet known liabilities, the amount of which canot be ascertained with substantial accuracy. Examples: Provisions for bad debts and depreciation.

*Reserves.* These are transfers made out of profits to meet no specific liability presently known to the directors of the company. Examples: Reserves for contingencies and the equalisation of dividends.

(ii) (a) Provisions are a cost of operating the business and appear as a deduction in arriving at profit for the year, i.e. they are charged 'above the line'. Reserves appear as appropriations of reported profit, i.e. they are deducted 'below the line'.

(b) In the balance sheet, provisions appear either as a deduction from the asset to which they relate or as a current liability; reserves appear as part of the shareholders' equity.

## Solution 10.2

(a) *Profit and Loss Account*

|  | 19X0 £000 | 19X1 £000 |
|---|---|---|
| Gross profit | 2,930 | 3,605 |
| Less: Administration expenses | 1,620 | 1,809 |
| Selling costs | 520 | 572 |
| Distribution costs | 140 | 164 |
| Depreciation costs | 250 | 300 |
|  | 2,530 | 2,845 |
| Net profit | 400 | 760 |
| Less: Proposed dividend | 100 | 200 |
| Transfer to general reserve | — | 500 |
|  | 100 | 700 |
| Retained profit for the year | 300 | 60 |
| Add: Retained profit at 1 January | 290 | 590 |
| Retained profit at 31 December | 590 | 650 |

*Balance Sheet at 31 December*

| | £000 | 19X0 £000 | £000 | 19X1 £000 |
|---|---|---|---|---|
| Plant and machinery at cost...... | | 1,840 | | 2,650 |
| Less: Depreciation.............. | | 520 | | 820 |
| | | 1,320 | | 1,830 |
| *Current Assets:* | | | | |
| Stock......................... | 724 | | 771 | |
| Debtors...................... | 570 | | 524 | |
| Bank......................... | 92 | | 305 | |
| | 1,386 | | 1,600 | |
| *Current Liabilities:* | | | | |
| Creditors .................... | 416 | | 480 | |
| Dividend..................... | 100 | | 200 | |
| | 516 | | 680 | |
| Working capital............... | | 870 | | 920 |
| | | 2,190 | | 2,750 |
| Financed by: | | | | |
| Share capital.................. | | 1,600 | | 1,600 |
| General reserve............... | | — | | 500 |
| Profit and loss account......... | | 590 | | 650 |
| | | 2,190 | | 2,750 |

(b) The revised accounts show that the *retained* profit is much lower in 19X1, but the *net* profit earned is almost twice as high as in 19X0. The draft accounts do not distinguish between *charges* against profit and *appropriations* of profit, and the revised accounts show that the lower retained profit is principally due to the large transfer to general reserve which was not made in the previous year. The fact that profits have substantially increased fully justifies the directors' decision to increase the dividend to £200,000. A further point which should be considered is whether there is sufficient cash available to finance the proposed distribution. However, there is £305,000 in the bank account and this suggests that the company will have no difficulty in meeting the dividend payment when it falls due.

# Solution 10.3

(a)  *Trading and Profit and Loss Account for 19X9*

|  | £ | £ |
|---|---:|---:|
| Sales | | 2,350,000 |
| Less: Opening stock | 206,300 | |
| Purchases | 1,650,000 | |
| Closing stock | (217,800) | |
| Cost of goods sold | | 1,638,500 |
| Gross profit | | 711,500 |
| Less: Director's remuneration | 60,000 | |
| Wages and salaries | 198,700 | |
| Motor expenses | 42,300 | |
| Rates (10,500 − 2,000) | 8,500 | |
| Legal expenses (9,100 − 7,900) | 1,200 | |
| General expenses | 86,000 | |
| Bad debts | 15,700 | |
| Loss on sale of motor van (1,750 − 1,000) | 750 | |
| Depreciation of motor vans | 48,000(1) | |
| Debenture interest | 37,500 | 498,650 |
| Net profit before tax | | 212,850 |
| Corporation tax | | 90,000 |
| Net profit after tax | | 122,850 |
| Less: Transfer to debenture redemption reserve | 25,000 | |
| Proposed dividend | 84,000 | 109,000 |
| Retained profit for the year | | 13,850 |
| Retained profit at the beginning of the year | | 17,500 |
| Retained profit at the end of the year | | 31,350 |

*Balance Sheet as at 31 December 19X9*

| *Fixed Assets* | £ | £ | £ |
|---|---|---|---|
| Freehold properties at cost | | | |
| (850,000 + 7,900)............................ | | | 857,900 |
| Motor vans at cost............................ | | 240,000(1) | |
| Less: Accumulated depreciation............... | | 140,950(1) | 99,050 |
| | | | 956,950 |
| *Current Assets* | | | |
| Stock....................................... | | 217,800 | |
| Debtors..................................... | | 166,500 | |
| Rates paid in advance........................ | | 2,000 | |
| Bank........................................ | | 96,900 | |
| | | 483,200 | |
| *Less: Current Liabilities* | | | |
| Trade creditors............................. | 159,800 | | |
| Corporation tax............................. | 90,000 | | |
| Dividend.................................... | 84,000 | 333,800 | 149,400 |
| Total assets less current liabilities............. | | | 1,106,350 |
| Less: 15% Debentures, repayable 19Y5......... | | | 250,000 |
| | | | 856,350 |
| *Financed by* | | | |
| Authorised share capital..................... | | | 700,000 |
| Issued ordinary shares of £1 each............. | | | 700,000 |
| Debenture redemption reserve................. | | | 125,000 |
| Retained profit.............................. | | | 31,350 |
| | | | 856,350 |

*Workings*

(1)

| | Cost | Depreciation |
|---|---|---|
| | £ | £ |
| Motor vans | | |
| Balance at 1 January.......................... | 225,000 | 101,200 |
| Sales......................................... | (10,000) | (8,250) |
| Additions..................................... | 25,000 | |
| Charge for year, 20% of £240,000................ | | 48,000 |
| | 240,000 | 140,950 |

(b) On 1 January 19X5 the company issued debentures which are repayable ten years later in 19Y5. It is the directors' policy to make annual transfers of £25,000, to a debenture redemption reserve, and these will accumulate to £250,000 over the period of the loan.

## Solution 10.5

The purpose of the bonus issue is to give formal acknowledgement to the fact that profits, retained by the directors in previous years, have been permanently invested in business assets and no longer remain available for distribution. At 31 March 19X6 the company has cash available of £268,000, of which £75,000 is required to finance the proposed dividend, and £120,000 is needed to pay for the plant recently purchased. This leaves a modest balance to meet operating expenses. It is therefore clear that the company has no surplus cash resources, and it was therefore perfectly reasonable to capitalise the bulk of the retained profits. It is possible to argue that a smaller bonus issue might have been made some years earlier, but certain formalities are involved and it is not a process which management will wish to undertake on a regular basis.

## Solution 10.6

(a)

*Profit and Loss Account, Year ended 31 Dec. 19X9*

|  | £ | £ |
|---|---|---|
| Gross profit on trading............................ |  | 416,500 |
| Less: Rent and rates (£30,000 − £6,000).............. | 24,000 |  |
| Office salaries............................. | 142,600 |  |
| Advertising costs........................... | 21,000 |  |
| Transport costs............................ | 23,600 |  |
| Depreciation.............................. | 37,500 | 248,700 |
| Net profit before tax............................. |  | 167,800 |
| Taxation........................................ |  | 83,900 |
| Net profit after tax................................ |  | 83,900 |
| Retained profit at beginning of year.................. | 278,500 |  |
| Less: Bonus issue............................... | 100,000 | 178,500 |
| Retained profit at end of year...................... |  | 262,400 |

*Balance Sheet at 31 December 19X9*

|  | £ | £ |
|---|---|---|
| Freehold property at valuation...................... |  | 650,000 |
| Furniture and equipment at cost..................... | 375,000 |  |
| Less: Accumulated depreciation £59,500 + £37,500 | 97,000 | 278,000 |
|  |  | 928,000 |
| **Current Assets** |  |  |
| Stock and work in progress......................... | 104,200 |  |
| Debtors and prepayments £105,000 + £6,000.......... | 111,000 |  |
| Deposit........................................... | 10,000 |  |
| Temporary investment............................. | 60,000 |  |
| Balance at bank................................... | 72,000 |  |
|  | 357,200 |  |
| **Current Liabilities** |  |  |
| Creditors an accruals.............................. | 85,300 |  |
| Taxation due 1 Jan. 19Y0.......................... | 103,600 |  |
| 1 Jan. 19Y1.......................... | 83,900 |  |
|  | 272,800 | 84,400 |
| Working capital................................... |  | 1,012,400 |
| Financed by: |  |  |
| Ordinary share capital £500,000 + £100,000.......... |  | 600,000 |
| Revaluation reserve............................... |  | 150,000 |
| Profit and loss account............................ |  | 262,400 |
|  |  | 1,012,400 |

(b) A dividend of 10 pence per share on the revised share capital of £600,000 would involve a payment of £60,000. There is no doubt that the bank balance at 31 December 19X9 appears sufficient to support this payment, and the after tax profits for the year are £83,900. Consideration must however be given to the company's future commitments. During January 19Y0, a tax payment of £103,600 must be made as well as £40,000 for the new equipment when delivery takes place. This would suggest that bank overdraft facilities will be required during January even if no dividend is paid, although the position would be partially alleviated by the sale of the temporary investment. Funds generated from trading operations during 19X9 amounted to £205,300 (profit £167,800 and depreciation £37,500), and this should soon make good any cash shortage if the results are repeated during 19Y0. Nevertheless a dividend payment of £60,000 is probably unwise at this stage.

# Solution 11.1

*(£000)*

| | Branch | | | Total |
|---|---|---|---|---|
| | 1 | 2 | 3 | |
| Sales......................... | 250 | 300 | 175 | 725 |
| Cost of goods sold............. | 125 | 160 | 67 | 352 |
| Gross profit.................. | 125 | 140 | 108 | 373 |
| Branch expenses............... | 60 | 85 | 47 | 192 |
| Branch surplus................ | 65 | 55 | 61 | 181 |
| Head office expenses............ | | | | 90 |
| Profit........................ | | | | 91 |

# Solution 11.2

### Rock Ltd - Forecast Results for Additional Sales

| Proposal | (i) | | (ii) | | (iii) | |
|---|---|---|---|---|---|---|
| Additional sales (in units) | 25,000 | 50,000 | 25,000 | 50,000 | 25,000 | 50,000 |
| Process X | | | | | | |
| Materials..................... | 5,000 | 10,000 | | | | |
| Wages........................ | 7,500 | 15,000 | 80p x | 80p x | | |
| Depreciation.................. | 12,000 | 12,000 | 25,000 | 50,000 | | |
| Rent......................... | 8,000 | 8,000 | | | | |
| To process Y..................... | 32,500 | 45,000 | 20,000 | 40,000 | | |
| | | | | | 180p x | 180px |
| Process Y...................... | | | | | 25,000 | 50,000 |
| Materials..................... | 2,500 | 5,000 | 2,500 | 5,000 | | |
| Wages........................ | 10,000 | 20,000 | 10,000 | 20,000 | | |
| Depreciation.................. | 12,000 | 12,000 | 12,000 | 12,000 | | |
| Rent......................... | 8,000 | 8,000 | 8,000 | 8,000 | | |
| Cost of Production.............. | 65,000 | 90,000 | 52,500 | 85,000 | 45,000 | 90,000 |
| General Expenses................. | 2,000 | 4,000 | 2,000 | 4,000 | 2,000 | 4,000 |
| Net Profit (Loss)................ | (17,000) | 6,000 | (4,500) | 11,000 | 3,000 | 6,000 |
| Sales......................... | 50,000 | 100,000 | 50,000 | 100,000 | 50,000 | 100,000 |

# Solution 11.3

| (a) | £ | £ | £ | £ | £ | £ |
|---|---|---|---|---|---|---|
| Sales............................ | | 46,000 | | 92,000 | | 138,000 |
| Variable Cost.................... | 25,300 | | 50,600 | | 75,900 | |
| Depreciation.................... | 3,600 | | 7,200 | | 10,800 | |
| General Expenses................. | 10,000 | | 14,000 | | 18,000 | |
| Interest*........................ | 3,900 | | 9,300 | | 14,700 | |
| | | 42,800 | | 81,100 | | 119,400 |
| Profit | | 3,200 | | 10,900 | | 18,600 |
| *Calculation: | | | | | | |
| Cost of plant.................... | | 36,000 | | 72,000 | | 108,000 |
| Available for investment........... | | 10,000 | | 10,000 | | 10,000 |
| Balance to be borrowed........... | | 26,000 | | 62,000 | | 98,000 |
| Borrowings at 15%.............. | | 3,900 | | 9,300 | | 14,700 |

(b)   Eagles can either retain ownership of the business or sell it to Troon Ltd and remain as manager. Under either of these options his income varies according to the level of sales, and is calculated as follows:

| Sales | £ Existing | £ + 46,000 | £ + 92,000 | £ + 138,000 |
|---|---|---|---|---|
| *Retain ownership:* | | | | |
| Existing profit................ | 20,000 | 20,000 | 20,000 | 20,000 |
| Profit from exports............ | – | 3,200 | 10,900 | 18,600 |
| Total Income.................. | 20,000 | 23,200 | 30,900 | 38,600 |
| *Sell to Troon Ltd:* | | | | |
| Invest proceeds of sale to earn annual interest............. | 12,000 | 12,000 | 12,000 | 12,000 |
| Salary as manager.............. | 14,000 | 14,000 | 14,000 | 14,000 |
| Bonus for additional sales........ | – | 3,000 | 6,000 | 9,000 |
| Total | 26,000 | 29,000 | 32,000 | 35,000 |

It can be seen that Eagles is better off to sell the business and work as manager unless the largest increase in sales under consideration can be achieved. He must consider whether this is likely. Also, the relief of no longer having the responsibility of both owning and managing the business may be attractive together with the possession of personal capital in the form of cash. These considerations may induce him to sell the business even if he considers the higher income from retention can probably be achieved.

## Solution 11.4

*Summary Profit and Loss Account*

|  | £000 |
|---|---|
| Sales (60,000 x £5).............. | 300 |
| Variable Costs (60,000 X £3*)..... | 180 |
| Total Contribution............ | 120 |
| Fixed Costs**.................. | 100 |
| Net Profit..................... | 20 |

\*   £5 (Selling Price) − £2 (Contribution) = £3 (Variable Cost)
\*\* Balancing figure

(b)
$$\frac{\text{Fixed Costs}}{\text{Contribution}} = \frac{£100,000}{£2} = 50,000 \text{ units}$$

50,000 x £5 = £250,000

(c)
$$\frac{\text{Fixed Costs}}{\text{Contribution}} = \frac{(£100,000 + £4,500)}{(£2 - £0.10)} = 55,000 \text{ units}$$

£55,000 × £5 = £275,000

# Solution 11.5

(a)

| | £ | £ |
|---|---|---|
| Sales | | 400,000 |
| Raw Materials | 100,000 | |
| Wages | 200,000 | |
| Depreciation | 20,000 | |
| | | 320,000 |
| Gross Profit | | 80,000 |
| General Expenses (20,000 + 15,000*) | 35,000 | |
| Interest | 10,000 | |
| | | 45,000 |
| Net Profit | | 35,000 |

(b)

| | £ | £ |
|---|---|---|
| Selling Price per Unit | | 2.00 |
| Variable costs: | | |
| Raw Materials | .50 | |
| Wages | .30 | |
| | | .80 |
| Contribution | | 1.20 |
| Fixed Costs: | | |
| Depreciation | | 20,000 |
| Interest | | 20,000 |
| Expenses* | | 15,000 |
| | | 55,000 |
| Additional Profit: | | |
| Profit under Plan 1 | | 35,000 |
| Existing Profit | | 20,000 |
| | | 15,000 |

Sales = $\dfrac{55,000 + 15,000}{1.20}$ = 58,333 units OR 58,333 x £2 = £116,667

* The increase in sales is greater than £100,000 and so the full additional general expenses are incurred.

(c)   The condition necessary for the company as a whole to make the same profit as in 19X6 is that the extra sales break even. This point is calculated as follows:

|  | £ |
|---|---|
| Fixed Costs of Plan 2: | |
| Depreciation ................ | 20,000 |
| Interest .................... | 20,000 |
| Expenses** ................. | 5,000 |
|  | 45,000 |

Break even sales = $\frac{45,000}{1.2}$ = 37,500 units OR 37,500 x 2 = £75,000

**   As the increase in sales is less than £100,000, the additional expenses are limited to £5,000.

## Solution 11.6

(a)

|  | Plan 1 £ | Plan 2 £ |
|---|---|---|
| Sales ......................................... | 84,000 | 112,500 |
| Expenses...................................... | 76,440 | 103,500 |
| Net profit.................................... | 7,560 | 9,000 |

(b)   The net profit percentages are:

| 19X5 | 19X6 Plan 1 | 19X6 Plan 2 |
|---|---|---|
| $\frac{5,600 \times 100}{56,000}$ | $\frac{7,560 \times 100}{84,000}$ | $\frac{9,000 \times 100}{112,500}$ |
| = 10% | = 9% | = 8% |

Both plans give a higher net profit than 19X5 together with a lower net profit ratio. Plan 2 gives the higher net profit, but has a lower net profit ratio. However, as Plan 2 involves a much greater capital investment than Plan 1, its results must be judged on the basis of relative return on capital employed, which is discussed in Chapter 12.

## Solution 11.7

|  | Jan £ | Feb £ | March £ | April £ | May £ | June £ |
|---|---|---|---|---|---|---|
| Receipts: | | | | | | |
| Sales ............. | – | – | 12,000 | 12,000 | 12,000 | 12,000 |
| Capital ........... | 20,000 | | | | | |
| Loan ............. | 8,000 | | | | | |
|  | 28,000 | – | 12,000 | 12,000 | 12,000 | 12,000 |
| Payments: | | | | | | |
| Fixed Assets....... | 20,000 | | | | | |
| Purchases......... | – | 16,000 | 8,000 | 8,000 | 8,000 | 8,000 |
| Expenses.......... | 800 | 800 | 800 | 800 | 800 | 800 |
| Drawings ......... | 200 | 200 | 200 | 200 | 200 | 200 |
| Interest .......... | – | – | – | – | – | 400 |
|  | 21,000 | 17,000 | 9,000 | 9,000 | 9,000 | 9,400 |
| Opening balance..... | – | 7,000 | (10,000) | (7,000) | (4,000) | (1,000) |
| + Receipts .......... | 28,000 | – | 12,000 | 12,000 | 12,000 | 12,000 |
| – Payments ......... | 21,000 | 17,000 | 9,000 | 9,000 | 9,000 | 9,400 |
| Closing Balance | 7,000 | (10,000) | (7,000) | (4,000) | (1,000) | 1,600 |

# Solution 11.8

*Forecast Trading and Profit and Loss Account*

|  | £ | £ |
|---|---|---|
| Sales(W2)................................................. |  | 72,000 |
| Less: Cost of Goods Sold (W3)...................... |  | 48,000 |
| Gross Profit..................................................... |  | 24,000 |
| Expenses (W1).................................................. | 4,800 |  |
| Loan Interest (.5 x 8,000 x 10%) | 400 |  |
| Overdraft Interest............................................... | 300 |  |
| Depreciation (.5 x 20,000 x 20%)................... | 2,000 |  |
|  |  | 7,500 |
| Net Profit...................................................... |  | 16,500 |

*Forecast Balance Sheet*

|  | £ | £ |
|---|---|---|
| **FIXED ASSETS** |  |  |
| Cost............................................................ |  | 20,000 |
| Less: Depreciation............................................... |  | 2,000 |
|  |  | 18,000 |
| **CURRENT ASSETS** |  |  |
| Stock (W3)...................................................... | 8,000 |  |
| Debtors (May + June sales)......................... | 24,000 |  |
| Cash (W1)....................................................... | 1,600 |  |
|  | 33,600 |  |
| **CURRENT LIABILITIES** |  |  |
| Trade Creditors (June purchases).................... | 8,000 |  |
| Accrued Interest................................................ | 300 |  |
|  | 8,300 |  |
| **WORKING CAPITAL** |  | 25,300 |
|  |  | 43,300 |
| **CAPITAL** |  |  |
| Capital Introduced.............................................. |  | 20,000 |
| Profit............................................................. |  | 16,500 |
|  |  | 36,500 |
| Less: Drawings (W1)............................................ |  | 1,200 |
| Closing Capital.................................................. |  | 35,300 |
| Loan.............................................................. |  | 8,000 |
|  |  | 43,300 |

*Workings*

W1. Forecast cash account produced by adding across the individual columns in the solution to question 11.7.

### Cash Account

|  | £ |  | £ |
|---|---|---|---|
| Capital................. | 20,000 | Plant................... | 20,000 |
| Loan.................. | 8,000 | Creditors.............. | 48,000 |
| Debtors............... | 48,000 | Expenses............... | 4,800 |
|  |  | Drawings.............. | 1,200 |
|  |  | Loan Interest........... | 400 |
|  |  | Balance c/d............ | 1,600 |
|  | 76,000 |  | 76,000 |

W2. Sales can be calculated in two alternative ways:

(a)  Sales = Cash from debtors + closing debtors*

= £48,000(W1) + £24,000(May + June sales) = £72,000

OR

(b)  £12,000(monthly sales) x 6 (number of months) = £72,000

W3. Cost of Goods Sold

Purchases can be calculated in two alternative ways:

(a)  Purchases = Payments to creditors + closing creditors*

= £48,000(W1) + £8,000(June purchases) = £56,000

OR

(b)  £16,000(January purchases) + (5 x £8,000) = £56,000

Cost of Goods Sold = Purchases − Closing Stock*

= £56,000 − £8,000** = £48,000

\*   As this is the first period of trading, there are no opening debtors, creditors or stocks.

|  |  | £ |
|---|---|---|
| ** | Purchases.......................... | 56,000 |
|  | Less:  Cost of Goods Sold: |  |
|  | $\frac{100}{150}$ x £72,000(sales)............. | 48,000 |
|  | Closing Stock........................ | 8,000 |

# Solution 12.1

(a) Gross profit margin $\qquad \dfrac{54,000}{180,000} \times 100 \qquad = 30\%$

Net profit as a % of sales $\qquad \dfrac{15,000}{180,000} \times 100 \qquad = 8.3\%$

Return on capital employed $\qquad \dfrac{15,000}{150,000} \times 100 \qquad = 10\%$

(b) An increase in the ROCE to 12.5% would require additional profit of £150,000 × 2.5% = £3,750. The gross profit margin is 30% and an additional turnover of £3,750 × (100 ÷ 30) = £12,500 would produce the required increase in net profit

# Solution 12.2

(a) *Workings:*

*Balance Sheet, 31 December*

|  | 19X1 | | 19X2 | |
|---|---|---|---|---|
|  | £000 | £000 | £000 | £000 |
| Fixed assets............................... |  | 500 |  | 550 |
| Current assets: Stock........................ | 150 |  | 200 |  |
| Trade debtors................. | 125 |  | 150 |  |
| Cash at bank.................. | 25 |  | — |  |
|  | 300 |  | 350 |  |
| Less: Current Liabilities: Trade creditors...... | 80 |  | 100 |  |
| Proposed dividend... | 20 |  | 60 |  |
| Overdraft........... | — |  | 20 |  |
|  | 100 |  | 180 |  |
| Working capital............................ |  | 200 |  | 170 |
| Shareholders' equity (capital employed)........ |  | 700 |  | 720 |

*Profit and Loss Account*

|  | | | | |
|---|---|---|---|---|
| Sales..................................... |  | 2,000 |  | 3,000 |
| Less: Cost of sales......................... | 1,000 |  | 1,450 |  |
| Overhead costs....................... | 800 | 1,800 | 1,300 | 2,750 |
| Net profit................................ |  | 200 |  | 250 |

|  |  |  | 19X1 |  |  | 19X2 |
|---|---|---|---|---|---|---|
| Return on capital employed................. | $\dfrac{200}{700}$ | × 100 | 28.6% | $\dfrac{250}{720}$ | × 100 | 33.3% |
| Working capital........... |  |  | 200 |  |  | 170 |
| Working capital ratio....... | $\dfrac{300}{100}$ | : 1 | 3:1 | $\dfrac{350}{180}$ | : 1 | 1.9:1 |
| Liquidity ratio............. | $\dfrac{125+25}{100}$ | : 1 | 1.5:1 | $\dfrac{150}{180}$ | : 1 | 0.8:1 |

(b) Lock Ltd. earned a high rate of return on the shareholders' investment during 19X1, which has been improved on during 19X2. The balance sheet, at 31 December 19X1, shows a strong financial position with the working capital and liquidity ratios each at a high level for a wholesale trading company. There has been a significant decline in the solvency position during the year. The ratios suggest that the company will find it difficult to meet its debts as they fall due for payment. The proposal to pay a final dividend three times last year's level may need to be reconsidered.

# Solution 12.3

(a)

|  | 19X2 | 19X3 |
|---|---|---|
| Current assets | 17,000 | 23,000 |
| Current liabilities | 6,000 | 10,700 |
| Working capital | 11,000 | 12,300 |
| Working capital ratio | 2.8:1 | 2.2:1 |

(b) *Work Sheet*

### Balance Sheets 31 December

|  | 19X2 £ | 19X3 £ | Differences Sources £ | Differences Applications £ |
|---|---|---|---|---|
| Fixed assets at cost | 25,000 | 30,000 |  | 5,000 |
| Less: Accumulated depreciation | 5,000 | 6,500 | 1,500 |  |
|  | 20,000 | 23,500 |  |  |
| Stock | 11,000 | 17,000 |  | 6,000 |
| Debtors | 5,000 | 6,000 |  | 1,000 |
| Cash at bank | 1,000 | — | 1,000 |  |
|  | 37,000 | 46,500 |  |  |
| Share capital | 20,000 | 20,000 |  |  |
| Reserves | 10,000 | 15,000 | 5,000 |  |
| Debentures | 1,000 | 800 |  | 200 |
| Trade creditors | 6,000 | 7,500 | 1,500 |  |
| Overdraft | — | 3,200 | 3,200 |  |
|  | 37,000 | 46,500 | 12,200 | 12,200 |

*Statement of Funds for 19X3*

|  | £ | £ |
|---|---|---|
| SOURCES | | |
| Profit........................................ | | 5,000 |
| Add: Depreciation.............................. | | 1,500 |
| | | |
| Funds generated from operations.................. | | 6,500 |
| APPLICATIONS | | |
| Purchase of plant............................. | 5,000 | |
| Repayment of debentures....................... | 200 | 5,200 |
| | | |
| INCREASE IN WORKING CAPITAL | | 1,300 |
| CHANGES IN WORKING CAPITAL ITEMS | | |
| Decreases in working capital | | |
| Trade creditors................................ | (1,500) | |
| Bank (£3,200 + £1,000)........................ | (4,200) | |
| Increases in working capital | | |
| Stock......................................... | 6,000 | |
| Debtors....................................... | 1,000 | 1,300 |

(c) The main feature is the heavy build up of stock. This has been financed partly by creditors but mainly by the bank with the result that the cash balance, at the beginning of the year, has been replaced by a large overdraft.

# Solution 12.4

| *Work Sheet* | *19X1* | | *19X2* | | *Differences* | |
|---|---|---|---|---|---|---|
| | | | | | | *Appli-* |
| | | | | | *Sources* | *cations* |
| | £ | £ | £ | £ | £ | £ |
| *Fixed Assets:* | | | | | | |
| Plant at cost............. | 52,000 | | 70,000 | | | 18,000 |
| Less: Depreciation........ | 16,500 | 35,500 | 22,700 | 47,300 | 6,200 | |
| | | | | | | |
| Transport at cost......... | 10,000 | | 10,000 | | | |
| Less: Depreciation........ | 3,600 | 6,400 | 4,800 | 5,200 | 1,200 | |
| | | 41,900 | | 52,500 | | |
| *Current Assets:* | | | | | | |
| Stocks.................. | 10,200 | | 12,600 | | | 2,400 |
| Debtors................. | 8,300 | | 13,700 | | | 5,400 |
| Bank................... | 4,900 | | — | | 4,900 | |
| | | 23,400 | | 26,300 | | |

*Less: Current Liabilities*

| | | | | |
|---|---|---|---|---|
| Trade creditors . . . . . . . . . . | 5,100 | | 5,800 | | 700 |
| Bank overdraft . . . . . . . . . . | — | | 1,300 | | 1,300 |
| | 5,100 | | 7,100 | | |
| Working capital . . . . . . . . . | | 18,300 | | 19,200 | |
| | | 60,200 | | 71,700 | |

Financed by:

| | | | | | | |
|---|---|---|---|---|---|---|
| Share capital . . . . . . . . . . . . | 50,000 | | 54,000 | 4,000 | |
| Profit and loss account . . . . | 10,200 | | 17,700 | 7,500 | |
| | 60,200 | | 71,700 | 25,800 | 25,800 |

### Statement of Funds for 19X2

| SOURCES OF FUNDS | £ | £ |
|---|---|---|
| Profit . . . . . . . . . . . . . . . . . . . . . . . . . . . . . . . . . . . . . | | 7,500 |
| Add: Depreciation . . . . . . . . . . . . . . . . . . . . . . . . . . . | | 7,400 |
| Funds generated from operations . . . . . . . . . . . . . . . . . | | 14,900 |
| Funds from other sources: | | |
| Share capital . . . . . . . . . . . . . . . . . . . . . . . . . . . . . . . . | | 4,000 |
| | | 18,900 |

| APPLICATIONS OF FUNDS | |
|---|---|
| Purchase of plant . . . . . . . . . . . . . . . . . . . . . . . . . . . . . | 18,000 |

| INCREASE IN WORKING CAPITAL | |
|---|---|
| | 900 |

CHANGES IN WORKING CAPITAL ITEMS

Decrease in working capital

| | | |
|---|---|---|
| Bank . . . . . . . . . . . . . . . . . . . . . . . . . . . . . . . . . . . . . . . | (6,200) | |
| Trade creditors . . . . . . . . . . . . . . . . . . . . . . . . . . . . . . | (700) | |

Increase in working capital

| | | |
|---|---|---|
| Stocks . . . . . . . . . . . . . . . . . . . . . . . . . . . . . . . . . . . . . | 2,400 | |
| Debtors . . . . . . . . . . . . . . . . . . . . . . . . . . . . . . . . . . . . | 5,400 | 900 |

# Solution 12.5

*Work Sheet*       *Balance Sheet 31 March*

|  | 19X3 £ | 19X4 £ | Differences Sources £ | Applications £ |
|---|---|---|---|---|
| Share capital................. | 500,000 | 600,000 | 100,000 | |
| Retained profit................ | 395,800 | 427,100 | 31,300 | |
| 10% Debentures.............. | 200,000 | 300,000 | 100,000 | |
| Creditors .................... | 179,800 | 207,500 | 27,700 | |
| Proposed dividend............. | 50,000 | 60,000 | 10,000 | |
| Bank overdraft................ | — | 36,900 | 36,900 | |
| | 1,325,600 | 1,631,500 | | |
| Plant at cost.................. | 658,300 | 796,900 | | 138,600 |
| Less: Depreciation............. | 263,500 | 371,600 | 108,100 | |
| | 394,800 | 425,300 | | |
| Freehold property............. | 300,000 | 350,000 | | 50,000 |
| Stock........................ | 327,100 | 608,300 | | 281,200 |
| Debtors...................... | 265,700 | 247,900 | 17,800 | |
| Cash at bank................. | 38,000 | — | 38,000 | |
| | 1,325,600 | 1,631,500 | 469,800 | 469,800 |

### Statement of Source and Application of Funds

| SOURCES OF FUNDS | £ | £ |
|---|---|---|
| Net profit...................................... | | 191,300(1) |
| Add: Depreciation............................. | 295,600(1) | |
| Loss on sale of plant and equipment.......... | 33,000(2) | 328,600 |
| | | |
| Funds generated from operations.................. | | 519,900 |
| Funds from other sources........................ | | |
| Debentures issued............................ | 100,000 | |
| Sale of plant and equipment...................... | 169,500 | 269,500 |
| | | 789,400 |
| APPLICATIONS OF FUNDS | | |
| Freehold property............................. | 50,000 | |
| Plant and equipment........................... | 528,600(1) | |
| Dividend proposed............................ | 60,000 | 638,600 |
| | | |
| INCREASE IN WORKING CAPITAL.............. | | 150,800 |

CHANGES IN WORKING CAPITAL ITEMS

Decrease in working capital

| | | |
|---|---|---|
| Creditors..................................... | (27,700) | |
| Dividend..................................... | (10,000) | |
| Bank......................................... | (74,900) | |
| Debtors...................................... | (17,800) | |

Increase in working capital

| | | |
|---|---|---|
| Stock......................................... | 281,200 | 150,800 |

**Workings:**

(1)

| | Plant £ | Depreciation £ | Profit £ |
|---|---|---|---|
| Net increase (work sheet).................. | 138,600 | 108,100 | 31,300 |
| Add: Sale of plant........................ | 390,000 | 187,500* | |
| Proposed dividend.................. | | | 60,000 |
| Bonus issue........................ | | | 100,000** |
| Gross changes.......................... | 528,600 | 295,600 | 191,300 |

\* Accumulated depreciation £187,500 = Cost, £390,000—Book value, £202,500.

\*\* The bonus issue is a book entry and does not result in a flow of funds. It must therefore be added back to profit so that funds generated from operations is stated correctly and so that the increase in share capital does *not* appear as a source of funds.

(2) Loss on sale, £33,000 = £202,500 (book value of plant sold) — £169,500 (sales proceeds)

*Note:* To comply with SSAP 10, entitled the Statement of Source and Application of Funds, dividends and tax must be accounted for on the *cash* basis rather than the *accruals* basis, i.e. the amount shown as an application would be the amount paid *during* the year rather than the amount paid and provided for the year. Use of the cash basis to account for dividends, in the above example, results in the payment of £50,000 reported as an application and the increase in the dividend provision omitted from the list of changes in working capital items. A disadvantage of this procedure is that the actual change in working capital does not appear in the statement of funds.

## Solution 12.6 (Work sheet omitted)

(a)                                      *Statement of Funds for 19X4*

| SOURCES OF FUNDS | £ | £ |
|---|---:|---:|
| Profit (£5,500 + £44,000)...................... | | 49,500 |
| Add: Depreciation.............................. | | 27,200 |
| | | |
| Funds generated from operations................. | | 76,700 |
| APPLICATIONS OF FUNDS | | |
| Purchase of fixed assets........................ | 30,000 | |
| Dividends..................................... | 44,000 | |
| Debentures repaid............................. | 80,000 | 154,000 |
| | | |
| DECREASE IN WORKING CAPITAL | | (77,300) |
| CHANGES IN WORKING CAPITAL ITEMS | | |
| Decrease in working capital | | |
| Decrease in trade debtors....................... | (2,700) | |
| Decrease in bank.............................. | (61,500) | |
| Increase in creditors........................... | (14,200) | |
| Increase in working capital | | |
| Increase in stock.............................. | 1,100 | (77,300) |

(b) The company plans to pay out nearly all of its profits in the form of dividends, while the funds retained in the business by way of the depreciation charge have been used to purchase fixed assets. There are no other long-term sources of finance and the debentures have been repaid by running down working capital. The result is a large bank overdraft and, probably, severe liquidity problems.

# Solution 12.7

(a)             *Statement of Funds for 19X8*

| SOURCES OF FUNDS | £000 | £000 |
|---|---|---|
| Net profit from ordinary activities.................. | | 720 |
| Add: Depreciation.............................. | | 350 |
| | | |
| Funds generated from operations.................. | | 1,070 |
| Funds from other sources | | |
| Share issue (500 + 200)........................ | 700 | |
| Long-term loan.............................. | 300 | |
| Sale of investment........................... | 130 | 1,130 |
| | | 2,200 |
| APPLICATION OF FUNDS | | |
| Purchase of plant............................. | 410 | |
| Dividends paid................................ | 400 | 810 |
| | | |
| INCREASE IN WORKING CAPITAL.............. | | 1,390 |
| CHANGES IN WORKING CAPITAL ITEMS | | |
| Decrease in working capital | | |
| Increase in creditors........................... | (200) | |
| Increase in working capital | | |
| Increase in stocks............................. | 1,220 | |
| Increase in debtors............................ | 40 | |
| Increase in short-term loans and deposits | | |
| at bank.................................... | 330 | 1,390 |

| (b) | | |
|---|---|---|
| Accounting ratios.............................. | 19X7 | 19X8 |
| Working capital............................... | 2:1 | 3.1:1 |
| Liquidity...................................... | 1:1 | 1.2:1 |

The financial position at the end of 19X7 appears satisfactory when judged on the basis of relevant accounting ratios. The liquidity ratio is 1:1 and the working capital ratio is 2:1, both of which are about right for an engineering firm. At the end of 19X1, the working capital appears to be too high and the company is verging on excess liquidity.

The statement of funds shows that the company both raised and generated long-term funds significantly in excess of present business requirements. Funds generated from operations more than cover the dividend and plant acquisition, yet the company has issued shares, raised a loan and benefitted from the sale of investments. A great deal of the surplus finance is tied up in stocks; a non-income producing asset. The company's system of stock control should be examined to check whether it is being operated efficiently.

The effect of financial developments during 19X8 is a very strong financial position at the end of the year, but there is some doubt whether available resources are being effectively employed. Perhaps additional resources have been raised to finance *future* expansion, but there is no indication that this is the case.

# Solution 12.8

(a)              *Trading and Profit and Loss Accounts for 19X5*

|  | Metalmax | | Precision Products | |
|---|---|---|---|---|
|  | £000 | £000 | £000 | £000 |
| Sales . . . . . . . . . . . . . . . . . . . . . . . . . . . . . . . . |  | 800 |  | 950 |
| Less: Variable cost of sales . . . . . . . . . . . . . . . . . | 640 |  | 760 |  |
| Depreciation . . . . . . . . . . . . . . . . . . . . . . . | 54 |  | 54 |  |
| Cost of sales . . . . . . . . . . . . . . . . . . . . . . . . . . . . |  | 694 |  | 814 |
| Gross profit . . . . . . . . . . . . . . . . . . . . . . . . . . . . |  | 106 |  | 136 |
| Less: Administration expenses . . . . . . . . . . . . . . | 30 |  | 30 |  |
| Selling expenses . . . . . . . . . . . . . . . . . . . . . . | 45 | 75 | 60 | 90 |
| Net profit . . . . . . . . . . . . . . . . . . . . . . . . . . . . . . |  | 31 |  | 46 |

*Balance Sheets at 31 December 19X5*

|  | Metalmax | | Precision Products | |
|---|---|---|---|---|
|  | £000 | £000 | £000 | £000 |
| Plant and machinery at cost . . . . . . . . . . . . . . . . . |  | 360 |  | 360 |
| Less: Depreciation . . . . . . . . . . . . . . . . . . . . . . . . |  | 164 |  | 164 |
|  |  | 196 |  | 196 |
| *Current Assets:* |  |  |  |  |
| Stocks and work in progress . . . . . . . . . . . . . . . . | 120 |  | 200 |  |
| Other current assets . . . . . . . . . . . . . . . . . . . . . . . | 120 |  | 200 |  |
|  | 240 |  | 400 |  |
| *Less: Current Liabilities* |  |  |  |  |
| Working capital . . . . . . . . . . . . . . . . . . . . . . . . . . | 120 | 120 | 320 | 80 |
|  |  | 316 |  | 276 |
| Share capital . . . . . . . . . . . . . . . . . . . . . . . . . . . . . |  | 200 |  | 200 |
| Reserves . . . . . . . . . . . . . . . . . . . . . . . . . . . . . . . . |  | 116 |  | 76 |
|  |  | 316 |  | 276 |

(b)

| Accounting ratios | Metalmax | Precision Products |
|---|---|---|
| Gross profit margin . . . . . . . . . . . . . . . . . . . . . . . . . . . . . | 13.3% | 14.3% |
| Net profit percentage . . . . . . . . . . . . . . . . . . . . . . . . . . . | 3.9% | 4.8% |
| Return on total capital employed . . . . . . . . . . . . . . . . . . | 7.1% | 7.7% |
| Return on owners' equity . . . . . . . . . . . . . . . . . . . . . . . . . | 9.8% | 16.7% |
| Working capital ratio . . . . . . . . . . . . . . . . . . . . . . . . . . . . | 2:1 | 1.25:1 |
| Liquidity ratio . . . . . . . . . . . . . . . . . . . . . . . . . . . . . . . . . . | 1:1 | 0.6:1 |

Metalmax is the more solvent whereas Precision Products is the more profitable.

Variable cost of sales is 80% in the case of both companies. Precision Products produces the higher gross profit margin because, on the basis of an identical investment in fixed assets, it produces a significantly higher level of sales. The selling expenses of Precision Products are much higher, perhaps due to the fact that they advertise their products more heavily and distribute them more widely. However, the company retains its advantage and achieves the higher net profit margin. The rates of return on both versions of capital employed are higher at Precision Products. The difference is substantial in the case of return on owners' equity. This is because a large proportion of Precision Products' current assets are funded out of the 'free' finance provided by trade creditors. The consequence of this, however, is that Precision Products's solvency position, at the end of 19X5, is extremely weak. Metalmax, with a working capital ratio and liquidity ratio in line with conventional 'norms', is in a sound financial condition.

## Solution 13.1

(a) *Balances at 31 March (£000).*

| | |
|---|---|
| Current assets | 27 + 13 = 40 |
| Current liabilities | 7 + 10 = 17 |
| Working capital | 40 − 17 = 23 |

(b) *Balance Sheet at 1 April, 19X4 (£000).*

*Fixed assets:*

| | | |
|---|---|---|
| At cost (80 + 10)............................. | | 90 |
| Less: Depreciation............................ | | 35 |
| | | 55 |

*Current assets:*

| | | |
|---|---|---|
| Stock (27 + 2 − 3)........................... | 26 | |
| Debtors (13 − 6 + 5)......................... | 12 | |
| Bank (− 7 + 6 − 10 − 1 + 18)................. | 6 | |
| | 44 | |

*Current liabilities:*

| | | |
|---|---|---|
| Creditors (10 + 2 − 1)....................... | 11 | |
| Working capital.............................. | | 33 |
| | | 88 |
| Long term loan............................... | | 18 |
| | | 70 |

*Financed by:*

| | | |
|---|---|---|
| Share capital................................ | | 60 |
| Profit and loss account (8 + 2)................. | | 10 |
| | | 70 |

# Solution 13.2

(a)                       *Balances Sheet at 1 January, 19X3*

| | £ | £ | | £ | £ |
|---|---|---|---|---|---|
| Capital (Assets – Liabilities) | | 19,110 | Business premises..... | | 12,000 |
| Creditors: stock.......... | 2,380 | | Delivery van.......... | | 2,600 |
| electricity...... | 240 | | Shop fittings.......... | | 3,000 |
| Bank overdraft........... | 290 | 2,910 | | | 17,600 |
| | | | Stock................ | 4,350 | |
| | | | Cash in till............ | 70 | |
| | | | | | 4,420 |
| | | 22,020 | | | 22,020 |

*Note:*
Personal assets and liabilities are excluded to comply with the entity concept.

(b)                       *Trading & Profit & Loss Accounts.*
                          *Year to 31 December, 19X3*

| | £ | £ | £ |
|---|---|---|---|
| Sales (57,390 + £40, increase in float)............................ | | | 57,430 |
| less: Opening stock............................................ | | 4,350 | |
| Purchases (£31,270 − £2,380 + £1,780)...................... | | 30,670 | |
| Closing stock............................................. | | ( 5,220) | |
| Cost of goods sold....................................... | | | 29,800 |
| Gross profit................................................. | | | 27,630 |
| Less: Wages................................................. | | 9,480 | |
| Electricity (£1,020 − £240 + £150)......................... | | 930 | |
| Motor expenses.......................................... | | 920 | |
| Depreciation: Shop fittings................................ | | 500 | |
| Van........................................ | | 650 | 12,480 |
| Net profit | | | 15,150 |

*Balance Sheet at 31 December, 19X3*

| | £ | £ | | £ | £ |
|---|---|---|---|---|---|
| Opening capital......... | | 19,110 | Business premises..... | | 12,000 |
| Profit.................. | | 15,150 | Shop fittings......... | | 4,500 |
| | | | Delivery van......... | | 1,950 |
| | | 34,260 | | | |
| | | | | | 18,450 |
| Drawings............... | | 11,480 | | | |
| | | | | | |
| | | 22,780 | | | |
| Creditors: stock......... | 1,780 | | Stock................ | 5,220 | |
| electricity...... | 150 | | Bank................ | 930 | |
| | | | Cash float........... | 110 | 6,260 |
| | | 1,930 | | | |
| | | 24,710 | | | 24,710 |

# Solution 13.3

(a)(i)   Calculation of profit

Assets at 31 December 19X0:

| | £ | £ |
|---|---|---|
| Motor vans............................. | | 2,700 |
| Stock................................. | | 2,836 |
| Debtors............................... | | 3,121 |
| Cash.................................. | | 1,121 |
| Insurance prepaid...................... | | 26 |
| | | 9,804 |
| Less: Liabilities: | | |
| Creditors for: Purchases............... | 1,811 | |
| Rates................... | 62 | 1,873 |
| Closing capital of partners................... | | 7,931 |
| Add:Drawings:Leyton..................... | | 1,712 |
| Woodford.................. | | 1,529 |
| | | 11,172 |
| Less:Opening capital....................... | | 8,000 |
| Net profit............................... | | 3,172 |
| Allocated equally: Leyton................... | | 1,586 |
| Woodford............... | | 1,586 |

(ii)    Capital Accounts:

|  |  | Leyton | Woodford |
|---|---|---|---|
|  |  | £ | £ |
| Balance 1 January 19X0 | | 4,000 | 4,000 |
| Add: Net profit | | 1,586 | 1,586 |
| Less: Drawings | | (1,712) | ( 1,529) |
| Balance 31 December 19X0 | | 3,874 | 4,057 |

(b)             *Trading & Profit & Loss Account for 19X1.*

| | £ | | £ |
|---|---|---|---|
| Purchases (£30,886 − £1,811 | | Sales (£48,123 + £3,211 − £3,121) | 48,213 |
| + £2,162) | 31,237 | | |
| Add: Opening stocks | 2,836 | | |
| Less: Closing stocks | (3,249) | | |
| Cost of sales | 30,824 | | |
| Gross profit | 17,389 | | |
| | 48,213 | | 48,213 |
| Depreciation | 900 | Gross profit | 17,389 |
| Rent and rates (1,200 − 62 + 71) | 1,209 | | |
| Insurance (211 + 26 − 29) | 208 | | |
| General expenses | 9,746 | | |
| Net profit | 5,326 | | |
| | 17,389 | | 17,389 |
| Leyton | 2,663 | Net profit | 5,326 |
| Woodford | 2,663 | | |
| | 5,326 | | 5,326 |

*Balance Sheet as at 31 December 19X1*

| Capital | Leyton | Woodford | |
|---|---|---|---|
| | £ | £ | £ |
| Opening Balances............... \. | 3,874 | 4,057 | |
| Add: Net profit.................. | 2,663 | 2,663 | |
| Less: Drawings................... | (1,924) | (1,863) | |
| | 4,613 | 4,857 | 9,470 |
| *Current Liabilities:* | | | |
| Trade creditors.................. | | 2,162 | |
| Rates.......................... | | 71 | 2,233 |
| | | | 11,703 |
| *Fixed Assets:* | | | |
| Vans at cost.................... | | | 3,600 |
| Less: Depreciation.............. | | | 1,800 |
| | | | 1,800 |
| *Current Assets:* | | | |
| Debtors........................ | | 3,211 | |
| Stock.......................... | | 3,249 | |
| Insurance...................... | | 29 | |
| Cash.......................... | | 3,414 | 9,903 |
| | | | 11,703 |

# Solution 13.4

(a)  *Bar Trading Account and profit and Loss Account for 19X5*

| | £ | | £ |
|---|---|---|---|
| Bar purchases............ | 38,970(1) | Sales ............... | 62,100 |
| Add: Opening stock...... | 5,100 | | |
| Less: Closing stock....... | (6,250) | | |
| Cost of sales............. | 37,820 | | |
| Wages and salaries........ | 11,250 | | |
| | 49,070 | | |
| Gross profit............. | 13,030 | | |
| | 62,100 | | 62,100 |
| Rents and rates........... | 3,600 | Gross profit.......... | 13,030 |
| General expenses......... | 3,770(2) | Subscriptions........ | 7,700 |
| Depreciation ............ | 1,630 | Interest.............. | 3,180 |
| | 9,000 | | |
| Surplus................. | 14,910 | | |
| | 23,910 | | 23,910 |

*Balance Sheet at 31 December 19X5*

| | £ | £ | | £ |
|---|---|---|---|---|
| Accumulated fund, | | | | |
| 1 Jan............... | | 49,690 | Investments at cost....... | 42,400 |
| Add: Surplus for year.. | | 14,910 | Furniture and equipment | |
| | | | at cost less depreciation.... | 14,670(3) |
| | | 64,600 | Bar stocks.............. | 6,250 |
| Creditors: | | | Bank balance............ | 4,220 |
| Bar purchases....... | 2,810 | | | |
| Expenses........... | 130 | 2,940 | | |
| | | 67,540 | | 67,540 |

*Workings:*

| | £ | | £ |
|---|---|---|---|
| (1) Payments for bar purchases | 38,870 | (2) Payments for expenses.... | 3,790 |
| Less: Opening creditors.... | (2,710) | Less: Opening creditors.... | (150) |
| Add: Closing creditors.... | 2,810 | Add: Closing creditors.... | 130 |
| Bar purchases........... | 38,970 | General expenses........ | 3,770 |

| | £ |
|---|---|
| (3) Furniture and equipment: | |
| At 1 January............. | 16,300 |
| Less: Depreciation........ | 1,630 |
| At 31 December.......... | 14,670 |

(b)(i)

| | £ | £ |
|---|---|---|
| Cost of building........................ | | 100,000 |
| Less: Bank of balance.................. | 4,220 | |
| Sale of investments................ | 35,000 | |
| Loan........................... | 10,000 | 49,220 |
| Amount to be borrowed on overdraft....... | | 50,780 |

(ii)

| | £ |
|---|---|
| Surplus in 19X5........................ | 14,910 |
| Add: Depreciation...................... | 1,630 |
| Rent from scout troop.............. | 200 |
| Rent and rates no longer payable | |
| (£3,600 – £900).................... | 2,700 |
| | 19,440 |
| Less: Loan interest (£10,000 x 10%)........ | 1,000 |
| Estimated annual surplus available for repayment | 18,440 |

## Solution 13.5

### Sales Ledger Control Account

| | £ | | £ |
|---|---|---|---|
| Balance 1 January 19X1...... | 74,090 | Balance 1 January 19X1...... | 667 |
| Sales...................... | 633,772 | Returns.................... | 3,740 |
| Balance 31 December 19X1.... | 798 | Cash received.............. | 605,107 |
| | | Bad debts................. | 4,173 |
| | | Balance 31 December 19X1.... | 94,973 |
| | 708,660 | | 708,660 |

### Purchase Ledger Control Account

| | £ | | £ |
|---|---|---|---|
| Balance 1 January 19X1...... | 461 | Balance 1 January 19X1...... | 58,487 |
| Returns.................... | 4,120 | Purchases................. | 454,406 |
| Cash payments.............. | 438,734 | | |
| Balance 31 December 19X1.... | 69,578 | | |
| | 512,893 | | 512,893 |

Note that cash sales, cash purchases and the increase in the provision for doubtful debts do not appear in the control accounts.

## Solution 13.6

(a)                          Balance sheet at 31 December 19X2

| | £ | £ | | £ | £ |
|---|---|---|---|---|---|
| Capital | | | Fixed assets.......... | | 37,500 |
| 1 January.......... | | 45,750 | Stock............... | 18,750 | |
| Profit*............ | | 21,660 | Trade debtors......... | 17,250 | |
| Drawings.......... | | (15,450) | Prepaid insurance..... | 60 | |
| | | | Cash............... | 750 | |
| | | 51,960 | | | 36,810 |
| Creditors........... | 15,750 | | | | |
| B Baker............. | 1,350 | | | | |
| Overdraft........... | 4,500 | | | | |
| I Left.............. | 750 | | | | |
| | | 22,350 | | | |
| | | 74,310 | | | 74,310 |

* £22,500 (draft profit) + £450 (stock drawings) − £1,350 (purchases) + £60 (prepaid insurance) = £21,660

(b)                                  *Suspense Account*

|                      | £     |                  | £     |
|----------------------|-------|------------------|-------|
| Opening balance......... | 1,500 | Trade debtors.............. | 2,250 |
| I Left.................... | 750   |                  |       |
|                      | 2,250 |                  | 2,250 |

## Solution 13.7(a)

|                                                              | £       | £       |
|--------------------------------------------------------------|---------|---------|
| Capital .......................................             |         | 48,642  |
| Debtors........................................             | 11,131  |         |
| Creditors ......................................            |         | 7,283   |
| Stock 1 January 19X4...........................             | 14,169  |         |
| Premises at cost................................            | 25,000  |         |
| Vans at cost....................................            | 10,000  |         |
| Sales..........................................             |         | 122,488 |
| Purchases......................................             | 89,952  |         |
| Rent and rates.................................             | 2,460   |         |
| Light and heat..................................            | 841     |         |
| Salaries and wages..............................            | 14,865  |         |
| General expenses................................           | 1,861   |         |
| Bad debts......................................             | 622     |         |
| Doubtful debts provision at 1 January 19X4...........       |         | 862     |
| Provision for van depreciation at 1 January 19X4............ |         | 6,000   |
| Motor expenses.................................            | 1,326   |         |
| Drawings.......................................             | 7,146   |         |
| Bank overdraft..................................            |         | 4,302   |
| Discounts received..............................           |         | 501     |
| Discounts allowed...............................           | 1,738   |         |
| Office equipment................................           | 2,000   |         |
| Provision for depreciation of office equipment at 1 January 19X4.................. |         | 400     |
| Suspense account...............................            | 7,367   |         |
|                                                              | 190,478 | 190,478 |

# Solution 13.7(b)

(i)

| | | Debit £ | Credit £ |
|---|---|---|---|
| Error | | | |
| a | Creditors ............................... | 60 | |
| b | Office furniture.......................... | 293 | |
| | General expenses.......................... | | 293 |
| c | Purchases ............................... | 372 | |
| d | Debtors................................. | 1,750 | |
| e | Capital ................................. | 5,000 | |
| f | Sales ................................... | 256 | |
| | Debtors................................. | | 256 |
| g | Discount allowed.......................... | 185 | |
| | Net effect............................... | | 7,367 |
| | | 7,916 | 7,916 |

(ii)

| | £ | £ |
|---|---|---|
| Capital ........................................ | | 43,642 |
| Debtors (W1)................................... | 12,625 | |
| Creditors (W2).................................. | | 7,223 |
| Stock 1 January 19X4............................ | 14,169 | |
| premises at cost................................ | 25,000 | |
| Vans at cost.................................... | 10,000 | |
| Sales (W3)...................................... | | 122,232 |
| Purchases (W4)................................. | 90,324 | |
| Rent and rates................................. | 2,460 | |
| Light and heat.................................. | 841 | |
| Salaries and wages.............................. | 14,865 | |
| General expenses (W5).......................... | 1,568 | |
| Bad debts...................................... | 622 | |
| Doubtful debts provision at 1 January 19X4........... | | 862 |
| provision for van depreciation at 1 January 19X4............................... | | 6,000 |
| Motor expenses................................. | 1,326 | |
| Drawings ...................................... | 7,146 | |
| Bank overdraft.................................. | | 4,302 |
| Discounts received.............................. | | 501 |
| Discounts allowed (W6).......................... | 1,923 | |
| Office equipment (W7).......................... | 2,293 | |
| Provision for depreciation of office equipment at 1 January 19X4................ | | 400 |
| | 185,162 | 185,162 |

*Workings:*

|     |                  | Original Balance |                                            |
| --- | ---------------- | ---------------- | ------------------------------------------ |
| W1  | Debtors............... | 11,131       | + 1,750 (error d) − 256 (error f) = 12,625 |
| W2  | Creditors ............ | 7,283        | − 60 (error a) = 7,223                     |
| W3  | Sales ................. | 122,488      | − 256 (error f) = 122,232                  |
| W4  | Purchases............. | 89,952       | + 372 (error c) = 90,324                   |
| W5  | General expenses....... | 1,861       | − 293 (error b) = 1,568                    |
| W6  | Discounts allowed...... | 1,738       | + 185 (error g) = 1,923                    |
| W7  | Office equipment....... | 2,000       | + 293 (error b) = 2,293                    |

# Solution 13.8

### Bank Account

|   |   | £ |             |             |           | £     |
|---|---|---|-------------|-------------|-----------|-------|
|   |   |   | 2  Jan 19X2 | Cutter Ltd  |           | 1,200 |
|   |   |   | 31 Dec 19X2 | Cutter Ltd  |           | 1,200 |
|   |   |   | 31 Dec 19X3 | Cutter Ltd  |           | 1,200 |
|   |   |   | 31 Dec 19X4 | Cutter Ltd  |           | 1,200 |

### Machinery Account

|             |             | £     |   | £ |
|-------------|-------------|-------|---|---|
| 2  Jan 19X2 | Cutter ltd  | 4,185 |   |   |

### Cutter Ltd

|             |             | £     |             |               | £     |
|-------------|-------------|-------|-------------|---------------|-------|
| 2  Jan 19X2 | Bank        | 1,200 | 2  Jan 19X2 | Machinery A/c | 4,185 |
| 31 Dec 19X2 | Bank        | 1,200 | 2  Jan 19X2 | H P interest  |       |
|             | Balance c/d | 2,400 |             | Suspense A/c  | 615   |
|             |             | 4,800 |             |               | 4,800 |
|             |             |       |             |               |       |
| 31 Dec 19X3 | Bank        | 1,200 | 1  Jan 19X3 | Balance b/d   | 2,400 |
|             | Balance c/d | 1,200 |             |               |       |
|             |             | 2,400 |             |               | 2,400 |
|             |             |       |             |               |       |
| 31 Dec 19X4 | Bank    '   | 1,200 | 1  Jan 19X4 | Balance b/d   | 1,200 |

*Hire Purchase Interest Suspense Account*

| | | £ | | | £ |
|---|---|---|---|---|---|
| 2  Jan 19X2 | Cutter Ltd | 615 | 31 Dec 19X2 | P & L A/c | 298 |
| | | | | Blance c/d | 317 |
| | | 615 | | | 615 |
| 1  Jan 19X3 | Balance b/d | 317 | 31 Dec 19X3 | P & L A/c | 208 |
| | | | | Balance c/d | 109 |
| | | 317 | | | 317 |
| 1  Jan 19X4 | Balance b/d | 109 | 31 Dec 19X3 | P & L A/c | 109 |

Note:
In the balance sheet, prepared at the end of each year, the credit balance on the hire purchase interest suspense account is deducted from the sum owed to Cutter Ltd to show the net amount due. An alternative approach is, each year, to debit the year's interest in the profit and loss account and credit it to Cutter Ltd's account; this avoids the use of a suspense account.

## Solution 13.9

(a)                           *Trading Account of Arno.*

| | 19X6 | 19X7 | 19X8 | 19X9 | 19Y0 |
|---|---|---|---|---|---|
| | £000 | £000 | £000 | £000 | £000 |
| Sales...................... | 40 | 92 | 162 | 174 | 480 |
| Less:Opening stock............ | – | 28 | 64 | 108 | 160 |
| Purchases ............... | 56 | 96 | 144 | 160 | 176 |
| Closing stock (workings).... | (28) | (64) | (108) | (160) | – |
| Cost of goods sold......... | 28 | 60 | 100 | 108 | 336 |
| Gross profit.................. | 12 | 32 | 62 | 66 | 144 |

(b)                           *Trading Account of Garland.*

| | 19X6 | 19X7 | 19X8 | 19X9 | 19Y0 |
|---|---|---|---|---|---|
| | £000 | £000 | £000 | £000 | £000 |
| Sales...................... | 40 | 92 | 162 | 174 | 480 |
| Less:Opening stock............ | – | 28 | 60 | 96 | 136 |
| Purchases ............... | 56 | 96 | 144 | 160 | 176 |
| Closing stock (workings).... | (28) | (60) | ( 96) | (136) | – |
| Cost of goods sold......... | 28 | 64 | 108 | 120 | 312 |
| Gross profit.................. | 12 | 28 | 54 | 54 | 168 |

| *Workings:* | 19X6 | 19X7 | 19X8 | 19X9 | 19Y0 |
|---|---|---|---|---|---|
| Units in stock: | | | | | |
| Total purchases to date.......... | 4,000 | 10,000 | 18,000 | 26,000 | 34,000 |
| Total sales to date............... | 2,000 | 6,000 | 12,000 | 18,000 | 34,000 |
| Closing stock.................. | 2,000 | 4,000 | 6,000 | 8,000 | – |
| | | | | | |
| Valuation of stock: | | | | | |
| FIFO: cost per unit.............. | £14 | £16 | £18 | £20 | |
| FIFO valuation, £000........... | 28 | 64 | 108 | 160 | |

| LIFO: cost per unit, | 2,000 at | £14 | £14 | £14 | £14 |
|---|---|---|---|---|---|
| | 2,000 at | | 16 | 16 | 16 |
| | 2,000 at | | | 18 | 18 |
| | 2,000 at | | | | 20 |
| LIFO valuation, £000 | | 28 | 60 | 96 | 136 |

(c)

| | Arno | Garland |
|---|---|---|
| Gross profit for: | £000 | £000 |
| 19X6.......................... | 12 | 12 |
| 19X7.......................... | 32 | 28 |
| 19X8.......................... | 62 | 54 |
| 19X9.......................... | 66 | 54 |
| 19Y0.......................... | 144 | 168 |
| Total gross profit | 316 | 316 |

(d) Over the five year period, the total gross profit of each company is identical. The allocation of profits, over the five year period, varies due to the fact that they use different stock valuation methods. Arno uses FIFO which means that, during a period of inflation, closing stock (valued at most recent purchases prices) is reported at a higher figure than is the case at Garland where the LIFO cost flow assumption is used. The result is that Arno reports higher profits each year, except 19Y0, when all the stock is sold and Garland's low value LIFO stock is matched with sales proceeds.

## Solution 13.10

*Manufacturing, Trading and Profit and Loss Account of Arthur Holland 19X0*

|  | £000 | £000 |
|---|---|---|
| Sales |  | 525 |
| Less: Stock of raw material at 1 January | 30 |  |
| Purchases | 175 |  |
| Stock of raw material at 31 December | (35) |  |
|  | | |
| Materials consumed | 170 |  |
| Manufacturing wages | 110 |  |
|  | | |
| Prime cost | 280 |  |
| Indirect expenses | 20 |  |
|  | | |
| Factory cost of completed items | 300 |  |
| Add: Stock of finished goods, 1 January | 90 |  |
| Less: Stock of finished goods, 31 December | (105)(1) |  |
|  | | |
| Cost of goods sold |  | 285 |
|  | | |
| Gross profit |  | 240 |
| Less: Office expenses | 82 |  |
| Selling and distribution expenses | 15 | 97 |
|  | | |
| Net profit |  | 143 |

*Workings:*
(1) No. of items in stock, 300 (opening stock) + 1,000 (items manufactured) − 950 (items sold) = 350

Finished stock valued on the basis of a factory cost of completed items as follows:

$$\frac{£300,000}{1,000} \times 350 = 105,000.$$

## Solution 13.11

(a)(i)

*Fixed Assets at Cost Account*

|  |  | £ |  |  | £ |
|---|---|---|---|---|---|
| 1.1.19X0 | Cash: Asset A | 5,000 | 31.12.19X0 | Balance c/d | 7,500 |
|  | Cash: Asset B | 2,500 |  |  |  |
|  |  | 7,500 |  |  | 7,500 |
| 1.1.19X1 | Balance b/d | 7,500 | 31.12.19X1 | Balance c/d | 7,500 |
|  |  | 7,500 |  |  | 7,500 |
| 1.1.19X2 | Balance b/d | 7,500 | 1.1.19X2 | Disposal account | 2,500 |
|  | Cash: Asset C | 7,000 | 31.12.19X2 | Balance c/d | 12,000 |
|  |  | 14,500 |  |  | 14,500 |
| 1.1.19X3 | Balance b/d | 12,000 |  |  |  |

(a)(ii)

### Provision for Depreciation Account

| | | £ | | | £ |
|---|---|---|---|---|---|
| 31.12.19X0 | Balance c/d | 1,500 | 31.12.19X0 | Profit and loss | 1,500 |
| 31.12.19X1 | Balance c/d | 3,000 | 1.1.19X1 | Balance b/d | 1,500 |
| | | | 31.12.19X1 | Profit and loss | 1,500 |
| | | 3,000 | | | 3,000 |
| 1.1.19X2 | Disposal account | 1,000 | 1.1.19X2 | Balance b/d | 3,000 |
| 31.12.19X2 | Balance c/d | 4,400 | 31.12.19X2 | Profit and loss | 2,400 |
| | | 5,400 | | | 5,400 |
| | | | 1.1.19X3 | Balance b/d | 4,400 |

(a)(iii)

### Diposal of Fixed Asset Account

| | | £ | | | £ |
|---|---|---|---|---|---|
| 1.1.19X2 | Fixed asset account | 2,500 | 1.1.19X2 | Provision for depreciation | 1,000 |
| | | | | Cash | 900 |
| | | | | Profit and loss | 600 |
| | | 2,500 | | | 2,500 |

(b)(i)

| | Asset A | Asset B | Asset C | Total |
|---|---|---|---|---|
| | £ | £ | £ | £ |
| Cost 1 January 19X0.................. | 5,000 | 2,500 | | 7,500 |
| Less: Charge for 19X0 (30%)........... | 1,500 | 750 | | 2,250 |
| Book value at 31 Dec. 19X0............. | 3,500 | 1,750 | | 5,250 |
| Less: Charge for 19X1 (30%)........... | 1,050 | 525 | | 1,575 |
| Book value at 31 Dec. 19X1............. | 2,450 | 1,225 | | 3,675 |
| Sale: 1 January 19X2.................. | | 1,225 | | 1,225 |
| | | | | 2,450 |
| Purchase: 1 January 19X2.............. | | | 7,000 | 7,000 |
| | | | | 9,450 |
| Book value at 1 Jan. 19X2............. | | | | 9,450 |
| Less: Charge for 19X2 (30%)........... | 735 | | 2,100 | 2,835 |
| | 1,715 | | 4,900 | 6,615 |

| | £ |
|---|---|
| Charge: 19X0........................ | 2,250 |
| 19X1........................ | 1,575 |
| 19X2........................ | 2,835 |

(ii)    Loss on sale of Asset B:

|  | £ |
|---|---|
| Book value at 1 January 19X2........... | 1,225 |
| Sale proceeds....................... | 900 |
| Loss on sale........................ | 325 |

(c) The purpose of charging depreciation is to ensure revenue bears the full cost of resources used up during the course of business operations. The result of making a charge is to produce a more useful measure of profit and to report the decline in the value of the asset, to the business, in the balance sheet. The method chosen should reflect the expected pattern of benefit from using the asset; if most benefit is received early on the reducing balance basis should be used.

## Solution 13.12

*Plan (a)*
*Forecast Profit and Loss Account 19X7*

| | £ | | £ |
|---|---|---|---|
| Variable cost of sales: | | Cash sales.................. | 200,000 |
| Cash sales............ | 160,000 | HP cash received............ | 75,000 |
| Hire purchase.......... | 80,000 | Stock out on HP c/d (W1)..... | 32,000 |
| Administration expenses... | 36,000 | | |
| Bank interest........... | 10,000 | | |
| Net profit.............. | 21,000 | | |
| | 307,000 | | 307,000 |

*Forecast Profit and Loss Account 19X8*
*and subsequent years*

| | £ | | £ |
|---|---|---|---|
| Stock out on HP b/f...... | 32,000 | | |
| Variable cost of sales: | | Cash sales.................. | 200,000 |
| Cash sales............ | 160,000 | HP cash recieved............ | 125,000 |
| Hire purchase.......... | 80,000 | Stock out on HP c/d (W1)..... | 32,000 |
| Administration expenses... | 36,000 | | |
| Bank interest........... | 10,000 | | |
| Net profit.............. | 39,000 | | |
| | 357,000 | | 357,000 |

*Workings*
W1 Stock out on HP:

$$£80,000 \text{(cost of sales)} \quad \times \quad \frac{£50,000 \text{(outstanding HP debt)}}{£125,000 \text{(HP sales for year)}} = £32,000$$

*Plan (b)*
*Forecast Profit and Loss Account for 19X7*
*and subsequent years*

| | £ | | £ |
|---|---|---|---|
| Variable cost of sales...... | 320,000 | Sales...................... | 395,000 |
| Administration expenses... | 36,000 | | |
| Bank interest........... | 10,000 | | |
| Net profit.............. | 29,000 | | |
| | 395,000 | | 395,000 |

Comments:

Hire Purchase Sales: the full gross profit on a year's sales is not credited in the profit and loss account until 19X8. The profit in subsequent years should continue at the 19X8 level and the choice between the alternatives should be based on the results of that year rather than on those of 19X7.

Cash Sales: Under this alternative, the full benefit is reflected in the results of 19X7, and there will be no increase in subsequent years.

Conclusion: Despite the fact that the 19X7 results are better under plan (b), the total profit for the first two years will be greater under alternative (a); this advantage will increase steadily in each successive year. Plan (a) should be selected.

# Solution 13.13

*Trout Ltd*
*Manufacturing, Trading and Profit and Loss Account 19X4*

| | £ | £ | £ |
|---|---|---|---|
| Stock of raw materials 1 January................... | | 52,200 | |
| Purchase of raw materials......................... | | 427,500 | |
| Less: Stock of raw materials 31 December............ | | (57,500) | |
| Cost of raw materials consumed.................... | | 422,200 | |
| Direct manufacturing wages....................... | | 432,400 | |
| Prime cost of manufacture........................ | | 854,600 | |

Factory overhead expenses:

| | | |
|---|---:|---:|
| Indirect expenses.............................. | 43,600 | |
| Rent and rates (12,000 x 2/3)...................... | 8,000 | |
| Depreciation — plant.......................... | 40,000 | |
| Light and heat (23,100 x 2/3).................... | 15,400 | |
| | | 107,000 |
| Total factory cost of production..................... | 961,600 | |
| Work in progress 1 January....................... | 71,800 | |
| Less: Work in progress 31 December................. | (81,600) | |
| Factory cost of finished goods..................... | 951,800 | |
| Sales........................................... | | 1,350,000 |
| Less: Returns................................... | | 13,100 |
| | | 1,336,900 |
| Finished stock 1 January.......................... | 76,200 | |
| Finished stock 31 December....................... | (69,000) | |
| Cost of goods sold............................... | | 959,000 |
| Gross profit.................................... | | 377,900 |
| Add: Discounts received.......................... | | 4,500 |
| | | 382,400 |
| Less: Depreciation — fixtures and fittings............. | 9,000 | |
| General administration expenses............... | 119,700 | |
| Salesmens' salaries.......................... | 22,400 | |
| Other selling expenses........................ | 43,700 | |
| Discounts allowed........................... | 10,300 | |
| Rent and rates (12,000 x 1/3)................... | 4,000 | |
| Light and heat (23,100 x 1/3).................. | 7,700 | |
| | | 216,800 |
| Net profit...................................... | | 165,600 |
| Profit brought forward........................... | | 168,100 |
| | | 333,700 |
| Less: Dividend.................................. | | (100,000) |
| Retained profit carried forward.................... | | 233,700 |

# Solution 13.14

## Cash Account for 19X4

| | £ | | £ |
|---|---|---|---|
| Opening balance........ | 20,200 | Payments to suppliers | |
| (W2)................. | 297,320 | | |
| Receipts from | | Wages and expenses....... | 96,920 |
| customers (W1).......... | 471,580 | Fixed assets.............. | 20,000 |
| | | Drawings .............. | 24,000 |
| | | Theoretical closing balance. | 53,540 |
| | 491,780 | | 491,780 |

| | £ |
|---|---|
| Theoretical closing balance................. | 53,540 |
| Actual closing balance..................... | 28,580 |
| Discrepancy............................. | 24,960 |

*Workings*

W1 Receipts from customers

| | £ |
|---|---|
| Sales.................................... | 480,000 |
| Add: Opening debtors...................... | 34,400 |
| Less: Closing debtors...................... | (42,820) |
| | 471,580 |

W2 Payments to suppliers

| | £ |
|---|---|
| Cost of goods sold.......................... | 300,000 |
| Add: Closing stock........................ | 73,160 |
| Less: Opening stock........................ | (60,600) |
| Purchases................................ | 312,560 |
| Add: Opening creditors..................... | 23,600 |
| Less: Closing creditors..................... | (38,840) |
| | 297,320 |

## Solution 13.15

### Trading and Profit and Loss Account 19X7

|  | £ | £ |
|---|---|---|
| Cash sales........................................... | 55,200 | |
| Credit sales (42,600 − 9,600 + 16,800)................... | 49,800 | |
|  | 105,000 | |
| Less: Cost of goods sold on cash and credit................. | 80,400 | |
| Gross margin on cash and credit sales...................... | | 24,600 |
| Receipts from H P Customers........................... | 15,000 | |
| Less: Apportioned cost of H P sales (W1).................. | 10,500 | |
| Gross margin on H P sales.............................. | | 4,500 |
| Rent received........................................ | 61,200 | |
| Less: Depreciation on rented out assets (W2)............... | 30,000 | |
| Gross margin on renting out assets....................... | | 31,200 |
| Total gross margin.................................... | | 60,300 |
| Bad debts........................................... | 600 | |
| Administration expenses............................... | 36,720 | |
| Depreciation (12,000 x 20%)............................ | 2,400 | |
|  | | 39,720 |
| Net profit........................................... | | 20,580 |

*Workings*

W1 Cost of H P Sales:

|  | £ |
|---|---|
| Total cost of goods sold on H P........................ | 42,000 |
| Stock out on H P $\dfrac{42,000 \times 45,000}{60,000}$ .................... | 31,500 |
|  | 10,500 |

W2 Depreciation on rented-out assets:

|  | £ |
|---|---|
| Rented-out 1 January: | |
| 48,000(cost) x 1/4(proportion of life expired) = | 12,000 |
| Rented-out 1 July: | |
| 144,000(cost) x 1/8(proportion of life expired) = | 18,000 |
|  | 30,000 |

# Solution 13.16

*Trading and Profit and Loss account of Ludlow Ltd for 19X9*

|  |  | £000 | £000 |
|---|---|---|---|
| Sales: |  |  | 2,060 |
| Less: | Opening stock | 246 |  |
|  | Purchases | 1,350 |  |
|  | Less: Closing stock | (286) |  |
|  | Cost of sales |  | 1,310 |
| Gross profit |  |  | 750 |
| Less: | Depreciation of plant and machinery | 50 |  |
|  | Amortisation of patents etc. | 9 |  |
|  | Debenture interest | 50 |  |
|  | Rent and insurance | 14 |  |
|  | Rates | 17 |  |
|  | Salaries and wages | 365 |  |
|  | Provision for doubtful debts (£6,000 – £2,000) | 4 | 509 |
| Trading profit |  |  | 241 |
| Add: | Income from investments |  | 15 |
| Profit before tax |  |  | 256 |
| Less: | Corporation tax |  | 76 |
|  |  |  | 180 |
| Less: | Dividends (20p x 560,000) |  | 112 |
| Retained profit for 19X9 |  |  | 68 |
| Retained profit at 1 January 19X9 |  |  | 260 |
| Retained profit at 31 December 19X9 |  |  | 328 |

*Balance Sheet of Ludlow Ltd. at 31 December 19X9*

| *Fixed Assets* | £000 | £000 |
|---|---|---|
| Land and buildings at revalued amount..................... | | 750 |
| Plant and machinery at cost............................ | 500 | |
| Less: Accumulated depreciation......................... | 200 | 300 |
| | | |
| Patents, copyrights and licences at book value.............. | | 54 |
| | | 1,104 |
| *Current Assets* | | |
| Stock................................................... | 286 | |
| Debtors (£120,000 − £6,000)........................... | 114 | |
| Temporary investments................................ | 300 | |
| Cash at bank......................................... | 70 | |
| | 770 | |
| *Current Liabilities* | | |
| Creditors ............................................ | 103 | |
| Interest due.......................................... | 25 | |
| Corporation tax....................................... | 76 | |
| Dividends............................................ | 112 | |
| | 316 | |
| Working capital...................................... | | 454 |
| Total assets less current liabilities........................ | | 1,558 |
| Less: 10% debenture repayable 19Y8..................... | | 500 |
| | | 1,058 |
| Financed by: | | |
| Share capital......................................... | | 560 |
| Share premium account............................... | | 40 |
| Revaluation reserve................................... | | 130 |
| Retained profit....................................... | | 328 |
| | | 1,058 |

# Solution 13.17

(a)                    *Fund Flow, 19X1−X4*

| Sources: | £ | £ |
|---|---|---|
| Net profit.................................... | | 214,700 |
| Add: Depreciation............................ | | 125,300 |
| Funds generated from operations.................. | | 340,000 |
| Funds from other sources: | | |
| Share capital..................................... | | 90,000 |
| | | 430,000 |

*Applications:*

| | | |
|---|---|---|
| Purchase of fixed assets.......................... | 260,000 | |
| Dividends..................................... | 81,000 | 341,000 |
| | | |
| Increase in working capital........................ | | 89,000 |
| Increase in current liabilities...................... | | 23,800 |
| | | |
| Increase in current assets.......................... | | 112,800 |
| Current assets at: 31 December 19X0................ | | 97,500 |
| | | |
| 31 December 19X4................ | | 210,300 |

(b)                              *Balance Sheet as at 31 December 19X4*

| | £ | | £ |
|---|---|---|---|
| Fixed assets at cost........ | 496,000(1) | Share capital............. | 360,000(3) |
| Less: Accumulated | | Share premium........... | 30,000 |
| depreciation............. | 165,500(2) | Retained profit........... | 73,400(4) |
| | 330,500 | | 463,400 |
| Current assets............ | 210,300 | Current liabilities......... | 77,400 |
| | 540,800 | | 540,800 |

*Workings:*
(1) £236,000 + £260,000 (purchases 19X1–X4).
(2) £40,200 + £125,300 (charged 19X1–X4).
(3) £150,000 + £150,000 (bonus) + £60,000 (new issue).
(4) £89,700 + £214,700 (profit 19X1–X4) − £81,000 (dividends) − £150,000 (bonus).

## Solution 13.18

(a)      *Profit and Loss Account for the Year to 31 December 19X4*

| RESORT | A | B | C | D | E | F | Total |
|---|---|---|---|---|---|---|---|
| | £ | £ | £ | £ | £ | £ | £ |
| SALES | 452,000 | 230,000 | 26,000 | 59,000 | 23,000 | 64,000 | 854,000 |

COST OF SALES

| | | | | | | | |
|---|---|---|---|---|---|---|---|
| Agents commission........ | 45,200 | 23,000 | 2,600 | 5,900 | 2,300 | 6,400 | 85,400 |
| Coaches from airports to resorts.......... | 900 | 700 | 1,200 | 1,000 | 1,500 | 700 | 6,000 |
| Cost of local representatives............ | 4,600 | 4,100 | 5,500 | 5,100 | 5,300 | 4,900 | 29,500 |
| Hotel accommodation..... | 300,600 | 147,600 | 17,000 | 39,800 | 4,600 | 38,200 | 547,800 |

| | | | | | | | |
|---|---|---|---|---|---|---|---|
| TOTAL COST OF SALES........ | 351,300 | 175,400 | 26,300 | 51,800 | 13,700 | 50,200 | 668,700 |

| CONTRIBUTION FROM RESORTS................. | 100,700 | 54,600 | (300) | 7,200 | 9,300 | 13,800 | 185,300 |
|---|---|---|---|---|---|---|---|

| COUNTRY | FRANCE | SPAIN | GREECE | |
|---|---|---|---|---|
| | £ | £ | £ | |
| Total contribution from resorts.............. | 155,300 | 6,900 | 23,100 | |
| Flight costs.............. | 25,000 | 35,000 | 30,000 | 90,000 |

| CONTRIBUTION FROM COUNTRIES .............. | 130,300 | (28,100) | (6,900) | 95,300 |
|---|---|---|---|---|

| HEAD OFFICE AND OTHER COMMON COSTS...... | | | | 101,000 |
|---|---|---|---|---|

| NET LOSS................ | | | | (5,700) |
|---|---|---|---|---|

(b)
Holidays at resorts A and B, in France, are the only profitable ventures; an overall profit would result if these were the only ones served:

| | £ |
|---|---|
| Contribution from France.. | 130,300 |
| Less: Central costs........ | 101,000 |
| Net profit............... | 29,300 |

Holidays at other resorts should be investigaged to see whether they can be made profitable, and give a positive contribution to central costs. If they cannot, then they should be discontinued.

# Solution 13.19

(a)                              *Profit and Loss Account 19X8*

|  | £ | £ |
|---|---|---|
| Sales (20,000 x £30)............................... |  | 600,000 |
| Materials (20,000 x £12.75)........................ | 255,000 |  |
| Labour (20,000 x £5.00).......................... | 100,000 |  |
| Variable expenses (20,000 x £2.75)................. | 55,000 |  |
| Fixed expenses.................................. | 47,600 |  |
|  |  | 457,600 |
| Gross profit.................................... |  | 142,400 |
| Selling expenses................................ | 58,700 |  |
| Administration expenses.......................... | 55,200 |  |
|  |  | 113,900 |
| Net profit...................................... |  | 28,500 |

(b)                              *Break Even Point 19X9*

|  | £ | £ |
|---|---|---|
| Selling price per unit............................ |  | 30.00 |
| Variable costs per unit: |  |  |
| Materials................................... | 13.25 |  |
| Labour (£5.00 x 1.12)........................... | 5.60 |  |
| Expenses.................................... | 2.75 |  |
| Commission (£30.00 x 3%)..................... | .90 |  |
|  |  | 22.50 |
| Contribution per unit............................ |  | 7.50 |

| Fixed expenses: |  |
|---|---|
| Factory (£47,600 − £13,500)..................... | 34,100 |
| Selling (£58,700 − (5 x £4,000))................... | 38,700 |
| Administration (£55,200 − 2,000)................ | 53,200 |
| Total fixed expenses............................ | 126,000 |

$$\text{Break even point} = \frac{£126,000}{£7.50} = 16,800 \text{ units at } £30 \text{ each} = £504,000$$

(c)                      *Sales to make a profit in 19X9 of £28,500*

Total required contribution:
£126,000(19X9 fixed expenses) + £28,500(19X8 profit) = £154,500

$$\text{Required sales} = \frac{£154,500}{£7.50} = 20,600 \text{ units at } £30 \text{ each} = £618,000$$

## Solution 13.20

(a)

*Trading and Profit and Loss Accounts 19X9*

|  | Potter | | Lenton | |
| --- | --- | --- | --- | --- |
|  | G | H | G | H |
|  | £ | £ | £ | £ |
| Sales......................... | 100,000 | 60,000 | 60,000 | 100,000 |
| Costs of sales................. | 90,000 | 45,000 | 54,000 | 75,000 |
| Product gross margin........... | 10,000 | 15,000 | 6,000 | 25,000 |

|  | £ | £ |
| --- | --- | --- |
| Company gross margin.......... | 25,000 | 31,000 |
| General expenses............... | 15,000 | 12,000 |
| Net profit.................... | 10,000 | 19,000 |

(b)

*Balance Sheets at 31 December 19X9*

|  | Potter | | Lenton | |
| --- | --- | --- | --- | --- |
|  | £ | £ | £ | £ |
| Fixed assets at cost.............. |  | 80,000 |  | 60,000 |
| less: Accumulated depreciation... |  | 24,000 |  | 18,000 |
|  |  | 56,000 |  | 42,000 |
| Current assets: |  |  |  |  |
| Stock....................... | 32,000 |  | 23,000 |  |
| Debtors..................... | 18,000 |  | 16,000 |  |
| Cash ....................... | 25,000 |  | 12,000 |  |
|  | 75,000 |  | 51,000 |  |
| less: Creditors................. | 14,500 |  | 19,500 |  |
| Working Capital............... |  | 60,500 |  | 31,500 |
|  |  | 116,500 |  | 73,500 |
| Share capital................... |  | 100,000 |  | 60,000 |
| Retained profit*............... |  | 16,500 |  | 13,500 |
|  |  | 116,500 |  | 73,500 |

* Balancing figure

(c)  Ratios:

|  | Potter | Lenton |
|---|---|---|
| Gross margin − G..........................10.0% | | 10.0% |
| Gross margin − H..........................25.0% | | 25.0% |
| Return on owners capital employed........... 8.6% | | 25.9% |
| Current ratio............................. 5.2:1 | | 2.6:1 |
| Liquidity ratio............................ 3.0:1 | | 1.4:1 |

Comments:

Lenton benefits from the fact that, while total sales, at £160,000, are the same as for Potter, it sells a larger share of H which carries a higher gross margin.

Lenton achieves a higher return on capital employed because it makes more profit from the same value of sales, and these sales are obtained from a smaller investment in assets.

Potter has better working capital and liquidity ratios than Lenton, but both companies are in a healthy financial position.

# Solution 13.21

(a) *Profit and Loss Accounts for 19X8*

| Product | A | B | C | D |
|---|---|---|---|---|
| | £ | £ | £ | £ |
| Sales........................ | 72,000 | 48,000 | 36,000 | 120,000 |
| Variable costs................. | 57,600 | 36,000 | 24,000 | 102,000 |
| Contribution................. | 14,400 | 12,000 | 12,000 | 18,000 |
| Fixed costs................... | 6,000 | 6,000 | 9,000 | 4,800 |
| Net profit.................... | 8,400 | 6,000 | 3,000 | 13,200 |

(b) *Forecast Profit from Additional Sales 19X9*

| Product | A | B | C | D |
|---|---|---|---|---|
| | £ | £ | £ | £ |
| Sales........................ | 108,000 | 108,000 | 108,000 | 108,000 |
| Variable costs................. | 86,400 | 81,000 | 72,000 | 91,800 |
| Contribution................. | 21,600 | 27,000 | 36,000 | 16,200 |
| Fixed costs................... | 8,400 | 9,600 | 15,000 | 6,000 |
| Net profit.................... | 13,200 | 17,400 | 21,000 | 10,200 |

(c) The fixed costs of product C are much higher than for the other products, but, at the assumed level of sales, this is more than compensated for by the high level of contribution. Product C should be chosen.

# Solution 13.22

(a)

| | Post Ltd | | Haste Ltd | |
|---|---|---|---|---|
| | Full Capacity £ | 4,500 units £ | Full Capacity £ | 4,500 units £ |
| Sales.......................... | 140,000 | 90,000 | 140,000 | 90,000 |
| | | | | |
| Materials................... | 70,000 | 45,000 | 70,000 | 45,000 |
| Labour..................... | 42,000 | 27,000 | 14,000 | 9,000 |
| Total variable costs............. | 112,000 | 72,000 | 84,000 | 54,000 |
| Contribution.................. | 28,000 | 18,000 | 56,000 | 36,000 |
| | | | | |
| Fixed costs.................. | 5,000 | 5,000 | 12,000 | 12,000 |
| Depreciation................ | 10,000 | 10,000 | 25,000 | 25,000 |
| Total fixed costs................ | 15,000 | 15,000 | 37,000 | 37,000 |
| Net profit (loss)................ | 13,000 | 3,000 | 19,000 | (1,000) |

(b) Post is labour-intensive while Haste is capital-intensive. Haste earns a greater contribution per unit sold (£8 compared with £4), but has to achieve a higher level of sales to reach its break even point; once Haste has passed this point, its profits rise at a faster rate than Post for each additional unit sold. Hence, Haste makes a higher net profit at full capacity, but Post still makes a profit while Haste makes a loss at the lower level of activity.

# Solution 13.23

(a)

| | (i) Prime cost of production £ | (ii) Total cost of production £ | (iii) Total cost of opertions £ | (iv) Total variable cost of production £ |
|---|---|---|---|---|
| Manufacturing wages........... | 120,000 | 120,000 | 120,000 | 120,000 |
| Raw materials................ | 160,000 | 160,000 | 160,000 | 160,000 |
| General administration......... | | | 32,000 | |
| Depreciation................. | | 45,000 | 45,000 | |
| Factory rent.................. | | 20,000 | 20,000 | |
| Factory administration......... | | 30,000 | 30,000 | |
| | 280,000 | 375,000 | 407,000 | 280,000 |

| | (v) Total fixed cost of production | (vi) Direct production cost per unit | (vii) Average indirect production cost per unit |
|---|---|---|---|
| | £ | £ | £ |
| Manufacturing wages........... | | 12 | |
| Raw materials................. | | 16 | |
| Depreciation .................. | 45,000 | | 4.5 |
| Factory rent.................. | 20,000 | | 2.0 |
| Factory administration.......... | 30,000 | | 3.0 |
| | 95,000 | 28 | 9.5 |

(b)

| | £ | £ |
|---|---|---|
| Sales (10,000 + 50%) x (£45 − 10%) | | 607,500 |
| Production costs: | | |
| Wages...................... | 180,000 | |
| Materials .................. | 240,000 | |
| Rent ...................... | 32,000 | |
| Depreciation ............... | 67,000 | |
| Factory administration........ | 41,000 | |
| | | 560,000 |
| Gross margin................. | | 47,500 |
| General administration.......... | | 35,000 |
| Net profit.................... | | 12,500 |

(c)   The expanison was not worth undertaking as it reduced profit. Most of the costs rose, in line with the increase in volume, by about 50%, but the revenue per unit was reduced.

If the selling price per unit had not been reduced, profit would have been:

| | £ | £ |
|---|---|---|
| Sales (15,000 x £45)........... | | 675,000 |
| Total production costs........ | 560,000 | |
| General administration........ | 35,000 | |
| | | 595,000 |
| Net profit.................. | | 80,000 |

The expanison would have been worth undertaking as the extra activity would have resulted in additional profit.

# Solution 13.24

(a)                    *Forecast Profit and Loss Accounts for 19X9*

|  | Plan 1 £ | Plan 2 £ |
|---|---|---|
| Sales...................... | 336,000 | 450,000 |
| Expenses.................. | 305,760 | 414,000 |
| Net profit................. | 30,240 | 36,000 |

*Forecast Balance Sheets at 31 December 19X9*

|  | Plan 1 £ | Plan 1 £ | Plan 2 £ | Plan 2 £ |
|---|---|---|---|---|
| Fixed assets at cost.............. |  | 304,000 |  | 354,000 |
| Less: depreciation.............. |  | 94,400 |  | 102,400 |
|  |  | 209,600 |  | 251,600 |
| Current assets.................. | 58,240 |  | 70,000 |  |
| Less: Current liabilities......... | 36,000 |  | 44,000 |  |
| Working capital............... |  | 22,240 |  | 26,000 |
|  |  | 231,840 |  | 277,600 |
| Share capital.................. |  | 128,000 |  | 168,000 |
| Retained profit brought forward.. | 73,600 |  | 73,600 |  |
| Profit for 19X9................ | 30,240 |  | 36,000 |  |
|  |  | 103,840 |  | 109,600 |
|  |  | 231,840 |  | 277,600 |

(b)  Ratios:

|  | 19X8 | Plan 1 19X9 | Plan 2 19X9 |
|---|---|---|---|
| Net profit as a percentage of sales.. | 10.0% | 9.0 | 8.0% |
| Return on capital employed...... | 12.5%* | 15.0% | 14.9% |
| Working capital............... | 2:1 | 1.6:1 | 1.6:1 |

\* Capital employed 1 January 19X8:
£201,600(balance 31 December) − £22,400(profit for 19X8) = £179,200.

Both plans give a higher return on capital employed than was earned in 19X8, and neither seriously reduces the working capital position; therefore, either of them could be accepted. Plan 1 is expected to give a marginally higher return than plan 2, but the difference is immaterial, particularly as forecasts cannot be relied upon to be totally accurate.

# Solution 13.25

### Summarised Trading Accounts

| | 19X3 £ | 19X4 £ | 19X5 £ | 19X6 £ | 19X7 £ |
|---|---|---|---|---|---|
| (a)   Stock................ | 150,000 | 112,500 | 168,750 | 318,750 | 506,250 |
| | | | | | |
| (b) | | | | | |
| Sales..................... | 450,000 | 675,000 | 975,000 | 1,500,000 | 1,875,000 |
| | | | | | |
| Purchases ................ | 487,500 | 468,750 | 787,500 | 1,350,000 | 1,687,500 |
| Stock movement........... | (150,000) | 37,500 | (56,250) | (150,000) | (187,500) |
| | | | | | |
| Cost of goods sold.......... | 337,500 | 506,250 | 731,250 | 1,200,000 | 1,500,000 |
| | | | | | |
| Gross profit............... | 112,500 | 168,750 | 243,750 | 300,000 | 375,000 |
| | | | | | |
| Selling  expenses........... | 11,250 | 16,870 | 24,370 | 45,000 | 65,630 |
| Rent | 37,500 | 37,500 | 37,500 | 75,000 | 75,000 |
| General  expenses.......... | 56,250 | 65,630 | 75,000 | 112,500 | 140,620 |
| | | | | | |
| Total expenses............. | 105,000 | 120,000 | 136,870 | 232,500 | 281,250 |
| | | | | | |
| Net profit................. | 7,500 | 48,750 | 106,880 | 67,500 | 93,750 |
| | | | | | |
| (c)   Relevant ratios:....... | 19X3 | 19X4 | 19X5 | 19X6 | 19X7 |
| Gross margin.............. | 25.0% | 25.0% | 25.0% | 20.0% | 20.0% |
| Net profit percentage....... | 1.6% | 7.2% | 11.0% | 4.5% | 5.0% |

The net profit rose between 19X3 and 19X4 in both relative and absolute terms. The value of sales increased and the gross margin held steady at 25%; the expenses did not rise at the same rate as sales, and so net profit rose faster than sales due to the spreading of fixed costs over higher sales.

In 19X6 it appears that expansion was undertaken. The greater rent suggests enlarged capacity and sales and selling expenses rose considerably. However, the gross margin fell, possibly because prices had to be reduced to sell the increased volume of goods.

In 19X7 recovery has begun, although the gross margin has not improved. The increased profit stems from spreading the fixed costs, which increased in 19X6, over an increased volume of sales in 19X7. The scope for further improvement depends on the firm's ability to increase sales without a further cut in the gross margin or increases in expenses.

## Solution 13.26

(a)

|  | Current Position £ | Alternative (i) £ | Alternative (ii) £ |
|---|---|---|---|
| Salary.......................... | 8,000 | 6,000 | 9,000 |
| Investment..................... | 5,500 | 3,300 | 1,100 |
| Profit/dividend.................. | – | 5,000 | 2,800 |
| Annual return................... | 13,500 | 14,300 | 12,900 |
|  | × 5 | × 5 | × 5 |
| Total return.................... | 67,500 | 71,500 | 64,500 |

On purely financial grounds, the advice is to choose alternative (i) which produces an annual return which is £800 per year higher than is currently earned, or £4,000 overall. Greenleaf should also take into account the greater risk probably involved in undertaking a business venture.

(b) Revised alternative (ii):

|  |  | £ | £ |
|---|---|---|---|
| Year 1.......................... |  |  | 12,900 |
| Years 2–: Salary................. |  | 12,000 |  |
| Investment............. |  | 1,100 |  |
| Profit................. |  | 4,800 |  |
| 4 × | 17,900 | 71,600 |
|  |  |  | 84,500 |

In the revised circumstances, alternative (ii) promises comfortably the best financial return.

## Solution 13.27

(a)

### Profit and Loss Account of Hudson for 19X4

|  | £ |  | £ |
|---|---|---|---|
| Cost of sales (by difference) ............ | 70,840 | Sales.............. | 88,000(2) |
| Administration expenses ............... | 5,400 |  |  |
| Depreciation (10% of £56,000).......... | 5,600 |  |  |
|  | 81,840 |  |  |
| Net profit | 6,160(1) |  |  |
|  | 88,000 |  | 88,000 |

*Balance Sheet as at 31 December 19X4*

| | £ | | £ |
|---|---|---|---|
| Fixed Assets: | | Share capital ......... | 30,000 |
| Cost .............................. | 56,000 | Profit and loss | |
| Less: Accumulated depreciation .......... | 17,600 | account ............ | 20,160 |
| | 38,400 | | 50,160 |
| | | | |
| Current assets........................ | 21,360 | Creditors ........... | 9,600 |
| | 59,760 | | 59,760 |

*Workings:*

(1) Capital employed on 1 Jan 19X3:

| | | |
|---|---|---|
| Share capital | | 30,000 |
| Retained profit £14,000 – £4,000 | | 10,000 |
| | | 40,000 |

Return on capital employed for 19X3: $\dfrac{£4,000 \times 100}{£40,000} = 10\%$

Forecast return on capital employed for 19X4: 10% + 4% = 14%.

Forecast profit for 19X4: 14% × £44,000 (capital employed at 1 January 19X4 = £6,160.

(2) Net profit percentage for 19X3: $\dfrac{£4,000 \times 100}{£50,000} =$      8%

Forecast net profit percentage for 19X4: 8% – 1% =      7%

Forecast sales for 19X4: $\dfrac{£6,160 \times 100}{7} =$      £88,000

(b)

| *Reconciliation* | £ | £ |
|---|---|---|
| Current assets at 31 December 19X3 .................... | | 12,400 |
| Add: Net profit ...................................... | 6,160 | |
|       Depreciation.................................... | 5,600 | |
| | | |
| Funds from operations ........................... | | 11,760 |
| Increase in creditors ............................ | | 3,200 |
| | | 27,360 |
| Less: Purchase of fixed assets ........................... | | 6,000 |
| | | |
| Current assets at 31 December 19X4 .................... | | 21,360 |

# Solution 13.28

(a)

Balance Sheets at 31 December

|  | 19X0 | 19X1 | 19X2 |
|---|---|---|---|
|  | £ | £ | £ |
| Fixed assets at cost................ | 240,000 | 400,000 | 400,000 |
| Less: Accumulated depreciation .... | 24,000 | 48,000 | 88,000 |
|  | 216,000 | 352,000 | 312,000 |
| *Current Assets:* |  |  |  |
| Stock and debtors ............... | 135,000 | 171,000 | 210,800 |
| Bank ......................... | 69,600 | — | 62,000 |
|  | 204,600 | 171,000 | 272,800 |
| *Less: Current Liabilities* |  |  |  |
| Trade creditors.................. | 77,900 | 95,000 | 121,000 |
| Bank overdraft.................. | — | 45,000 | — |
|  | 77,900 | 140,000 | 121,000 |
| Working capital................. | 126,700 | 31,000 | 151,800 |
|  | 342,700 | 383,000 | 463,800 |
| Share capital.................... | 300,000 | 300,000 | 300,000 |
| Retained profit 1 January.......... | — | 42,700 | 83,000 |
| Profit for year .................. | 42,700 | 40,300 | 80,800 |
|  | 342,700 | 383,000 | 463,800 |

(b)

|  | 19X0 | 19X1 | 19X2 |
|---|---|---|---|
|  | £ | £ | £ |
| Net profit ...................... | 42,700 | 40,300 | 80,800 |
| Add: Depreciation ............... | 24,000 | 24,000 | 40,000 |
| Funds generated from operations ... | 66,700 | 64,300 | 120,800 |

(c)   The main cause of the bank overdraft and the shortage of working capital at the end of 19X1 was the purchase of fixed assets costing £160,000 on 31 December. A day earlier working capital was approximately £191,000 (£31,000 + £160,000), and a balance sheet prepared at that date would have shown a healthy cash balance. Funds generated and retained in the buisness during 19X2 restored working capital and cash to acceptable levels by the end of the year.

# Solution 13.29

(a)

|  | Cost | Accumulated depreciation |
|---|---|---|
|  | £ | £ |
| Balance at 31 December 19X1.......... | 120,400 | 45,600 |
| Disposals........................... | (49,000)(1) | (42,600)(1) |
| Additions........................... | 124,500 |  |
| Charge for the period 19X1 – 19X4..... |  | 63,530 |
| Balance at 31 December 19X4.......... | 195,900 | 66,530 |

*Workings:*

| (1) Plant scrapped and sold: | Scrapped | Sold | Total |
|---|---|---|---|
|  | £ | £ | £ |
| Cost ........................... | 30,000 | 19,000(2) | 49,000 |
| Less: Written down value ··········· | 2,000 | 4,400(3) | 6,400 |
| Accumulated depreciation........... | 28,000 | 14,600 | 42,600 |

(2) £14,600 (accumulated depreciation) + £4,400 (book value).

(3) £3,400 (sales proceeds) + £1,000 (loss of sale).

(b)

### Statement of Funds for 19X1-19X4

| Sources | £ | £ |
|---|---|---|
| Net profit (£46,400 - £17,600).......................... |  | 28,800 |
| Add: Loss on disposal of plant (£2,000 + £1,000)......... |  | 3,000 |
| Depreciation .................................... |  | 63,530 |
| Funds from operations .............................. |  | 95,330 |
| Funds from other sources |  |  |
| Sale of plant ................................... | 3,400 |  |
| Share capital ................................... | 30,000 | 33,400 |
|  |  | 128,730 |
| Applications: |  |  |
| Purchase of plant ............................... |  | 124,500 |
| Increase in working capital........................... |  | 4,230 |
| Analysed as follows: |  |  |
| Increase in stock ............................... | 13,380 |  |
| Increase in debtcrs ............................. | 10,690 |  |
| Increase in creditors ............................ | (7,600) |  |
| Decrease in cash ............................... | (12,240) | 4,230 |

(c)

| Solvency ratios: | 19X1 | 19X4 |
|---|---|---|
| Working Capital ratio ............................... | 2.5:1 | 2.2:1 |
| Liquidity ratio...................................... | 1.3:1 | 0.9:1 |

The financial developments over the three year period have been satisfactory. A significant investment in fixed assets has been adequately covered by funds generated from operations and an issue of share capital. There have been modest declines in both solvency ratios, but they remain at reasonably satisfactory levels.

## Solution 13.30

Assessment to deal with the following matters:

CALCULATIONS:

### Statement of Source and Application of Funds

| Sources: | | £ | £ |
|---|---|---|---|
| Net profit (£4,900 + £2,500) | | | 7,400 |
| Add: Depreciation | | | 6,700 |
| Funds generated from operations | | | 14,100 |
| Funds from other sources | | | |
| Loan | | | 10,000 |
| | | | 24,100 |
| Applications: | | | |
| Purchase of plant | | 37,400 | |
| Dividends | | 2,500 | 39,900 |
| Decrease in working capital | | | (15,800) |
| Analysed as follows: | | | |
| Increase in stock | | 11,120 | |
| Increase in debtors | | 9,420 | |
| Increase in creditors | | (15,020) | |
| Decrease in cash (£6,210 + £15,110) | | (21,320) | (15,800) |

*Accounting Ratios.*

| | | 19X5 | 119X6 |
|---|---|---|---|
| Solvency: | Working Capital | 1.7:1 | 0.9:1 |
| | Liquidity | 0.9:1 | 0.4:1 |
| | Debtors to Sales | 13 times(28 days) | 8 times(48 days) |
| Profit | Net profit percentage | 7.3% | 5.9% |
| | Return on net assets | 9.5% | 9.9% |

COMMENTS:

*Financial policy and solvency*

1. Investment in fixed assets has been partly financed out of working capital. This has caused the working capital ratio to fall to a dangerous level.
2. The liquidity position has also deteriorated due to the investment in fixed assets, referred to above, and also because there has been a heavy transfer of resources from cash into stocks, i.e. the structure of the current assets has become less liquid.
3. A significant decline in the rate of collection of debtors has added to the company's cash problems.

4. The company is clearly not paying its creditors as they fall due for payment; these are up by 150% despite an increase in activity in the region of only 30%.
5. The company has over-traded.

*Profitability*
1. The net margin on sales has declined. This may be due to price cutting in an attempt to generate extra sales.
2. The rate of return is low, making it difficult to recover on the basis of internally generated funds; 19X7 may be a better year but an immediate injection of cash is needed.

# Index